They Used to Call Us Witches

They Used to Call Us Witches

Chilean Exiles, Culture, and Feminism

Julie Shayne

LEXINGTON BOOKS
A division of
ROWMAN & LITTLEFIELD PUBLISHERS, INC.
Lanham • Boulder • New York • Toronto • Plymouth, UK

Published by Lexington Books
A division of Rowman & Littlefield Publishers, Inc.
A wholly owned subsidary of The Rowman & Littlefield Publishing Group, Inc.
4501 Forbes Boulevard, Suite 200, Lanham, Maryland 20706
http://www.lexingtonbooks.com

Estover Road, Plymouth PL6 7PY, United Kingdom

British Library Cataloguing in Publication Information Available

Library of Congress Cataloging-in-Publication Data
Shayne, Julie D., 1966–
 They used to call us witches : Chilean exiles, culture, and feminism / Julie Shayne.
  p. cm.
 Includes bibliographical references and index.
 ISBN 978-0-7391-1849-8 (cloth : alk. paper) —ISBN 978-0-7391-1850-4
 (pbk. : alk. paper) — ISBN 978-0-7391-4413-8 (electronic)
 1. Women—Political activity—Chile. 2. Exiles—Political activity—Chile. 3.
Feminism—Chile. 4. Human rights movements—Chile. 5. Chile—Politics and
government—1973- I. Title.
 HQ1236.5.C5S53 2010
 305.48'969140896883071133—dc22

                                                        2009039387

◎™ The paper used in this publication meets the minimum requirements of American
National Standard for Information Sciences—Permanence of Paper for Printed Library
Materials, ANSI/NISO Z39.48-1992. Printed in the United States of America

In memory of my beloved father, Barry

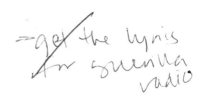

Contents

Acknowledgments

Writing this book was an intellectually and emotionally arduous project that would not have been possible without the help of many people. First, I would like to express my gratitude to the many people who gave me initial encouragement and contacts that allowed me to begin my research: Susan Franceschet, Gerardo Otero, Alejandro Rojas, and Pablo Policzer. Carmen Rodríguez was the first Chilean woman exile I contacted and without Carmen and all of her subsequent contacts I literally could not have written this book. Carmen's support did not stop with initial contacts. She sent me her personal archives, answered my clarification questions consistently for the past five years, and greatly enhanced my understanding of the Chilean community in Vancouver. Irene Policzer is another very early Chilean contact who also helped to expand my list of interviewees considerably. She too opened her home, personal archives, and email inbox to me. I also want to offer my deep appreciation to Cecilia Boisier for allowing me to visit her art studio. Looking at and talking to her about her paintings gave me a clearer picture of the exile experience and I thought about her work constantly as I wrote this book.

Additionally, I want to acknowledge the graciousness of every person I interviewed for this book. The Chilean women opened up some very painful memories and shared things with me that were much more than history; their pain was never far from the surface and I greatly appreciate them reliving and retelling what was often the most traumatic and emotionally difficult part of their lives. I was constantly touched by their warmth and courage to walk through memories that many had chosen to avoid, often for decades.

A thank you is also due to Emory University's Institute for Comparative and International Studies, who provided research and travel funds. I also must offer my deepest appreciation to my wonderful transcriber, Paola Wakeford, who worked tirelessly to transcribe every interview within days, often just hours, of receiving the tapes. Additionally, I am grateful to Patrick Blaine for answering my random, varied, and frequent questions with perfect detail and speed.

I also wish to acknowledge Gary Cristall, whose decades of involvement in the Vancouver Left gave me a great historical understanding of the solidarity movement. Gary took me to his storage space and let me pour through boxes, and boxes, and boxes of documents from the solidarity movement. He went one by one with me to help explain what they all were and trusted me to borrow and copy them. Gary's archives and generosity greatly enhanced this book.

Recognition is also due to the many people who helped me think through this project in its very early stages: Nancy Eiesland, Jose Moya, Girija Sankaranarayanan, Tim Dowd, and Chris Bobel. I also want to convey my gratitude to the many colleagues and friends who read (and reread) drafts of the book in its various forms, offering careful and insightful feedback: Carolina Palacios, Sarah Kishpaugh, and Tom Wright, with a very special thanks to Serena Cosgrove, Margaret Power, and Jeff Goodwin, who worked with me literally until the very end. Serena, Margaret, and Jeff graciously allowed me to interrupt their own book writing, family visits, and sabbatical with my never-ending "last" requests to read just one more chapter. Their combined feedback made this book much, much stronger.

Finally, I want to thank my family: My mom, Lynda, and stepdad, Frank, for their permanent, unwavering, and inordinate amount of faith in me (and, for driving and ferrying all over the northwest to take care of my daughter while I did interviews). My father, Barry, who offered me so much support his whole life that eight and a half years after his death I can still feel his glowing pride. My wonderful children, Barrie and Aaron, who taught me that there is a family-friendly way to be an academic, and my husband Dave, now, my everything plus-one.

Preface

Why Witches?

"Aquelarre means 'illegal gathering of witches.' They used to call us witches. What do they call us now? Arpilleristas, weavers, union leaders, women in exile, political prisoners, mothers of the disappeared, artists. . . ." The title of my book comes from this quote. These words appear in every issue of the Latin American feminist magazine *Aquelarre,* started by a collective of women in Vancouver, under the leadership of Chilean exiles. (I discuss the magazine in great detail in Chapter Six.) I chose this title for several reasons. First, the quote comes directly from the women who are the subject of this book. Additionally, it speaks to the political evolution of women and resistance, a theme that is central to understanding the intersection of leftist politics and feminism. And finally, all of the things "they call women now" are central to the story that this book tells. In the rest of this book we will meet the self-identified twentieth-century "witches" as artists, activists, exiles, and mothers. As every issue of their magazine says, "Let us begin the AQUELARRE."

Introduction

Theoretical and Methodological Background

As the taxi drew out of the courtyard, a school friend of Manuela's whose father had also been killed came rushing to say good-bye . . . "Please go and tell people outside what is happening."

—Joan Jara, closing line of her husband Victor Jara's biography

Exile "encompasse[s] expulsion and oblivion, a sentence and rare pardon. I was able to pin down the sensation of alienation as an unbearable suspicion that I had left the world, but with the additional factor of my being alive."

—Protagonist in *A Secret for Julia* by Patricia Sagastizábal

INTRODUCTION

On the morning of September 11, 1973, Carmen Aguirre, the six-year-old daughter of leftist parents, woke to the sound of the radio and her parents crying. She remembers being a bit confused by the stillness in the house. Why were the adults not doing their morning routines? How come her parents did not wake her and get her dressed for school? Why was the whole neighborhood quiet when children are usually playing in the streets, waiting for the adults who readied themselves for work? She went into her parents' bedroom, eventually joined by her five-year-old sister, Alejandra, and the two of them joined their parents on their bed as they listened to Salvador Allende's last speech to the Chilean people. They watched their parents sob as they heard the military planes and bombs in the background as Allende spoke. Carmen explained that she and her sister remained quiet because they had some sense that this was "an historic moment." Her mother then told them "something terrible has happened; the president has been killed" (personal interview 2004).

This is Carmen's first memory of the Pinochet dictatorship. On September 11, 1973, Army General Augusto Pinochet, with the help of the United States government, orchestrated a coup against democratically elected Marxist Salvador Allende. Under the guise of a "state of war" and an around-the-clock curfew, the military launched a reign of terror against leftist activists and sympathizers, government officials, intellectuals, union leaders, and the poor. They used mass arrests, beatings, torture, summary executions, and military sweeps of shantytowns to terrorize the population into submission. The military took control of the media and broadcast calls demanding that specified individuals immediately turn themselves in to the new authorities. Santiago's two major soccer stadiums were converted in to mass jails, torture, and death chambers filled with prisoners, while the hospitals overflowed with the wounded, and the morgues with dead bodies. The CIA's own sources reported on September 20, just nine days after the coup, "4,000 deaths have resulted from the September 11, 1973, coup action and subsequent clean-up operations" (quoted in Kornbluh 2003, 153). Just four days later the CIA estimated civilian deaths anywhere between 2,000 and 10,000 (Kornbluh 2003, 153). These numbers were actually inflated and are higher than post-dictatorship reports have since confirmed.[1] Chileans who escaped death were also terrorized by the junta. Carmen recalls her first experiences with the military. She explained:

> The military completely raided our house and my parents were not home. Later I found out that they were in hiding; I do not know how long they were hiding . . . but we [she and her sister] were with the nanny and the military raided the house. In my memory they spent the whole day there but it might have been an hour; you know when you are six an hour is much longer. They basically went through the entire house. The nanny was crying in the kitchen. They had her in the kitchen with the door locked and she was this older Mapuche [indigenous] woman. Then they literally went through the entire house, turned everything over. They broke our dolls and . . . they kept trying to bribe us. They would offer us chocolate and then . . . we would grab the chocolate and they took it away. [They would say] "Tell us where your parents are," that kind of thing.
>
> Then they decided to have some fun so they kept the nanny in the kitchen and they took my sister and me outside and put us against the wall and kept pretending that they [were] going to do the firing squad with us. So they put us against the wall and then they stood behind us and they would do the whole counting to ten, "fire!" and they would not fire and they all started laughing because they thought that was hilarious. I am sure we pissed our pants.

Then they went across the street and raided my friend's house. They were a
working-class family and [the military] took her older brother and her father
away with blindfolds in a jeep . . . [but first they did] the firing squad thing. This
kid, who was about fourteen, who was also a working-class kid, came running
out of his house and insulted them. . . . He was very brave. . . . We had our face
towards the wall [and could not see what they were doing]. . . . Then they took
him to the woods and they beat the shit out of him. We thought they killed him
but they did not and then eventually they left.

Carmen and her family's story is quite common. By the middle of 1978
experiences like these forced nearly thirty thousand Chileans into exile in
Western Europe[2] alone, and by the end of the decade an estimated two hundred thousand Chileans (nearly 2 percent of the population) had fled their
country for political reasons. By the end of the dictatorship approximately
one million Chileans (of a population of ten million) fled their country to
every continent in the world. At least two hundred thousand left because they
were blacklisted and politically forced from the country, while the others fled
because the economic situation under the dictatorship made life unlivable.
Canada was one of the 140 countries where Chileans fled (Wright 1995, 198;
Wright and Oñate 1998).

Carmen remembers leaving Chile:

The next memory is in the middle of the night, which must have been days
later . . . going to somebody's house and saying goodbye . . . and everybody is
crying but everything is very quiet. . . . We did not say goodbye at the school.
We did not say goodbye to anybody basically. [The next memory I have] . . . is
just being at the airport and my parents being very, very nervous . . . going up
to the counter, and they . . . had no idea if they were going to get out. . . . The
airport was crazy; you could not move . . . thousands of people . . . crying, and
desperate.

She and her family were able to leave and eventually ended up in Vancouver,
British Columbia.

This book is a study of women exiles like Carmen's mother who fled Chile
for Canada during the dictatorship. Specifically, I use a gendered lens to
analyze the anti-Pinochet solidarity movement organized by Chilean exiles
in Vancouver, British Columbia, during the 1970s and 1980s and the feminist movement that followed in the 1990s. Within this historical framework
there are several specific issues I will address: The roles and experiences of
Chilean women in the solidarity movement; the place of emotions in birthing
the movement; the power of culture to articulate and sustain resistance; the
intersection of emotions, gender, and culture with respect to organizational
strategies; and the significance of feminism and feminist activism to Chilean

women exiles, especially in the post-Pinochet period. In this chapter I will offer a brief theoretical and conceptual introduction to some of the different themes and definitions, including the meaning of *culture*, that are relevant to understanding the data I present in the rest of this book. I begin by speaking to the importance of studying exile. Then I will discuss what I mean by culture. Next, I introduce social movement theories of culture and emotions that help explain why and how the solidarity movement came about in the first place. I save the gender and feminist theory for Chapters Five and Six respectively. I conclude the theoretical discussion with a note on studying diaspora and then offer an overview of my methodology and organization of the book.

WHY STUDY EXILE?

A recent issue of *Latin American Perspectives* was devoted entirely to exile [2007, 155, 34(4)]. In the introduction the editors highlight a number of trends in the literature on exile. In short, they maintain that most of what has been written thus far either falls into the biography/testimony category or the literary analysis/theoretical realm. The evolution of both types of literature makes perfect sense and the readings are often quite compelling. That said, the scholarship remains largely underdeveloped and in great need of disciplinary expansion and cross-fertilization. The editors of the issue maintain that exile has "played a vital part in shaping the forms and styles of Latin American politics." The editors thus propose that the systematic study of exile "promises to lead to new readings of history and society in Latin America, away from the traditional readings of national histories toward more regional, transnational, or even continental perspectives" (Roniger and Green 2007, 4). The articles that make up the volume are an exciting beginning in this new direction of exile scholarship. The authors address a variety of issues including colonialism and exile as a political tactic; exiles in home country politics; exiles and their social and political networks, and reconstruction of identities. They draw on Chilean, Argentine, and Brazilian cases and offer other scholars of exile an excellent map from which to pursue related questions. Not surprisingly, the editors conclude the issue by posing a series of questions that might further scholarship in this area, several of which I take up in this book. They maintain:

> More attention needs to be given to the impact of exile groups, solidarity committees, and human rights efforts on the internal dynamics and political contradictions within the military regimes that expelled their opponents. We need more studies analyzing the role of exiles in the international campaigns against

torture. . . . What tangible effects did activities to isolate dictatorships have on the political processes in those countries? . . . To what extent did exile offer political activists innovative ways to think about political and social change beyond renewed activism in political parties and left-wing movements? . . . While scholars are looking toward the macro-dynamics of exile, continued consideration should be given to the detailed study of émigrés from different countries living abroad. At the same time, researchers should pay special attention to gathering and preserving personal and institutional archives and eliciting oral histories from those who experienced exile (Green and Roniger 2007, 107–8).

The study of Chilean women exiles in Vancouver lends itself to addressing many of their questions and concerns. For example, the anti-Pinochet solidarity movement is an ideal case to analyze the roles of exiles in international anti-torture campaigns (Chapter Four). Additionally, studies of gender and feminism are exceptionally fertile intellectual terrain to analyze "innovative" ways of doing politics (Chapters Five and Six). And finally, the editors charge researchers with supplementing macro-historical studies with case studies that rely on oral histories and create archives from this period. This is one of my most pressing goals with this book, to help archive and document a social movement that was fundamental in the histories of Chilean exiles, Chilean politics in the inside of the country, and arguably Canadian left politics as well.

THEORETICAL AND CONCEPTUAL BACKGROUND

This book uses a gendered lens to understand the place of culture and emotions in the Chilean solidarity movement. That is, I work from the experiences of Chilean women exiles to understand why and how culture and emotions worked together to inspire, sustain, and embody the solidarity movement. This chapter is meant to provide context to the culture and emotions aspect of this equation. I save the discussion of gender as an analytic category for when I look specifically at the roles of women in the solidarity movement (Chapter Five).

Collecting Chilean women's stories made it abundantly clear that one needs to analyze the political place of culture to truly understand the solidarity movement. As we will see throughout this book, cultural events, institutions, and productions were central to sustaining the solidarity movement and articulating its message. Women exiles also played a special role as the producers and ambassadors of exile political culture. In order to understand the significance of all of this we need to understand several things: the meaning of culture; the inherent political power of culture, and the place of culture in social movements. I take these up in turn.

What Is Culture?

What do we mean by culture? Defining culture is a particularly difficult task. Raymond Williams postulates that one reason offering a definition of culture is so complicated, or as he says, "culture is one of the two or three most complicated words in the English language," is due to the fact that several different intellectual disciplines use the concept often in what he considers "incompatible systems of thought" (1983b). There are three aspects of the meaning that I use throughout the book. First, what is *culture*? Second, how is culture represented? Finally, why does culture matter? In this book I draw from three main theorists to help answer these questions.

The conception of culture I find most compatible with the solidarity and feminist movements and my own subsequent analysis of them comes from Manuel Jofré, a Chilean literary theorist. Specifically, I draw on an article (1989) he authored about cultural production in Chile between 1973 and 1985. I suspect the common historical time and place renders Jofré's analysis so compatible with that which I offer in this book. Jofré posits that in the case of Chile, and I would add in the Chilean diaspora, culture is the way in which human activity continuously produces meaning. In this sense, it is a complex multidimensional process of communication that articulates and symbolizes a people's way of life. Culture embodies worldviews, linguistic markers, material objects, and social practices. In other words, because culture refers to the way communication is symbolized it thus includes all aspects of life since humans individually and collectively communicate in a multitude of ways. This premise hints at the power of culture, which I will take up in a moment. For Jofré, "culture is the whole set of signifying practices and products that convey meaning to a total society . . . culture is nothing but society signifying" (1989, 71). Working from Jofré's logic we might deduce that communication is a key component in cultural production, particularly when fused with symbolization, individual and collective, and identity formation. Or, as Jofré argues, culture is "the collective self of a community" (1989, 70). This idea resonates strikingly well with the anti-Pinochet solidarity movement organized by Chilean exiles in Canada.

Jofré's argument is also quite parallel to Raymond Williams', particularly the implicit attention to agency, or what Williams calls "lived experience" (1983a).[3] Similarly, they both see culture as symbolizing processes. Williams in part borrows from what he calls the anthropological and sociological sense of culture, which asserts that it is "the *signifying system* through which . . . a social order is communicated, reproduced, experienced and explored" (1981b, 13 [italics in original]). For Williams this signifying process is a convergence of traditional anthropological and sociological views of culture as a "distinct way of life" and the more commonsense notion of culture as "artistic and intellectual activities" (1981b, 13). To assume culture is merely a way of life or a material representation of that life removes the human agency, or what Jasper calls "artful creativity" (1997, 11), from cultural processes. That is, if culture is "something out there" made by "other people," then it is something that we watch rather than participate in. Such a formulation implies cultural stagnation and human apathy and is thus highly incompatible with social movements, which ideally represent change and pro-action.

Another parallel way to think about culture comes from James Jasper. He argues, similar to Williams and Jofré, that culture is "shared mental worlds and their physical embodiment" (1997, 12). For Jasper, culture is made up of three subcomponents, cognitive beliefs, emotional responses, and moral evaluations. According to Jasper culture does several things: It provides a collection of discrete feelings, beliefs, images, and the like. It helps us define social action while also providing patterns of acting, thinking, judging, and feeling. And it offers what he calls "the building blocks and dynamics of creativity" (1997, 12). Combined we might assume that Jofré, Williams, and Jasper are saying that culture is everything. However, Jasper clearly demarcates what culture is not. He reminds us that culture is not physical resources, nor the money to buy them. Neither is it strategic interactions between groups and individuals, or their individual biographies. Culture, Jasper argues, helps define and shape the aforementioned but it is not the same thing.

Culture and Power

In order to understand the relationship between culture and power I turn to Antonio Gramsci. Culture is central to Gramsci's analysis of everything—education, philosophy, the State, religion—or a nexus of hegemony. Living in prison in fascist Italy and being exposed to the Catholicism of that period was pivotal in cultivating his belief that "political power rests upon cultural hegemony" (Duncombe 2002, 58). For Gramsci the ruling elite maintained its power through hegemony, or a process that involves subaltern groups in their own disempowerment. The method of choice for cultivating self-compliance in one's own oppression is cultural hegemony. For Gramsci, everything is ideological and political. As a result even the seemingly benign institutions like schools are ideological centers for the ruling class. Since they circulated cultural beliefs, citizens subjected to these institutions, willingly or not, were thus inundated with cultural values, or, the political ideology of the elite. As a result, for Gramsci, true revolutionary change can only be realized via the development of a counter-hegemonic culture, a culture that saturates all institutions. According to Gramsci, such endeavors need be collective. That is, a series of atomized individual counter-hegemonic cultures does nothing to undermine the concentrated power of the State vis-à-vis education, religion, and philosophy. In his discussion of philosophy in *The Prison Notebooks* Gramsci argues:

> Creating a new culture does not only mean one's own individual "original" discoveries. It also, and most particularly means the diffusion in a critical form of truths already discovered, their "socialisation" as it were, and even making them the basis of vital action, an element of co-ordination and intellectual moral order. For a mass of people to be led to think coherently and in the same coherent fashion about the real present world, is a "philosophical" event far more important and "original" than the discovery by some philosophical "genius" of a truth which remains the property of small groups of intellectuals. (1971, 325 [quotation marks in original])

It is Gramsci's vision of the power of culture to oppress and liberate that is central to what I argue throughout the rest of this book.

Culture and Social Movements

History has certainly shown that culture and cultural production play central roles in social movements. A social movement is a grassroots, collectively organized series of events that register opposition to a given set of circumstances or structures. In this next section I look at what scholars have argued about the place of culture in social movements. Rather than offer an exhaustive overview of the entire field of culture and social movements in this section I focus on the scholarship I find the most useful in explicating the case study I analyze in this book.[4] Specifically, I discuss culture as a resource (Swidler 1986; Selbin 1997; Taylor and Whittier 1995), political cultures of resistance and opposition (Foran 1992; 1997; Reed and Foran 2002), and the place of culture in facilitating group identity and solidarity (Roscigno et al. 2002; Eyerman 2002; Taylor and Whittier 1992).

Culture is manifested in a variety of forms: rituals, linguistic markers, material objects, social practices, as well as the less apparent ones like worldviews, beliefs, and value systems. The aforementioned ultimately serve as the infrastructure of politics. Culture and cultural production are thus fluid sociopolitical processes. Culture in the context of social movements can be seen as a "characteristic of a movement's environment that functions to channel or constrain its development and that defines what behaviors are legitimate and acceptable" (Johnston and Klandermans 1995, 5). In other words, cultures are manifest in social movements just as much as movements are manifestations of cultural forms.[5]

Culture as a Resource

We must begin by establishing the utility of culture as a tactical tool in social movements. I find Eric Selbin's (1997) analysis of this subject particularly insightful. He borrows from Swidler's "tool-kits for strategies of action" (1986) and Tilly's "repertoires of collective action" (1978) to offer an agency-driven analysis of the revolutionary potential of a given population. Selbin is most centrally concerned with Revolutionary movements, with a capital "R," and his conclusions are thus drawn from the Cuban, Nicaraguan, and Mexican revolutions, among others. The leftist cultural fabric that permeates Latin American resistance movements, Revolutionary and otherwise, is transnational and transgenerational, which is precisely one of Selbin's points. That is, actors draw from the possibilities they see available and their interpretations of their options are largely based on their collective memories of the past. Potential activists, Selbin argues, know if revolutionary activity is a possibility based on a "long-standing history of rebellious activities being celebrated in folk culture or to revolutionary leaders having created, restored, or magnified such traditions in the local culture" (1997, 125). Taylor and Whittier's analysis of feminist movements in the United States lead them to draw similar conclusions. They argue "that ideas and symbols can also function as resources that supply opportunities for activists to mobilize concrete struggles for social change" (1995, 186). In other words, memories, ideas, and symbolic politics fill the "tool-kits" and "repositories of collective action" which are eventually deployed in radically tactical ways. The Chilean solidarity movement very much demonstrates this point as exiles relied heavily on their leftist cultural roots to keep their movement alive.

Political Cultures of Resistance and Opposition

Another useful analytical tool quite central in understanding the solidarity movement is "political cultures of opposition" (Foran 1992; 1997; Reed and Foran 2002). According to Foran and Reed, political cultures of opposition capture everything from shared history, to collective memory, to nascent ideology, or ideas of what individuals suffered through. Specifically they refer to collective oppositional sentiment in revolutionary movements. According to Foran, a revolutionary movement will not triumph without the presence of vibrant political cultures of opposition (1992). Foran and Reed's understanding of what brings about political cultures of opposition is quite applicable to the solidarity movement. They propose that "organizational capacity, lived experience, emotions, culture, and ideology come together under certain circumstances to produce revolutionary political cultures" (Reed and Foran 2002, 340). Additionally, political cultures of opposition both draw from and are reflected in a plethora of cultural productions—folk art, ideology, idioms, historical experience, and the like. In the case of the solidarity movement, Chilean exiles experienced the New Song movement before being exiled and then brought it with them into the diaspora once they began organizing against the dictatorship (see Chapter Three). In short, Foran and Reed propose that culture is both a catalyst to and a manifestation of political mobilization. My analysis of the exile-led anti-Pinochet movement reflects the convergence of emotional, cultural, ideological, and lived experiences that ultimately resulted in a social movement that can in part be characterized by its political cultures of opposition.[6]

Culture, Group Identity, and Solidarity

Another theme noted by scholars in the field and relevant to my study is the place of music in promoting group identity and solidarity in collective action (Denisoff 1983; Eyerman 2002; Eyerman and Jamison 1998; Jasper 1997; 1998; Kaplan 1992; Eder et al. 1995; Roscigno et al. 2002; Taylor and Whittier 1992). According to Polletta and Jasper collective identity refers to "an individual's cognitive, moral connection with a broader community, category, practice, or institution. It is a perception of a shared relation. . . . Collective identities are expressed in cultural materials. . . . And unlike ideology, collective identity carries with it positive feelings for other members of the group" (2001, 285). Scholars have been successful in investigating the influence of music as a cultural production in social movements and social movement culture, especially in promoting mobilization and maintaining solidarity vis-à-vis the development of collective identities. Roscigno et al.'s (2002) work on the textile workers' mobilization in the rural southern United States and Eyerman's (2002) study of the role of song in the Civil Rights movement are instances of such efforts. Drawing from Durkheim, Roscigno et al. (2002) argue that cultural production is best exemplified by rituals that create group solidarity and set group boundaries. Musical productions in the context of worker mobilization contribute to boundary generation and maintenance by singing collectively. Similarly, Taylor and Whittier hold that music is integral to social movements because it promotes group identity, provides an alternative approach to understanding grievance, and gives the group a "sense of political efficacy" (1992). Related to this, Ron Eyerman's study of the cultural aspects to social movements operates from the basic argument that cultural expressions, such as songs, blur the boundaries between culture and politics when studying social movements and that such expressions are political in their form, scope, and content (2002). The findings are similar to Roscigno et al.'s in that Eyerman too argues that music and songs bring hitherto disparate groups of people together, promotes solidarity, and becomes a symbol of collective protest, all issues that I argue are germane to the Chilean solidarity movement.

In sum, social movement theorists have articulated a variety of ways to make sense of culture and social movements. Culture provides a "tool-kit" of resources from which social movement actors borrow. Furthermore, cultural production can serve as its own form of resistance. Additionally, cultural events, especially music, play a central role in developing collective identity and solidarity, both central in the development of a viable social movement. The anti-Pinochet movement organized by exiles, which I describe in the rest of this book, helps to illuminate various complementary pieces of these aforementioned arguments.

Emotions and Social Movements

As I collected the personal and political stories of Chilean women exiles I confronted a plethora of emotions; they expressed sorrow, anger, guilt, despair, and so forth. After my first summer of fieldwork I decided to turn to the literature on social movements and emotions to help explain the various patterns I saw emerging in my interviews.[7] Emotions help us understand why activists choose to get and stay involved in social movements and help to partially explain why social movement actors use the different tactics they do. The literature is relatively new and offers an explanatory power that was until recently overlooked by social movement theorists. It is particularly useful for understanding mobilization against a dictator like Pinochet since under his rule leftists and their sympathizers were virtually guaranteed to experience varying levels of abuse, which resulted in emotional trauma. They were emotionally shaken by the tactics of the dictatorship and those experiences fueled a fire that in many cases translated to protest. Many exiles, and especially those who lost loved ones, felt emotionally compelled to get involved with the solidarity movement. In some cases they felt guilty that they were able to leave Chile safely while others were deeply pained by their own and others' losses. They were also outraged with Pinochet and the United States government for trampling upon their hard-fought-for dream. But despite these potentially debilitating emotions some exiles also carried with them a sense of hope—hope that Pinochet would eventually be ousted, that they would inevitably return to their homes and families, and even in some cases that their beloved socialist state would somehow be rebuilt.

Perhaps it is due to and the result of my decade-plus of interviewing Latin American revolutionaries and feminists who exude palpable passion for their projects, but I have always been dissatisfied with many of the highly cognitive models that dominate Western social movement theory.[8] Indeed, as Goodwin, Jasper, and Polletta point out even the cultural turn in social movement theory has, for the most part, "taken a cognitive form, as though political participants were computers processing symbols" (2000, 66). In an attempt to challenge the still-dominant paradigms, or what Aminzade and McAdam call the "structural environmental perspectives" (2001, 14), several theorists propose various concepts that highlight emotions. Social movement scholars have drawn on the work of social psychologists about the sociology of emotions (e.g., Hochschild 1975; 1979; Kemper 1978) and critiques and analyses from feminist theorists (Campbell 1989; Frye 1983; Hercus 1999; Jagger 1989; Jay 1991; Kleinman 1996; Marx Ferree 1992; Rorty 1980; Scheman 1980; Taylor 1995; Thiele 1986) as they shape this growing body of literature.

According to Goodwin, Jasper, and Polletta, "if emotions are intimately involved in the processes by which people come to join social movements, they are even more obvious in the ongoing activities of the movements. The richer a movement's culture . . . the greater those pleasures" (2001, 18). This is not to suggest that all social movement activity breeds pleasure; indeed political mobilization, even in the most peaceful of times, can be a painful process. Rather, Goodwin et al. are attempting to highlight the connections between culture and emotions in social movements. As I will demonstrate in Chapter Three, the solidarity movement is a quintessential example of this premise and the literature on emotions and social movements is quite helpful in illuminating why.

What are emotions? Arlie Hochschild, drawing from Peggy Thoits (1990), argues that emotions are an awareness of four elements usually experienced simultaneously: "(a) appraisals of a situation, (b) changes in bodily sensations, (c) the free or inhibited display of expressive gestures, and (d) a cultural label applied to specific constellations of the first three elements" (1990, 119). Aminzade and McAdam (2001, 18) also work from this definition, adding a fifth dimension they borrow from Michelle Rosaldo: "Emotions are embodied thoughts, thoughts seeped with the apprehension that 'I am involved'" (1984, 143). Randall Collins offers another complimentary perspective, arguing that emotions are "the 'glue' of solidarity—and what mobilizes conflict—the energy of mobilized groups" (1990, 28).[9] Together I find these definitions quite helpful in understanding social movements. In the case of the Chilean solidarity movement the emotions with which I am most concerned are outrage, sorrow, and hope. Hope initially sounds at odds with the two former emotions. However, many scholars have noted that hope is a necessary emotion or actors would not choose to mobilize (e.g., Jasper 1997; Aminzade and McAdam 2001).

Moral Shocks and Outrage

Moral shocks (Jasper and Poulsen 1995; Jasper 1997; 1998) and moral out-rage (Nepstad and Smith 2001) help explain why anger propels some to lead and join social movements. "Moral shocks," according to Jasper and Poulsen, "refer to an event or situation [that] raises such a sense of outrage in people that they become inclined toward political action, even in the absence of a network of contacts" (1995, 498).[10] In my estimation Pinochet's coup very much embodies the sort of event of which they speak. The shock Chileans ex-perienced, however, was not the result so much of the actual day, September 11, 1973, because for the most part no one was surprised by the coup, so in a sense "shock" is the wrong word. However, intellectually understanding the political inevitability of the coup did not prepare Chileans for the emotional shock and anger they felt once they started seeing their own relatives and friends disappear, their own lives directly threatened, and/or the dead bodies of strangers lining the streets that were only recently filled to capacity with Allende's supporters. These experiences shook Chilean leftists and their sup-porters to their core and exiles took the visions, memories, and nightmares with them when they fled. As a result, the "absence of a network of contacts" became a highly surmountable obstacle, which was replaced in part by the political fuel generated by the moral shock of the dictatorship. Indeed, Jasper and Poulsen argue that "moral shocks can serve as the functional equivalent of social networks, drawing people into activism by building on their existing beliefs" (1995, 498). This part of the equation is particularly true when we try and understand how Canadians and Chileans found one another. That is, there were leftist Canadians already organizing against the dictatorship before most Chileans even arrived and the common sense of outrage at witnessing the end of Chilean socialism and democracy engendered a cross-national solidarity network based on ideology rather than acquaintance.

Nepstad and Smith (2001) offer a similar analysis and indeed draw on Jas-per (1998) as embodied by their argument that moral outrage was the essential motivating factor for many activists in the Central American peace movement, especially people "of faith."[11] Like most theorists of emotions and social move-ments Nepstad and Smith find the irrationally emotional versus overly rational decision maker "erroneously dichotomous" (2001, 158). Indeed, for Nepstad and Smith "moral outrage was a logical emotional response to information about human rights abuses and atrocities in Central America" (2001, 158). In other words, it made perfect cognitive sense to be angry. They argue that a variety of structural factors influenced who had access to this information and furthermore that one's values and identity shape the way the information was perceived and thus acted upon. Again, similar conclusions can be drawn from the exiles' solidarity movement. The "information" exiles received was more concrete than what the Canadian activists, for the most part, had access to in that exiles were directly and indirectly the victims of the human rights violations. But again, this did not mean that all Chilean exiles automatically joined the solidarity movement. The political values and identity of exiles prior to arriving in Canada also helped create the lens they used to help them process what they witnessed while helping them decide what to do with the information. For many Chileans, all but two in my sample, their (or their families') leftist political values and identity definitely shaped the likelihood of their getting involved and indeed, having access to the information.

Shared Emotions and Rituals

Shared emotions (Jasper 1997; 1998) and rituals (Taylor 1995; Taylor and Whittier 1995) also help explain the ability of social movements to ease sorrow and thus illuminate the mobilizing capacity of emotions. According to Jasper, shared emotions are those that a group consciously holds at the same time. He maintains that collectively a group can generate or articulate "anger toward outsiders, or outrage over government policies. It [the group] trusts certain individuals and institutions and mistrusts others. The power of shared emotions comes from expressing them together, from recognizing and proclaiming that they are shared" (1997, 187). This assertion helps us further understand how emotions pull individuals into social movements but in the case of the solidarity movement it explains more; it helps shed light on why the solidarity movement relied so heavily on cultural events, namely the *peñas*. Peñas, political gatherings that operated like parties, were a staple event for exiles and their supporters. They were political statements articulated via culture, specifically music, *empanadas* (Chilean meat pies), and wine. In addition to providing a space to denounce the dictatorship peñas also provided a space for sorrow-filled Chileans to, as Jasper notes, collectively share and articulate their sadness. They also provided a space that confirmed their politics, hopes for the future, and support for the resistance movement. For many Chileans the peñas served as a place to collectively heal the emotional and political pain brought on by exile. And as Jasper notes, it was precisely the opportunity to collectively proclaim these shared emotions that engendered peñas with a power to partially mediate the pain and motivate activists.

Understanding rituals also helps us analyze the place of emotions in mobilizing and sustaining social movements and their actors. Taylor and Whittier (1995) are by no means the only theorists who address this question (see also Hunt 1984; Kim 2000; Steadman 1994; Wuthnow 1987) but their analysis is most illuminating to patterns I found in the solidarity movement. According to Taylor and Whittier, social movement scholars need to designate ritual as central to our theorizing because they are "cultural mechanisms through which collective actors express emotions . . . that mobilize and sustain conflict" (1995, 176). Based on their research on U.S. feminist organizations, Taylor and Whittier argue that rituals serve as cultural mechanisms whereby subordinate groups transform and express emotions resultant from such subordination. Furthermore, they argue that rituals provide the space for actors to redefine dominant feelings to express more positive individual self-conceptions and group solidarity. Taylor and Whittier argue that in certain types of events, for example, films, plays, and concerts (many of which exiled Chileans organized), "ritual is used to express emotion [and] dramatize inequality and injustice" (1995, 178). In other words, rituals help transform potentially alienating and individually experienced emotions to proactive feelings with collective mobilizing potential, precisely what we saw in the solidarity movement.

Pride, Pleasure, and Mobilization

Finally, I borrow from Wood's conclusion (2001) that pride is a politically motivating factor. From her analysis of peasant mobilization in the Salvadoran guerrilla movement she concludes that "moral outrage, pride, and pleasure, along with more conventional reasons such as access to land, impelled the insurgency despite the high risk and uncertainty" (2001, 268). It is important to qualify what she means by *pleasure*. Indeed, she is speaking about guerrilla warfare, which certainly is anything but a pleasure-filled experience. Rather, Wood means "the pleasure subordinate people may take in exercising agency, a human function from which they had long been excluded" (2001, 281). Again, and similar to what the other theorists are postulating, the process of mobilizing serves to transform the alienation and potential sense of political defeat into emotions like hope, which ultimately prove central to mobilizing and sustaining social movements. I observed similar patterns when looking at the Chilean solidarity movement. That is, Chilean exiles received a powerful assault to their political dignity as a result of the coup; their hard-fought-for socialist dream was violently toppled in what felt like a matter of hours. Getting involved in the solidarity movement allowed them the space to collectively claim and reframe that sorrow and anger into a quest for dignity or hope.

In short, emotions help us understand why actors join and stay in social movements and why they choose the various organizational tactics they do. We have seen that anger in the form of moral shocks and moral outrage is

xxviii   *Introduction*

central in catalyzing movements. We have also seen that often the anger and even acute assault on one's political dignity is experienced and articulated collectively, specifically through rituals. The rituals then provide the space to transform the potentially demobilizing emotions into a place of healing and hope which serve to further recruit new activists and fuel others reeling from the pains of, in this case, exile.

A NOTE ON STUDYING DIASPORA

Chilean exiles active in the solidarity movement deserve much of the credit for the cultural and political face of the Chilean diaspora. Initially it was the exiles who served as the architects of this very vibrant transnational community. (As we will see in Chapters Three and Four, Chilean architects literally did play a role in institutionalizing the diaspora by designing housing cooperatives.) Studying exiles and the solidarity movement helps illuminate the fluidity of diasporas in all senses, including reasons for mass exodus and modes of extranational reconstruction. Ironically, much of the literature on diaspora tends to underacknowledge such political, cultural, and emotional fluidity. The conception of diaspora I find most useful comes from Jose Moya (2004). Moya argues that diasporas refer to both "situation and process" and that the two most central criteria for defining a normative type are "dispersion and connectivity" (2004, 6). These ideas capture the mutability of diasporas while also conveying the shared experience ("connectivity") that is at the roots of diasporic communities. Perhaps an even simpler and more straightforward description is "a forced dispersion of a defined group to multiple sites that last a substantial time during which transnational ties to the homeland were maintained" (Wright and Oñate 2007, 31). For Moya, "the novelty in diaspora studies lies not in a new approach to the study of diasporic peoples but in shifting the subject of study" (2004, 7). My goal here is to bring scholarly attention to an undertheorized social movement situated within a diaspora, rather than the Chilean diaspora per se.

As a result, this study does not purport to articulate a new typology for diaspora. Rather, it is my intention to study exile politics and feminism at the nexus of social movement theories of gender, culture, and emotions, and Latin American and transnational feminist history. (I discuss feminism in Chapter Six.) As I have attempted and will continue to outline, each literature has much to offer my analysis. However, each remains sociogeographically limited in its object of inquiry and, as this study will help demonstrate, exile and diaspora politics constitute the perfect bridge to foster cross-disciplinary dialogue.

METHODOLOGY

As I noted earlier Green and Roniger (2007) encourage scholars of exile to take care to collect oral histories and institutional archives from exile communities. I absolutely concur and thus my data comes predominantly from primary interviews and the political archives of the activists themselves. Specifically, data for this study was collected in four ways: (1) one-on-one interviews and focus group discussions; (2) content analysis of primary documents from the movements and media coverage of the events; (3) minimal participant observation with a Vancouver-based email group composed of Latinos/as and Latin Americanist activists and scholars, and (4) secondary sources. Because I am studying a period of time thirty years in the past, I was quite mindful of corroborating information gleaned through my subjects; thus the variety of methods. For example, wherever possible I spoke with more than one woman per family about her recollections of fleeing Chile in order to more accurately capture the story of how and why the family left. I also did a handful of focus group discussions and follow-up interviews with women with whom I already conducted one-on-one interviews to try and better assemble the parts of a given story. These follow-up discussions were with the more seasoned activists and focused on the specific histories and structures of the solidarity and feminist movements. I also spoke to Canadians who were active in the movement and could offer a semi-outsider's perspective. Additionally, I collected and examined media coverage of the period and compared the accounts offered by the press to those of the activists. Similarly, I compared the discourse used in newsletters and flyers, for example, to the recollections shared with me by my informants. That is, I looked to see if the movements' documents told the same stories as did the activists' memories. Ultimately, however, the narrative I share in this book is the story of the Chilean solidarity and feminist movements in Vancouver, British Columbia, told from the perspective of some of the women activists themselves.

I conducted the fieldwork in Vancouver and Victoria, British Columbia, in June 2004 and 2005.[12] I located the informants via a snowball sample. Initially, parameters for inclusion in this purposeful sample included (1) Chilean women, (2) connected to the Left in Chile pre-exile, and (3) affiliated with the solidarity movement while in exile. However, as the fieldwork progressed I saw a need to speak to Canadians who were very central to the solidarity movement, as well as Chileans who were not necessarily leftists at the time of the coup but were in Canada during the dictatorship nonetheless. I also attempted to speak to Chileans who chose not to get involved with the movement, though they proved harder to locate given the highly leftist tendencies of the majority of my informants and my reliance on snowball sampling. In total I spoke with twenty-five women, all Chilean save one, and one Canadian man, who ranged in age from twenty-seven to seventy-one, with the majority currently in their fifties.[13] Class status was fairly heterogeneous; on one side of the spectrum was a woman whose family's economic situation propelled her to begin working at the age of seven, while at the other end were those who came from several generations of the privileged, professional classes. Social class is somewhat hard to determine when talking about exile. For example, many Chilean women left behind prestigious jobs with attendant class and social privilege but were pushed into domestic service once they arrived in Canada. To the best of my knowledge, all my informants are heterosexual, and of the Chilean women, only four are married to the same men with whom they left Chile.[14] Most have long since divorced (at least once) with only two of them remarrying and staying married. Two married after they arrived in Canada and only one of those marriages lasted. Of the six that were children at the time of exile, four are currently married, one divorced and did not remarry, and one, the youngest of the entire sample, never married. Only one of the Chilean women who left as an adult has never married. Of the two Canadians, both are currently married. The woman was divorced once and remarried a Chilean. (We will meet the exiles more personally in Chapter Two and the appendix, where I share their testimonies.)

Some of the Chilean women were literary, visual, and/or dramatic artists in the formal sense, others were self-taught, and still others had no artistic inclinations whatsoever. One of the Canadians is a folk-music festival organizer and historian, and the other a part-time fiction writer. Many of the Chileans left Chile as a direct result of threats to their lives for their involvement in a variety of political projects. Other women left as young children (or, in one case, in utero) when their parents' lives were being threatened, while others followed their partners. Nearly the entire sample remains politically active in some capacity, be it through their course of study, their cultural productions, and/or their paid and voluntary involvement in progressive organizations.

Interviews and focus group discussions lasted between two and four hours, in a place chosen by the interviewee, and all but one were in English. Unless otherwise noted, given the informants' permission I have used their real names. In some cases, however, women came married and were assigned their husband's last name by the Canadian government once their papers were processed (not the norm in Chile). Since then, most have divorced and many have changed or are in the process of changing their names back to their given ones. All of the interviewees were given the transcripts to read, and in some cases edited the transcribed version of their interviews before I used any of their quotes in this book. Additionally, at the request of the informants, all fillers such as "like" and "um" have been removed and grammar corrected where necessary.

Participant observation is a difficult method to incorporate into an historical study based on nonethnographic fieldwork. That is, I was researching the past so there is not much of a contemporary setting in which to participate and observe. However, early on in my research (May 2004), as I was pursuing all of my initial contacts (a son of an exile whose mother I later interviewed), invited me to join an email list in Vancouver comprised of Latino/as and Latin Americanist activists and academics. Initially postings were relatively infrequent, perhaps bi-weekly, and eventually they ceased all together. Over the course of this research the list did not generate a significant amount of data. However, it gave me insight into the contemporary political priorities of some activists in the region. Of the limited posting a considerable amount were from Chilean exiles. For example, there were several events commemorating the death of Victor Jara (see Chapter Three), or films about Salvador Allende to acknowledge the anniversary of the coup. The activism of Chilean exiles has most certainly tapered off but their presence is a permanent part of the Vancouver sociopolitical landscape and participating in the email list allowed me a glimpse into that world.

I also draw on interviews with Chilean leftists and feminists in Chile that I conducted in 1998–1999 for my first book (Shayne 2004). Those interviews were the original impetus for my interest in exile but at the time of those interviews this book was nowhere on the horizon. I visited Chile in October of 1998 and stayed for seven months working from very solid contacts from colleagues in the United States and easily initiated a snowball sample. In total I interviewed twenty-three Chilean women, in Chile. These women held leadership positions of various levels in leftist parties and organizations and/or the feminist movement. I interviewed women who were active during the Allende years as government functionaries and grassroots activists, leaders of the anti-Pinochet movement, feminist and otherwise, members of the contemporary women's movement, and various combinations thereof. Though I had not planned it, the subject of exile came up in nearly every interview since most of the women were exiled during the dictatorship and eventually returned to Chile. The women I interviewed varied in age from twenty-nine to seventy-eight, with levels of education that ranged from secondary schooling to Ph.D.s. Their social classes spanned the spectrum, though the majority reside in the Chilean middle- and upper-middle-classes. The interviews lasted between one and three hours, were cassette taped, and conducted in Spanish, in Santiago, Chile. In sum, data for this book was collected in a variety of ways. I conducted formal interviews with forty-nine people for this project, sometimes twice, some in Chile some in British Columbia, and did an additional four focus group discussions. I did content analysis of primary documents from the solidarity and feminist movements as well as Canadian media coverage of both. Finally, I did a limited amount of participant observation in Canada via a Latin Americanist email list.

ORGANIZATIONAL OVERVIEW

The rest of the book is organized as follows. In the first chapter, I offer an historical overview of the Allende government and Pinochet dictatorship in Chile to provide the context for understanding why exiles left and what about their experiences propelled them to organize en masse. In Chapter Two I introduce the reader to a sampling of women I interviewed in Canada for this project. This chapter focuses on personal testimonies regarding leaving Chile and early experiences in Vancouver or other parts of Canada. In Chapter Three I provide a detailed overview of the anti-Pinochet solidarity movement in global and national perspective in order to foreground the next chapter, which focuses specifically on the Vancouver case. I discuss the movement's emergence, structure, goals, tactics, and efficacy. Chapter Five is dedicated to gender and the movement. I look at the roles of women in the different organizations and the gendered division of leftist labor. I also address the relationship between gender, emotions, and culture as embodied by women's experiences in the solidarity movement. Chapter Six focuses on exile feminism in the diaspora, particularly in the post-Pinochet era. I then conclude the book by asking two questions: How did a gendered lens enhance our understanding of the exiles' solidarity movement, and is exile permanent? I have also included an appendix with the women's testimonies not included in Chapter Two.

NOTES

1. According to the 1993 Rettig report 2,279 people were killed during the dictatorship. Steve J. Stern puts the number at between 3,500 and 4,500. He provides a detailed explanation regarding this discrepancy with the Rettig Report. Raúl Rettig Guissen et al., (1993), *Report of the Chilean National Commission on Truth and Reconciliation, Vol. 1 and 2* (Notre Dame: Center for Civil and Human Rights, Notre Dame Law School); Steve J. Stern, (2004), *Remembering Pinochet's Chile: On the Eve of London 1998* (Durham, N.C.: Duke University Press), xxi and 158–61, fn 3.

2. It is noteworthy that less than half of Chilean exiles ended up in Europe.

3. For an extensive discussion of agency, see Mustafa Emirbayer and Ann Mische, (1998), "What is Agency?" *American Journal of Sociology* 103(4): 962–1023.

4. One of the most oft-cited texts in this field is Hank Johnston and Bert K. Klandermans, ed., (1995), *Social Movements and Culture* (Minneapolis: University of Minnesota Press). For a concise overview of the evolution of the sociology of culture

and cultural studies within sociology, see Ann Swidler, (1995), "Cultural Power and Social Movements," in *Social Movements and Culture,* ed. Hank Johnston and Bert K. Klandermans (Minneapolis: University of Minnesota Press), 25–40.

5. See, for example, Jacqueline Adams' ethnographic work on Chilean *Arpilleristas*: Jacqueline Adams, (2000), "Movement Socialization in Art Workshops: A Case from Pinochet's Chile," *The Sociological Quarterly* 41(4): 615–38; Jacqueline Adams, (2001), "Art in Social Movements: Shantytown Women's Protest in Pinochet's Chile," *Sociological Forum* 17(1): 21–56; Jacqueline Adams, (2002), "The Makings of Political Art," *Qualitative Sociology* 24(3): 311–48.

6. Almeida and Urbizagástegui (1999) offer similar observations based on their empirical analysis of popular music in the Salvadoran national liberation movement. Paul Almeida and Rubén Urbizagástegui, (1999), "Cutumay Camones: Popular Music in El Salvador's National Liberation Movement," *Latin American Perspectives* 105, 26(2): 13–42.

7. See Jeff Goodwin, James M. Jasper, and Francesca Polletta, (2000), "The Return of the Repressed: The Fall and Rise of Emotions in Social Movement Theory," *Mobilization* 5(1): 65–84, for a discussion of social movement scholars, renewed interest in emotions. Ron Aminzade and Doug McAdam, (2001), "Emotions and Contentious Politics," in *Silence and Voice in the Study of Contentious Politics*, ed. Ronald R. Aminzade et al. (Cambridge: Cambridge University Press), 14–50, also offer a comprehensive overview of the emotions literature with respect to earlier social movement theories, namely political process.

8. Similarly, David Slater outlines three persistent problems with Euro-American social movement theory: "(1) The persistence of absence, (2) assumptions of universality, and (3) the problem of 'worlding.'" For Slater, the persistence of absence refers to the ability of scholars to develop arguments "as if the West were a self-contained entity; as if somehow it could be apprehended and comprehended of and by itself." Assumptions of universality refer to "the peculiarity and specificity of the Euro-American 'universal' [that] remain invisible, submerged beneath assumptions of generality." And "worlding" refers to the

> double bind of ethnocentric universalism. Thus there is not only the supposition that the West acts as the primary referent for theory and philosophical reflection but also the frequent inclination to express an interest in the periphery in the context of information retrieval, the incorporation of token, often stereotyped themes such as 'the culture of tradition' or 'violence,' and above all the simplification of the heterogeneity of the periphery."
> (1994, 20)

Slater accurately credits feminist theorists, specifically Chandra Mohanty (1988) for some of his critiques. Though both theorists critiques still ring true there has been a concerted attempt by many social movement scholars, particularly feminists, to empirically and theoretically challenge the aforementioned problems. David Slater, (1992), "On the Borders of Social Theory: Learning from Other Regions," *Environment and Planning D: Society and Space* 10: 307–27; David Slater, (1994), "Power and Social Movements in the Other Occident: Latin American in an International Context," *Latin American Perspectives* 81, 21(2): 11–37.

9. James M. Jasper also works from Collins's definition. James M. Jasper, (1997), *The Art of Moral Protest: Culture, Biography, and Creativity in Social Movements* (Chicago: The University of Chicago Press); James M. Jasper, (1998), "The Emotions of Protest; Affective and Reactive Emotions In and Around Social Movements," *Sociological Forum* 13(3): 397–424.

10. "Moral shocks" are similar to Edward Walsh's conception of "sudden grievances." However, a sudden grievance implies a cognitive response whereas a moral shock reflects the emotional dimension. Edward Walsh, (1981), "Resource Mobilization and Citizen Protest in Communities around Three Mile Island," *Social Problems* 29(1): 1–21.

11. I would extend their argument beyond the religious sector of the peace movement to include the secular as well—students, and so forth.

12. I discuss the significance of Vancouver as a case study in Chapter Four.

13. Unless otherwise noted, the demographic data I share in this, that is, age, marital status, number of children, etc., all refer to the informants at the time of the interview.

14. I did not ask explicitly about sexual orientation but the comfort level was high and the conversation open-ended enough that the women would have most likely shared their sexual preference with me were they not heterosexual.

Chapter One

Political Seeds of Exile and Resistance

It is possible they will smash us, but tomorrow belongs to the people!

President Salvador Allende (in Dorfman et al. 2003, 86)

I don't see why we need to stand by and watch a country go communist because of the irresponsibility of its own people.

—Henry Kissinger, National Security Advisor to Richard Nixon
(in Galeano 1998, 313)

Chile was one of the first countries in the world to abolish slavery. Now our country has broken the chains of totalitarian Marxism, the great Twentieth-Century Slavery, before which so many bow their heads without the courage to defeat it. We are thus once again pioneers in Humanity's fight for liberation.

—General Augusto Pinochet (in Loveman 2001, 262)

INTRODUCTION

Why did hundreds of thousands of Chileans, a fervently patriotic people, leave their homeland en masse? What was it about their political experiences in Chile that led them to rapidly organize anti-Pinochet movements in virtually every of the hundred-plus countries they inhabited? In order to answer these questions we must look at political histories and ideologies that ultimately marked them as exiles and the modus operandi of the dictatorship that caused their collective expulsion. In a study of Chilean exiles in Belgium, Marcela Cornejo explains the importance of history to the exiles she interviewed. Cornejo concludes that "what [the exiles] did during their exile was strongly influenced by what they had done before" (2008, 341). In this chapter I intend to establish the connection between exiles' collective political and ideological lives pre-exile to their political experiences once in the diaspora. In Chapter Four I will make the case that the exiles' anti-Pinochet solidarity movement was borne from intense emotions, namely moral outrage, combined with political cultural histories. I will argue that the exiles' anger over Pinochet's assault on their political dreams combined with the symbolic/cultural resources they brought into exile catalyzed the solidarity movement. In this chapter I hope to illuminate how the exiles' pride in the Popular Unity's (Unidad Popular, UP) accomplished and future goals eventually led to an anger that propelled them to organize once their dream was wholly and violently decimated. I also intend to shed light on how their political exposure during the UP's tenure ultimately translated into ideological resources they would use in the solidarity movement. In what follows I discuss Salvador Allende's tenure as president of Chile, focusing specifically on his coalition's goals and accomplishments, and the rise and fall of Pinochet, particularly the role of women in ousting him from power. I focus on Salvador Allende and the Popular Unity coalition to provide a window into the leftist agendas, passions, accomplishments, and obstacles that exiles internalized and ultimately brought with them into the diaspora. I also look at Pinochet's rise and fall from power to understand why there were hundreds of thousands of exiles in the first place, what they and their compatriots experienced, and to provide the context for understanding their role in Pinochet's ultimate demise; the focus of the remainder of the book.[1]

CHILE'S BUMPY ROAD TO SOCIALISM

In 1952 long-time socialist Dr. Salvador Allende ran for president for the first time and lost to former dictator Carlos Ibáñez. Thus began Chile's uphill battle toward socialism. A year later he was re-elected to the senate and became that body's vice-president. In 1958 he ran for president again and lost by a mere thirty thousand votes to right-wing candidate Jorge Alessandri. Allende ran again in the 1964 elections. Since Allende was so close to victory in the 1958 race the United States government actively intervened to help secure a victory for centrist Christian Democrat candidate Eduardo Frei, who ultimately won the election.[2] While Frei was president, Allende served as the president of the Senate. In 1969 Allende helped organize the Popular Unity coalition and victoriously ran as its presidential candidate in the 1970 election. Allende won 36.5 percent of the vote, Jorge Alessandri 35.2 percent, and

Christian Democrat Radomiro Tomic 28.0 percent. In other words, Allende received only a slim plurality.

According to the 1925 Chilean constitution, if the victorious candidate failed to receive a majority the Congress chose the president from the top two candidates. Tradition dictated that Congress would choose the candidate who garnered the most votes. However, because Allende was a revolutionary Marxist it would not have been surprising if Congress broke with tradition (Oppenheim 1999, 38–39). The Christian Democrats controlled the deciding votes and thus had much bargaining power with both candidates. They pressured the UP parties to agree to constitutional amendments that would limit the future power of the Allende government. While these negotiations were happening right-wing extremist groups like the neofascist *Patria y Libertad* (Fatherland and Liberty),[3] the United States government and corporations, the CIA, and right-wing political parties plotted to prevent Allende's inauguration. U.S. Congressional hearings eventually demonstrated that President Nixon and his foreign policy advisors, particularly Henry Kissinger, were actively involved in an effort to undermine the work of Chile's congress.[4] (Recall the opening quotes in this chapter.) In an attempt to block Allende's confirmation by congress the U.S. government initiated a plot with two distinct tracks known as Track I and Track II. The first track involved attempted manipulation of the Chilean congress to prevent them from selecting Allende. The second track encouraged an outright coup (Qureshi 2009, 58). Toward that end between September and October 1970, the CIA encouraged anti-Allende officers to stage a coup. The plan failed because René Schneider, commander-in-chief, refused to disregard the Chilean constitution by involving the military in politics. As a result, on October 22 "a right-wing group kidnapped Schneider and killed him, using weapons supplied by the CIA" (Power 2002, 26). On November 3, 1970, less than two weeks later, despite his slim victory and the formidable political, economic, military, and U.S./ CIA opposition to his inauguration, Allende was recognized the victor and sworn into office.

The Popular Unity's Program

In order to capture the exile situation we need to understand the Popular Unity's ideology, agenda, structure, and even tensions. The grandiose nature of the UP's political aspirations and accomplishments helps to explain the deep-seated anger exiles brought with them and later applied to the solidarity movement. Similarly, its structure and conflicts illuminates the intraparty tensions that also found their way into exile. The Popular Unity coalition was made up of six leftist parties representing workers, peasants, urban shantytown dwellers, intellectuals, and middle-class sectors. The parties included the Socialist Party (*Partido Socialista*, PS), represented by Allende, the Communist Party (*Partido Comunista*, PC), the Radical Party (*Partido Radical*, PR), the Movement for United Popular Action (*Movimiento de Acción Popular Unitaria*, MAPU), the Independent Popular Action (*Acción Popular Independiente*, API), and the Social Democratic Party (*Partido Socialista Demócrata*, PSD). The Christian Left Party (*Izquierda Cristiana*, IC) became the seventh party in the coalition in August of 1971 when it split from the Christian Democrats.

The UP was formed through intense negotiations in 1969 and 1970. The two main tasks in their initial meetings were to choose a candidate and draft a program, including rules of governance. The UP ultimately agreed upon a program that "promised to bring to an end the rule of the imperialists, the monopolists and the landed oligarchy and to initiate the construction of socialism" (Unidad Popular [UP] 1970; in Cockroft 2000, 257).[5] Allende and the UP shared their program with the electorate predominantly through Allende's campaign speeches and through "Popular Unity Committees" that were set up in virtually every place of work or neighborhood during the electoral campaign. According to the UP, the Popular Unity Committees were to "be run by militants of the left-wing movements and parties and to be composed of the thousands of Chileans who are in favor of fundamental change. These . . . Committees . . . will interpret and fight for the immediate claims of the masses and above all they will learn to exercise power" (UP 1970, 262).

From the UP's perspective the Chilean state and political system had failed its people. Allende and his coalition placed the blame squarely on capitalism and imperialism. Their program explicitly addressed this so-called failure:

What has failed in Chile is the system—a system which does not correspond to present day requirements. Chile is a capitalist country, dependent on the imperialist nations and dominated by bourgeois groups who are structurally related to foreign capital and who cannot resolve the country's fundamental problems—problems which are clearly the result of class privilege which will never be given up voluntarily. (UP 1970, 258)

For the UP, one manifestation of this failure was violence directed at the poor. Their program states: "People living in luxurious houses while a large part of the population lives in unhealthy dwellings or has no shelter at all also constitutes violence; people who throw away food while others lack the means to feed themselves also commit violence" (UP 1970, 259). For the UP, unequal distribution of plentiful resources is violence against the consistently underserved.

The UP was concerned with eradicating these inequities and the subsequent substandard living conditions experienced by much of Chile's poor and working class. In order to accomplish this, the UP's first concern was to empower the poor who had historically been politically disenfranchised vis-à-vis capitalism. The UP proposed what they called Popular Power: "Revolutionary changes required by Chile can only be carried out if the people of Chile take power into their own hands and exercise it in a true and effective manner" (UP 1970, 263). Similarly, democracy was fundamental to their vision:

> The People's Government will guarantee the exercise of democratic rights and will respect the social and individual liberties of all sectors of the population. . . . In order to put this into practice . . . the unions and social organizations . . . will be called upon to participate in government decision making at the relevant level. (UP 1970, 263–64)

The UP sought to make democracy available to all, not just the privileged sectors of society who had direct access to politicians. The UP also proposed changes to the state in order to create "The People's State," which included the creation of a Popular Assembly that would ultimately appoint the justices of the Supreme Court. Additionally they proposed changes in Chile's understanding of national defense, the central tenet being sovereignty from imperialism, militarily, economically, and otherwise, claiming it "will be necessary to provide the armed forces with the necessary material and technical means and to establish a just and democratic system of remuneration, promotion and retirement, which guarantees economic security to personnel in all ranks while serving in the forces" (UP 1970, 267). The respect the UP pledged to the military is sadly ironic given it ultimately played such a critical role in undermining Chilean democracy.

Much of the program was dedicated to explicating the UP's vision of "The New Economy." The main goal "of the united popular forces will be the search for a replacement for the present economic structure, doing away with the power of foreign and national monopoly capital and of the *latifundia* in order to initiate the construction of socialism" (UP 1970, 268). The restructured economy would increase the scope of the public sector through expropriating farms equivalent or in excess of eighty hectares of irrigated land and nationalizing financial institutions like banks, insurance companies, and "all those activities which have a strong influence on the nation's social and economic development" (in Loveman 2001, 246). The ambiguity of this last category provided the UP the space to socialize the channels of production and distribution. To accomplish all of this, the UP proposed the creation of a three sector economy, the socially owned, the privately owned, and the mixed sector. According to the UP the first step in transforming the economy should be the application of a policy intended to create a dominant state sector [socially owned sector], comprising those firms already owned by the state and the businesses which are to be expropriated. As a first step, we shall nationalize those basic resources like large-scale copper, iron, and nitrate mines, and others which are controlled by foreign capital and national monopolies. (UP 1970, 268)

The UP pledged to protect the interests of small shareholders during the process of expropriating industries from the private sectors. Similarly, the privately owned sector was a central component to their economic model. Indeed, "in terms of numbers these enterprises will constitute the majority" (UP 1970, 268). Under the UP program, "the firms which compose this sector will benefit from the overall planning of the national economy" (UP 1970, 269). The mixed sector was also important to their vision and was intended to include enterprises combining state and private capital. Though their economic model was quite progressive, particularly with respect to nationalizing key industries and expropriating businesses, it did have enough emphasis on privately owned sectors, mixed or otherwise, to offer some appeal to the non-Marxist parties in the coalition, and thus, their electorate.

The final component of their economic plan was the acceleration of the agrarian reform initiated but not completed by the Christian Democrats. The UP believed agrarian reform was fundamental to their overall goals for social, political, and economic restructuring. They outlined seven specific steps that they believed would enable Chile to complete land reform. First, they pledged to accelerate the entire process by continuing to expropriate land that exceeded the maximum size as established by the Frei administration but without giving the original landholder the final say regarding which area he would retain and which would go to the State. Similarly, the expropriation may also include any or all of the farm's assets, including machinery and livestock. This differed from the Christian Democrats' plan, which left the farm's assets to the original land holder. Next, they called for the immediate cultivation of abandoned or misused land. Third, they believed the expropriated land should be organized based on cooperative ownership. However, the UP maintained that in "certain qualified cases land will be allocated to small farmers, tenants, sharecroppers and trained agricultural workers." Fifth, the UP believed that small land parcels (or *minifundias*) should be reorganized "by means of progressively cooperative forms of agricultural work." Next, the UP wanted to guarantee that small- and medium-size peasant-run farms had access to services provided by the larger cooperatives in their geographic areas. And finally, the UP wanted to guarantee the defense of Mapuche (indigenous) communities that they believed were "threatened with usurpation of their land" while guaranteeing the "democratic conduct of these communities, the provision of sufficient land and appropriate technical assistance and credit to the Mapuche people and other indigenous groups" (UP 1970, 269–270).

Another part of their program addressed what the Popular Unity called "Social Tasks." This included social services like equal access for all Chilean citizens to rent-controlled housing, education, from preschool to university level, stable employment with adequate wages, medical care (this was quite important to the president given that Salvador Allende was a medical doctor), street lighting, decent sewage systems, drinking water, roads, police, and recreation, including sport fields, holidays, tourism, popular beach resorts, and "a just and efficient social security system, which is not based on privilege and which does not provide starvation level pensions" (UP 1970, 271). In other words, for the UP "basic needs" were not simply about daily survival like food and housing, but long-term comfort and security. The UP was deeply opposed to the class inequities that provided some sectors of society not only economic advantage and success but also access to so-called luxuries like vacations and higher education. For the UP "'reformist' and 'developmentalist' solutions . . . promoted by the Frei Government . . . have not changed anything of importance in Chile" (UP 1970, 258). The Popular Unity believed temporary solutions were nothing but distractions from the systematic, structurally maintained inequities that subjugated the working and poor classes in all social realms — everything from access to a living wage to a holiday on the beach. The UP vowed to rectify these inequalities by replacing one economic system, capitalism, with another, socialism.

The next section of the Popular Unity's program was what they called "Culture and Education." Their goal here was two-fold. First, the UP sought to "develop a new culture which considers human labor with the highest regard" (UP 1970, 273). Related to this, they vowed to provide access to what had formerly been considered "high-culture" and thus reserved for society's elites.

> If, today, the majority of intellectuals and artists fight against the cultural distortions of capitalist society and attempt to convey their creative efforts to the workers and link themselves to the same historical destiny then, in the new society, they will continue this effort but from a vanguard position. A new culture cannot be decreed. It will spring from the struggle for fraternity as opposed to individualism, for the appreciation rather than the disdain of human labor, for national values rather than cultural colonization, and from the struggle of the popular masses for access to art, literature and the communications media and the end of their commercialization. (UP 1970, 273)

The UP had several tactics for implementing these ambitious goals. One component of their program was to create a large network of "Local Centers for Popular Culture" in order to encourage ordinary people to organize themselves and thus participate in the creation and promotion of culture. In the Latin American context Popular Culture has a different meaning than in the Global North. In Latin America "popular" typically refers to that which comes from the people, specifically, the poor and working class. It does not necessarily equal leftist but the connection is typically implied. Related to this, the UP also sought to create a "national system of popular culture [that] will be particularly concerned with the development of the film industry and the preparation of social programs for the mass media" (UP 1970, 276).

The UP also sought to build a "Democratic, Integrated and Planned Educational System." Within this system they proposed national scholarships for university tuition and the construction of new schools in expropriated luxury buildings. They also pledged to pay specific attention to the urban poor and rural areas, both of which the UP believed were consistently and systematically marginalized. Additionally, they pledged the construction of nursery schools, particularly for poor families, for the dual purpose of creating a healthy developmental atmosphere for children and to "facilitate the incorporation of women into productive work" (UP 1970, 274). Since the nursery schools provided day care, they also offered women who may not have otherwise had the opportunity the chance to go to college. The UP's final educational/cultural agenda was to strongly back the university reform process in order to incorporate universities into "the revolutionary development of Chile" (UP 1970, 275).

The final component of the Popular Unity's program was what they called "The People's Government's Foreign Policy." Their main goals were to foster Chilean autonomy and national independence and provide international solidarity to other nations and movements attempting to do the same. According to the UP,

> the active defense of Chilean independence means that we must denounce the present Organization of American States as an agent and tool of American imperialism, and fight against all forms of Pan-Americanism which are implicit in this organization. . . . The government will reject and denounce foreign aid and loans which are extended for political reasons, or involve conditions requiring the investments derived from those loans to be made in ways which prejudice our sovereignty. (UP 1970, 276–77)

In short, the Popular Unity pledged to take Chile on the path to socialism, free from outside intervention. At its core their agenda was about the elimination of structural inequalities as perpetuated by capitalism and the social class system inherent to it. They sought individual, collective, and domestic sovereignty with respect to the economy, social services, and national security. The language of their program was extremely radical and their tactics highly pluralistic. It is certainly easy to understand why the elite classes within Chile and the United States government were threatened and reacted with undeniable hostility to the project that UP ambitiously sought to realize.

The Popular Unity's Accomplishments

Salvador Allende took office with a minimal plurality and formidable obstacles. The Popular Unity's goals were anything but modest, while their political infighting was at times paralyzing. Their political and economic agendas alienated the more privileged classes and empowered formerly marginalized sectors of Chilean society. The Supreme Court was staffed by pre-Allende appointees. Foreign corporations were threatened with expropriation. Foreign governments, namely the United States, refused to, in the words of Kissinger, "stand by" and watch this "test case" (Loveman 2001, 249) and thus potential role model of electoral Marxism succeed and subsequently represent a failure of the U.S. war against communism. In other words, Salvador Allende and his coalition assumed the presidency in the face of great obstacles. Bearing this in mind, how much was he able to accomplish in his brief tenure as president? From the perspective of many leftists, specifics aside for a moment, Allende and the UP were tremendously successful; the UP created a feeling among its supporters never before or since cultivated in the Chilean electorate. According to folk musician Angel Parra (discussed below),

> those 1,000 days seemed like one single day, one single day and one single night—until September 11. All that had been elation, street parties, dance, murals of that time became overshadowed by another reality, like a magnificent sunny day that suddenly begins to cloud over, and there is a horrible storm. (Quoted in Pottlitzer 2001a, 4)

Similarly, when Alicia Basso, former Communist Party leader, and member of Allende's presidential advisory group, reflected on her feelings about his presidency, she explained, "I always say that I had the sensation that we tried to touch the sky with our hands. We had the feeling we were about to touch the sky but the storm came and we got all wet" (personal interview 1999). What happened during Allende's tenure that made leftists feel that they could reach a sunny sky simply by throwing their arms in the air?[6]

Allende's first year in office was marked by enthusiasm and optimism. He started with a series of "redistributive measures" (Wright 1991, 143). For example, free milk for children and nursing mothers, rent reductions, and subway renovation to better serve working-class neighborhoods. Workers also benefited from increases in social security and pension payments combined with salary adjustments designed to help them manage inflation. The middle class also benefited from the elimination of taxes on modest income and property. Combined, these changes spawned a purchasing spree, which led to a boom in industry and services and subsequently raised employment levels.

An early move toward reclaiming Chile's resources and redistributing the wealth among Chileans rather than American businessmen was a constitutional amendment to nationalize the copper industry, including U.S.-owned copper companies. Copper accounted for 80 percent of all of Chile's foreign exchange produced from exports, and of that, half came from three U.S.-owned companies. By 1971 there was nearly a national consensus about the need for Chile to control its principal resource, a process that began under Allende's predecessor, Eduardo Frei, who attempted to "Chileanize" the copper industry. The bill to nationalize the industry passed in Congress unanimously. Leftists considered Allende's success in nationalizing the hitherto U.S.-controlled copper industry a major victory against economic imperialism.

Another accomplishment of the UP was agrarian reform. The 1967 Agrarian Reform Law passed during the Frei administration had yet to be fully realized when the UP took office. The law specified all farms greater than 80 hectares (about 200 acres) were eligible for expropriation and redistribution to peasants. Owners were entitled to keep 80 hectares, livestock, and machinery for themselves and would be compensated for the rest. Eduardo Frei's accomplishments pale in comparison to Allende's in this regard. By the end of Frei's six-year term 3,408,788.3 hectares of land had been expropriated. During the first six months of Allende's tenure he had already accomplished nearly half that, or, 1.5 million hectares of land. By the end of 1972, just two years into his term, Allende expropriated nearly all of the eligible land in accordance with the 1967 law.

Many of the UP's other economic goals, namely the creation of a socialized sector of the economy, were much less successful. However, according to Pedro Vuskovic, minister of economic affairs for the UP, by early 1972 the UP had many economic achievements of which to boast, particularly if one bears the circumstances in mind (in Zammit 1973, 49–56). For example, output grew from 8 percent to 9 percent in 1971 with estimates of growth in real volume in manufacturing between 12 and 14 percent. Under the UP there was also a significant decrease in unemployment within the first year in office. In Santiago unemployment declined from 8 percent when Allende assumed the presidency to less than 4 percent by the end of 1971, one year later. The rate of inflation also decreased from 35 percent in 1970 to 20 percent in 1971. Furthermore, the National Planning Office reported that wage earners' share in national income rose from 51 percent to approximately 60 percent, again, between 1970 and 1971. In other words, the basic premises of Vuskovic's plans included: raise workers' salaries, eliminate unused industrial capital, keep prices for basic goods low and thus attainable for the working class, and implement redistribution mechanisms so that basic goods were available in working-class neighborhoods.

In May 1973 Allende presented his annual congressional address and re-counted his government's accomplishments: The UP expropriated 3,570 rural properties, or 35 percent of Chile's total agricultural surface, which left only a small number of holdings exceeding the legal maximum. The government nationalized 200-plus of Chile's largest businesses, or over 30 percent of Chilean production. Additionally, 90 percent of bank credit was under state control, and income had been markedly redistributed. That is, Allende was making significant progress toward his goal of placing Chile firmly on the road to socialism. However, while some sectors of the population, particularly the working class, were experiencing political, economic, and cultural access like never before, the country's economy was on a downward spiral toward an insurmountable crisis. Needless to say, the UP's advances toward social-ism alienated Chilean capitalists who still held significant power over the economy through their potential business decisions. Rather than investing in the Chilean economy, private entrepreneurs sold off their inventory, disposed of farm machinery and cattle herds, and invested in foreign hard currencies, including U.S. dollars. Together these factors—rising demand, capital flight, and deficit spending—compounded by U.S. intervention in the political and economic workings of the country, eventually led to staggering increases in inflation, reduction in employees' real income, less goods produced, and thus a short-fall in government revenues.[7]

Allende's Downfall

Few leftists were surprised by the coup but most were completely unprepared for its gravity and staying power. For example, María Elena Carrera, a Sena-tor and member of the Socialist Party Central Committee at the time of the coup, recalled having her and her family's "coup bags" packed in case they were forced into hiding:

> We had a plan, with the central committee of my party, to gather in a certain place if there was a coup. . . . I [had] what we called in my family the "coup bag," and in the bag were the essentials you need when you go on a picnic or when you are going to camp out on the mountain. . . . [T]his meant that all the children had their bags for the coup and my mother-in-law also. (Quoted in Wright and Oñate 1998, 15)

The Popular Unity was plagued with political, economic, and even military troubles since before Allende took office, but especially in the last two years of his tenure. Recall, the U.S. government/CIA and right-wing extremist groups tried to prevent his inauguration; U.S. and Chilean capitalists were vehemently opposed to the UP's economic agenda and had the economic power to challenge it at every turn; Allende had no electoral mandate, nor did his party control the supreme court or the Congress. In this section I focus on the political and economic issues that led to Allende's executive vulnerability.[8]

One of the first issues that plagued the UP was political conflict within the coalition.[9] As early as 1971 the UP was starting to divide into two factions, the moderates and the radicals. The moderates' strategy was to work within the constitutional limits while simultaneously moving to create an electoral majority for socialism. The radicals on the other hand did not believe in waiting for an electoral majority. Rather, they believed in mobilizing the grassroots to inspire change from below. The sectarianism was both intra- and inter-party. In some cases party leaders and those they represented were at odds with one another while other tensions existed across the different parties that made up the UP coalition.

In addition to internal fractures, by the end of the first year opposition forces began to mobilize. As Allende's term progressed the opposition grew from extreme right-wing groups like Patria y Libertad to include moderates like the Christian Democrats, who had initially been sympathetic to the UP. Allende was also faced with public dissent from the grassroots. One of the most notable protests happened in December of 1971 when women organized the first "March of the Empty Pots and Pans." Women, elite as well as middle- and working-class, marched in downtown Santiago, banging empty pots and pans in protest of Allende's economic policies. The women maintained that they were going hungry, as evidenced by the less-plentifully stocked shelves and long lines in their local markets. Allende's redistribution of foodstuffs to poorer neighborhoods, anti-Allende shopkeepers hording goods, and politically calculated anti-Allende strikes did in fact mean that women, especially wealthy women, were confronted with the unfamiliar experience of long lines and fewer choices.[10] The short supply of everything from diapers to meat, however, had more to do with the mobilization of anti-Allende forces than the UP's economic policies.

The second year of Allende's presidency was plagued by economic unrest. Domestic production did not keep up with consumer demand for basic goods while Chile could not afford to import all that it needed. The inability of Chile to import goods was in large part due to the U.S. government's decision to terminate all loans and credit to Chile. According to Nixon, this secret plan was designed "to make the Chilean economy scream" (quoted in Oppenheim 1999, 66). One of the most devastating economic events during Allende's presidency was the 1972 October *paro* (strike). The strike began in early October when the forty-thousand-member association of truck owners went on a nationwide strike. With the support of the National Party, the Christian Democrats, the CIA, other groups like bank clerks, members of professional and economic associations, students, and even some working-class and *campesino* groups, strikers essentially shut down the economy. Shop owners closed their doors in support of the strike, making goods unavailable and thus fomenting anger toward the government and its economic policies, rather than the trucking companies and their supporters. The strike lasted a full month and crippled the system of distribution of all goods, including food. This led to hoarding and relentless lines where goods were available. The shortages touched all social classes and thus spread the dissent hitherto concentrated primarily in the elite and extreme right-wing sectors to the middle and working classes. The public dissent was met by mobilization of Allende's supporters, which contributed to the country's already polarized political mood. The strike ultimately ended as a result of Allende inserting the military into his cabinet. Involving the Chilean military in the government's politics was extremely counter to Allende's core political principles and speaks to the perceived urgency of the situation. Sadly, and perhaps not surprisingly, the expansion of the military's political powers left an indelible mark on Chile's future governing.[11]

In March of 1973 the congressional elections further emboldened anti-Allende political forces. The right-wing National Party formally joined with the Christian Democrats in an electoral coalition. At the same time, though the Left publicly supported the socialist project, the UP was speaking with several different voices, undermining their unity and political credibility. The election results illustrate that Chile was virtually divided in two unequal parts: The UP garnered 43.5 percent of the vote while the center-right won 54.6 percent. But the center-right did not receive the mandate it had hoped; if the coalition obtained a two-thirds congressional majority they would have had sufficient votes to impeach Allende. Without this option they ultimately agreed that if nothing else worked, a military coup was necessary to remove Allende from power. By the middle of 1973 both anti- and pro-Allende street protests were becoming commonplace while anti-UP strikes became a normal part of politics. The most damaging strike began in July of 1973 and lasted until the coup, when the truckers, accompanied by the rest of the private sector, went on strike again. Nothing short of the resignation of Allende would persuade them to end the strike. Throughout all of this instability, including acts of sabotage orchestrated by Fatherland and Liberty, the United States was intimately involved. Declassified documents confirm that the Nixon administration and Secretary of State Henry Kissinger instructed CIA personnel to promote a coup in Chile. On the morning of September 11, 1973, the anti-UP forces triumphed in a military coup that resulted in the death of Salvador Allende.[12] Thus began seventeen bloody years of the Pinochet dictatorship.

PINOCHET AND OUTRAGE

During Allende's presidency, Chileans connected to the UP's agenda felt politically passionate about and protective of their vision for a just future. *Allendistas* and UP supporters internalized the program both politically and viscerally and felt personally attacked once their dream was intentionally, permanently, and violently derailed. Those who fled Chile brought that sense of attack with them into exile. The dictatorship, which began September 11, 1973, further entrenched the anger brought on by the coup. According to the junta, they were assuming "supreme rule over the nation with the patriotic commitment to restore the Chilean way of life, justice, and institutional order that have been shattered" (quoted in Rettig et al. 1993a, 73).[13] "Institutional order" translated to mass terror and targeted repression. According to Loveman, there were several overlapping stages in the junta's policies designed to carry out a "thorough 'modernization' and 'cleansing' (*depuración*) of the Chilean polity." The first phase was marked by ad hoc measures of political and economic restructuring in order to establish political control and economic stability. The second stage began in 1975 and served to consolidate Pinochet's control through the secret police and security apparatus combined with an economic "shock treatment." The third stage institutionalized "authoritarian democracy" by introducing a series of "constitutional acts" that eliminated parts of the 1925 Constitution without fully replacing it. Finally, the fourth stage began in 1980 when Pinochet sought to manage the resurgence of political opposition and ultimately complete the "presidential term," which, according to the junta's 1980 Constitution, would end in 1989 (2001, 263–65).[14]

What happened during the dictatorship that left physical and psychological scars upon individual Chileans and their democratic infrastructure? Not even two full weeks after the coup the CIA acknowledged that civilian deaths were anywhere from 2,000 to 10,000 (Kornbluh 2003, 154).[15] These numbers are in stark contrast to the junta's claim of 244 deaths. The 1993 Rettig Report has since confirmed that 2,279 people who disappeared during the dictatorship were subsequently murdered for political reasons. Steven Stern (2004) suggests that the numbers of detained, disappeared, and/or murdered are substantially higher. According to Stern, based on a conservative methodology, a reasonable estimate for deaths and disappearances at the hands of state agents and those in their employ is 3,500–4,500, with political detentions between 150,000 and 200,000, and torture estimates surpassing 100,000. Stern details the process by which he calculated these numbers, which, in short, are the result of formal human rights reports, namely the Rettig Report, media archives, and first-hand accounts from the detained (2004, 158–61, fn. 3).

The detainees were held at approximately twenty different make-shift detention camps spread throughout the country, one of the most infamous being the National Soccer Stadium in Santiago. In the first six weeks following the coup 7,612 prisoners were processed through the stadium. All were held incommunicado and many were interrogated in the locker rooms or luxury skyboxes that were turned into torture chambers. After the abuse many were then executed, buried in secret/mass graves, dropped into the ocean or the Mapocho River, or left on the city streets at night.[16] These tactics were designed to terrorize the population into submissiveness and exile. In addition to those murdered or disappeared by the military, hundreds of thousands more were subjected to and survived egregious physical and psychological abuse, namely torture, arbitrary detention, and forced exile.

The junta immediately banned all political activities, shut down Congress, suspended political parties, took control of the universities, and closed all but the most right-wing of media outlets. Within weeks of the coup Pinochet created a secret police force empowered to "eliminate" enemies of the regime. According to a CIA memo written ten days after the coup: "Severe repression is planned. There is no indication whatever that the military plans any early relinquishment of full political power in Chile" (in Kornbluh 2003, 154). Indeed, the junta stayed in power for over a decade and a half. Shantytowns were particularly vulnerable as they had typically been very supportive of Allende. Shantytown dwellers were some of the Popular Unity's earliest beneficiaries with respect to everything from a new sense of dignity to concrete gains designed to better the abject conditions under which the poor lived. Blanca, a woman from the *La Victoria* neighborhood in Santiago, interviewed by Patricia Politzer, explains: "The period of Popular Unity was the most fruitful era we have ever known. What little we have now, we saved from that time: the refrigerator, the gas range, a twelve-inch television, a washing machine. . . . I never imagined my children would each have their own bed" (quoted in Politzer 2001, 159)! As a result of this sort of pro-Allende sentiment, entire shantytowns were deemed subversive by the junta. Blanca continues:

> September 11, 1973, is an unforgettable date for us. Everyone went out into the street, airplanes began to fly overhead, swooping so low that the tin roofs shook and the noise was deafening. Women began to cry. . . .
>
> I was furious. I was crying with fury. . . .
>
> I was so angry and so sad! I was afraid, but I felt I had to do something. . . .
>
> On the fifteenth, for the first time, the soldiers came into the neighborhood during the day. They arrived, firing their guns, at nine o'clock in the morning; they were looking for priests. These were working-class priests, and they were branded Communists. Hundreds of soldiers were shooting in the streets. The noise was awful. They shot at roofs, and pieces of tin and wood were flying

everywhere. . . . That day made me understand what the following years of terror would be like. (Quoted in Politzer 2001, 154–55)

The members of *La Victoria* and other similar communities watched not only their political dreams evaporate but their concrete advances abruptly turn upside down as well. And as Blanca explains, the assault left them riddled with anger, which propelled many of them to resist.

Pinochet's regime will be held in infamy for several reasons. One reason includes a series of massacres known as "The Caravan of Death." Between October 16 and 19, 1973, General Sergio Arellano Stark coordinated a death squad of military officers that traveled throughout the central and northern parts of the country. Their objective was to "expedite justice" (Kornbluh 2003, 155). At each stop the leader of the caravan identified a series of prisoners—regional representatives of the Popular Unity government, mayors, police chiefs, prominent leaders in the trade union movement, and civic leaders—removed them from their cells, had them taken away, brutalized, and shot. Over the four days sixty-eight individuals were killed, most thrown into common graves while their families were denied permission to bury them. Fourteen of these bodies have yet to be recovered.

The Pinochet dictatorship is also notorious for the Directorate of National Intelligence (*Dirección de Inteligencia Nacional*, DINA). After Pinochet, the DINA was the main pillar of the regime's power. The DINA unofficially came into being November 12, 1973, but would not become an official institution until decree 521 was passed on June 14, 1974. The DINA had a large organizational infrastructure and was infamous for three types of human rights violations: secret detention camps, systematic practices of torture, and the disappearances of thousands of Chileans. All of the detention camps dealt with the prisoners in similar fashion: victims were blindfolded once kidnapped from their homes or on the street by plainclothes DINA agents in unmarked, civilian vehicles. They were then brought to the camps and severely abused. According to Kornbluh, each detention center specialized in a particular form of torture. For example, at Londres No. 38, a facility in Santiago housed in the former Socialist Party headquarters, DINA agents rounded up the prisoner's family and sexually abused them while the prisoner was forced to watch. According to a Chilean human rights organization the DINA used seventeen different types of torture (Wright 2007, 65). Some that were commonly used on the prisoners include:

• The Grill: prisoners would be tied to a metal bedspring and electrical current applied to sensitive body parts, including genitals.

- La Parilla: a bar on which victims were suspended by the wrists or by wrists and knees for long periods of time. While suspended, victims received electric shocks and beatings.
- The Submarine: forced immersion in a vat of urine and excrement, or frigid water.
- The Dry Submarine: use of a cloth bag roped around the head to bring victims to the point of suffocation. This practice was often accompanied with burning victims with cigarettes to accelerate loss of air.
- Beatings: administered with gun butts, fists, and chains. In one technique, called "the telephone," according to a survivor, the torturer "slammed his open hands hard and rhythmically against the ears of the victim," leaving the prisoner deaf (Kornbluh 2003, 162–63; Muñoz 2008, 46–47).

A woman Patricia Politzer calls "Raquel" recalls her and her husband's detention:

> I still had the blindfold on so I wouldn't recognize the torturers. . . . They applied the electric prod to Jorge's [her husband] penis, to his anus, to his eyes . . . it was terrible. I knew what was happening from his awful screams and the way he was moving . . . every scream went straight to my soul. (Quoted in Politzer 2001, 82)

Torture was designed to get prisoners to confess to the so-called crimes they were accused of and to extract information about other suspected or real leftists. It was also meant to terrorize those in the victim's political and familial circles. Torture victims however rarely provided confessions or information about their *compañero/as* (comrades) because refusing to do so conveyed resistance to the dictatorship. Defying the dictatorship and protecting their cause often took priority over the immediate relief of a loved one's pain. Raquel continues:

> The only prayer I had was that they wouldn't go too far with the torture. That he wouldn't die. But I would be lying if I said that I had for one second thought about saying something to save him. It never crossed my mind. The only thing I longed for was that he continue to resist. . . . I couldn't be an informer; I couldn't betray the cause that I loved my entire life, the cause I had been defending since I was fourteen years old. For me, betrayal is the ultimate sin. If I would have talked, I would have been like a piece of trash, and moreover, I would have felt Jorge's contempt. (Quoted in Politzer 2001, 82–83)

Raquel eventually went into exile. Raquel, like hundreds of thousands of other exiles, brought with her the conviction that prevented her from saying anything that might betray her beloved and lifelong cause, even if were to stop her husband's soul-touching screams.

Rape was also a common tactic. Many women prisoners were brutally raped and at least a dozen were impregnated by their torturers. Some women had rodents inserted into their vaginas as a regular course of action (Muñoz 2008, 47). Rape as a torture tactic had a particularly vile psychological element as rape survivors carry around a shame that can never be shaken.[17] A woman who spoke to the Chilean National Commission on Truth and Reconciliation about her father's murder explains: "When they took my father, they took my husband and me as well. I was raped by a whole group that was guarding me. I never told my husband. That was fifteen years ago" (quoted in Rettig et al. 1993b, 782).

Most of the thousands who disappeared did so at the hands of the DINA. "Some were killed and buried in secret graves; others were airlifted in a helicopter and thrown into the ocean by DINA agents 'after first cutting their stomach open with a knife to keep the bodies from floating'" (Kornbluh 2003, 163). The disappearance of victims was a mode of psychological torture designed to terrorize the opposition more generally, while psychologically injuring the victim's family. Ironically, it was precisely the tactic of disappearing that led to the formation of the Association of the Relatives of the Detained and Disappeared (*Agrupación de Familiares de Detenido y Desaparecido*—AFDD), which served as a major catalyst to the movement against Pinochet. (I discuss this in greater detail below.)

Exile was another tactic employed by Pinochet (Angell and Carstairs 1987, 148; Wright 1995, 199; 2007, 68–69; Wright and Oñate 2007, 34–35). What do we mean by exile? Exile is a person, a place, and a process. Formally we can think of an exile as one who has been forced out of her country for political reasons. According to this definition then all exiles would be refugees. Refugees differ from immigrants in their causes for leaving their home country. *Refugee* has a political connotation, whereas an immigrant is presumably motivated by opportunism. Similarly, different programs exist for political refugees to which economic immigrants may not have access. However, the distinction does not work for Chileans under Pinochet. For example, a person may have left because she became unemployable after the coup, a very common occurrence. If someone was a member of a union it was a virtual certainty that her employer fired her and her name ended up on a blacklist. The junta may have overlooked her but she still became unemployable for the duration of the dictatorship. (In Chapter Two we will meet a few women who were in this position as a result of their husbands' political activities.) In other words, their economic predicament was a result of their political convictions, making the cause for leaving Chile political. In this book I define *exile* as one forced to leave Chile because of the dictatorship.[18] That is, if one's life became unlivable due to the dictatorship, be it financially, psychologically, or physically, I consider her an exile.

Exile was certainly less dramatic a punishment than imprisonment, torture, assassination, and/or disappearance, yet it was extremely common for exiles to have experienced any number of the aforementioned atrocities prior to being exiled. For example, many Chileans, both those who stayed and those who fled, disappeared for finite periods of time. That is, they were captured and detained incognito for varying periods—days, weeks, months, or more. Their families suffered but were eventually reunited with their loved ones, something that did not happen for the thousands declared "disappeared." It was often these same temporarily disappeared people who eventually fled the country after being released, knowing that the likelihood of being captured again was high and next time they would likely not be as "lucky."

According to Dominguez (1984) exile involves a series of psychosocial consequences. With respect to exile, consequences include: an "abrupt rupture of life projects; the loss of social and emotional networks of family, friends, and co-workers; the loss of a familiar landscape and geography; and the end of active participation in the everyday life of one's country and, therefore, the loss of personal history, biography, and a sense of identity" (cited in Espinoza 2004, 77). Indeed, exile was one of Pinochet's many tactics replete with psychological devastation.

By the middle of 1978 nearly 30,000 Chileans had been forced into exile in Western Europe alone, and by the end of the decade an estimated 200,000 Chileans fled their country for political reasons. According to Wright and Oñate, by the end of the dictatorship one million Chileans had left their country. They suggest that 200,000 were political exiles while the remaining 800,000 fled for economic reasons (1995, 198; 2007, 31). However, as I noted, I find the distinction somewhat blurry. Marcela Durán also maintains that one million Chileans left their homeland as a result of the coup, though her article was written in 1980, so by the end of the dictatorship she may have adjusted her numbers up (1980, 13). One of the immediate results of this mass exodus was the dispersion and displacement of over a tenth of the population, the majority of whom were leftists or leftist sympathizers. Their absence was partially responsible for Pinochet's rapid consolidation of power (Wright 1995, 199; Wright and Oñate 2007, 34; Angell and Carstairs 1987, 157). However, as I and others have argued, banishing the leftists from Chile did not eliminate their desire and ability to participate in Chilean politics, as the exile community eventually represented a major sector of the movement to oust Pinochet.

Who are the exiles? Demographic and political data regarding the exiles remains somewhat imprecise. In a general sense, exiles were forced out of

Chile due to their real or suspected political opinions and past activities. They ranged in age from the very young (even in utero) to the elderly. Race was somewhat diverse since the numbers include a sizeable presence of Mapuche Indians. Approximately three thousand Chileans went into exile directly from prison, while many others had been detained for short periods of time. Others fled because they either received detention orders or heard that they were being pursued. Others left because political pressures made it impossible for them to work. That is, they ended up on blacklists or worked in industries shut down or privatized by the military, for example, universities or newspapers. The majority of exiles were members, sympathizers, or family members of left or center-left parties. Social class was somewhat diverse though middle- and professional-class Chileans were definitely in the majority[19] (Wright and Oñate 2007, 37; Angell and Carstairs 1987, 153). The women (or their partners) I interviewed for this book reflect these same overarching demographic trends. This becomes more apparent in Chapter Two and the appendix, which include the testimonies of the different women I interviewed.

THE MOVEMENT AGAINST PINOCHET INSIDE CHILE

What did that movement look like from inside Chile, or the "interior," as it was known by exiles? In this section I will discuss the movement against Pinochet, paying specific attention to women and culture. I will also offer an introduction to the place of exiles in the anti-Pinochet movement. The significant role played by women in bringing down Pinochet has been well documented (for example, see Baldez 2002; Chuchryk 1984; 1989a; 1989b; 1994; Fisher 1993; Franceschet 2005; Frohmann and Valdés 1995; Gaviola, Largo and Palestro 1994; Noonan 1997; Palestro 1991; Shayne 2004). Thus, this section is not meant to be an exhaustive discussion, but rather a brief sampling of women's mobilization against Pinochet.[20] Specifically, I will look at the human rights and feminist sectors of the movement.

According to all of the women I interviewed for my first book and other feminist histories of the period, women were the first to take to the streets to oppose the Pinochet dictatorship. By July of 1975, the Association of the Relatives of the Detained and Disappeared (AFDD) was established.[21] Like their counterparts in Argentina and Central America, these women often met repeatedly in line at police stations, detention centers, or government offices, trying desperately and determinedly to ascertain the whereabouts of their disappeared husbands, fathers, brothers, and/or children.[22] There were women political prisoners as well, but the majority were men.[23] While in Chile in 1999 I interviewed Viviana Díaz, president of the AFDD.[24] Viviana's father, an Allendista, was disappeared after the coup and she has been involved with the AFDD ever since. She explained how the AFDD initially began taking to the streets:

> We eventually conquer[ed our] fear to go out in the streets. We started to use . . . pictures because we were told that the people we were looking for were fabricated family members, so we had to show people these were the people who we were looking for, and tell us where they are, because if they have gone clandestine, well then locate them and tell us; here they are. They were never able to do this and that is how we started to go out in the street; we were the first organization that conquered the fear of going out in the street and having small, simple demonstrations. We would sit on the park on the side of the *Moneda* palace. . . . That is where we started to go and sit and we would have small signs that said: "Where is my father?" "Where is my son?"

The AFDD played an important role in the anti-Pinochet movement through their ability to minimize the fears of those supportive of but uncomfortable with the idea of participating in the protests. As a result, the women of the AFDD are typically identified as responsible for catalyzing the movement against Pinochet.

Another important part of the human rights movement was the *arpilleristas*. Arpilleras, literally meaning burlap, are tapestries handmade from scraps of fabric by women residing in the *poblaciones* (shantytowns) and elsewhere in Santiago. Each arpillera conveyed a woman's interpretation of life under the dictatorship, many of which had some image of the permanent loss of their children and loved ones (see the cover of this book). Or, as Emma Sepúlveda, herself a Chilean exile, explains: "the *arpilleras* were compact records of the misery and suffering of all Chileans" (1996, 21). These arpilleras, compact and portable as they are, were then smuggled out of Chile and sold abroad by Chilean exiles, who used the folk art to articulate life under the dictatorship while raising funds to support the anti-Pinochet movement in Chile (Adams 2000; 2001; 2002; Agosín 1987; Moya-Raggio 1984; Sepúlveda 1996). The National Vicariate of the Catholic Church in Chile was quite instrumental in helping to form the committees of women that eventually made the arpilleras. The church helped women organize a series of workshops in detention centers and shantytowns so that people could help earn some extra money to feed their families. The crafts that were made in the workshops were then disseminated by the Vicariate and provided women a small source of desperately needed income. Some women who got involved with the arpilleras workshops were also members of the AFDD. By 1975 they started making and distributing their tapestries, which served to express what the Chilean media refused to say. According to Emma Sepúlveda, "this utterly silent social art was soon converted into the most effective clandestine means of communication to resist the military dictatorship of General Augusto Pinochet" (1996, 25).

Feminists also played a central role in bringing down Pinochet. In 1983 the organization the Movement for the Emancipation of Women '83 (*Movimiento Pro Emancipación de la Mujer 83*, MEMCH'83) emerged as a leading women's umbrella organization who framed their actions in explicitly feminist terms. At the time that MEMCH'83 was formed the women's organizations were structured around three central goals: human rights, self-help, and feminist groups. These sectors were represented by three separate federations: the Committee for the Defense of Women's Rights (*Comité de Defensa de los Derechos de la Mujer,* CODEM), Women of Chile (*Mujeres de Chile,* MUDECHI), and the Movement of Shantytown Women (*Movimiento de Mujeres Pobladores,* MOMUPO) (Baldez 2002, 149). The first two were from left-wing parties, with the central focus being to end the dictatorship. Both organizations initially declined to identity as feminist despite the fact that they focused on women. CODEM eventually changed its position. MOMUPO worked with *pobladoras* (shantytown dwellers) from the northern part of Santiago and were initially concerned with devising economic survival strategies (Valdés and Weinstein 1993). All three emerged as grassroots organizations that worked to unite and coordinate the activities of smaller neighborhood groups (Chuchryk 1994; Frohmann and Valdés 1995). The focus on neighborhood organizations was more politically significant than might be assumed. Because the dictatorship forced political parties underground, political activities moved from the national/formal sphere to the very local, community level. Here the presence of women was particularly noticeable as their assigned roles as nurturers positioned them to collectively organize soup kitchens and the like (Mattear 1997, 86). The absence of male-controlled political parties meant that this new and highly untraditional locale for doing politics was women-centered and -dominated.

Another women's organization central to the movement against Pinochet was Women for Life (*Mujeres por la Vida*)—a pluralistic coalition of women's and feminist organizations that spanned the political spectrum from the Movement for the Revolutionary Left (*Movimiento de Izquierda Revolucionario,* MIR) to the Christian Democrats. It was established in December of 1983, six months after the birth of MEMCH'83. On one political end were the Christian Democrats, many of whom had been vehemently anti-Allende, and in some cases, at least initially, in favor of the coup. On the other extreme was the MIR, who, even prior to the coup, was a proponent though not necessarily practitioner of armed struggle and criticized the Chilean Left for relying on elections to gain power. That is, for the members of the MIR the strategies of the Popular Unity were not militant enough. (The MIR did support Allende's 1970 electoral victory.)

Artist activists are often overlooked for their contributions to bringing down Pinochet (Pottlitzer 2001a; Moya-Raggio 1984). Because censorship was so intense and political meetings deemed illegal, art played an important role in conveying what was happening and bringing people together in legal ways (Blaine 2009; Loveman 2001, 279; Mattern 1997). This was especially true in the case of popular theater (Ochsenius 1991). Ramón Griffero, a director and playwright, believes that art played a role in ousting Pinochet. He recalls:

> When all the communications media were controlled, live performance was almost the only one that existed with its own voice, without censorship. Even though there was a certain level of self-censorship, and shows were closed now and then. . . . Those live performances were artistic shows, but they were not merely nonpolitical recitals. They were political meetings as well. . . . I think art contributed [to bringing down Pinochet] by being able to subsist and generate autonomous spaces during all that time. (Quoted in Pottlitzer 2001b, 12)

Playwrights re-crafted language to make explicit political points for members of the audience sympathetic to their position. On the other hand, many of the anti-Pinochet messages were so veiled that right-wingers in the audience did not even realize the message was there. As a result, it was legal to perform and attend the plays and it gave leftists a relatively safe gathering space to find one another and sustain their vision of a Chile without Pinochet.

It is important to remember, however, that though the same explicit mechanisms for censorship did not apply to theater as television and print media, the junta did find ways to both monitor the content of productions and intimidate theater companies and their audiences from performing "subversive" stories. For example, David Benavente, a sociologist, playwright, filmmaker, and director of communication arts at the Alberto Hurtado Jesuit University, recalls the subtle forms of censorship that limited the poetic license of playwrights and actors/actresses.

> We didn't have to pass the script by any censor, the way they had to in Spain or in Brazil. What did exist was a commission created in 1974 to enforce a tax law called the IVA [aggregate value tax] that subjected theater productions to a 22 percent tax on gross box office receipts unless the productions were approved as "highly cultural" and therefore exempt. This subtle form of censorship counted on the accurate assumption that the financial burden of such a tax would be prohibitive to most independent theaters, whose survival relied on ticket sales. (Quoted in Pottlitzer 2001b, 25)

Benavente goes on to explain how playwrights made sometimes successful attempts to adhere to this requirement while receiving a certification that their plays were indeed "cultural pieces." For a play to be considered a cultural piece was "really a euphemism for saying if this play is produced, the military won't come and kill a lot of people, which would mean killing that person [the one who declared it a 'cultural piece'], too, because he or she said it was OK" (quoted in Pottlitzer 2001b, 25).

In addition to serving as a form of political communication, as was the case for the arpilleras and theater, art also served as a way to feed and ultimately revitalize the spirit of politically demobilized leftists, particularly political prisoners. Angel Parra, composer and singer, recalls the importance of art to what he calls the "cultural agitators" who were incarcerated after the coup:

> We created mural newspapers. There were many journalists in the jails and ex-
> cellent illustrators and caricaturists, so we didn't need photographers—besides,
> we didn't have cameras. . . . Some of us wrote poetry. . . . We didn't have a radio,
> but we had music, the music we made ourselves. . . . There was also intense
> activity in popular culture. . . . Jewelry and other crafts were made out of scrap
> metal, cloth and pebbles. This form of cultural work began to occur in all the
> jails. It was the only form of power there was to maintain our spirit, maintain a
> state of mind that belonged to us and not to those who dominated us—or who
> wanted to dominate us. (Quoted in Pottlitzer 2001a, 5)

In other words, cultural production and art played a variety of roles for Chilean leftists during the dictatorship—it helped them find each other, to sustain their collective leftist spirit the dictatorship worked so tirelessly to destroy, and it served as a form of communication to denounce Pinochet and his regime. Cultural production also played a central role in the solidarity movement organized by exiles, meeting some of these very same needs. (I discuss this more in Chapters Four and Five.)

By 1983 the aforementioned sectors—human rights activists, arpilleristas, feminists, and artists—in conjunction with labor unions and political parties resurfacing from underground, were collectively and consistently mobilizing against the dictatorship. As the protesters swelled in numbers, so too did the repression. After three years of visible protests Pinochet's power remained fully entrenched. Opponents of the regime, including hitherto squelched political parties, eventually changed tactics and focused their efforts on defeating Pinochet in the upcoming plebiscite. According to the dictatorship's 1980 constitution voters would register their approval (a Yes vote) or disapproval (a No vote) for the junta's candidate—presumably Pinochet—for president from 1989 through 1997. Though the task of electorally defeating Pinochet was an onerous and indeed politically contentious one, the opposition successfully waged it. The first campaign of the center-left was to get people to register to vote. The second was to create legal parties, two tasks in which women were quite active. By early 1988 the various committees who organized Chileans to vote "no" to Pinochet's continued power-hold formed an organization called the Coalition for No (*Concertación por el No*). Graciela Borquez was one of the co-founders of the aforementioned feminist coalition Women for Life. She explained the role of her organization in the No Campaign to me:

> We had to do something so that people knew that they had to vote No. So we started to throw out ideas until we got one that became known worldwide, and then many copied us, it was good: black silhouetted images of a person that said: "so that you do not forget me, have you forgotten me?" And we wrote the name of a persecuted person. We made one or two thousand . . . we filled downtown Santiago with the figures.

The silhouettes lined the streets, urging Chileans to cast their "no" votes for the disappeared, whom lacked the opportunity to do so.

The No movement carried out a well-organized campaign and received international support, much of which was secured through the sustained efforts of exiles. While Chileans inside of Chile organized in the aforementioned ways, exiles coordinated parallel demonstrations, media campaigns, and fundraising efforts to support their compañero/as who did not leave Chile. Many exiles even returned to Chile, some only temporarily, precisely to work with the movements that were organizing to oust Pinochet. Six million Chileans went to the polls on October 5, 1988 and rejected Pinochet—55 percent voted "no" and 44 percent "yes." Among women voters, despite the fact that polls predicted the majority would vote "yes," 52.5 percent voted "no" (Baldez 2002, 174; Oppenheim 1999, 182). Begrudgingly, Pinochet stepped down and in December of 1989 the first elections since the dictatorship occurred. Patricio Aylwin, a Christian Democrat with solid support from the Left, including the Communists, who were prevented from running, was victorious and in 1990 assumed a presidency plagued with insurmountable problems. A diverse group of actors and forces ultimately brought an end to the dictatorship and ushered in the transition to democracy: women, human rights activists, the church, artists, intellectuals, labor, grass-roots community leaders, politicians, non-Chilean internationals, exiles, and various combinations thereof. Without this cross-section of activists, Pinochet may have remained in power until 1997.

PINOCHET'S FATE

October 16, 1998, is a most historic date for Chileans. That night, two Scotland Yard detectives served Augusto Pinochet a "priority red warrant" on behalf of the Spanish government for crimes of "genocide and terrorism."[25]

Spanish lawyers had been working for two years assembling a case against Pinochet. They confronted a number of barriers including resistance from the U.S. government, but their most concrete challenge was physically apprehending Pinochet. Spanish law forbids trials in absentia and though they could have legally extradited Pinochet from Chile it was a virtual certainty that the Chilean Supreme Court, staffed with Pinochet appointees, would never expel him for such a trial. Fortuitously, Pinochet traveled to London with his wife in late September 1998. While there he did an interview with a journalist from the magazine *The New Yorker.* In the article he made reference to the fact that he would be seeking medical care in London and staying on for a while. Once the article hit the news stands members of Amnesty International Britain learned Pinochet was in London. Eventually the Spaniards learned of the information as well and coordinated an effort to formally detain, question, and extradite the general. Chilean officials pressured the British government to release Pinochet to Chile rather than extradite him to Spain. Over the sixteen months he was under house arrest in the estate he and his wife were renting for sixteen-thousand dollars a month, the British Law Lords debated the legality of extraditing Pinochet. Once it finally looked as though he would be sent to Spain to stand trial, a final wave of pressure exerted on the British government led British Home Secretary Jack Straw to announce, "following recent deterioration in the state of Senator Pinochet's health, [he is] unfit to stand trial"[26] (quoted in Kornbluh 2003, 461). Additionally, some argued it would be in violation of his human rights to subject him to the tedium and duress of a trial given his physically and mentally compromised state.

Many found assertions about Pinochet's failing health and the humanitarian appeal highly unbelievable and painfully ironic. David Aaronovitch, a columnist for the London daily *The Independent*, responded to the calls for humanitarianism: "Your beloved general is safe with us. He will not be tortured, stabbed or shot, or have electrodes attached to his genitals. We will not drop him from a helicopter into the sea, kidnap his grandchildren, break his hands or gouge his eyes" (cited in Muñoz 2008, 260). Once arrested, all media coverage of Pinochet showed him wheelchair bound. However, as soon as he returned to Chile via air force jet, he disembarked onto a red carpet lined with a military marching band, "smiling and spry, rose from his wheelchair and walked across the tarmac to shake the hands of the generals who played such an important role in securing his release" (Kornbluh 2003, 462). In March 2000 Pinochet was finally criminally charged under Chilean law and placed under house arrest.[27] He died at the age of ninety-one on December 10, 2006. According to Heraldo Muñoz, high-level Allendista, Chilean diplomat, and long time politico: "Nobody won with Pinochet's death. It was a draw. The courts did not sentence him and the remains of many prisoners who disappeared have still not been found; . . . but Pinochet spent his last years on the defensive, a helpless witness to the destruction of his reputation" (2008, 302).

CONCLUSION

As I have attempted to demonstrate in this chapter, the political seeds of exile and resistance were planted in Chileans long before they left their homeland en masse. The abrupt rise and fall of socialism in Chile explains the mass exodus of exiles and their political goals once outside of their country. As we saw, the Popular Unity's agenda and ambitions were far reaching. Allende put Chile firmly on the path toward socialism. In the process many leftists and their sympathizers were politically energized as they grew more and more invested in a dream that was producing real results. The Left helped unravel decades of Chilean capitalism over the course of one thousand days. As they advanced toward their goal Chilean leftists grew more politically and emotionally attached to the project and what they envisioned as an economically and socially just future for all Chileans. As Allende and the UP moved Chile toward socialism, opposition forces grew, created alliances, and ultimately were successful in ending Allende's life and forcing the Popular Unity permanently from power. However, the opposition forces, even with the backing of the U.S. government, CIA, and Chilean military, were entirely incapable of eliminating the Chilean Left's vision of egalitarianism. The violent assault on their hard-fought-for dream left a political and emotional scar that many have yet to heal from but it did not lead to full-scale surrender. Rather, the coup and dictatorship catalyzed anger, resistance, and ultimately public mobilization against the junta, not at all what Pinochet had intended.

The hundreds of thousands of Chileans forced out of their country during the dictatorship were both architects and beneficiaries of the Popular Unity project. The exiles brought their political histories, convictions, alliances, and even divisions with them into the diaspora. Though many Chileans were traumatized both physically and politically by the violent assault on their dream, they converted this emotional pain into political mobilization. To many of the exiles Allende was more than a president and the Popular Unity more than a political coalition; both were emblematic of something much bigger and from the exiles' perspectives needed to be defended and vindicated if only from afar. Kicking the leftists out of Chile meant that the Chilean Left was distributed and dispersed around the world, arguably expanding its reach rather than squelching its momentum, as Pinochet and his junta originally intended. In the rest of this book we will see how the exiles' political histories, cultures, and emotions translated into a transnational movement mobilized to oust the dictatorship.

NOTES

1. This chapter is not meant to be an exhaustive overview of twentieth-century Chilean history. I point the reader to Lisa Baldez, (2002), *Why Women Protest: Women's Movements in Chile* (Cambridge: Cambridge University Press); Susan Franceschet, (2005), *Women and Politics in Chile* (Boulder: Lynne Rienner Publishers); Brian Loveman, (2001), *Chile: The Legacy of Hispanic Capitalism, 3d ed.* (New York: Oxford University Press); Margaret Power, (2002), *Right-Wing Women in Chile: Feminine Power and the Struggle Against Allende 1964–1973* (University Park, Pa.: Pennsylvania State University Press); Thomas C. Wright, (2007), *State Terrorism in Latin America: Chile, Argentina, and International Human Rights* (Lanham, Md.: Rowman & Littlefield Publishers). Combined, these books provide the reader with a detailed analysis of Chilean history, including the place of women in shaping it.

2. See Margaret Power, (2008), "The Engendering of Anticommunism and Fear in Chile's 1964 Presidential Election," *Diplomatic History* 32(5): 931–53, for a detailed and gendered account of U.S. intervention in the 1964 elections.

3. According to Peter Kornbluh, Patria y Libertad was an "avowedly pro-fascist group that modeled itself after Hitler's Brownshirts." Peter Kornbluh, (2003), *The Pinochet File: A Declassified Dossier on Atrocity and Accountability (A National Security Archive Book)* (New York: New Press), 168.

4. See Lubna Z. Qureshi, (2009), *Nixon, Kissinger, and Allende: U.S. Involvement in the 1973 Coup in Chile* (Lanham, Md.: Lexington Books), for the most recent and thorough documentation of U.S. involvement in Chilean politics during this period.

5. All quotes from the Popular Unity's program come from a reprint in James Cockcroft, ed., (2000), *The Salvador Allende Reader: Chile's Voice of Democracy* (Melbourne, Australia: Ocean Press), 257–85. Future references to the program will be cited as follows (UP 1970, 257), with the page number referring to the reprint.

6. Details for the following discussion regarding the accomplishments of the UP come from Loveman, *Chile,* 243; Lois Hect Oppenheim, (1999), *Politics In Chile: Democracy, Authoritarianism, and the Search for Development* (Boulder: Westview Press), 54–83; Thomas Wright, (1991), *Latin America in the Era of the Cuban Revolution* (Westport, Conn.: Praeger Publishers); Ann J. Zammit, ed., (1973), *The Chilean Road to Socialism* (Brighton, England: The Kensington Press).

7. See, Loveman, *Chile,* 249–57, for a detailed overview of the economic crises during Allende's tenure.

8. For an excellent overview of the pre-coup military activities, see Mary Helen Spooner, (1999), *Soldiers in a Narrow Land: The Pinochet Regime in Chile* (Berkeley: University of California Press), and for the role of the U.S. in bringing and keeping Pinochet in power, see Kornbluh, *The Pinochet File*; Qureshi, *Nixon, Kissinger, and Allende.*

9. Information for this discussion, unless otherwise noted, comes from Loveman, *Chile*; Oppenheim, *Politics in Chile,* 62–83; Power, *Right-Wing Women in Chile*; Wright, *Latin America in the Era of the Cuban Revolution,* 145–53.

10. Much has been written about the roles of right-wing women in the movement against Allende and the UP. For the most comprehensive and recent analysis, see Power, *Right-Wing Women in Chile.*

11. The film *Machuca* does a beautiful job capturing the economic and political tensions of the period. Andres Wood, (2004), *Machuca* (Barcelona, Spain: Cameo Media; DVD).

12. Dr. Patricio Guijón, a member of Allende's team of medical doctors, watched from the shadows as Salvador Allende put an automatic rifle under his chin and pulled the trigger. The president's cranium was destroyed and his face unrecognizable. According to Allende's now-deceased widow, Hortensia Bussi de Allende, "He always said he would never abandon La Moneda [the presidential palace] and would kill himself rather than betray his ideals" (quoted in Spooner, *Soldiers in a Narrow Land,* 51).

13. This discussion intends to provide a brief overview of the repression and resistance under Pinochet. For a more detailed overview of the period, see Pamela Constable and Arturo Valenzuela, (1991), *Chile Under Pinochet: A Nation of Enemies* (New York: W.W. Norton); Spooner, *Soldiers in a Narrow Land*; Wright, *State Terrorism in Latin America.* For a good overview of the economic, institutional, political, and gendered nature of the dictatorship, see Paul W. Drake and Iván Jaksić, ed., (1995), *The Struggle for Democracy in Chile, rev. ed.* (Lincoln, Nebr.: University of Nebraska Press).

14. Loveman, *Chile*, provides great detail regarding the various decrees, laws, and economic policies passed by the junta that operationalized these stages.

15. Unless otherwise noted, data for this section comes from Kornbluh, *The Pinochet File*, Chapters Three and Six. Other excellent sources on human rights violations and resistance under Pinochet include: Rodrigo Atria et al., (1989), *Chile: La Memoria Prohibida: La Violaciones A Los Derechos Humanos, 1973–1983* (Santiago, Chile: Pehuén); Ascanio Cavallo Castro, Manuel Salazar Salvo, and Oscar Sepúlveda Pacheco, (1989), *Chile, 1973–1988: La Historia Oculta del Régimen Military* (Santiago, Chile.: Editorial Antártica); John Dinges, (2004), *The Condor Years: How Pinochet and His Allies Brought Terrorism to Three Continents* (New York: New Press); Mark Ensalaco, (2000), *Chile under Pinochet: Recovering the Truth* (Philadelphia: University of Pennsylvania Press); Mónica González and Héctor Contreras, (1991), *Los secretos del Comando Conjunto* (Santiago, Chile: Ediciones del Ornitorrinco); Pamela Lowden, (1996), *Moral Opposition to Authoritarian Rule in Chile, 1973–1990* (New York: St. Martin's Press); Patricio Orellana and Elizabeth Quay Hutchinson, (1991), *El Movimiento de Derechos Humanos en Chile, 1973–1990* (Santiago, Chile: Centro de Estudios Políticos Latinoamericanos Simón Bolívar (CEPAL)); Patricia Politzer, (2001), *Fear in Chile: Lives Under Pinochet, rev. ed.*, translated by Diane Wachtell (New York: Pantheon Books); Raúl Rettig Guissen et al., (1993), *Report of the Chilean National Commission on Truth and Reconciliation, Vol. 1 and 2* (Notre Dame, Ind.: Center for Civil and Human Rights, Notre Dame Law School); Hernán Vidal, (1996), *Dar la Vida por la Vida: Agrupación Chilena de Familiares de Detenidos Desaparecidos* (Santiago, Chile.: Mosquito Editores); Wright, *State Terrorism in Latin America.*

16. See Elizabeth Farnsworth and Patricio Lanfranco, (2008), *The Judge and the General* (New York: The Cinema Guild; videorecording), regarding disposing bodies into the ocean.

17. For a detailed and disturbing overview of South American women and torture during this period, see Ximena Bunster, (1993), "Surviving beyond Fear: Women and Torture in Latin America," in *Surviving beyond Fear: Women, Children and Human Rights In Latin America,* ed. Marjorie Agosín (New York: White Pine Press), 98–125.

18. See Alena Heitlinger, (1999b), "Émigré Feminism: An Introduction," in *Émigré Feminism: Transnational Perspectives,* ed. Alena Heitlinger (Toronto: University of Toronto Press), 5; Marcela Durán, (1980), "Life in Exile: Chileans in Canada," *Multiculturalism* 3(4): 14, for similar arguments.

19. Landolt and Goldring see far less diversity among Chilean exiles in Canada than might be suggested here. They maintain: "Chilean exiles [in Canada] are an incredibly homogenous group both in terms of demographic profiles and political experience. . . . Despite some heterogeneity in class background, Chileans generally held shared experiences and views of political participation." Patricia Landolt and Luin Goldring, (2006), "Activist Dialogues and the Production of Refugee Political Transnationalism: Chileans, Colombians and Non-Migrant Civil Society in Canada" (paper presented at Second International Colloquium of the International Network on Migration and Development. Cocoyoc, Morelos, Mexico), 16–17.

20. Much of the data reported here comes from the twenty-three interviews I did with Chilean women in Chile in 1998 and 1999.

21. Patricia Chuchryk (1989b) puts the date at 1974 in "Subversive Mothers: The Women's Opposition to the Military Regime in Chile," in *Surviving beyond Fear: Women, Children and Human Rights in Latin America*, ed. Marjorie Agosín (New York: White Pine Press), 86–97.

22. For more information regarding the mothers and grandmothers in Argentina, see Rita Arditti, (1999), *Searching for Life: The Grandmothers of the Plaza de Mayo and the Disappeared Children of Argentina* (Berkeley: University of California Press); Margarite Guzmán Bouvard, (1994), *Revolutionizing Motherhood: The Mothers of the Plaza de Mayo* (Wilmington, Del.: Scholarly Resources Inc.); Jo Fisher, (1993), *Out of the Shadows: Women, Resistance, and Politics in South America* (London: Latin American Bureau); Susana Muñoz and Lourdes Portillo, (1986), *Las Madres: The Mothers of the Plaza de Mayo* (Los Angeles: Direct Cinema); regarding Chile, see Chuchryk, "Subversive Mothers"; Patricia Chuchryk, (1994), "From Dictatorship to Democracy: The Women's Movement in Chile," in *The Women's Movement in Latin America: Participation and Democracy,* ed. Jane Jaquette (Boulder: Westview Press), 65–107; regarding Guatemala, see Jennifer Schirmer, (1993), "The Seeking of Truth and the Gendering of Consciousness: The COMADRES of El Salvador and the CONAVIGUA Widows of Guatemala," in *"Viva": Women and Popular Protest in Latin America,* ed. Sarah A. Radcliffe and Sallie Westwood (New York: Routledge), 30–64; regarding El Salvador, see Mariclaire Acosta, (1993), "The Comadres of El Salvador: A Case Study," in *Surviving beyond Fear: Women, Children, and Human Rights in Latin America,* ed. Marjorie Agosín (New York: White Pine Press), 126–39; Lynn Stephen, ed., (1994), *Hear My Testimony: María Teresa Tula, Human Rights Activist of El Salvador* (Boston: South End Press); Lynn Stephen, (1997), *Women and Social Movements in Latin America: Power from Below* (Austin, Tx.: University of

Texas Press); regarding Latin America in general, see Nikki Craske, (1999), *Women and Politics in Latin America* (New Brunswick, N.J.: Rutgers University Press); Francesca Miller, (1991), *Latin American Women and the Search for Social Justice* (Hanover, N.H.: University Press of New England); Julie Shayne, (2004), *The Revolution Question: Feminisms in El Salvador, Chile, and Cuba* (New Brunswick, N.J.: Rutgers University Press).

23. AFDD president Viviana Díaz explained that in the first year of their work, of the 1,198 detained and disappeared, seventy-four were women (personal interview 1999).

24. At the time of the interview she was the vice president. Then-president Sola Sierra passed away while I was in Chile.

25. For an excellent and detailed overview of the arrest, detention, and attempted extradition of Pinochet, see Heraldo Muñoz, (2008), *The Dictator's Shadow: Life Under Augusto Pinochet* (New York: Basic Books).

26. According to Pinochet's 1980 constitution, after the transition to democracy he would serve as a so-called "Senator for Life." During the week of March 10–17, 1988, the Spanish and English press in the United States reported that Pinochet finally stepped down as the head of the armed forces and assumed the position of senator for life in Chile. This transition and refusal to relinquish power was met with protest. One senator proclaimed his opposition, stating that Pinochet has never been elected to any position in Chile and certainly did not deserve to be a senator for life. Street protesters echoed this same sentiment and were met with riot police.

27. See Farnsworth and Lanfranco, *The Judge and the General,* for an intimate look at the case against Pinochet under Chilean criminal law.

Chapter Two

Testimonies

We did not want to leave of course . . . but I guess our legacy . . . [of] being
Jewish [gave] us a different way of seeing things.

—Patricia Gomberoff

This chapter serves to introduce the reader to a sampling of the women I met
in my Canadian fieldwork. The women in this chapter serve as some of the
many "experts" I rely on throughout the rest of the book. Some I interviewed
only once and some I met again during focus group discussions and/or regular
email follow-up. I should note that though I do not rely on direct quotes from
all the women I interviewed, their stories, impressions, and interpretations are
woven throughout the book, even if their words verbatim are not. Who are
the Chilean women we meet in this book? As I explained in the introduction,
in total I spoke with twenty-four Chilean women in British Columbia who
ranged in age from twenty-seven to seventy-one, with the majority currently
in their fifties. There is more variety in the sample than sweeping generaliza-
tions allow. Before introducing the individual women I will provide a sense
of the entire sample (see table 2.1).

Thirteen of the women were in their early twenties and thirties when they
left Chile; four were in their late teens and left independent of their parents;
one was in her early forties; and the remaining six were children of exiles.
The youngest child was in utero and the oldest was fifteen. Their political
backgrounds and reasons for leaving are varied. Almost all the women who
left as adults, regardless of their political involvement in Chile, told me
they left because of their husbands/boyfriends' political involvement and
thus risks. Some women knew their political involvement put them at risk
whether they were coupled with a particular man or not. The women who

were involved in leftist politics were often affiliated with the student movements or youth sectors. A handful were formally members of political parties while others were merely exploring that possibility. The women came
from politically heterogeneous families. For example, one's father was a
radical but her uncle or aunt was conservative. Or, their parents were radical
but some of their siblings were conservative, even to the point of supporting
the coup. Some of the women left because they received warnings alerting
them that despite the fact that their names may not appear on any public
lists, they were indeed being watched. In some cases the warnings were
obvious—police coming to their homes in the middle of the night—while
in other cases a colleague may have learned that the woman or her family
was on the military's radar and passed the information on to her. The children I spoke to generally recall either desperately not wanting to leave, or
being confused by the whole process, aware that something life altering and
unpleasant was about to begin.

The social class background of the women is also relatively diverse. Two
women came from decidedly elite backgrounds backed by generations of
education and social status. On the other end, two came from several generations of the working poor where they worked as child paid laborers. The
majority were somewhere in the middle. There were many first-generation
students who eventually held professional and semi-professional jobs,
while others who never gained access to post-secondary education remain
in working-class jobs. The issue of social class is complicated for all immigrants, exiles included, as one's social class standing does not automatically
translate when one crosses borders, particularly when the primary language
changes. In some cases, established professionals such as architects and educators lose their status when they move from country to country, finding their
certifications are often no longer relevant. I found that for the most part, even
the most professionally established women (or their husbands) went to the
bottom of the social hierarchy once they arrived in Canada. Race, social class
in Chile, and linguistic skills all played roles in this. For example, the much
fairer-skinned Chileans, particularly if they already spoke English, tended to
receive better treatment than their dark-skinned, non-English-speaking *compañeras*. For some of the women, this is still the case.

The women ended up in Canada, and more specifically Vancouver, for varied reasons. Just like exiles all over the world, many Chileans went wherever
they were first offered safe passage. Some people applied to as many countries as possible and some knew of friends or family members who made it to
Canada and were at least somewhat happy there. Many Chileans tried to stay
as close to Chile as possible, but many South American countries were politically dangerous as well. Some of the women came on student or temporary

visas, which eventually became permanent, some came as political refugees, and others as landed immigrants. Currently most hold dual Canadian-Chilean citizenship. Almost half of the women I interviewed did not start their exile in Vancouver, rather in different Canadian cities/provinces or other countries all together. Those who started elsewhere in Canada knew they eventually wanted to get to Vancouver for what they understood was a politically and physically friendly climate.

Presently the women's lives are very different from when they first left Chile. Almost none of them are married to the men with whom they left, the same men who in many cases were responsible for them needing to leave their homeland in the first place. Many are grandmothers now or at least mothers of adult children. Nearly all were (at least) bilingual, some with virtually no accents and others with perfect yet accented English. Some hold professional positions in Vancouver as social worker, medical technician, writer, or playwrights, while others remain in fleeting service sector jobs. Several have remarried (and remain married to) Canadians, while others remarried and divorced again. Most miss Chile but feel at least partly Canadian, and at this point in their lives can no longer imagine returning to Chile.

Many people often wonder why the exiles do not return to Chile, since Pinochet has been out of power for nearly twenty years and dead for almost three. The reasons for this are complicated, and though I did not intend to talk to most of the women about this issue, the subject invariably came up. Nearly all the women intended to eventually return to Chile and did for brief periods of time but felt they no longer belonged there. Chile post-Allende was not the Chile they left behind. They felt like outsiders as more and more time passed. Some women hoped to return to Chile but, once their children grew up, either married and had children with Canadians, and/or established careers in Canada, and they decided they could not leave their families again and decided to stay in Vancouver. One woman I interviewed had successfully returned to Chile and was in Vancouver visiting her son, his Canadian wife, and her grandchild. Another woman was just about to leave Vancouver to return to Chile and felt very confident that she would stay there this time. I take this topic up further in the conclusion, when I discuss exile's permanence.

Due to page limitations I am unable to include the story of every woman and man I interviewed in this chapter. Rather, I have chosen fourteen women's testimonies based on a series of criteria: the extent to which I rely on her words throughout the book, the representative nature of her experiences and the amount of detail she shared. All but two of the remaining testimonies are included in the appendix. The women are introduced in the order they arrived in Vancouver.[1]

Table 2.1: Overview of Exiles

Name[1]	Left Chile[2]	First stop after Chile	Political affiliation at time of departure	Arrived in Vancouver	Age[3]
Ana María Quiroz	1968	California	Active in university student politics and affiliated with the Socialist Party	1968	60
Patricia Gomberoff	Sept 8, 1973	Madrid	Active in university politics	1973	61
Carmen Rodríguez	Dec 15, 1973	California	Leftist, unaffiliated with a party	August 7, 1974	56
Carmen Aguirre	Dec 15, 1973	California	Carmen Rodríguez's daughter	August 7, 1974	36
Alejandra Aguirre	Dec 15, 1973	California	Carmen Rodríguez's daughter	August 7, 1974	35
Sacha Rodríguez[4]	Dec 15, 1973	Argentina	Member of the Communist Party youth sector; connections to the MIR and Socialist Party	1982	54
Isabel López	Feb 1974	Vancouver	Worked in a school run by the Federation of University Students	Feb 1974	49
Carla Gutiérrez	June 1974	Edmonton, Alberta	Member of the Socialist Party youth sector	1997	50
Magaly Varas	June 1974	Vancouver	None; voted for Allende	June 1974	62
Marilyn Gutiérrez-Diaz	1974	Vancouver	None, right-leaning	1974	51
Cecilia Boisier	1974	Argentina	Active with the MAPU	1992	61
Irene Policzer	1975	Vancouver	Independent Allende supporter	1975	62
Cecilia Tagle	Feb 26, 1976	Toronto	University student	1981	52
María José Valenzuela	Feb 26, 1976	Toronto	Cecilia Tagle's daughter	1981	33
Rebeca Jimenez	Aug 1976	Chicoutimi, Quebec	Leftist, unaffiliated with a party	July 15, 1978	58

Table 2.1: Overview of Exiles

Name[1]	Left Chile[2]	First stop after Chile	Political affiliation at time of departure	Arrived in Vancouver	Age[3]
Angélica Gutiérrez	Aug 1976	Chicoutimi	Rebeca Jimenez's daughter	July 15, 1978	40
Patricia Andrade	Sept 9, 1976	Vancouver	Member of the Socialist Party	Sept 9, 1976	~63
Lina de Guevara	1976	Toronto	Leftist, unaffiliated with a party	1977 (Victoria)	71
Patricia Andrade	N/A	Argentina	Member of the Socialist Party	N/A	N/A
Ursula Andrade	N/A	In utero	Patricia Andrade's daughter	N/A	27
Lorena Jara	July 1977	Vancouver	Student/youth activist	July 1977	46
Nina Vaca	Dec 31, 1978	Brandon, Manitoba	MIR collaborator	1984	48
Andrea Diaz[4]	1979	Argentina	Daughter of well-known union and Communist Party activist	August 1981	42
Amanda[4]	1983 or 1984	Vancouver	Organized a soup kitchen in a shantytown	1983 or 1984	45

[1] This chart includes all of the women interviewed, not just the ones in this chapter.
[2] Some women recalled and/or shared the actual date, while others only refer to the month and/or year.
[3] Age refers to that at the time of the interview.
[4] Pseudonym; all pseudonyms were chosen by the interviewee.

Ana María Quiroz

Ana María comes from a well-educated family. She explained: "[M]y parents did not have [a] university education but [that was] the case with that generation; not many people were going to university. . . . My father was doing very well in Chile and my mother [stayed] at home; she never worked." Ana María is one of six siblings. Three of her sisters attended the university and one did not, and they all married and "had lots of kids," while her "brother was into making money." As was typical, Ana María's family was politically divided. Of her siblings, "three were into supporting Allende and two were right-wing." In 1968 Ana María was studying at the University of Chile in the southern part of the country when she met her now ex-husband, an American Peace Corps volunteer. She left Chile with him for the United States and not long after they fled the U.S. for Canada when her ex-husband became a Vietnam war draft-dodger. At the time of the coup she was already living in Vancouver, working toward her Ph.D. in Latin American Literature at the University of British Columbia. Eventually politics and divorce took priority over her studies and she dropped out of graduate school.

In 1984 Ana María returned to Chile. She tried earlier than that but was denied entry because the government revoked her citizenship as punishment for political organizing in Vancouver. She stayed in Chile until 1988, at which point she was forced to leave for the United States to care for her daughter, who eventually died of cancer. She returned to Chile in 1990 after this tragic incident that, as she explains, "really changed my view of everything, the world, politics, [everything]." She worked in the Santiago office of the Latin American Consul for Adult Education and was eventually asked to represent the organization in Toronto, Canada, for a few years. She happily agreed and when she returned to Chile in 1995 she began working with the Ministry of Education in their international relations division. At the time of our interview in 2005 she was sixty years old. Currently she directs multilateral relations and is in charge of relations with the Organization for Economic Co-operation and Development (OECD) and Asia-Pacific Economic Cooperation (APEC). She loves her job and living in Chile but I asked if she misses Canada: "Yeah, very much. My son is here [Vancouver] so my family is all split up; my only son and his baby. . . . That is the consequence of this horrible history we went through."

Patricia Gomberoff

Patricia comes from a family of Ashkenazi Jews who left Germany in 1938. In their search for a country that would take them they ended up in Chile, as did many other Jews, where Patricia was born. Her parents were in the garment industry; her father the business side and her mother a hat maker. Eventually her mother stopped working because her father's business was quite successful. Neither of Patricia's two siblings (an older sister and younger brother) are university educated. After high school Patricia was married and had three children.[2] She decided to go to college and was studying social work, on track to receive her degree, but due to the coup was never able to finish. She would have been the first person in her immediate family to receive a college degree were the political situation different.

At the time of the coup Patricia and her husband were both politically active. Her husband had already completed his studies and was a certified architect. However, he worked in her father's garment business for about seven years. She explains:

We were both politically active in different ways. He was quite politically active but on the side of the work[er]. . . . Chile was in turmoil to say the least . . . and because of the United States we had a terrible, terrible boycott. . . . So here is the factory that was making garments and they did not have needles to . . . sew [with]. [My husband] was quite politically active; he . . . went with Allende to the Soviet Union and to other places because they were trying to . . . replace everything that they could not get from the States. . . . So, it was pretty bad but he was quite involved in that. And I was involved more in university which looking back now I think, "well [it] was not much" but . . . [as] you know . . . they [the Left] need[ed] you at work but . . . I was [at] a university.

Patricia is quite typical of the women with whom I spoke in respect to downplaying her own political contributions as secondary to those of her husband's or other activists.[3] I asked Patricia if she was always political. She explained that being raised as a conservative Jew and exposure to her husband's politics converged to create her political consciousness:

Well I was not always political, no. . . . Because in my family, my father, mother, they were not political and life taught them not to get involved in too many things. . . . But then in school I started dating my husband when I was very young, I guess I was about 15, 14, and his family was quite involved, especially his father [who] strongly identified as a socialist and worked for them . . . on Allende's side. . . . They [her father-in-law and Allende] went to university together in Valparaíso and they knew each other. . . . So I guess my husband started opening my eyes a little bit. But at the same time I was sort of opening my eyes a bit and I thought it was not fair between men and women, but more I started [seeing it] in the religion, the Jewish religion. I started [seeing this] at a very young age, 12, 13, 14. I felt very segregated because my parents went [to temple] for the High Holidays [or] for whatever and . . . women sat on one side and men on the other; I could not give my hand to the Rabbi. [And] you know religious women had to go and take baths after their period.

Patricia, her husband, and three children ended up leaving Chile a few days before the coup. Because the garment business was largely a right-wing industry her husband was privy to inside information that they took very seriously. She explained:

He [my husband] had to leave . . . because they had already menaced him before, way before the coup because all the people in the garment industry were [from] the Right and they were against Allende of course. . . . They had already threatened him [my husband] many, many times "just wait, just wait for things to turn around." So he had to leave and I did not want to stay either. We got out a few days before the coup. . . . [H]e was privy to . . . information. [Some of the right-wing lawyers] who were quite involved, we found out later, . . . told

my husband: "Listen it is not going to be nice;" they told him this [the coup] is
coming. . . . We did not want to leave of course . . . but I guess our legacy again
[of] being Jewish had given us a different way of seeing things.

In other words, Patricia did not want to be in a position like her parents,
forced to flee a country knowing it may be too late. She, her husband, and
children first went to Spain but decided not to stay there since Franco was
still in power. Her sister, who left Chile because Allende was president, was
already in Vancouver. Patricia and her family arrived in Vancouver in 1973.
Her husband started as a carpenter, and once again worked himself up the
architecture ladder. They now live in an exquisite home, high atop a hill, with
a breathtaking view of Vancouver. At the time of our interview in June 2005
she was sixty-one years old. Her three grown children are successful: her two
sons with children of their own live in Vancouver, and her daughter was off
to Cuba to explore politics and life.

Carmen Rodríguez

Carmen's parents were both teachers. She explains, "My mom never had a
chance to work in the system, she worked with us." Carmen's father came
from a very poor family; he was one of thirteen children, only four of whom
survived into adulthood. Her father was an extremely intelligent man who
never had the chance to go to school. Carmen explained of her father: "He
was a reader, an incredibly curious person. One of his main things was always, in our house there might not be a lot of clothing or furniture . . . but
there was [always] food and . . . books." She continues: "We were fairly poor
because teachers in Chile do not make any money so we were lower middle-
class and my mom was always a housewife. Having been trained as a teacher
she did go to normal school . . . [and] never got to work outside home."
   Carmen grew up in the south of Chile and she and her siblings were the
first in her family to attend university. She is the youngest sister of two older
brothers, one who died while in exile in Vancouver. After her oldest brother,
Carmen, was the next to attend the University of Chile. She explains:

I got married in between my first and second year; I had my kids while going to
university. I am one of those people that did everything at the same time; do not
ask me how because I do not remember anymore. I was really young [laughs].
I was young, you know that kind of energy you have when you are so young. I
guess I never questioned it. When I think about it now I get really tired but back
then I just did it!

In other words, she married for the first time at eighteen, had her first
daughter at nineteen, and her second one at twenty. At the time of the coup

Carmen was teaching English at the University of Austral in the south of Chile. When I asked if she was involved in politics at the time she said: "Who wasn't? I was not formally involved; I did not belong to any political party. I was flirting with the MAPU and . . . I liked their politics and [was] also was flirting with the MIR." Carmen was vocal about her support for the socialist project and thus ended up on the junta's list of people required to turn themselves in. Her house was raided, and, as she says, "the writing was on the wall" so she and her family decided to leave Chile on December 15, 1973. (I opened the book with Carmen's daughter's memories about that raid.) They started in the United State due to the connection of friends she met in Chile. After seven months there they received legal status in Canada and arrived in Vancouver on August 7, 1974. While in exile, she enrolled in graduate school at the University of British Columbia, studied literature, became extremely active in the solidarity movement, divorced her first husband, and got involved with a Canadian man, Bob.

Carmen and Bob left Vancouver for South America and stayed there from 1979 until 1984. They took Carmen's two teenage daughters and had a son while there. Carmen and her family lived in Bolivia and Argentina while she and Bob (now deceased) collaborated with the armed resistance organization, the Movement for the Revolutionary Left (MIR).[4] Carmen explains:

> We went to Argentina and we were there for a year and a half and continued to do *"cosas raras"* as my friends would say, strange things. And I know that my kids . . . the two girls have questioned. . . . "How could you love the Revolution more than you love us? How could you put us in such risk? Did you ever think that we could have been killed?" Yeah, I did and you know you can get run over by a car crossing the street and besides I still believe, "Would I do it all over again? Yes. Does that mean that I did not love my kids? No!" I love my kids with passion and I would defend them to the death but again, I am not one of those people that will make a list and say this is what I love the most, and then this, and this . . . no! I am one of those people that will do everything and I did that.

Carmen shared very little detail about what exactly she and Bob did while in South America though her daughters later provided some insight. (Her daughters' testimonies are in the appendix.) Carmen and her family returned to Vancouver in 1984 and resumed their participation in the solidarity movement. Toward the end of the movement, once Pinochet was ousted from power, she became very active in feminist issues, namely the magazine *Aquelarre*, which I talk about in Chapter Six. Carmen is now a published poet, fiction writer, and educator. She is fifty-six, remarried, and her three kids all live in Vancouver. Each of her daughters has a son and Carmen thoroughly enjoys being a grandmother.

Sacha Rodríguez

Sacha, a pseudonym, comes from a poor, working-class family. In her family, women worked all of their lives and she never understands why North Americans assume Latinas do not work. Her mother worked as a clerk in a grocery store and on the side she was a flamenco dancer/singer who performed at parties. Sacha's grandmother worked her whole life as a seamstress. Sacha was raised by her aunt, though she did not explain why. Her biological father came from a wealthy family but died when she was only three years old, by which time her parents were divorced. Her stepfather was a longshoreman. Sacha was aware of the class disparities on the different sides of her family and believes this reality contributed to her becoming a leftist. She explains: "It was part of my influence, my questioning: 'Why is life like this [with] so much difference between rich and poor; and the rich sometimes did not work, and my family were hard working and poor?'"

Sacha has a high school education and was a student at the Chilean French Institute at the time of the coup. She loved French but really wanted to study philosophy. At the time, her now-ex-husband was an engineering student and that took priority over her academic desires. She explains: "My ex-husband said, 'ok you help me and I will help you later' which is not true!" At the time of the coup they were both twenty-two years old and student activists. She was a member of the Communist Party youth sector and her ex-husband belonged to one of the factions of the Socialist Party. She was also becoming interested in the MIR, since most of her friends were members. One public project she and her ex-husband were both involved in was a popular theater group. Their goal was to share the arts with all sectors of society: they performed in jails and slums with the intention of bringing "the arts and theater and everything to the street." From Sacha's perspective, "it was not such a big deal but for . . . the military it was; everything was . . . suspicious; anything that could make [you] think or question."

Right after the coup Sacha's ex-husband was captured and their apartment searched. She still finds it a bit perplexing given their relatively unimportant positions in the movement. She explains: "We were not . . . big shots, we were just from the base, from the very, very base so I do not know why my ex-husband was picked up, or . . . why he was suspicious, or me, because we were not really big shots." Several of the women I spoke with conveyed this same sentiment and basically concluded that the military had the resources to pursue even the seemingly inconsequential activists. Sacha's ex-husband was abducted from the university he was attending and taken to the War Academy where he was tortured. While he was being held their apartment was searched when Sacha was home. For whatever reason the soldiers did not take Sacha but she decided rather than test her luck again it was time to go into hiding and even her family did not know where she was.

Once her husband was released they decided to leave Chile immediately. On December 15, 1973 they left for Argentina. Sacha explains: "The situation was impossible for us. I mean all the people around us, our friends, were disappeared and he [had] already [been] in jail, our apartment was searched . . . so we escaped to Argentina. [We started in] . . . Mendoza [and] we were received by the Socialist Workers Party. They gave us the shelter and food." Like so many of the other Chileans who fled, they thought their exile would be short lived: "We did not think that this could last too long; we thought that we could come back to Chile." They were legally in Argentina but remained scared, especially when the Argentine government started collaborating with Pinochet. Eventually they found jobs and Sacha got pregnant. Both of her children were born in Argentina but by 1976 they knew they had to leave. They applied to several countries but Canada granted them status first, so in February 1976 they left Buenos Aires for Edmonton with their two kids, a three-month-old son and his one-year, three-month-old sister.

Sacha and her ex-husband got involved with the solidarity movement almost immediately. In 1980 she divorced her husband and in 1982 left Edmonton for Vancouver with her two children. Upon arriving in Vancouver she got involved in the movement immediately. By 1989 she missed Chile so much and thought she could live there again since Pinochet was out of power. She returned with her two kids, ages fourteen and fifteen at the time. She explains: "I went back in 1989 [and] until 1989 my heart [and] my mind were in Chile and my body was here [Canada]." But like so many other exiles, while she was there she realized Canada was home: "I [thought], 'what are you doing here [Chile]?' and for the first time in my life, in 1989, when I came back to Canada . . . I [was] here with body [and] my spirit; I was totally here [for the] first time [in] 1989." She now loves Vancouver partly because it physically reminds her of Chile (something many Chileans told me), combined with the fact that it is a culturally diverse, and a politically open-minded city. At the time of our interview Sacha was a very young fifty-four. Her son is twenty-nine and teaches English and Spanish in Japan and her daughter is a thirty-year-old drug addict. They have been out of touch for some time but Sacha is optimistic that her daughter will make it through safely and they will eventually be reunited. Sacha works as a hypnotherapist and does translation on the side. Her hope is to write and publish progressive children's books.

Isabel López

Isabel's father was a Spaniard, sixty-two years old when she was born. Her mother was twenty-two years his junior and was always politically active for the right wing, including Pinochet. Isabel's father worked as a sports-journalist and her mother, though not formally educated, was an entrepreneur and worked until her children were born. Her older brothers were university educated and her eldest one very active with the Left. At the time of the coup Isabel was working at a business school run by the Federation of Students of the University of Concepción. The UP government turned it into a public school that served working people who worked in commerce and wanted to upgrade their skills and/or change jobs. Students worked during the day and went to school in the evenings. Isabel's oldest brother was one of the founders of this school and had worked as both its principal and vice principal. A few days after the coup her brother and the current principal of the school were abducted from the premises. Isabel explained that her brother was taken to the "Regional Stadium of Concepción for six months which was a concentration camp in Chile."

In 1972 Isabel had spent some time in Vancouver visiting her cousins. She loved it there but was also excited by the changes she saw in Chile upon her return. Even before the coup she toyed with the idea of returning to Vancouver for a prolonged stay. Though she had not decided for sure, she began the immigration process to obtain papers if she did choose to return to Canada. Before the coup she was not very politically involved but she had long-term goals in Chile. "For me [it] was . . . very exciting, this new government was just starting and . . . I thought I would study medicine and be a rural doctor; that is what I was going to do. So I got this job and I was studying to apply to the university but then the coup came and that was a big, big, big earthquake."

On the day of the coup Isabel was en route to Santiago for an interview with the Canadian Embassy about her immigration papers. Eventually she ended up in a hotel near the center of all the violence. She explains:

> The day of the coup . . . I was traveling from Concepción to Santiago to the embassy for my interview for immigration and I was caught in the middle of the coup actually. We were on a train on the way out in another city so we actually hitchhiked all the way to Santiago and we arrived there when the curfew time came, right at curfew time we arrived in Santiago. So it was big; I saw a lot of people dead on the streets, there was shooting everywhere, it was like a war zone.

I asked Isabel if she knew what was going on in Santiago before she arrived. She explains:

We left at about 6:00 am and half way through to the next big city we were listening to the radio and they were already talking about the coup so when we arrived in this next city, Chillán, the train was stopped there so we did not know whether the train would go or not. . . . So we were left there not knowing what to do [laughs] and there were a couple of other girls about my age or a little bit older that were going back to Santiago and I went with them, I just did not know what was happening. Should I go back to Concepción? What is going to happen with my brothers? Because they were more involved, especially my older brother, but I lived with my younger brother at that time and we were very close to the other one too. . . . So I ended up going to . . . Santiago but we ended up in a little hotel; we were three girls . . . and we went and talked to a policeman, or military or something and they just kind of put us in this little hotel [and] we stayed there for two days but there was a lot of shooting around that area.

She explains hitchhiking to Santiago:

We had hitchhiked and there was . . . this SUV . . . from one of the [UP] government agencies and this man wanted to get back home in time before the curfew, so he was rushing, but there were stops everywhere in every little town you had to get out and get searched and you did not know if they will stop you or what.

Taking a ride from a government official was perhaps the most dangerous choice Isabel and her friends made that day; virtually all members of the government because of their default association with the Popular Unity were targets of the military. It is not entirely clear how they made it safely through all the checkpoints but, fortunately for Isabel and her friends, they did. Isabel eventually got permission to enter Canada and in February 1974, at the age of nineteen, she arrived in Vancouver, alone. Not long after arriving she got very involved in the solidarity movement and eventually met her husband, a Chilean to whom she is still married. They went back to Chile between 1985 and 1997, spending some time in Vancouver working and some time in Chile doing political organizing. She now has two sons in their early twenties. Isabel works in the medical profession as a Technical Lab Assistant and performs Electrocardiograms. At the time of our first interview in 2004 she was forty-nine years old.

Carla Gutiérrez

Carla, not her real name, comes from a very politicized family and became interested in politics around the age of twelve. She describes her family as "laborers," though her dad "made his way to have a better standard of living than a usual laborer." He was always active in union politics and after a year of law school dropped out to work full time. Her mother received an elementary school education and neither she nor her three siblings attended college. Carla's father was an administrative worker at the time of the coup and was arrested in December 1973 for his union activities. He was held in a concentration camp in the North of Chile until August of 1974.

Carla was a high school student at the time Allende was elected and got involved with the Socialist Party youth sector. Carla explains that even though it was high school, "everything got very politicized; we elected the student board by political parties, the school was full of pamphlets and banners all over, and all over Santiago high school students were involved in politics. [It was] something new, never seen before in Santiago, or for that matter in the country, high school students participating so actively in politics." After the coup she was targeted for her active participation in the Socialist youth. Early into the dictatorship she was picked up on the street in an industrial belt for "waiting" with her sister and a high school student friend also active with the Socialist youth. The girls were taken to the National Stadium. Carla explains:

I was detained right after the coup in the stadium of Chile. We were [there] almost a week and we had in front of us, we [sigh], I can not begin to tell you, I was nineteen years old and in front of us was a machine gun that had a bullet at least twenty centimeters long that shoots, I do not . . . remember any more how many bullets per minute . . . . I guess [we were] the youngest in this stadium that was almost full of people precisely to explain to us what would happen to us if we did anything wrong and this machine gun . . . was literally two meters long and [sat] on top of a tripod, in front of us, to shoot [at] any moment. . . . [There was a] whole side [in the stadium] with students from different countries in Latin America.

I asked Carla how she, her sister, and her friend were able to get out of the stadium:

We were interrogated by an officer and we were clever enough to look like who we were, [just] . . . a bunch of crazy girls [not] . . . really knowing what was going on. But it also was part of the officer's attitude too; he gave us the room to say something like that; I think he was quite shocked to see that we were so young, so involved in something. . . . I guess as they went by they realized that we were not the only ones! Because a lot of people my age went to jail because of their participation but they released us after they sort of checked names, addresses, and whatever else they wanted to check.

Not long after Carla's detention, her house was searched a couple of times but she and her family happened to not be home at the time the military showed up. She explains: "[I was] very lucky, very lucky to not be at home; actually none of my family was at home. . . . A few of my friends were already in jail, so I knew that was coming . . . so I left for Argentina and came to Canada in 1976."

Carla went to Edmonton and stayed there for the first twenty years of her exile except when she traveled back to Chile. She was very active in the solidarity movement while living in Edmonton. But in 1983 she returned to Chile and worked underground with the MIR until 1985 when she returned to Canada. Carla was fifty at the time of our interview in June 2004, living in Vancouver with her twelve-year-old daughter. She has only sporadic work, generally in retail, and has not been able to find a job that utilizes her training as an engineer.

Magaly Varas

Magaly comes from a very politically conservative Catholic family. While in Chile she received a high school education and at the time of the coup was working as a secretary at the Catholic University in Santiago. In retrospect, she considers herself a "rightist" at the time of the coup; however, she was a very open-minded rightist and voted for Allende. She explains: "I voted for Allende in 1970 because I thought maybe something can happen with the poor people but I was not [a leftist], I mean my family, all my family, are rightists." Magaly was twenty-eight at the time of the 1970 elections and it was the first election she ever voted in. She explains that the anti-Communist propaganda actually led her to vote for Allende because it was so extreme that it really made her think about politics in a way she had not prior to this election:

> The propaganda was awful and . . . I was very scared of communism. If you were there you could have seen the posters with the Russian tanks parked right there in front of the government palace. So we were very, very scared. But at one point I thought "I do not have any properties, I do not have any money, they will not get anything from me because all I have is my job" so I said: "Let's see what happens if we elect . . . a socialist president, and see if the poorer people get something."

Magaly's now-ex-husband was a leftist sympathizer not active in politics at the time of the coup. But he decided, and Magaly agreed, that they should leave Chile. They were not directly targeted but felt that living under a military dictatorship, particularly in contrast to Chile's democratic and peaceful past, was no way to live. So in June 1974 Magaly, her husband, and their four-month-old daughter left Chile for Vancouver. Not long after they arrived they literally stumbled upon the solidarity movement when they saw a flyer for a film about Chile. Magaly got very active with the movement, including the women-centered and feminist projects.

Magaly had a series of low-paying and unsatisfying jobs, including wait-ressing, nanny/domestic helper, and housekeeper. In 1975 she and her hus-band split up and she went on welfare to support herself and her daughter. As time progressed she was able to land jobs in the professional sector, includ-ing translating and working on the census, but she knew she had not found her calling. She went to college in 1993 and 1994 and got a certificate as a community social worker and currently works with Latino senior citizens in a job she loves and finds quite satisfying. Magaly's daughter is now living in Chile with her husband and their infant daughter, studying sociology at the University. She left Vancouver in 1998 and Magaly blames herself for this painful separation: "[It] is my fault that she is living in Chile right now because I [raised her] as a Latin American person, as a Chilean person, and I did not know I was going to be so influential in her life and politics; I did not know, otherwise I would have kept my mouth shut [laughs] and she would [still] be here." Magaly always assumed she would retire in Canada. She is one of the only women I interviewed who knew the minute she left Chile she would never return permanently, in contrast to most of the other women, who assumed their exile would be temporary. Now, after she retires (she was sixty-two at the time of our interview in July 2005) she plans to live half-time in Chile and half-time in Vancouver so she can get her retirement benefits while still having time with her daughter and granddaughter. In the meantime, she purchased a digital camera for her daughter and made her promise to send pictures of her granddaughter every day.

Irene Policzer

Irene comes from a very professional family. Her father was French and earned his engineering degree in France but practiced in Belgium. He never renewed his title in Chile so he was not formally an engineer there but worked as one nonetheless. In contrast, Irene described her mother as "very Chilean." She never received any post-secondary education and neither Irene nor her sister (I interviewed both) were sure if she even finished the twelfth grade. At the time of the coup Irene and her husband, Adam, were both Allende sup-porters. Irene was a certified architect and worked with the government. She explains: "I was a supporter of Allende of course but I was not in any political party; I was an independent supporter of Allende. I worked in the Ministry of Public Works. . . . My husband [Adam] was a member of the Socialist Party and he was a union leader." She explained that her husband eventually ended up incarcerated for a year and half.

> He spent a year and a half more or less; he was detained when he was [de-livering] somebody to an embassy . . . trying to get the friend into the French

embassy and they were caught and ironically the friend was released in three days while Adam stayed in prison for a year. He was in different concentration camps [throughout the country] and then for a half year he was under house arrest. He was released with the understanding that it would be a good idea to get out so we came [to Canada].[5]

Luckily, Irene and Adam had already started the process to come to Canada before he was detained. Irene explains:

We had heard about the Canadian embassy before he was detained. In fact, it was the day before he was detained that we actually submitted the papers to the embassy and so I managed to keep that file open. They could not make a decision without actually having an interview with him but they kept the file open so after he was released the process of completing it was relatively fast because of the history.

Irene knew nothing of Canada prior to arriving there. As she explains, "For me Canada was snow and the mountain police." However, she and Adam were quite proactive about deciding what part of Canada to move to: "When we made the application we had a choice, so where would we go? We did not have a clue so we looked at the map. We knew Canada was cold so we looked at the temperature chart [laughs]." In 1975 they ended up in Vancouver with their three children, who were four, six, and eight at the time. Due to Canadian bureaucracy Irene's last name was assumed to be the same as her husband's and changed upon arrival in Vancouver. She explains: "When you come from Chile you are scared to death; you do not do anything that would upset anybody. . . . The first information that we had here when we arrived in Canada [is] you use your husband's name; you do not use your own [as you do in Chile] and I said 'ok, ok' [laughs]!"[6]

Early on Irene and her husband got very involved with the Chilean community and have remained so ever since. Both participated in solidarity events and Irene eventually became active in the feminist movement. She also attended UBC's Planning School and then worked as a city planner for about ten years. Eventually she started doing community work and now calls herself a "'Community Worker' and [is] basically working for people who are disenfranchised, a lot of them immigrants and refugees." Her children are all grown up. Her oldest, Pablo, is a political scientist. He earned his Ph.D. from Massachusetts Institute of Technology and now teaches at Calgary University.[7] Pablo has two children. Irene also has two daughters. Her oldest is an architect and studied at UBC and McGill and currently works in Vancouver at an architecture firm. Her youngest daughter is also university educated. She earned her BA in Canada and then went to Chile because, as Irene says, "she wanted to look for her roots so she studied history [and] she got a masters in history. But . . . she decided she wanted to [return] to Canada again so she is here [Vancouver]." At the time of our first interview in 2004 Irene was about to turn sixty-two and she loves living in Vancouver.

Cecilia Tagle

Cecilia grew up in a very political house. Her parents (mother and stepfather) were both active with "Christians for Socialism," an organization that combined Catholic and Marxist ideology. Her stepfather was an artist and at the time of the coup he had a position with the UP as the Minister of Tourism for the Region of Antofagasta and served as the Dean of the Arts department at the University of Northern Chile. Her mother had a high-school education and for the most part was a housewife. She was also very socially conscious and while Allende was president she ran a UP-sponsored craft market in Antofagasta where she sold things from the small towns in the Andes where the majority of the people were indigenous. The goals were to educate people about their way of life and promote fair trade for their crafts in order to highlight the importance of knitting, weaving, carving, or things like traditional medicine. Cecilia is the oldest of seven children, three from her mother's first marriage and four from her stepfather. One of her sisters is an artist, studied art at a young age, and was never very involved in politics. She also has a brother who left home on the day of the coup to join the right-wing group *Patria y Libertad*, which I discussed in Chapter One. He never finished school because he was young when he left home and eventually started using drugs and alcohol. As Cecilia says: "He was the black sheep of the family." She also has another brother who is a priest and keeps with the liberation theology tradition. Sadly, Cecilia feels particularly distant from the rest of her siblings, as they were quite young when she left Chile and she missed virtually all of their growing up.

At the time of the coup Cecilia was twenty-one years old, married, with a daughter. She was a second-year university student at the same school where her father was a dean. Her now-ex-husband was a member of the Socialist Party and held a government position in his capacity as an architect. According to Cecilia: "I was not an activist then but I was the daughter of and the wife of [laughs]." Her ex-husband lost his job, was blacklisted, and unable to find work in Chile, and Cecilia was expelled from the university. But the event that traumatized her the most was her father's disappearance. Her father was held for two months in a Catholic school that was converted into a clandestine torture center. He was blindfolded the entire time he was there. Cecilia explains his release:

My father was detained for a while. . . . He had disappeared at the hands of the police in 1974 and it was . . . that event [that] shook me up because the day he was released he was left on the street. I was with my mom at the time. I am the oldest of seven and my youngest brother was only three or four years old and very attached to my dad. (I say my dad but [he is] actually my stepdad). . . . [On] the day he was released he came home, knocked at the door, and he took us, my mom and all of us, to the bedroom and he took off his clothes and showed us his tortured body. It was *so* shocking but I think that was the best thing to do for us as children. Each one [of us] reacted differently to his disappearance; my youngest brother was very upset when he saw him, he started to kick him, and one of my sisters she jumped on him and hugged and kissed him.

After her father was released he told Cecilia's husband that he should leave Antofagasta because when he was picked up he heard the soldiers reading a list that included his son-in-law's name. Cecilia and her husband left Antofagasta for Santiago, hoping the capital would provide some anonymity and thus safety. She worked as a secretary for a year before coming to Canada but her husband could not find work since he was blacklisted. So, on February 26, 1976 they left Chile for Toronto, Ontario, where they were sponsored by a church.

They both got involved with the solidarity movement almost immediately upon arrival in Canada. But Cecilia explains she was:

> *so* emotionally sick, I was crying every day, I became pregnant immediately . . . [and my] son was born in December of that year. . . . [For] me it was very difficult being from a large family and especially in those days I did not know what was happening to them because you could not phone because you did not know if the phone was tapped . . . and letters came and arrived open with a stamp saying: "We opened your letter."

Many, many years later Cecilia eventually felt at home in Canada. She was a very active member of the solidarity movement in both Toronto and Vancouver, including with women's and feminist projects and the Chilean Housing Cooperative, which I will discuss in Chapter Four. She has lived in Vancouver since 1981, where both of her adult children live. At the time of our first interview in 2004 Cecilia was fifty-two years old.

Rebeca Jimenez

Rebeca comes from a working-class background of women-headed households. She was one of seven children that her mother, who lacked any formal education, raised without the help of the children's father. (Rebeca's parents were separated when she was ten years old.) She saw her father occasionally but for the most part was raised by her mother and older sister. Her maternal grandmother was in a similar position to her own mother, that is, being a single mother to a large family with virtually no help from the children's father. Rebeca was very influenced by the strength of her mother and maternal grandmother. She explains:

> Those women, despite all of the struggles they [had, they also had] a very tremendous will; and so powerful. . . . [M]y mom died when she was eighty-two and the last time when I saw my mom it was maybe two . . . or three months before [she died] when I went to Chile for the first time after being here five years. . . . And I saw her, and she was helping us to stop the bus, she ran [after the bus]; a very tiny lady, she became tiny because she was dealing with cancer, but she ha[d] that . . . will that made her do incredible things.

Her mother and maternal grandmother still influence Rebeca with respect to her strength and approach to the world. I discuss this more in Chapter Six.

While in Chile, Rebeca did not work outside of the home: "I was a housewife all my life. In Chile not too many women at that time worked, for most of them the expectation was to be a good wife, and a good mother, and housekeeper." Rebeca received a secondary and vocational education while in Chile. She was trained as a sewing instructor, a skill that later proved quite useful in securing employment while in exile. Her younger sister studied to become an accountant, the only one of her siblings who earned a professional degree.

Rebeca was twenty-four at the time of the coup. From her perspective she and her family left Chile because "we were pretty much involved in politics and so [there comes this] moment that you leave or die." Her now-ex-husband belonged to the Communist Party but Rebeca did not have any formal party allegiance. She explains: "I did not have any affiliation. I always tried to keep my thought[s] independent and . . . not be ruled by any particular party." She and her husband participated in the types of activities that called a lot of attention to themselves within their neighborhood. For example: "We participated in meetings, we campaigned for candidates. We opened our house for . . . parties . . . to raise money . . . for any particular candidate." As a result they feared that right-wing neighbors would pass their names on to the police, a common practice during the dictatorship. But Rebeca explains that she and her husband were never arrested and she believes it was due to the fact that her husband worked as a longshoreman and whenever packages were damaged from the ships he unloaded he shared the goods with his neighbors—everything from food to medical supplies. She believes that her neighbors did not want to interrupt their access and thus did not report him to the authorities. Her husband eventually lost his job as a result of his political activities and had a very hard time finding a new and secure one.

Rebeca explains: "The situation was terrible and . . . they knew [when people] were laid off for some reason that was politic[al] so nobody want[ed] to risk hir[ing him]." So in 1976 when the situation became too desperate Rebeca, her husband, and two children left for Canada. They went to a town called Chicoutimi in Quebec first and then in 1978 her husband insisted they move to Vancouver since he had friends there who repeatedly explained how beautiful the city was and how much more pleasant the weather was in contrast to Quebec. Not long after arriving in Vancouver, Rebeca got divorced and her children stayed with her, making her a single mother much like her own mother and grandmother.

She worked a series of jobs to support her family, including in a cannery cleaning fish, as a seamstress, housecleaner, and chambermaid in a hotel. She eventually became a union activist while working at the hotel. She also got involved in the solidarity movement after her divorce and believes she would not have gotten involved if she stayed married because her husband controlled everything and simply would have forbade it. Rebeca eventually went to college in Vancouver and graduated from the programs of Domestic Violence and then Alcohol and Drug Counseling. Currently she works as a domestic violence counselor and has for about the past twelve years. She counsels the women who come to her shelter to flee violent family lives and also helps to integrate them in society independent of their ex-partners. Rebeca also has two children, a thirty-eight-year-old son and a forty-one-year-old daughter, whom I also interviewed. At the time of our interview in 2005 she was fifty-eight and repeatedly told me she intends to live to be 130 years old.

Patricia Andrade

Patricia comes from a politically active family. Her father was an accountant who specialized in cooperatives and worked for the Ministry of the Treasury under Allende. Her mother received only a sixth-grade education but, according to Patricia, "She read a lot and educated herself." In the 1940s her mother fought for women's suffrage in Chile. (Women gained the right to vote in municipal elections in 1931 but were not granted full suffrage until 1949.) Patricia finished high school while in Chile and took some college-level secretarial classes in Vancouver but never earned a college degree.

At the time of the coup Patricia was working in a bank and very active with the Socialist Party. While Allende was president she worked with other women in her bank to establish a daycare center. She explains: "That was my baby; working hard to get a daycare [center] because I knew when I was working with my children . . . it was very [hard]. My mother had to look after them [but] my mother was old and sick and [that was a] problem." Women at the bank initiated the project and appealed to the UP for support. Predictably, Patricia was fired from the bank after the coup. She recalls: "[T]hey told me . . . I was not treating the . . . customers well and . . . [that] I did not forget that I was a member of the UP." She lost her job, was blacklisted, and unable to find another one.

During the dictatorship Patricia was politically terrorized in addition to suffering through economic hardships. Her entire apartment building (a downtown, fifteen-floor highrise) was searched. She was home at the time but luckily was able to escape arrest. She believes this was largely due to good luck. She explains how the building's super helped her by speaking very loudly outside her door to alert her that the military were on their way:

> [The] day when they searched my apartment they were taking people out. . . . [A]nd the day before I took . . . out all of the papers that I had, everything. . . . I took them to the patio. . . . [T]he building's caretaker . . . was a retired military man . . . and he could have told them and that would have been enough for me to be out and never seen, missed, lost; nobody would have found me ever; that would have been enough. . . . But this guy was the opposite [and] he helped me. I could hear him at the door. . . . [I] . . . had this thing [with] my identity from the [Socialist] Party [a laminated card] and I tried to burn it but it did not burn; I tried to flush it and it did not flush. [So] we unrolled a toilet paper and put in the middle . . . because if they found [it] I would have been dead. . . . [So] I could hear [the building's care taker] outside telling [the solider]: "You do not have to go in this apartment, she is a lady, a beautiful lady with two kids, . . . you do not have to go [in] there, she works in a bank. . . . [He was] very loud. I knew already because . . . you could hear they were coming . . . and you could see they were all over.

The military ultimately passed her over but after this incident Patricia decided she was too frightened to stay in Chile and on the ninth of September 1976 left Santiago for Vancouver with her two boys, who were fourteen and fifteen at the time.

Life was very difficult once in Vancouver. Her boys were utterly depressed and cried every day for years, according to Patricia. Additionally, she had a very hard time securing work with a guaranteed and decent wage. She explains: "I had to work three jobs to make the money [to support my boys]. I was making six hundred dollars a month in one place, and I worked in places that . . . never paid me; . . . when I went for the pay [check], I never got it!" Patricia used what little spare time she had to participate in the solidarity movement. For her this was most important for her boys' emotional well-being, as the movement provided a community and extended family they so desperately missed from Chile. Her sons are now forty-four and forty-three, one married to a Canadian, one to a Venezuelan, both in Vancouver. Patricia, now in her early sixties, has been married to a Canadian man for the past fifteen years. She remains active in politics working with the provincial sector of the New Democratic Party (NDP).

Lorena Jara

Lorena comes from a working-class background. Her mother and grandmother were both union activists and street venders. When Lorena was seven and her sister nine they started working with their mother, after her father died. Her first memory of politics, beyond listening to her family debate issues at dinner, was attending a union meeting with her mother. She recalls: "When I was nine years old my mom took me to the union because she did not know how to write properly, [even though] she knew how to read. And she asked me to take notes in meetings." In her first year of high school, at fourteen, Lorena started getting involved with student politics. She started as the secretary of the class, was then elected president, and eventually got involved at both the schoolwide and regional level. By the time the coup happened she was thoroughly involved in student politics. Rather than stopping her organizing, the dictatorship made her get more involved. She explains:

> [There was] the sense that [the dictatorship] was going to be a temporary situation. [So] . . . I started to get more involved. . . . I started hearing more and more stories and I got in contact with the church in my barrio. . . . This [was] 1974 . . . and then [my] . . . teacher . . . approached me and he started to warn me to be careful because I was rebelling too much. We had no notion to be careful with what we were saying; basically we still sang songs that we were not supposed to be singing. So he talked to me and he started sort of looking after me.

Within a year the twenty-eight-year-old teacher, a mentor to Lorena and the other student activists, was killed by the DINA. Lorena found herself wanting to get more involved but also started being very careful. She was married to a young man with the Communist youth and he was having serious problems. So in 1977 the two of them left Chile for Vancouver. Lorena was nineteen years old and left behind her mother, three sisters, and one brother.

Not long after arriving in Vancouver she got involved with the solidarity movement and she and her husband divorced. Like most of the exiles, she had a series of unsatisfying jobs, including chambermaid, janitor, and hotel cafeteria worker. In 1987 she was finally able to study part time at a university. At the time she left Chile she was in her first year of college and as she explains, "I was the first in my whole family ever [attending a] university so I had this huge weight on my shoulders that I had failed them so I decided to go back to university." While in school she took time off and traveled to Mexico, Central America, and Chile, which prolonged her studies. On this trip she realized Vancouver is where she belongs. She explains: "It was in Chile when I decided 'That's it! My home is in Vancouver, I belong there, I have all my friends there, I have my life there! I love my family a lot, the culture of my country, but I just cannot live there. And on top of it I had no degree.'" She returned to Vancouver and graduated from Simon Fraser University with her BA in 1998 and when I interviewed her in 2004 she was about a year from finishing her masters in communications. She is forty-six years old and considering pursuing a Ph.D. but as of our interview had not yet decided.

Andrea Diaz

Andrea (a psuedonymn) comes from a working-class background. Her mother earned a vocational degree in dress making while in Chile and her father is a technical electrician. As she says: "We were not affluent at all. I guess by . . . comparison we were not considered to be poor or even borderline. . . . [M]y dad was a laborer and my mom . . . contributed from her work from home so we were not at all a family that had any money." She has one older brother and the two of them are college educated. For a variety of reasons, however, her brother never finished his degree. Andrea on the other hand has a university degree with a double major in Spanish and psychology from UBC and she did part of her masters in Spanish literature at the University of Santiago.

Andrea's family was in danger immediately after the coup. She explains:

> At the time of the coup [my dad] was the national president of the Railway Workers Union in Chile and so obviously he was a supporter of the Allende government. . . . [O]ur last name is not very common in Chile so my dad and my uncle were very well-known in the city [San Bernardo] where we lived. . . . [T]hey were both members of the Communist Party at the time.

Andrea was only ten at the time of the coup but she has some particularly vivid memories of the period.[8] She went to school during the afternoon shift and was home on the morning of September 11th. Andrea explains:

> I remember my brother putting his uniform on early in the morning and going to school. I was at home; I was wearing my yellow pants. I remember my dad coming back from work very early in the morning and saying to my mom that the military was attacking the government palace. I remember being there but I . . . cannot remember who went to get [my brother]. All I know is that they took me to my grandparents' house right away; my mom's brother came and they got us. . . . [T]he next memory that I ha[ve], I cannot remember if it was the same day, or the next day, we were burning pictures and books. I remember being

really upset because some of those pictures I really liked. My dad had hosted at his parents' place a delegation from the Soviet Union and I remember some beautiful pictures of these people with my grandparents and us; holding us. . . . I remember crying when we were burning those. . . . [M]y dad's family was the family that was well known and my mom's family was not, so they took us to my mom's parents' place. . . . I remember being there with one of my uncles and there was this container with this huge thing and they were just throwing [in] all those books, pictures, whatever could be burned.[9]

While Andrea and her brother stayed with their maternal grandparents her parents went into hiding. "[M]y uncle . . . was arrested right away and my dad went into hiding for a while. . . . [H]e was only hiding for the first few months. . . . I guess, however, it was decided that [it] was probably safe . . . to come out and he just . . . tried to [live]." But he was out of work and black-listed because of his Communist Party affiliation and in 1975 he was taken as a political prisoner for about a year. Andrea recalls the night of his arrest:

We were there when my dad was arrested. . . . [I]t was in the middle of the night so I remember lying in bed and . . . being threatened with a machine gun but I could not get out while they were questioning my dad. [T]hey would not even let him get his clothes on and I remember my mom crying and yelling and saying, "at least let him get his clothes on!" so they did. . . . [M]y brother was being held at gun point in his room and I was in my room. . . . I could not see anything but I could hear the whole [thing]. . . . [T]hey did not just knock on the door, they broke the door down. . . . [Y]ou do not really react right away. [W]e were scared but out of fear you . . . do not say anything. . . . I remember them going through my drawers and my night table and they were just pulling [everything] out and going through everything that was in there. I was probably eleven or twelve at the time and I was a girl-guy [Girl Scout] at the time as well . . . and I had one of my books with all the codes, the Morris code, and whatever the codes we used. . . . I remember they took it because . . . they thought there were some secret messages in there. . . . I was quite upset that they took my book.

Her father was then held for a year. For the first few months of his detention he was disappeared and his family did not know where he was or if he was dead or alive. Andrea's mother did not share this information with her children until many years later. Andrea later found out that the DINA came back to their house and returned her dad's watch, money, and I.D. and told her mother that he was dead. (This was a common tactic to which many family members were subjected.) Andrea's mom never believed them. Instead, she looked for him for about two or three months, day after day, trying to find him in every concentration camp and detention center. Eventually she was successful.

Her father was eventually released but could not find work nor did he and his family ever feel safe in Chile. Andrea's parents went to Argentina while they waited for permission to go to Canada. She and her brother stayed with their grandparents in Chile and spent their vacations with their parents in Argentina. Two years later, in 1979, Andrea and her brother joined their parents in Buenos Aires before they left for Winnipeg. Andrea was fifteen years old at the time and extremely depressed about leaving. It did not take her family long to realize they did not want to stay in Winnipeg and heard about Vancouver from other Chileans. They left Winnipeg for Vancouver in the summer of 1981. By that point Andrea and her brother were heavily involved in the solidarity movement and became even more so upon arrival in Vancouver. In 1990 Andrea married a Canadian she had been seeing for four years. Within a year she was pregnant and seven years later they divorced. Their son is now a teenager and lives with Andrea, who is forty-two years old. They live in Victoria on Vancouver Island, the capital of British Columbia. Her brother and parents still live in Vancouver.

Amanda

Amanda is a pseudonym. She has six sisters, all of whom had access to higher education. Her family's politics span the spectrum. She explains: "Growing up in Chile . . . you can [not] avoid being political. . . . [In] my family . . . some of them were on the Right, some of them were on the Left, some [in] the center. My oldest sister was more involved in the Left; she and her boyfriend at the time were from the MIR." Amanda was only thirteen at the time of the coup but lived in Chile under Pinochet for about ten years, longer than any of the other women I interviewed for this book. Though she became involved with the opposition during the dictatorship, she finds her own political history "uneventful." She explains: "I do not find it at all heroic or tragic . . . it was just a thing to do. . . . I did not have a very strong [party] militancy because I was so young." However, in recalling her experiences and the clear danger in which she found herself it seems as though Amanda understates the significance of her contributions. Indeed, in retrospect she does admit that she made some risky decisions: "I do not know if I would do the same things that I did then, when I was young, in terms of taking so many risks, [like] going to the protests and helping people."

In 1979 Amanda started her university degree in education studies.[10] At the time, education had a different meaning. For example, the dean of the university was part of the military and knew nothing about university administration. The previous dean was killed after the coup. She and her fellow students got involved in a variety of projects, which, according to Amanda, "seemed so Mickey Mouse at the time. I mean they seemed important, but

I guess compared to what other people were doing [they seemed insignificant]." For example, she and some friends wrote and distributed a newsletter. The professor who helped them was eventually fired from the university. Eventually Amanda started to realize that she and her friends were in danger. She explains: "[We knew] that we were being followed and monitored and everything. And they [the military] knew who were . . . involved. . . . A couple of friends disappeared from my group of friends . . . and I think that we were in denial big time about the danger that we were in." The first incident that really brought her pause was a warning she received from her leftist brother-in-law, which came via his right-wing university colleague. She explains her brother-in-law's colleague was a "Pinochet supporter but they managed to have a good friendship and working relationship and . . . he told my brother-in-law: 'Tell your sister-in-law to be careful because she is in all the records, they know where she lives,' and I think that is when I realized, 'Oh my God! This is serious!'"

Realizing the gravity of the situation, however, did not cause Amanda to stop organizing. After graduating she began a job teaching English in the shantytowns, a job she found utterly "stupid" given the unlikelihood that shantytown dwellers would have any use for English. All of the teachers were young like herself (early twenties), and "of course we were all leftist." Once again she got involved politically, starting with the "little things. . . . Like everyday at noon we would walk to the middle of the school yard and just sit there for five minutes and protest. . . . That meant that we could be fired for doing that. But someone had to do it, right?" Amanda explains the emotional and physical state of mind of her students: "They all had relatives killed or disappeared. . . . It was atrocious how the really poor people suffered. . . . So all these kids were, . . . I realize [now], completely traumatized in many ways, and also just plain hungry." Being confronted with this reality made the dictatorship even more concrete to Amanda and her colleagues so they decided to start a communal kitchen for their students. She explains:

[The students] made it more concrete for us. [Now] there was something that we could do, so we started organizing a communal [kitchen] for the kids because across the street from the school there was this woman who had [turned] her house . . . into . . . a [makeshift] cafeteria. . . . [S]he had basically one table and she would cook for the teachers and charge [us] monthly. . . . So we started talking about how can we set up something for the kids? . . . [W]e started with other teachers [and] at the beginning we were bringing our own two potatoes, one onion, whatever [was needed] and some of the other women there got involved in that they were helping with the cooking. . . . I believe that the toughest part was deciding which kid would eat and which would not.

Not long after they started the kitchen the professor who had taken the lead was disappeared. Amanda explains:

> He came back obviously tortured, aggressively tortured, so the message I think was clear: [This] . . . is what is going to keep happening here. . . . I knew . . . [I was] living in some form of denial; that "no, this is not happening." . . . You do not want to see this happening but it is happening. I knew they were follow-ing me but I . . . could not imagine why they would bother with me; I am just so puny; I am so little; there were other people doing other [bigger] stuff. . . . I guess they had plenty of people to do this kind of stuff. . . . It was fairly obvious that they were following me; they talked to my mom, at that time I lived with my mom, she was a widow, and I think that is when I realized how serious this was. . . . So she freaked out of course and so did I and I thought, it is basically a threat . . . . I did not see myself in danger but yet the danger was so immediate.

Amanda had some friends in Vancouver and finally decided to leave in either 1983 or 1984 (she could not recall for sure.) Her papers went through relatively quickly so she left Chile within six months of realizing it was time. She absolutely did not want to leave so she decided she would come to Canada and stay "just for a little while." That was twenty years ago. She was miserable in Vancouver. She missed her family and often wondered why she left in the first place. She married a Canadian not long after arriving which she describes as "an absolute fiasco." They eventually divorced. On top of missing her family and Chile, Amanda also had a series of, as she says, "shitty jobs, like [in] restaurants and dishwasher; you know, the same stuff that we all do here." Eventually she got more connected with other Chileans, became involved with the solidarity movement, and other political projects, and thus started feeling a bit better in Vancouver. She eventually went back to college and was forced to start all over again despite her post-secondary education in Chile. At the time of our interview, Amanda was forty-five years old, and a graduate student preparing to leave for Chile to do her dissertation research. She intends to temporarily return to Vancouver to defend her dissertation, but hopes to remain in Chile for the duration.

As we can see the Chileans I interviewed for this project come from a variety of social classes and educational backgrounds. They entered politics at different times and for different reasons, some remaining explicitly active while others having "retired." Their stories vary in many ways but regardless of structural and familial differences they hold many similarities as well. De-spite the trauma of exile we also get a sense of the women's strength to get through the political, emotional, and economic instability inherent in exile. Most experienced some sort of serious and even prolonged depression upon arrival. Most long for their families in Chile but at this point in their lives do not intend to move back. I hope that the reader will keep their personal histories and testimonies in mind when reading the rest of this book, which is based in large part on the recollections and political interpretations of the women we just met.

NOTES

1. Marcela Cornejo wrote a very interesting and related article entitled "Political Exile and the Construction of Identity: A Life Stories Approach" (2008). Her article is based on interviews with Chileans who lived their exiles in Belgium. She finds many similar patterns that the women note here. I have chosen not to incorporate her article into this chapter because this is meant to be the women's explanations of their own experiences. See Marcela Cornejo, (2008), "Political Exile and the Construction of Identity: A Life Stories Approach," *Journal of Community & Applied Social Psychology* 18(4): 333–48.

2. Patricia is one of only four women I interviewed who left Chile married and never divorced.

3. See Chris Bobel, (2005), "'I've never defined myself as an activist, though I've done a lot of it': Doing Activism, Being Activist and the Gendered 'Perfect Standard' in a Contemporary Movement" (paper presented at the American Sociological Association conference, Philadelphia, Pa.).

4. Carmen shared part of the story of her work with the MIR with me without being prompted. However, when she read the transcript some time later she originally asked me not to include any of the discussion in my book. After thinking about it more and discussing the need to archive this history she later agreed to let me include part of the story in the book. As she said during our original conversation: "Even though it has been so long, because of the nature of the work we did, I still have a lot of trouble talking about it; there was clandestine stuff, so I did not talk about it, and I never talk about it." But as Ana María Quiroz said during our focus group discussion, which included Carmen: "We owe it to the next generation [to share these stories] because they really suffered through all of this. . . . They were left you know, the kids were left." Carmen responded: "Or they were taken with us and exposed to the danger and that is something that I have also been coming to terms with."

5. In an email correspondence Irene wanted to make sure I understood the different types of detention centers:

There were several types of incarceration places for political prisoners: 1. Secret places, such as *Villa Grimaldi*, which were the places of interrogation with torture, run by the military, the *desaparecidos* were generally people taken to those places, and Pinochet consistently denied the existence of those places. The interrogations in those places had a heavy emphasis on giving names of other people, information that could be used to catch others. 2. Police stations, in which the prisoners were treated just as regular criminals; they were also places of interrogation, but the treatment was a lot better, done by policemen (the Military Junta also included the police forces), and they were not as secret. The interrogations there, as with regular criminals, [were] more about finding grounds for laying charges. 3. Waiting places, such as *Estadio Chile* National Stadium and *Chacabuco*, where prisoners were "filed" or kept in waiting until the Junta decided what to do with them. These spaces were publicly known, the Red Cross and other humanitarian groups had access to them, [and] the Junta saw them as POW camps. So Adam [her husband] was never a "desaparecido" really; he was lucky in that sense.

6. Irene was one of many women who told me that her name was changed by Canadian immigration officials upon entering the country. Some women, particularly those who have since divorced their husbands, have started and/or completed the extremely lengthy process of getting their original names back. Irene is one of the few women I interviewed who is still married to the man with whom she left Chile.

7. See Pablo Policzer, (2009), *The Rise and Fall of Repression in Chile Under Pinochet: Organization and Information in Authoritarian Regimes* (Notre Dame, Ind.: University of Notre Dame Press).

8. This is in contrast to her older brother, who remembers very little of the period, including leaving South America, at which point he was in his late teens.

9. Though I do not include all of the testimonies here, many of the women I interviewed recalled the same exact process of burning everything and thinking about it later. Many also explained how they burned their New Song album covers but kept the albums in different cases. Destroying their intellectual, political, and familial archives was a particularly difficult part of the early days of the dictatorship.

10. I intentionally leave out the specifics regarding which universities, in Chile and Canada, given Amanda's desire to stay anonymous.

Chapter Three

The Chilean Solidarity Movement in Trans/national Perspective

There is no important city in the world where you will not find a Chilean, nor a city that is not familiar with empanadas [traditional Chilean meat pies] and peñas.

—Juan Pablo Letelier (in Wright and Oñate 1998, 91)

INTRODUCTION

As of late the term *diaspora*, originally meaning "a scattering or sowing of seeds," has gained much academic credence. Indeed, as Jose Moya suggests, "the 'diaspora bandwagon' became a rollercoaster after 1990" (2004, 2). Such popularity potentially leads to an overuse of the term and thus the analytically watering down of its explanatory potential. However, the case of Chilean exiles most certainly captures the image of scattered and sowed seeds as they resettled and rebuilt their communities throughout the world. The Chilean diaspora differs significantly from other immigrant groups who tend to concentrate in one country or even city, for example, Cubans in Miami, Florida.

As we know, approximately one million Chileans fled their country by the end of the dictatorship. Two hundred thousand were forced out for political reasons, while the remaining eight hundred thousand left for economic reasons directly connected to the dictatorship (Wright 1995, 198). They went to at least 110 and as many as 140 different countries (Wright and Oñate 1998, 91; 2007), including Algeria, Angola, Argentina, Australia, Bangladesh, Brazil, the Cape Verde Islands, Colombia, Costa Rica, Cuba, East Germany, England, France, Greenland, Holland, Israel, Italy, Japan, Kenya, Mexico, Mozambique, the Netherlands, Nicaragua, Peru, Scotland, the former Soviet Union, Spain,

Sweden, the United States, Uruguay, Venezuela, West Germany, and of course Canada. The diversity of host cities and countries certainly led to a variety of experiences; however, according to Wright and Oñate "the effects of exile were fundamentally similar whether one was in Costa Rica or Sweden, Mozambique or Canada, the USSR or the United States" (1998, 94; 2007, 36). It is hard to know the exact numbers per country for a variety of reasons: most statistics collected only counted official refugees; many Chileans remained uncounted, and people moved around a lot. For example, many Chileans started in Argentina but were forced to leave once the coup happened in that country, while others tried to resettle elsewhere in Latin America but found the economic conditions insufficient to guarantee stability (Sznajder and Roniger 2007, 22).

For a great majority of these Chileans, exile became permanent. Indeed, exile remains such a normalized part of Chilean national and transnational politics that a webpage entitled "*Exilio Chileno*" still exists and was updated sometime in 2009 (chile.exilio.free.fr/index.htm). The current president of Chile, Michelle Bachelet, was an exile from 1975 until 1979. It is estimated that currently one million Chileans still live abroad. The country is divided into thirteen regions, each numbered, and Chileans abroad, many of whom were/are exiles, are said to make up "Region XIV." Chileans in Region XIV remain active in politics in their homeland with varying degrees of efficacy (Arriaza 2005, 291). The current political clout of Chileans abroad is arguably tied to their political efficacy during the dictatorship. In this chapter I offer a global and national overview of the solidarity movement. I begin with a discussion of the historical place of culture in Chilean politics, a trend that we will see in the solidarity movement as well. Next I provide an overview of the global solidarity movement outside of Canada. I conclude this chapter with an examination of the Canadian case in general in order to properly situate the Vancouver case, the subject of the next chapter.

CULTURE AS POLITICS IN CHILE

Cultural expression has long been central to leftist politics in Chile. It is important to highlight this part of Chilean political history as it offers much insight into the strategies and tactics Chileans eventually used in their protest movement once in exile. Perhaps the most concrete manifestation of the coupling of leftist politics with cultural production is the Chilean New Song movement. The New Song movement is best described as "music intended to support and promote social change" (Morris 1986, 117). The person deserving of the most credit for cultivating the New Song movement is Violeta Parra. Parra was born during the First World War in the south of Chile. She grew up in a farming town in close contact with indigenous music. She came from a very poor family of musicians and poets. Indeed, her father was known as the region's best folklorist. Rather than teaching his children to play guitar, he locked his in the closet. Violeta eventually stole the key to the closet and taught herself to play. Her brother, Nicanor Parra, was also culturally literate and became a famous poet. Violeta later set many of his verses to music.

Violeta Parra befriended some of the older folk singers in her community, who eventually taught her their songs. This initial introduction to Chilean folk music inspired Parra to eventually travel throughout Chile in search of disappearing folk songs. She tape-recorded hundreds of songs and eventually compiled a two-volume collection for the University of Concepción, where she was a researcher for the Folklore Department. Due to the pressure of a colleague and professional singer, Chilean radio stations, under the control of the right-wing business-class, begrudgingly allowed Parra to perform on the air. Violeta Parra was responsible for reintroducing, archiving, and legitimizing a piece of Chilean culture that would have likely disappeared without her efforts.

Though Violeta Parra was never formally trained in music in 1954 she traveled to Warsaw, Czechoslovakia, and England to participate in youth festivals. She also lived and performed in Paris. While in Paris she became more involved in composing contemporary folk music, "which she saw as a weapon against oppression" (Kirchheimer 1973, 8). It was Parra's music from this period that proved most influential for the New Song movement in the late 1960s and early 1970s.

Jeffrey Taffet (1997) explains that the New Song movement in Chile passed through four distinct phases, the first of which I just described. According to Taffet the 1950s and 1960s symbolize what he calls the discovery and protest period. In addition to archiving and thus arguably saving folk music from cultural extinction, it was also during this period in 1965 that Violeta Parra and her two children, Angel and Isabel, founded the first *peña*, or café, in a house they had recently bought, "Peña de los Parra."[1] This became a physical space to house New Song musicians, their progressive lyrics, and their followers. Eventually peñas appeared in cities throughout the country, exact copies of this first one: low tables, carafes rather than bottles of wine, candles, with *empanadas* (Chilean meat pies) and croquettes for sale during intermission (Pottlitzer 2001a).

The second period of the New Song movement was an electoral one in which the musicians more or less formally became the cultural representatives of the Left. That is, they wrote campaign songs and performed at political rallies in support of the Popular Unity (UP) and Salvador Allende. Indeed, according to the liner notes of the album *Canto al Programa*, the New Song movement was "part of an effort to use 'all available means of communication' to present the

UP program in a language and style that were accessible to the people" (cited in Morris 1986, 121–22, 134). Once Allende triumphed and he began to lead Chile down his "path to Chilean socialism," the New Song musicians became less directly tied to political parties and sang of everyday themes, including the glorification of labor. However, as we know it did not take long for the Left to realize that the Popular Unity's project was under attack. As a result, while the New Song musicians were celebrating the electoral triumph they were also put on the defensive, which was conveyed through their lyrics. After the coup, the fourth phase of the New Song movement, the *Canto Nuevo* [also translated New Song] movement began.[2] By this time, the power of leftist popular culture was so evident that one of the most infamous attacks during the dictatorship was against New Song musician Victor Jara. Within twenty-four hours of the coup Jara was one of the estimated thousands of Chileans detained, beaten, and/or tortured, publicly and behind closed doors in the National Stadium.[3] His murder was an unambiguous statement from the junta declaring New Song musicians, and by extension their fans, the enemy.[4]

Angel Parra (Violeta's son) believes the only reason he was not killed was because of Victor Jara's murder. Parra, reflecting on his detention from September 14, 1973 until the middle of 1976, explains:

> A next-door neighbor turned me in. But I knew they had to find me sooner or later. I think there were two people the military wanted to use as examples: Victor and me. That day [September 11] Victor was at the Technical University, and that very day they arrested him. I fell [was arrested] three days later. I've always said, very seriously, that I'm alive thanks to the death of Victor. It was about who they got first, who to use as an example: "This is what happens to singers who get involved in politics." (Quoted in Pottlitzer 2001a)

Other famous New Song musicians were spared simply because they were on tour in Europe at the time of the coup, including *Inti-Illimani, Quilapayún,* and Isabel Parra (Violeta's daughter/Angel's sister). They stayed in exile and it is in the Chilean diaspora that the Canto Nuevo period truly took shape. Eventually bands were able to play inside Chile as well but needless to say the censorship, surveillance, and repression made their shows much less frequent and public than those that happened in exile (Morris 1986; Cobos and Sater 1986).

Inti-Illimani means sun (Inti) of a mountain in the Bolivian Andes (Il-limani) in Ayamara dialect. They were one of the most important bands in the New Song movement. Five students from Santiago Technical University joined together in 1967 to form the band. For Inti-Illimani and the New Song movement more generally there is a direct connection between their music and the fight against cultural imperialism (Kirchheimer 1973, 8). Quilapayún is another group central to the New Song movement. A group of six men committed to the working class, their "aim was to help transform art, once the sanctified domain of the upper classes, into a revolutionary weapon" (Kirchheimer 1973, 12). Quilapayún did not accept payment for their performances. Rather, they performed at union events and on outdoor stages in public parks frequented by the working class. In addition to their long hair and beards they wore black *mantas* (traditional Chilean ponchos worn by peasants) during their performances. Chilean women exiles later formed their own musical group in Vancouver and emulated this same style, as they too wore the mantas when they performed.[5]

New Song musicians were such recognized popular ambassadors of the Left that after the coup owning their albums became cause for repression. Several of the women I interviewed explained how in the beginning of the dictatorship, as the brutality and intensity became more and more evident, they ended up burning their New Song album covers because being caught with them would have been as dangerous as owning a copy of *The Communist Manifesto*. One woman recalls destroying the covers but saving the albums because she did not want to lose them; she placed a Victor Jara LP in a Bee Gees album cover. Jan Fairley captures the political significance of the New Song movement quite well:

> The power and potency of this music is underlined not only when you consider the torture, imprisonment and death suffered by many of its creators but also the knowledge that . . . while politicians, unionists and many others [were eventually] allowed to return from exile to Chile . . . musicians—the public face and expression of solidarity and resistance movement—remain[ed] . . . on the excluded lists. (1985, 310)[6]

Music was not the only articulation of leftist popular culture. As we know, during the brief tenure of Salvador Allende, there was a quasi-attempt to institutionalize revolutionary culture. Simply put, Allende wanted everyone to have access to everything, including what is typically considered "high-culture." Recall Carla Gutiérrez who became active in politics at the age of twelve. Her father was a member of the Communist Party and he was detained for nine months during the dictatorship. She grew up in a typical working-class family and from her perspective,

> many people voted for Allende looking for a more [humane] society; one in which people had access to education, to healthcare; one with improved libraries, with more access to the theater, to cinema, to musical concerts and many other aspects of life that were [previously] denied to many.

In other words, Allende's agenda of treating cultural events just like a basic need as fundamental as health care or education appealed to many working-class Chileans. Article 40 of the UP's Program stated that "the class struggle would be fought out in the field of culture just as it was on the heights of the economy" (in Gonzalez 1976, 106). Toward this end, the UP implemented a variety of projects, some more successful than others. Mireya Baltra, secretary general of the *Allendista* Women's Unit, explained to me that "with Allende, there were culture trains, so that every sort of artistic manifestation could reach even the most remote villages where they had never before had a ballet, an opera, a symphony" (personal interview 1999). The impact of these campaigns was not particularly significant. However, the point of interest for this study is that the Chilean women forced into exile fled a country with a leftist government that was directly supported by a vibrant and radical New Song movement, a country where it was common for their president to appear in front of a banner that read "*No hay revolución sin canciones*" (there is no revolution without songs) (Fairley 1985, 307), and a country whose government valued leftist popular and mainstream "high" culture so much that its national platform included the support of them. This cultural context was central in influencing how Chilean exiles would later organize their movement.

GLOBAL SNAPSHOT OF THE SOLIDARITY MOVEMENT

According to Smith, Pagnucco, and Chatfield, social movements are transnational "when they involve conscious efforts to build transnational cooperation around shared goals that include social change" (1997, 60). Most social movement scholars would agree with this or a variant of this definition. Related to this, political transnationalism, according to Landolt and Goldring, refers to "activities aimed at participating in or changing the political situation in the home country, regardless of geographic orientation, . . . scale, . . . or interlocutors" (2006, 6). There is much agreement that (1) growth in democratization, (2) increased global integration, (3) convergence of values,[7] (4) the proliferation of transnational organizations (Kriesberg 1997, 3), and (5) advances in technology are the main causes for the growth in transnational mobilization. However, these causes are quite incongruent with the Chilean solidarity movement's reality. Indeed, (1) dictatorship not democratization provided the impetus for Chilean exiles to organize; (2) Chileans organized at the height of anti-global integration, that is, the Cold War; as such (3) values were highly polarized rather than converging; (4) transnational organizations did exist but certainly had not yet proliferated; and (5) technological advances were virtually nonexistent, most specifically the internet. However, I argue the Chilean solidarity movement was a quintessential transnational social movement. This is especially noteworthy given the political, geographical, and technological obstacles at the time. In this next section I provide an overview of the movement focusing on three specific themes: the role of political parties in the movement, transnational networks between exiles and Chileans in Chile ("the interior"), and support from non-Chileans. Throughout this discussion I offer a handful of examples from different countries around the world, and cities in Canada, in order to foreground the discussion of Vancouver.

Political Parties

One of the primary goals of the dictatorship was to destroy leftist parties and their irrefutable influence on Chilean politics.[8] The junta's main tactic of course was to remove all of the leaders from the country, either by murdering or disappearing them, or forcing them into exile. In other words, a great majority of the exiles were politically active and networked leftists. Once they arrived in their destinations party militants reconstituted their parties. This was the case for the bigger Socialist (*Partido Socialista,* PS) and Communist (*Partido Comunista,* PC) parties as well as the smaller Movement for United Popular Action (*Movimiento de Acción Popular Unitaria,* MAPU), and the Movement for the Revolutionary Left (*Movimiento de Izquierda Revolucionario,* MIR). Not long after establishing local party units, party militants then created regional, national, and international bodies. Even unions reorganized themselves in exile, namely the Communist Party–controlled Central Workers Confederation (*Central Única de Trabajadores,* or CUT), as well as the Allendista Women's Unit, which reorganized in at least thirty-five countries. Women also organized nonparty organizations like the Mothers' Centers (*Centros de Madres*).[9] Within months the Chilean Left replicated itself in dozens of countries around the world.

As I noted in Chapter One, Chile is a notoriously sectarian country. Perhaps its rich democratic history and plethora of political parties and coalitions is responsible for this reality but certainly Chilean *político/as* keep it alive. Not surprisingly, Chilean exiles brought their party alliances and thus sectarianism with them in exile.[10] Much of the political battles in exile revolved around placing blame on one another for the coup. Some parties argued the Popular Unity coalition moved too slowly, while others claimed they advanced their agenda much too quickly. Initially, party-based political organizing made the most sense to the exiles; indeed, it was the way they knew how to do politics. As Eduardo Montecinos, a Socialist Party member exiled in Costa Rica, noted: "This form of organization was important because of the lack of confidence that grew up around a person if that person could not show in some way what connections they had, or where they had been active" (quoted in Wright and Oñate 1998, 154). In other words, just being Chilean was not enough to earn the trust of other exiles; one needed explicit party alliances and history to demonstrate her connection to the project and thus her trustworthiness. This actually presented a problem for some Chilean women who were not active with parties at the time of the coup but once arriving in exile wanted to get involved. Chilean politics, including the Left, tend to be viewed as men's work. As a result, women had less formal political experience than men and lacked the same automatic political credibility that many of their male *compañeros* had. They were eventually able to overcome this obstacle but it does speak to the power of traditional party politics in marginalizing women.[11]

Parties continued to function as if they were still in Chile. For example, the Socialist Party (PS) was the largest in many exile communities just as it was in Chile prior to the coup. Berlin, the capital of the former German Democratic Republic, became the headquarters of the Socialist Party. The PS issued strict rules of conduct regarding the proper behavior of party militants in exile and the relationship with the underground PS still in Chile. Despite the repression within Chile, the party's main objective remained intact: "To overthrow the Capitalist regime of the country and construct socialism by organizing and directing the working class and Chilean masses" (in Eastmond 1997, 97). The job of the PS in exile was to support the struggle in the interior while ceding control to the underground party in Chile. The parties were also strict about their membership. For example, as a rule the PS did not let in new militants in exile. That is, only those who were members of the Party at the time of the coup and reaffirmed their commitment once in exile held the status of members. This was the case for leaders as well. Local leaders were appointed or authorized from the top and needed a substantial record of militancy, free of disciplinary sanctions. To be sure, over time there was some variation in these rules but in the beginning this model was advanced by the parties in the interior and respected by those in exile. The passage of time also led to much fragmentation in the parties, particularly the Socialist Party (PS).

The situation for the Communist Party (PC) was slightly different than it was for the Socialists. Exile did not divide the PC as significantly as it did the PS. The main reason for this is the orthodox nature of the party and long-time loyalty to Moscow. Most PC leaders were exiled in Eastern Europe and the former Soviet Union, with their headquarters in Moscow. The PC also depended on Moscow for financial support, which was certainly not lacking during the dictatorship. In other words, the PC was more centrally located and financially secure and thus better able to weather the sectarian battles that the exiles brought into the diaspora. Interestingly, the PC also coped reasonably well with the new situation in the interior. The PC has not always been legal in Chile and thus had some familiarity with clandestine organizing prior to the coup, a reality totally new to the Socialists.

Over time the role of the parties in exile shifted. While the parties in the interior put some of their differences aside, many in exile became more fractured and eventually demobilized. Many activists left their parties and joined organizations autonomous from the political parties because the dogmatic methods adhered to in Chile made little sense in exile. Some of the women I interviewed laughed as they recalled the "documents from the interior" and never-ending splits in the parties, especially the Socialist Party. The men's persistent ideological bickering, which, among other things, ultimately wasted a lot of time women did not have, compounded by a sense of masculine political arrogance combined to further alienate women from party politics. These practices are quite entrenched inside Latin America and many of these same trends were apparent in exile as well.

It was not just women who became frustrated with party politics, however; male activists did as well. For example, Eduardo Montecinos had a lengthy history with the Socialist Party including leadership positions prior to his exile in Costa Rica. But once in Costa Rica he explained that he and many of his friends "never believed in party activity by remote control. We could be sympathetic to the Chilean parties, but we couldn't be active party members in Costa Rica . . . [and] that created a separation from the other, more orthodox groups that met as Socialists, as Communists, and so forth" (quoted in Wright and Oñate 1998, 154). Gabriel Sanhueza, a MIR party militant both in and outside of Chile, had similar feelings about the party structure and exile. He recalls his experience in West Germany where he finally broke with the MIR in 1977: "I felt totally distanced from the MIR as far as what we wanted: from the utopia of the MIR, from the mission of the MIR. But what motivated me to leave it was that, as an instrument, it was undemocratic in the sense that they didn't discuss the mission or the objective of the party . . . [y]ou had to serve and respect and accept" (quoted in Wright and Oñate 1998, 157). In Chile this approach made more sense, as the political climate was so closed, but not for the exiles, since they had the space to question the tactics that favored dogmatism over democracy. Despite the fissures and political obstacles resultant of the party structures, they also helped create a transnational infrastructure to keep exiles networked with Chileans in the interior and one another regardless of their geographic locale.

Transnational Networking

The degree of coordination among exiles with their compañeras and compañeros in Chile was quite remarkable given the absence of the internet, combined with the politically dangerous terrain in which Chileans in the interior organized. The two primary goals of the solidarity movement, regardless of the city or country in exile, were (1) to provide material and (2) political support to the anti-Pinochet movement in the interior. The money from even the smallest of fundraising events was sent back to Chile to support the movement there. One woman exiled in Montreal recalls, "I worked in the solidarity movement for Chile. We made 500 empanadas every Saturday to collect money and . . . to send it to the women in Chile" (quoted in Wright and Oñate 1998, 150). Salvador Allende worked for a revolution "*a la Chilena* with 'empanadas and red wine.'" Exiles took this declaration to heart and transformed empanadas into a universal symbol of exile and resistance. Cooking and selling empanadas were never-ending and time-consuming tasks that typically fell to women exiles. Indeed, in the words of Margaret Power, some women had "empanada fatigue" by the end of the dictatorship (personal communication 2008)! As one exile recalled, "I don't plan to ever make another [empanada] in my life" (quoted in Wright and Oñate 2007, 39). I met many women who conveyed that exact sentiment. Certainly selling empanadas did not generate the same amount of funds that the Soviet Communist Party was able to channel to the PC in the interior but from the perspective of the activists in exile and the interior, it was equally integral to their movement. (I discuss this more in the next chapter.)

An interesting dynamic of the transnational relationship was the role exiles played in educating Chileans in the interior. In the early years after the coup censorship was so intense in Chile that if one was not living or witnessing the dictatorship firsthand she had no way of knowing its severity. Exiles addressed this by sending reports back to Chile about the situation there. One man exiled in Montreal recalls: "There was the uphill battle to keep the Chileans in the country informed. We used as a source of information the telephone books from different cities in Chile. Pages were distributed around the world and envelopes sent constantly with information "as to what was really happening in that country" (quoted in Wright and Oñate 1998, 152).[12] An interesting manifestation of this opposite direction of media exchange is the fact that some exiles learned upon arriving in Canada (and presumably elsewhere) that their exile was likely to be far longer, if not permanent, as opposed to what they initially believed as they left Chile. For example, one man Matthew Scalena interviewed explained that when he left Chile he "thought it would be a short period of time, maybe two or three years at the most, because the government is going to change and things are going to change. So it wasn't really something that I thought was going to be permanent" (quoted in 2005, 32). However, after spending some time in Winnipeg he realized that Pinochet continued to further entrench his power hold with absolutely no intention of relinquishing it. In other words, a speedy return to Chile for a persecuted exile seemed unlikely. Interestingly, this realization came from following the Canadian press's coverage of Chile—which was in part the result of the solidarity movement's efforts—rather than directly from the interior (Scalena 2005, 33).

Eventually Chileans were organized and networked enough to smuggle information from Chile into the diaspora and vice versa, leading to a transnational exchange of information. María Elena Carrera, a Socialist Party leader and elected senator at the time of the coup, recalls the way information was ultimately sent from Chile to the exterior. (After passing through Peru and Cuba, Carrera spent the rest of her exile in Berlin, East Germany.) "We had reports that we received from people who traveled clandestinely or sent news by secret mail. Then with this kind of report we would inform the United Nations and we had, in this respect, a good organization, an office in Rome and an office in New York, and we had people who were very well connected in Geneva" (quoted in Wright and Oñate 1998, 160). In this case we can see the links between Chileans in the interior with exiles as well as the transnational networks created in the movement.

The transnational component of the movement was quite important. That is, when Chileans in the interior and exiles attempted to design an appropriate political strategy they attempted to take the entire exile community into consideration. As a result, the networking needed to be sound. For example, Gabriel Sanhueza was a journalist and militant with the MIR at the time of the coup. He spent the first part of his exile in Argentina. While there he was recruited to organize for the MIR in West Germany. He arrived in West Germany in November of 1974. Sanhueza explained that the MIR

> had not been able to set up the work outside that would help them stay in Chile, something which the Communists, the Socialists, all the parties on the left, had. Then a compañero from the MIR who was in Argentina made me a very concrete proposal: "You have to go to Europe, you have the ability to put something together, to get something. Get money. We have a great number of prisoners, of people disappeared, so you go to Germany and wait there for orders." (Quoted in Wright and Oñate 1998, 156)

This request, as Sanhueza calls it, included Chileans in at least three different countries: Chile, Argentina, and West Germany. He arrived in Germany in November 1974, just thirteen months after the coup. By then organizational strategies were well into the implementation phase and as this testimony suggests transnational networking was fundamental to advancing the movement's goals.

Transnational networking among exiles also helped with the distribution of funds raised by exiles. Patricio Rivas, a leader of the MIR, recalled how some of that networking occurred:

> We had annual meetings in Mexico of all the exterior committees to coordinate and plan the work. Our [MIR in exile] tasks consisted of the development of our international relations . . . and financial responsibilit[ies] which consisted of collecting funds for the resistance in Chile. We sent the money by zones.[13] For example, [MIRistas in] Italy sent money to the Regional in Concepción and another country to Santiago. (Quoted in Wright and Oñate 1998, 160)

This level of coordination both provided efficiency with respect to the distribution of funds and, according to Rivas, also contributed to group spirit among the exiles.

Another impressive example of transnational networking among the exiles comes from the organization *Chile Democrático* based in Rome. Chile Democrático was founded by the leaders of different political parties in December of 1973 and according to Wright and Oñate, Chile Democrático was the "original and, most influential of several multiparty organizations fighting for the restoration of democracy in Chile" (1998, 163). It was a federation of party members and had a council where all the members of the Chilean Left were represented. The organization was quite pluralistic with members from the center to the far Left. They also reached out to the Christian Democrats in exile despite the fact that they were not formally represented in the organization. This is particularly significant if we recall that the majority of Christian Democrats originally supported the coup. Chile Democrático had committees in some eighty countries around the world, including Australia, Mexico, Algeria, Sweden, and Italy. They divided their activities into sections. For example, one section was dedicated to direct contact with international organizations, including the whole system of the United Nations, where they had human rights specialists based in Geneva. Others worked with what they called the "national committees" in any given country with special attention to unions or artists and intellectuals, for example. This entire structure was coordinated from Rome, Italy (Wright and Oñate 2007, 40).

Benjamin Teplizky Lijavetzky was director of Chile Democrático. He was arrested the day of the coup for his high-level presence in the UP and held until January 1975. In his estimation, the exiles

> were sure that this work of an international diplomatic nature that we were doing, by itself was not going to overthrow the military junta, that this would be determined inside the country—as, in fact, it was—but the force of this solidarity movement was such that we realized that it had become a force in favor of Chilean democracy. (Quoted in Wright and Oñate 1998, 165)

All of Chile Democrático's efforts were financed by aid from many international organizations, which were in turn funded by governments via Non-

Governmental Organizations (NGOs). According to Lijavetzky, "The country that gave the most money in solidarity with Chile was Holland, because it has a culture of real political solidarity; also the Scandinavian countries" (quoted in Wright and Oñate 1998, 164). This leads me to the last point I wish to discuss regarding the anti-Pinochet movement in a transnational context: international solidarity from non-Chileans.

INTERNATIONAL SOLIDARITY FROM NON-CHILEANS

We might think of international solidarity as the political opportunity (Mc-Adam 1982; Tarrow 1988; 1995) that was partially responsible for Chilean exiles organizing so rapidly, effectively, and transnationally. Certainly international solidarity created resources not otherwise available, namely material and formal political support, but it is virtually a given exiles would have organized even in its absence. (I discuss this further in the next chapter.) One of the first acts of solidarity came from countries opening their embassies to persecuted Chileans before they were able to leave the country. At least thirty-five hundred Chileans took asylum in embassies until the junta blocked access and cut off this important source of refuge. Once that happened some Catholic and Protestant churches in conjunction with the International Organization for Migration, the United Nations High Commission for Refugees, and the International Red Cross helped those safely in the embassies eventually flee into exile (Wright and Oñate 2007, 33–34). The leftist eyes of the world had been on Chile since 1970 and thus news of the coup inspired quick response from non-Chileans everywhere.[14] As a result of the international leftist community's familiarity with the Chilean socialist experiment, exiles were greeted by enthusiastic and sympathetic supporters. Anselmo Sule was a lawyer, professor, senator, president of the Radical Party, and president of the UP coalition at the time of the coup. Not surprisingly his very high-profile position in the UP led to his imprisonment from November 1973 until August 1974. In February 1975 he was then expelled from Chile and went first to Venezuela and later Mexico. While in exile he served as a vice-president of the Socialist International. Sule explains his view of international solidarity:

> Chile was considered a priority for all democratic solidarity movements in the world because Chile was like the Switzerland of America, in the sense of being a peaceful country, a democratic country. . . . Also a stability that was almost unique in Latin America, and the coup—because of its bloody nature—had a very great impact worldwide. . . . Allende's gesture, his suicide, Allende's final words—all those things reached all parts of the world. They caused an impact in the strangest, most exotic countries; in the smallest towns, people knew about

the Chilean experience and the dictatorship. I made a trip through Turkey, both the Asian as well as the European part, and everyone knew who Pinochet was and who Allende was. (Quoted in Wright and Oñate 1998, 168–69)

In a similar vein Jorge Arrate maintains that the far-reaching and unwavering solidarity of European leftists was the result of the preexisting sympathy for the Popular Unity project (in Wright 1995, 203).

The Chile-Canada Solidarity Newsletter published in October of 1973 reported actions of international solidarity with Chile in fourteen different countries including Peru, Costa Rica, Argentina, Mexico, Colombia, Venezuela, France, North Vietnam, Italy, Hungary, Cuba, Honduras, the United States, and Canada.[15] According to this report some of the more noteworthy actions include:

> Mexico—Mexican students shouted in front of Chilean embassy "United States is backing the Coups" [*sic*]. They were ready to give blood to support Allende's Socialist cause. . . . Paris—Representatives of the European Progressive and antifascist organizations met Sept. 22 to co-ordinate Continental Action in solidarity with the Chilean people. Decisions will be made to do with political, moral, and material solidarity. Hanoi—Top leaders in North Vietnam voiced strong protest against the fascist coup. Le Duan, First Secretary of the Vietnamese Workers' Party said he was confident of the people's struggle. . . . Honduras—A bomb exploded in gardens of the U.S. Embassy in Tegucigalpa—large demonstrations in support of Chilean people. (CCSN 1973(a); underlines in original)

Additionally, Margaret Power explains that in the days following the coup:

> 250,000 people marched in Buenos Aires, 100,000 demonstrated in Mexico City and burned the U.S. flag, as did 5,000 angry marchers in San Juan, Puerto Rico. Activists in Venezuela, Switzerland, Italy, and New York City firebombed offices of the International Telephone and Telegraph (ITT) Company because of its financial and political support of the opposition to Allende. Hundreds of thousands of people protested Allende's overthrow in Rome and Paris. A much smaller number, roughly some 5,000 people marched in U.S. cities such as Boston, New York City, Chicago, Pittsburgh, Cleveland, Memphis, and San Francisco. (2009, n.p.).

In January 1974, in the eighth issue of the aforementioned newsletter, contributors reported:

> More than 20,000 people gathered in Paris for an international demonstration called by the Committee to Support the Revolutionary Struggle of the Chilean People. Demonstrators came from most western European countries, including Holland, Italy, Britain, and West Germany. (CCSN 1974)[16]

In other words, international solidarity from non-Chileans was rapid and massive. In this section I will share some impressions from exile activists (most of whom we just met in the preceding section) about the tremendous solidarity they encountered around the world, as well as the concrete forms it took.

As Sule's above testimony about Turkey suggests, wherever Chilean exiles went they received a warm leftist welcome. Gabriel Sanhueza conveys virtually the same sentiment:

> The concern in [West] Germany about the situation in Chile was very great. Three days after arriving [Nov 1974], I was already talking at least to students, telling them what had happened in Chile, what the coup was like, and we formed an aid committee. I was very impressed at how the different sectors of German society converged in their concern for Chile. . . . [T]his was because Chile represented many dreams, dreams of a free socialism, a critical church, a labor movement creating a different kind of labor relations. This and many other dreams were present in the Chilean process, and, as a result, the great interest in being in solidarity with Chile. (Quoted in Wright and Oñate 1998, 156–57)

East Germans were equally welcoming to Chileans. María Elena Carrera arrived in Berlin in June 1974. She recalls:

> The welcome I received in the German Democratic Republic was incredibly good. There was a tremendous solidarity in all the countries that I visited, and from the stories that I heard, I think that the solidarity with Chile worldwide was more even than that given to Vietnam in the period of the war. The solidarity with Chile was very extensive in Europe and the United States. (Quoted in Wright and Oñate 1998, 158)

Anselmo Sule corroborates María Elena Carrera's assessment. He spent the majority of his exile in Mexico, where, he recalls, "The truth is that we were really overwhelmed by the support that they gave us" (quoted in Wright and Oñate 1998, 167). As I explained above, Sule was a vice president of the Socialist International while in exile. In that capacity he gained a thorough sense of international solidarity. He recalls:

> [W]ithout a doubt, the most unrestricted, unconditional, massive, automatic, obvious support for Chile was on the part of the socialist countries and the Communist International. But what was decisive and really very important was that of the Socialist International. . . . The Socialist International had a significant presence that countered that of the United States; we had easy access to the international decision-making organizations and to the United Nations, and in this aspect there was a total commitment to the cause of Chilean democracy on the part of the Socialist International. (Quoted in Wright and Oñate 1998, 168)

In other words, the socialist parties and organizations around the world provided support geographically, politically, and materially far reaching enough to counter the pro-Pinochet policies of the United States.

Much of the solidarity non-Chileans offered the exiles was material. In some cases it meant paying for copying newsletters and in others it included direct donations of cash. Julio Pérez was a *MIRista* who spent his exile in Montreal. He recalls: "The solidarity of the people of Quebec toward the Chilean resistance was very great. The union central committees often gave instructions to their members to contribute an hour's salary for the struggle in Chile; this fact alone meant a great deal of money" (quoted in Wright and Oñate 1998, 153). The amount of money paled in comparison to that provided by communist governments but the gesture did embody both a material and political contribution. That is, union-initiated projects such as this one alerted exiles that they were not alone in their struggle even once arriving in a brand new country that spoke a different language and lived a different culture. The solidarity undoubtedly helped ease some of the alienation inherent in exile.

The Chilean resistance movement also received international solidarity from guerrilla organizations. For example, in 1978 the MIR decided on a policy of returning exiles to Chile to fight in the underground resistance there. In order to prepare for this MIRistas were sent to Latin America to train with the guerrillas in Nicaragua, El Salvador, Guatemala, or Colombia to learn urban and rural guerrilla combat. According to MIRista Patricio Rivas, "These organizations demonstrated extraordinary solidarity with us, especially the Salvadorans" (quoted in Wright and Oñate 1998, 161). Though MIRistas benefited tremendously from the training, these relationships were eventually strained due to ideological and political differences. From Rivas's perspective: "They [Central American and Colombian guerrillas] were very militaristic—for them, it was a matter of firing more shots, more bombs; for us, it was a matter of masses, of greater participation. We were seen to be too 'intellectual'" (quoted in Wright and Oñate 1998, 162).

In sum, international solidarity came from all parts of the world and took on all different shapes. Chilean exiles received material support from a range of donors, including individual union members in Canada and Eastern Bloc governments. Regardless of the dollar amount this outpouring of solidarity translated into political support in the diaspora that Chileans tapped as a resource to pressure the Pinochet dictatorship. The political support also created a momentum necessary to keep the movement flourishing, particularly in the face of much political infighting. And finally, international solidarity was even delivered in the form of guerrilla combat training. Regardless of the varied political and ideological battles present in all of these sorts of relationships exiles benefited tremendously from international solidarity and, as the above testimonies suggest, were never oblivious to its presence and significance.

THE CANADIAN SOLIDARITY MOVEMENT

When I started this project I mistakenly assumed it would be relatively easy to find data regarding the numbers of Chileans in Canada. After all, the Canadian government keeps well-organized, frequently updated, public demographic data. Furthermore, most Chileans entered Canada legally and were thus visible to researchers. However, much to my chagrin, it is surprisingly difficult to find consistent statistics about the numbers of Chileans in Canada. In what follows I attempt to provide an overview of the breadth and subsequent inconsistencies in the data regarding Chileans in Canada. There is general consensus of their migration patterns but little agreement with respect to the actual numbers of Chileans in Canada.

Chilean migration to Canada occurred in three or four waves: The first wave, 1973–1978; second, 1979–1982; and third, 1987–1992 (Da 2002, 2). Diaz argues that it happened in four waves: first, 1974–1978; second, 1979–1982; third, 1983–1986, and fourth, 1987–1992 (1999, 349–50). The influx of Chilean refugees to Canada started out slowly due predominantly to the Canadian government's initial refusal to let in Chileans. In the first three months immediately following the coup (September 11, 1973) the Canadian embassy received 1,400 applications for asylum and approved only 184 of them (Landolt and Goldring 2006, 12–13). Statistics Canada reports that by the end of 1973 493 Chilean refugees arrived in Canada (cited in Da 2002, 2). Throughout the first wave the numbers increased steadily. According to a report dated February 1974 entitled "Immigration," published by *International Canada*, in January of 1974, 140 Chilean refugees arrived on a government-chartered aircraft. By the middle of February numbers had grown to 275 and 302 more had visas but had not yet arrived. One year after the coup 1,098 refugees had arrived in Canada. By February 1975 the total number of refugees reached 1,188 (Dirks 1977, 248; 250). However, Statistics Canada's numbers differ from these. By 1975, according to Statistics Canada, 2,082 Chileans were in Canada and by the end of the first wave, 1978, the total reached 8,302. Another series of data is provided by Patricia Landolt (1993). She reports that by 1975 Canada accepted 3,400 refugees directly from Chile. Yet another source estimates that by 1978 10,000 Chileans became permanent residents in Canada (Magocsi 1999, 355).

Another source, *Employment and Immigration, 1985* reports the numbers of entries for the same years as follows: 1974: 1,884, and 1975: 2,297, or a

total of 4,181 by the end of the year (Gilbert and Lee 1986, 123). Additionally, in 1974 the Canadian government established a special program for Chileans called *The Special Chilean Movement,* which mandated that up to five
thousand registered refugees were to be accepted in Canada and helped to resettle. By November 1976 this movement was responsible for bringing 4,600
Chileans to Canada. Of these, 100 were part of the One Hundred Prisoner
List, a program established by the Inter-Church Committee on Chile, which
arranged for refugees (and their families) to come directly from internment
camps where they were being held as political prisoners (Multiculturalism
Directorate 1979, 42). By 1978 the *Employment and Immigration* report for
the period 1969 through 1979 reported that 6,225 additional refugees had registered with this program, including 200 political prisoners who had arrived
in Canada directly from jail (Gilbert and Lee 1986, 125, 127). The 1981 Canadian Census reported that there were 15,330 Chileans in Canada with about
10 percent of them in British Columbia (mainly the Vancouver metropolitan
area) (Gilbert and Lee 1986, 122), while *Employment and Immigration*'s
1985 reported only 14,883 Chileans in Canada by the end of 1981. By 1984
the same report stated that 15,673 Chileans were in Canada. This number is
only 343 more than what the Canadian Census reported for three years prior
and for those same three years *Employment and Immigration*'s 1985 report
states that 2,432 new Chileans arrived (Gilbert and Lee 1986, 123).

As these variations suggest, it is hard to find accurate and consistent statistics for the numbers of Chilean exiles in Canada (or anywhere for that matter)
during the dictatorship. One problem with these numbers is they only reflect
Chileans who entered with formal "refugee" status. Some Chileans were able
to enter Canada as landed immigrants rather than refugees even though they
too should be counted as exiles. Additional problems result from inconsistencies in terms used in data collection. For example, some sources use the term
ethnic identity, others *country of origin,* while others rely on *country of last
permanent residence* (Da 2002, 3; Diaz 1999, 348).[17] Though the actual number of Chileans in Canada remains unclear, the political significance of their
presence is anything but ambiguous. In Canada at least 140 organizations
representing a cross-section of sectors, including exiles, formed to organize
against the dictatorship (Wright and Oñate 2007, 40). The actions they organized were varied, well coordinated, and rapid.

Pressuring the Canadian Government

Thomas Wright, leading historian of the Chilean diaspora, maintains that
Canada "was the setting of one of the largest and most politically active
exile communities" in the world (personal communication 2006). Indeed,

the solidarity movement is in large part responsible for Canada's ultimately welcoming immigration policy for Chileans fleeing the dictatorship. I specify "ultimately" because initially the Canadian government recognized Pinochet as the formal leader of Chile and ignored the human rights violations for which he was responsible. Indeed, the day after the coup Canadian Ambassador to Chile, Andrew Ross, urged the Canadian government to recognize Pinochet: "I can see no useful purpose in withholding recognition unduly. Indeed such action might even tend to delay Chile's eventual return to the democratic process" (quoted in Hanff 1979, 120). Accordingly, the Canadian government was hostile to the idea of letting leftist refugees into Canada. Many Canadians were vocally opposed to the government's initial policy toward Pinochet and Chilean refugees. For example, according to a memo to Mitchell Sharp, Secretary of State for External Affairs, "As of September 28, approximately 150 individual letters or telegrams have been received . . . about half a dozen letters are in favor of the coup; the remaining are strongly against recognition of the Junta, and many urge you to facilitate the immigration of Chilean refugees to Canada" (quoted in Hanff 1979, 117). Similarly, "approximately 80 per cent [*sic*] of the cables received by the government from individual Canadians opposed the move" (Hanff 1979, 121). A Canadian activist in Toronto recalls her frustration at the time:

> That Chile got no response on the part of [the] government was offensive. [It was the] idea of the riff raff of the left. The inadequacy of Canadian representation in Chile is what provoked reaction in Canada; [there was] no willingness on [the] part of the government to respond to what many people in society saw as a horrible situation. This was offensive to . . . people who'd been involved in church resettlement experiences. . . . There were a number of NGOs that pushed the churches as well, and internally within the churches there was a push to do something: that is when delegations go to Ottawa with concern about absence of response to [the] situation in Chile. Lobbying in Canada was preempted by the Chilean refugees who stormed the embassy in Santiago. (Quoted in Landolt and Goldring 2006, 19)

As a result of the Canadian government's stance toward Chile and its refugees, the solidarity organizations, particularly the Canadian Council of Churches, put so much pressure on the government they ultimately had to change their policies (personal interview, Gary Cristall, 2005; Gilbert and Lee 1986, 123–27; Dirks 1997, 244–53; Da 2002, 7; Johnson and Johnson 1982, 229).[18] (I discuss this in much greater detail in Chapter Four.) By October 1973 demonstrations had happened throughout Canada, including Toronto, Waterloo, Regina, Saskatoon, Edmonton, Winnipeg,[19] Vancouver, and Ottawa. Additionally, within the first few weeks, actual committees were formed in at least Toronto, Waterloo, Regina, and Vancouver and were in the process of being organized in the remaining aforementioned cities. Perhaps most noteworthy, however, is that national networks were in place so quickly that this information was centralized and disseminated by the Toronto-based Chile-Canada Solidarity Newsletter in what appears to be their first edition. (According to Da the newsletter began in Toronto in 1973 and ceased in 1974 [2002, 8].) In the sixth edition, dated October 29, 1973, or approximately six weeks after the coup, the Chile-Canada Solidarity organization explains who they are:

> Chile-Canada Solidarity was initiated just after the military coup by the Latin American Working Group [L.A.W.G], an independent research, education and action collective active since 1966. Chile-Canada Solidarity was established to give a focus to work which grew out of the membership of Chileans studying in Canada in L.A.W.G, members and other Canadians. . . . Chile-Canada Solidarity seeks to serve and inform committees and action groups across Canada, to work in concert with them, and to assist them in working together. . . . We are not an umbrella group, nor are we a part of an umbrella, nor related to a particular political movement or party in Canada. . . . Chile-Canada Solidarity seeks to re-inforce efforts across Canada, and is working internationally through continued co-operation with the Chilean students and exiles here in Canada, through our contacts with comparable groups in the U.S., and with the networks of contacts established over the years. (CCSN 1973[b])

The solidarity movement remained unsatisfied with their government's stance on Chile. On November 19, 1973, the Chile-Canada Solidarity Committee organized another national demonstration where they occupied government offices in Vancouver, Winnipeg, Toronto, and Montreal. In Winnipeg the protesters were forcibly removed and charged with assault and in Toronto they were dragged from the premises and charged with trespassing. In other words, Chile-Canada Solidarity had national and international links with both Chileans and non-Chileans, and networks they activated immediately after the coup. Once again, all such networking was accomplished before the internet, fax machines, and cell phones.

The solidarity movement was made up of a cross-section of sectors, including academics. The efforts of the academic community in part suggest the cross-class nature of solidarity Canadians offered Chileans. Academic groups throughout Canada started organizing immediately to support Chilean refugees. They focused on finding academic positions for professors forced to flee the country as well as spots for college students to resume their studies.[20] As early as October 1973, Canadian academics attempted a Canada-wide coordination of their efforts. It was at that time that the Canadian Association of University Teachers (CAUT) passed a resolution that sought assistance from the Departments of External Affairs and Manpower and Immigration demanding treatment for Chilean exiles comparable to refugees of "earlier national political revolutions" (Carroll 1974, 1). The resolution was largely symbolic in terms of concrete results for exiles but significant for its ability to create national networks within a month of the coup. In that same month Canadian academics were invited to participate in an international effort initiated by the Social Science Research Council in New York City. Two professors from the Canadian Association for Latin American Studies (CALAS) attended as representatives for Canadian faculty. However, since "it turned out that this 'international' group was restricted to U.S. groups with Canada as an appendage, it was decided that an independent Canadian effort might achieve better success" (Carroll 1974, 1).

In November 1973, the World University Service of Canada (WUSC) sponsored two meetings that resulted in the formation of the Canadian University Committee for Refugee Chilean Professionals and Students. This group was a cooperative effort of seven other previously existing organizations, including the National Union of Students. From the perspective of its leaders, this group's approach was entirely humanitarian rather than ideological or political. Within a month the member groups contributed to a fund that was complemented by a grant from the Canada Council. Funds were used to send a Canadian professor to South America to assess the situation for Chileans, and write and distribute a report. The professor first traveled to Buenos Aires to meet with refugees there and then Santiago to see the conditions inside the country. The intention was to produce an objective document.

While the fact-finding mission was underway a professor with the Association of Universities and Colleges of Canada (AUCC) approached university presidents with the goal of locating positions for Chilean refugees. Qualified refugees poured into Canada much more quickly than positions were located. Because of this, a few months later the committee solicited funds to staff professionals willing to coordinate the effort. Ultimately, the Ford Foundation offered some support for the effort. A Canadian professor and Chilean woman exile worked collaboratively in these funded positions to place Chileans in academic jobs. As of October 1974, the committee's efforts resulted in the placement of forty-five persons, or 20 percent of the eligible refugees. Many of these placements were due to the coordinated efforts of faculty across Canada who acted as liaisons at their universities during the summer months. Despite the limited success the program (at least as of October 1974), it sent a clear message to Chilean exiles and Canadian government officials that the Canadian intelligentsia was prepared and committed to this politically contentious cause.

Grassroots activists across Canada, not necessarily representing a particular sector or party, also joined forces rather quickly. By December 1973 seven solidarity committees across Canada, including the Chile-Solidarity Committee and the Canadian University Services Overseas, joined together to sponsor a tour for Salvador Allende's widow, Hortensia Bussi Soto de Allende. The tour included the following cities, which represent nearly every Canadian province, Montréal, Québec, Toronto, Ottawa-Hull, Winnipeg, Regina, and Vancouver. While in Canada she met with the Prime Minister to discuss a more favorable policy toward Chilean refugees (Hanff 1979, 126). By this time Chileans started arriving in Canada and collaborated with Canadians in organizing this tour. An open letter from the former First Lady was circulated; in it she appealed "to the conscious of you, the people of Canada, to denounce the grotesque events occurring in my homeland, Chile" (1973, 1). She passionately urged a number of tactics, including boycotts: "We call upon the moral consciousness of the workers to boycott every ship, every plane, coming and going to and from Chile with copper and other goods" (1973, 2). Shortly thereafter, economic tactics became central to the solidarity movement and her words were invoked by labor leaders in the interior when appealing to activists abroad.

By the late 1970s Canada, as well as Sweden and Australia, actually encouraged immigrants to come in an attempt to augment their labor forces. Additionally, Canada and Sweden both gave preference to political exiles (Wright and Oñate 1998, 93). In Canada the government established free hotels for Chileans to live in once arriving and prior to locating permanent housing. (One of the women I interviewed, Carmen Aguirre, authored a play about the Vancouver incarnation of this hotel and the experiences of Chileans who were housed there entitled "The Refugee Hotel." She and her family lived there for the first few weeks they were in Vancouver.) The government also provided English classes for one member of the family upon arrival in Canada, winter clothing, transportation assistance, and job placement services (Hanff 1979, 125).

The Exiles' Organizational Presence

Once Chileans were welcomed by the Canadian government, with only minor legal barriers, the movement's tactics began to change, especially as exiles themselves became more active in the organizations. Economic protests were organized by a cross-section of organizations. For example, Toronto-based Noranda Mines Ltd. moved aggressively to collaborate with the Pinochet dictatorship on investments in Chile's copper industry. Rather than accept this, a coalition of churches, labor unions, Catholic teachers, academics, women, and members of parliament joined forces to denounce the proposed investment alliance. Similarly, the Canadian Labour Congress (CLC) urged the government to withhold aid and credit from the Chilean junta (Da 2002, 7). In April 1977 protesters and concerned shareholders attended a meeting in Toronto with Noranda managers about their plans for Chile (VCA 1978b, 2). A variety of parallel protests happened throughout Canada to denounce Noranda's plans. According to LAWG Letter (IV, 5/6) reprinted in "Chile Conference: Boycott and Canadian Investments in Chile," the week before the meeting with Noranda, the Toronto city council passed a resolution calling for an end to Canadian investment in Chile. Additionally,

> [t]he Student Christian Movement organized a Toronto demonstration on the twenty-ninth [of April], when about 300 people gathered at Commerce Court, the site of Noranda's head office. Over 200 Torontonians attended a liturgical act in support of the campaign. On the same day, about 40 people—including trade union representatives and members of Amnesty International—occupied Noranda's Montreal office, demanding some answers about the company's plans. . . . During the week before the meeting, demonstrators in Vancouver assembled at Noranda's local offices while campaigners in Winnipeg picketed banks that have extended aid to the junta. In Calgary, church groups and members of Amnesty International marched from church to church, a procession that ended in a large public gathering. The issue was discussed at public meetings in St. John's, Edmonton and Regina. Letters and telegrams poured in Powis' [President and CEO of Noranda] office. A telegram from Vancouver included 1,043 signatures; 750 people in Calgary signed a telegram protesting the investment. The story was carried by newspapers, radio programs, and television stations from coast to coast. (LAWG Letter; IV, 5/6)

Additionally, solidarity committees across the country pressured the Canadian government to ban the sale of airplane engines and parts to the Chilean air force (Wright and Oñate 2007, 40). As with the other activities at the time, Canadian committees coordinated with one another throughout the country as well as Chilean exile organizations that were well established in Canada by mid-1977.

Partisan politics were central to Chileans organizing in Canada just as in the rest of the diaspora (Diaz 1999, 352). For example, Landolt and Goldring explain that in Toronto Chileans organized via one of two patterns of party-based organizing: party and intra-party organizations. Each type varied in strategies but remained united in their opposition to the junta. Party-based organizations were formed by party militants who maintained and promoted their party's line. Each party worked through at least one community organization. For example, the Socialist Party formed the *Centro Cultural Orlando Letelier*,[21] which lasted from 1977 until 1995, the Communist Party, the *Grupo Cultural Victor Jara*, formed around the same time and it still exists today, and in 1980 the MIR formed an outreach organization called the Chile Ontario Information Centre (CHOIC). Just like the Chilean party-politicking in the rest of Canada and diaspora more broadly, these organizations enabled parties to interact with a variety of institutions and organizations nationally and transnationally, including inside of Chile. Intra-party organizations operated in a more formal manner, serving as bridges to the Canadian parliamentary system, lobbyists, and institutional bodies. For example, the Toronto Chilean Association *(Asociación de Chilenos de Toronto)* began in 1974 and lasted until 1980. It was a community institution that included members from different parties and ultimately laid the groundwork for many political initiatives and served as a precursor to the Toronto Chilean Society of the 1980s and the twentieth-first-century *Casa Salvador Allende*. Despite their partisan tendencies, Chileans, at least in Toronto, did not develop formal relationships with Canadian political parties; they had informal alliances, particularly with the New Democratic Party (NDP), but no formal agreements (2006, 30–32, 35).[22]

As Chileans became further entrenched in Canadian society they began to organize a series of educational, cultural, and housing collectives. For example, the Toronto Chilean Association created programs to help maintain Chilean history and literature. Their school lasted from the late 1970s until the early 1980s. Another small school was established in Regina. Assuming these two schools paralleled the ones in Vancouver, they were aimed at exiles' children. Chileans also organized religious centers to help provide stability. For example, in Toronto the Scarborough Christian Community was established in 1976 and lasted until 1980; it offered a place for introspection and social action, again, specifically for Chilean Christian children. Chileans also created at least three housing cooperatives in Toronto, one in Arcadia (Da 2002, 10; Diaz 1999, 353; Landolt and Goldring 2006, 33) and one in Vancouver.

In addition to the aforementioned projects, many of which I learned about through the primary documents I collected from the movement, many of the Chilean women I interviewed started their exile outside of Vancouver and organized similar events across Canada. For example, Cecilia Tagle, leader of the solidarity and feminist movements in Vancouver, spent the first five years of her exile in Toronto where she was involved in the same types of activities as the women in Vancouver and would later help Vancouver committees with projects similar to those in Toronto, including the housing co-op. Similarly, Carla Gutiérrez (a pseudonym), former member of the solidarity movement in Canada and anti-Pinochet resistance movement in Chile, spent the first twenty years of her exile in Edmonton, which also had very similar events to those in Vancouver. Andrea Diaz, former president of the Communist Party youth sector, started her exile in Winnipeg and she too explained that the same organizations and structures existed there. Angelica Guitérrez, an activist with the Socialist Party youth sector, traveled throughout Canada as an organizer and explained that there were representatives of the leftist parties everywhere she went; together they helped circulate information that had been smuggled clandestinely from Chile:

> Documents . . . would be reproduced here [Vancouver], and then sent throughout the country [Canada] because there were parties in every city in Canada; very organized in Toronto; big, very big in Montreal; very big, [in] Calgary, Alberta, Edmonton; in every major city there was a party: Communist, the MIR, Socialist. Then the other ones, like when the Socialists started to split up. . . . It was very, very organized; very organized.

Carmen Rodríguez, a Chilean poet, educator, and leader in the solidarity and feminist movements, echoed the same exact sentiment as she and her musical band were able to travel throughout Canada performing their revolutionary repertoire because there were solidarity organizations everywhere that set up the events.

CONCLUSION

In short, Chilean exiles and their supporters all over the world joined forces to denounce and dethrone Pinochet. The leftist eyes of the world had been upon Chile since Salvador Allende's election and that heightened attention immediately translated into international solidarity. Wherever Chileans fled they were greeted by internationals willing to help. The exiles eventually reconfigured their parties and networked with Chilean exiles all over the world as well as with Chileans in the interior. Canadians and Chileans worked together to organize committees across Canada and remained quite networked with one another. Just as in the rest of the world, their actions started immediately and became progressively more nationally and internationally coordinated as the movement developed and Chileans started to enter Canada en masse. The movement was cross-class, incorporating everyone from laborers to academics, as well as multi-sector, including everyone from religious folks to politicians. The movement initially began with Canadians and the few Chileans who were in Canada at the time of the coup but within months of September 11, 1973, it began to readily incorporate exiles. The rapid, organized response of Canadians and Chileans in Canada to the news of the coup and ongoing repression of the junta was, as we have seen, quite similar to what happened in the other one-hundred-plus countries where Chileans fled. In the next chapter I discuss the Vancouver manifestation of this vibrant transnational movement.

NOTES

1. Peñas became central to the anti-Pinochet movement in the diaspora, as I will explain in Chapter Four.

2. This term is not as commonly used among Chileans as academics. For example, I interviewed a woman for this book who was very central to the anti-Pinochet resistance movement both in Canada and in South America. She co-founded and performed in two different New Song bands while in exile and had never heard the term "Canto Nueva" before I asked her about it. For this woman, the political music created and performed pre- and post-coup were both considered part of the original Nuevo Canción movement.

3. In 2001 the stadium was renamed the Victor Jara Stadium and was turned over to the Victor Jara Foundation as a venue for cultural events (Pottlitzer 2001a).

4. See Carmen Luz Parot, (1999), *El Derecho de Vivir en Paz/The Right to Live in Peace* (Santiago, Chile: Fundación Víctor Jara; videocassette); Joan Jara, (1998), *Victor: An Unfinished Song, 2d ed.* (London: Bloomsbury Publishing), for biographies of Victor Jara's very influential life.

5. For additional overviews of the New Song movement and its musicians, see Simon Broughton and Mark Ellingham, ed., (2000), *World Music, volume 2* (London, England: Rough Guides Ltd.), 363–74; Eduardo Carrasco Pirard, (1982), "The Nueva Canción in Latin America," *International Social Science Journal* 3(4): 599–623; Karen Linn, (1984), "Chilena Nueva Canción: A Political Popular Music Genre," *Pacific Review of Ethnomusicology* 1: 57–64; Mark Mattern, (1997), "Popular Music and Redemocratization in Santiago, Chile 1973–1989," *Studies in Latin American Popular Culture*, 16: 101–13; Ana María Cobos and Ana Lya Sater, (1986), "Chilean Folk Music in Exile/Nueva Canción Chilena en el Exilio," *Intellectual Migrations: Transcultural Contributions of European and Latin American Émigrés,* 295–339. Papers of the Thirty-First Annual Meeting of the Seminar on the Acquisition of Latin American Library Materials, ed. Iliana L. Sonntag (Madison: Memorial Library, University of Wisconsin); Cobos and Sater's article includes an extensive bibliography.

6. Fernando Reyes Matta expresses a similar sentiment: "At the hour of repression, the life of a politician or notorious government official may be pardoned, but never that of Victor Jara" (1988, 450). Fernando Reyes Matta, (1988), "The 'New Song' and Its Confrontation in Latin America," in *Marxism and the Interpretation of Culture*, ed. Cary Nelson and Lawrence Grossberg (Urbana, Ill.: University of Illinois Press), 447–60.

7. I find the term and concept of *values* terribly problematic but to remain consistent with the literature I use it here.

8. In addition to my own interviews and primary sources, information in this section comes from Alan Angell and Susan Carstairs, (1987), "The exile question in Chilean politics," *Third World Quarterly* 9(1): 159–66; Marita Eastmond, (1997), *The Dilemmas of Exile: Chilean Refugees in the U.S.A.* (Göteborg, Sweden: ACTA Universitatis Gothoburgensis), 97–107; Manuel Antonio Garretón, (1995), "The Political Opposition and the Party System under the Military Regime," in *The Struggle for Democracy in Chile,* ed. Paul W. Drake and Iván Jaksić (Lincoln, Nebr.: University of

Nebraska Press), 215; Margaret Power, (2009 [forthcoming]), "The U.S. Movement in Solidarity with Chile in the 1970s," *Latin American Perspectives;* Thomas Wright and Rody Oñate, (1998), *Flight from Chile: Voices of Exile* (Albuquerque: University of New Mexico Press); Thomas Wright and Rody Oñate, (2007), "Chilean Political Exile," *Latin American Perspectives* 155, 34(4): 38–43.

9. See Julie Shayne, (2004), *The Revolution Question: Feminisms in El Salvador, Chile, and Cuba* (New Brunswick, N.J.: Rutgers University Press), Chapter Three, for a lengthy discussion of the Mothers' Centers.

10. In *The Dilemmas of Exile,* Eastmond, drawing on Lewis (1965), Fagen (1973), and Patterson (1977), argues that all exile communities are plagued with political conflicts and Chile is therefore not unique in this regard.

11. Most of the literature about Latin American feminism speaks to this phenomenon and its connection to inspiring women to mobilize as feminists outside of male-dominated organizations. I discuss this in my first book, Shayne, *The Revolution Question,* and touch on it in Chapters Five and Six in this book.

12. See also Power, "The U.S. Movement in Solidarity with Chile in the 1970s," for an account of this tactic in the United States.

13. Chile is divided into zones, like states or provinces in other countries.

14. The academic community had been monitoring Chile as well. In the Autumn 1975 issue of *Latin American Research Review,* a review essay entitled "Visions of Chile" appeared. In it, the authors reviewed twenty-eight books published by the end of 1974 about Allende, the Popular Unity, and/or the coup. They were published in Latin America, Europe, and the United States and were written in Spanish, English, and French (Valenzuela and Valenzuela 1975, 155–75). Arturo Valenzuela and J. Samuel Valenzuela, (1975), "Visions of Chile," *Latin American Research Review* 10(3): 155–75.

15. Report originated with "Prensa Latina, Cuban Wire Services."

16. Original source: P.T.S., December 12, 1973.

17. See Fernando G. Mata, (1985), "Latin American Immigration to Canada: Some Reflections on the Immigration Statistics," *Canadian Journal of Latin American and Caribbean Studies* 10(20): 27–42, for further discussion of Latin American demographic data in Canada.

18. For a detailed overview of the Canadian government's policy changes toward Chileans, see George Hanff, (1979), "Decision-Making Under Pressure: A Study of the Admittance of Chilean Refugees by Canada," *NorthSouth* 4(8): 116–35.

19. For an overview of the solidarity movement in Winnipeg, see Stuart D. Johnson and Cornelia B. Johnson, (1982), "Institutional Origins in the Chilean Refugee Community in Winnipeg," *Prairie Forum* 7(2): 227–35.

20. The information about university mobilization comes from William Carroll, (1974), "The Response of the Canadian Academic Community to the Chilean Crisis," *Bulletin of the Canadian Association of University Teachers* 23(2/October).

21. Orlando Letelier was a member of the Popular Unity cabinet. He was murdered in Washington D.C. in 1976 as part of Operation Condor. According to John Dinges: "Letelier was the most typical victim—targeted as a dangerous democrat rather than a violent terrorist, a man who worked against Pinochet not in secret but in public

corridors of power in the United States and Europe" (2004, 15). John Dinges, (2004), *The Condor Years: How Pinochet and His Allies Brought Terrorism to Three Continents* (New York: New Press).

22. Some twenty-plus years later the efforts of Chileans exiles and Canadian activists in Toronto are still felt in the city: In September of 2006, a city street was publicly named "Victor Jara Lane." This event was due to the collaboration between the City of Toronto and the Salvador Allende Arts Festival for Peace (Landolt and Goldring 2006, 39). Patricia Landolt and Luin Goldring, (2006), "Activist Dialogues and the Production of Refugee Political Transnationalism: Chileans, Colombians and Non-Migrant Civil Society in Canada" (paper presented at Second International Colloquium of the International Network on Migration and Development, Cocoyoc, Morelos, Mexico).

Chapter Four

The Chilean Solidarity Movement in Vancouver

Music was a tool. . . . It was sort of like what Victor Jara says in one of his songs . . . 'yo no canto por cantar o por tener buena voz' . . . 'I do not sing because I just like to sing or because I have a good voice' . . . we sang because that was a tool, it was a means to an end, . . . which does not mean that we did not enjoy it; we loved it, we had great fun doing it. But if we thought that standing on our heads was more efficient we would have done that too.

—Carmen Rodríguez

INTRODUCTION

As we know Canada was home to one of the largest and most politically active exile communities. So, why focus on Vancouver? Vancouver was often the first choice of Chileans, particularly given its agreeable climate, not much different than Santiago and elsewhere in Chile (Gilbert and Lee 1986, 143). Indeed, many Chileans granted entry into Canada were first sent by the government to the Prairies, but a significant portion of them went to Vancouver as soon as they were able. Vancouver also lends itself to a study of this sort particularly given my interest in both culture and gender. Firstly, Vancouver was one of only a handful of cities where Chileans set up and owned their own housing cooperative. Additionally, to the best of my knowledge, Vancouver is the only city we know of where women organized a feminist collective and magazine published primarily after the dictatorship.[1] Later in this chapter I will use the housing co-op as a way to understand the importance of culture and cultural institutions to the exile community and in Chapter Six we will see the importance of the feminist Aquelarre collective in the collective identity of Chilean women exiles. Given the lack of documentation and plethora of solidarity movements in the Chilean diaspora this study could have been done in practically any major city in the world. As of yet, only a few books in English exist (Eastmond 1997; Kay 1987; Wright and Oñate 1998) to help document this vibrant and historically important movement. Understanding the case of Vancouver will be another building block in the future synthesis of the greater Chilean exile experience, particularly if culture and gender remain central foci in the analysis.

As Chapter Three demonstrates, data regarding the actual numbers of Chilean exiles is extremely imprecise. Based on my data, the only number I have for Vancouver during the dictatorship is 1,525. However, due to the inconsistencies between "refugees" and "immigrants," combined with under-reporting in formal statistical data collection, I argue this number significantly understates the reality. For example, most of the Chileans I interviewed for this project had not been counted in any formal surveys, including the census. If we work from the 1981 Canadian Census estimate that 10 percent of Chileans are in British Columbia then based on the last number I have for the dictatorship, 17,315 total in Canada by 1984, we can assume approximately 1,700 or so Chileans were in Vancouver by the mid-1980s. However, even this logic is faulty because by the mid-1980s many Chileans had left other parts of Canada for Vancouver and I would suspect the ratio was higher than 10 percent by 1984.

The numbers become more imprecise when we look at contemporary data. The former Chilean consul general in Vancouver informed me that there are 6,000 Chileans registered with the consulate while the majority are not registered (personal communication February 6, 2004). This would lead us to assume that there are at least 6,000 more Chileans in Vancouver not registered. But according to the 2001 census, there are only 2,525 Chileans in British Columbia, most of whom are in the greater Vancouver area (Statistics Canada 2001). That is, the census reports nearly 3,500 less than the Chilean consulate's official number. Informants and colleagues in the area believed that estimates tend to range between 15,000 and 16,000 Chileans in Vancouver. However, these are current numbers that are not necessarily the same as those during the dictatorship. For example, children of Chileans who were born in Canada boost the numbers. I suspect that this current figure (anywhere between 6,000 and 16,000) is relatively comparable to the numbers during the dictatorship. That said, it is not the amount of Chileans residing in Vancouver that render it an interesting case in understanding the Chilean diaspora globally, but the political organizing that exiles did once they arrived. In this chapter I offer an overview and analysis of the solidarity movement in Vancouver, BC. I conclude this chapter by returning to the discussion I began in the book's introduction regarding the place of emotions and culture in the solidarity movement.

THE SOLIDARITY MOVEMENT IN VANCOUVER

The immediate response of Canadians and Chileans in Canada to the news of the coup was quite similar to what happened in the other one hundred-plus countries where Chileans fled. Vancouver was a microcosm of the rest of Canada, exhibiting the same sorts of coalitions, party politicking, and rapid response. A unique feature of Vancouver, however, was once Chileans learned of it, it tended to be the first choice of Chileans. The Canadian government, once they started letting Chileans in, liked to send them to places like Edmonton or Winnipeg in an attempt to more evenly distribute the population and enhance the already-existing labor pools. However, for many Chileans, given the chance, they left the more politically and socially isolated, and indeed significantly colder, parts of Canada for Vancouver.

To suggest that the Chilean solidarity movement was spontaneous would of course be sociologically shortsighted. However, from the perspective of the Chileans and Canadians who participated in the movement one certainly gets the sense that it was politically inevitable. Gary Cristall, a Canadian and (at least) third-generation leftist, spent a year and a half in Chile while Allende was president. He returned to Vancouver in late summer 1973 to drum up support for a leftist magazine he and others were forming in Chile. He was scheduled to return to Chile on September 11 and, while packing his suitcases, heard a newsflash on the radio that Salvador Allende was dead and Chile now controlled by a military junta. He recalls, "I turned on the radio and it was literally one of those stupid things that says 'In international news, the military has given the president in Chile, Salvador Allende five minutes to surrender, now in sports!" Even upon hearing this news Gary wanted to return to Chile and support the movement from inside of Chile. However, he was advised by colleagues in the interior that he could do more good from abroad rather than return and be detained and/or killed. While visiting Vancouver he gave a talk about the situation in Chile just a week prior to the coup. Indeed, the eyes of leftists everywhere were focused on Chile. Gary explained that the coup happened on a Tuesday (about a week after his talk), and by Saturday, September 15, he and his colleagues organized the first protest in Vancouver.

Ana María Quiroz, who we met in Chapter Two, explained that a reporter from the Canadian Broadcasting Corporation (CBC) contacted one of her professors the day after the coup looking for a comment. Ana María's professor then put her in touch with the journalist and despite Ana María's lack of political background or training in public speaking she emerged as a leader and spokesperson of the movement on behalf of the soon-to-arrive Chilean exiles. Similarly, Patricia Gomberoff (also introduced in Chapter Two) explains:

> People [started] getting together from the Left and we . . . saw each other at a movie for instance . . . there were two or three Chileans and it was a movie to do with Chile of course! It was not just any movie right? So . . . we started talking and then you know we started getting together, they started to say "ok . . . we are getting together, we are forming this, we are forming that" and then you started slowly and . . . then the group would get together at that house and then something would come out of that. . . . That is how it all started, really just adding one thing with the other and then spontaneously, totally spontaneous and seeing that more people were getting in and this fellow knew another fellow who knew somebody else and then . . . we started getting [more and more] organized.

The movie was likely organized by Ana María's or Gary's groups, or both, so it was not "totally spontaneous," as it felt to Patricia, but the commonality of experiences among Chilean exiles and deep sense of solidarity from Canadian left led to the rapid emergence of the movement.

The Chilean solidarity movement had many goals. For the Canadians the main objective was to pressure their government to let in Chileans, which they were ultimately very successful in achieving. While this objective was certainly crucial to the exiles, they, however, were more focused on their *compañeros* and *compañeras* in Chile and thus worked tirelessly to denounce and dethrone the dictatorship and pressure the governments and citizens of other countries to do the same. All of the individual and collective projects that made up the movement served to advance these goals. A related objective of the movement was to provide material and political support to the thousands of political prisoners and their families. In this next section I will talk about the structure, tactics, and strategies of the movement. I begin with an overview of the Canadians' projects since their actions preceded the Chileans' and then move on to discuss the agendas and tactics of the exiles.

Structure, Goals, and Tactics: Canadians

Canadians in Vancouver started organizing against Pinochet and in support of the Chilean people immediately after the coup. Indeed, according to one of the main organizations, the Vancouver Chile Solidarity Committee's own literature, they were founded on the very day of the coup (1974b). There were two main Canadian organizations in Vancouver, the Vancouver Chile Solidarity Committee (CSC)[2] and Canadians for Democracy in Chile (CDC). There was also a third organization, which was multi-issue but devoted a good deal of its efforts to the Chilean cause, the Revolutionary Marxist Group (RMG). Much of the leadership of the RMG played a role in founding the Chile Solidarity Committee though they maintained separate identities. The organizations each had their own party alliances and ideological leanings. For example, the Vancouver Chile Solidarity Committee and Revolutionary Marxist Group were largely Trotskyist organizations, whereas Canadians for Democracy in Chile were most sympathetic to the Communist Party. Similarly, they each aligned themselves with different Chilean parties, the Vancouver Chile Solidarity Committee and Revolutionary Marxist Group predominantly with the MIR, and the more militant parts of the Socialist Party and Canadians for Democracy with the Communist Party. (See table 4.1 for a summary of these organizations.)

In reading the organizations' literature, particularly their internal documents, the sectarianism is quite notable. For example, the disharmony between the Canadian Communist Party (CP) and thus Canadians for Democracy in Chile with the Revolutionary Marxist Group was quite pronounced. In one internal document dated April 12, 1974, the RMG, speaking nationally, refers to the CP's organizational tactics as "right-wing maneuvers" (1974b, 2). In another internal document dated July 22, 1974, in which the Vancouver committee is reporting to the national branch about Chile work, the author says: "The RMG had won political hegemony (slogans and general analysis) and moreover its members were the accepted leadership of the committee [Chile Solidarity Committee]. . . . The CP had been forced to work with us" (1974d, 1).

In the publicly disseminated literature both Canadians for Democracy in Chile and the Chilean Solidarity Committee implicitly and explicitly rejected sectarianism. From the very beginning, the Chile Solidarity Committee (CSC) attempted to project itself as a non-sectarian organization open to everyone regardless of party affiliation. In every issue of their newsletter it reads: "The CSC is open to you if you are opposed to the military dictatorship in Chile and support the resistance to it." However, based on the literature produced and circulated by Canadians for Democracy in Chile, one gets the sense that despite its rhetoric the CSC was indeed a sectarian organization. For example, in June 1977, Canadians for Democracy in Chile launched its newsletter "Chile News." In its introduction to "Chile News," John Radosovic, the Executive Secretary of the CDC, writes:

> As a solidarity organization in support of the POPULAR UNITY, the CANADIANS FOR DEMOCRACY IN CHILE will not be drawn into sectarian debate in respect to the methods and forms of struggle whereby the people of Chile will overthrow the Junta and restore freedom. The road to freedom will be chosen by the people of Chile. . . . (1977a, 2, capitals in original)

Table 4.1:   Some Canadian Solidarity Organizations in Vancouver

Vancouver Chile Solidarity Committee[1]

Self-description of work

"Raised money for the resistance in Chile and worked to aid refugees. . . . [M]ake available information about the struggle in Latin America. . . . We also raise the political questions involved and their relevance to Canadians."

Membership

Independent leftists; Vancouver American Exiles Association; the League for Socialist Action; the Revolutionary Marxist Group; the Spartacus Bookstore Collective; Women's groups

Collaborating organizations

Vancouver Area Council of the NDP; Canadians for Democracy in Chile; B.C. Federation of Labour; University of British Columbia Arts Undergraduate Society; Simon Fraser University Department of Latin American Studies; Revolutionary Marxist Group; Vancouver Chilean Association; Vancouver & District Labour Council

Canadians for Democracy in Chile[2]

Self-description of work

"Our job is to help the heroic people of Chile in their struggle for freedom. We will promote solidarity actions in Canada and do everything we can to prevent the Canadian government and Canadian banks and corporations from helping to prop up the Junta by loans, investments in Chile and trade with that country."

Membership

Communist Party; labor activists

Collaborating organizations

Vancouver and District Labour Council; Workers Central Union of Chile (CUT), *Comisión Exterior*; Canadian Labour Congress; Chile Solidarity Committee; NDP Area Council; Vancouver Chilean Association; Vancouver & District Labour Council

Revolutionary Marxist Group[3]

Self-description of work

"(1) To continue to push for united action of the left & to develop a political debate on the differences between the Stalinist position on Chile and our own, within the framework of the united front. (2) To place a strong emphasis on building and consolidating the Chile Solidarity Committee with a view to pushing a broader understanding of Latin American struggles within that. (3) To maintain our independence of initiatives within the framework of the coalition, specially [sic] concerning the longshore, and to build a good relationship with the Chilean Association."

Membership

Trotskyist; anti-imperialist activists

Collaborating organizations

Chile Solidarity Committee; Chilean Movement of the Revolutionary Left (MIR); Communist Party; Canadians for Democracy in Chile

[1] Information comes from leaflets and newsletters distributed by the organization.
[2] Information comes from their newsletter "Chile News: Solidarity With Chile."
[3] Information comes from internal documents and public reports.

The quote from page 95 was published nearly four years after the coup. By this time party politics and ideological leanings were firmly entrenched. This was especially the case given the substantial number of exiles living in Vancouver by that time, most of whom brought their party affiliations with them. In other words, the CDC's leadership is clearly responding to the already-occurring debate about tactics in the interior by denouncing sectarianism. Despite the tensions, sectarianism, and often seemingly petty debates, the committees were able to work in coalition around common goals and tactics.

A goal implicit to all of the actions was to bring attention to the situation in Chile. That is, in addition to the practical goal of demanding asylum for refugees or forcing the Canadian government to stop doing business with the junta, was the desired press coverage to keep Canadians abreast of the situation in the Southern Cone, the logic of course being that once people started learning about the situation in Chile they too would want to start organizing in support of the resistance there and in opposition to their government's policies. Indeed, we might assume that Canadian solidarity activists attempted to generate "moral shocks" (Jasper and Poulsen 1995; Jasper 1997; 1998) and "moral outrage" (Nepstad and Smith 2001) to inspire nonactive Canadians to join their organizations. Canadians accomplished this in a variety of ways—speaking tours with Chilean activists and/or former political prisoners, films, educational events, conferences, newsletters, street leafleting, and the like. Additionally, the media coverage generated by their specific campaigns also served to keep nonactive Canadians aware of the situation in Chile.

Legal Entry

In the very beginning, the main goal of the Canadian solidarity organizations was to pressure the Canadian government to let in all Chileans seeking asylum.[3] (This was the priority of a cross-section of organizations ranging from leftist political organizations, to nonpartisan professional associations, to churches throughout Canada, not just in Vancouver.) In early October 1973 the Canadian government had yet to take a stand on its policy toward Chilean refugees. However, by this time the government formally recognized Pinochet (Allen 1973b; CP 1973; Mallory 1973; Winsor 1973). Needless to say, human rights advocates, regardless of their political, social, professional, or ideological affiliation, were outraged by these positions. For example, the Canadian Council of Churches stated:

> It [their appeal to let in Chileans] is based upon humanitarian and not political considerations. Since these refugees are in danger of their lives, under a very repressive military regime, we have only one option: to do what we can to save these lives. Canada opened her doors to refugees from Hungary, Czechoslovakia

and Uganda. If we refuse to open our doors to people who are in danger under another type of political regime, this would mean that we had acted from political rather than humanitarian motives. (Quoted in Dirks 1977, 246)

In late November 1973 an immigration team arrived in Chile to screen and process applications from Chileans and non-Chileans hoping to resettle in Canada.[4] However, the bureaucratic procedures, security screenings, and insufficient staff, namely translators, slowed everything down and thus kept the number of Chileans permitted to enter Canada rather insignificant, particularly in contrast to the numbers who applied. For example, by December 20, 1973, approximately 1,400 applications were received by Canadian officials, whereas only 184 refugees were granted visas. The security clearances were particularly unacceptable to the solidarity activists given that the process of requesting one from the Chilean authorities virtually served as a way to turn oneself in. As Gary Cristall explained to me:

Their [the Canadian government] whole thing was to not let as many people in as they possibly could and they wanted them to get police certificates. . . . You need a certificate of good behavior so [you] should go to your local police station and ask them for a certificate of good behavior, you know? Well why don't you hang yourself while you are there and save them the trouble?

Apparently these tactics worked, as the initial numbers of Chileans granted entry was quite miniscule. In January 1974, 140 arrived on a government-chartered aircraft. By mid-February, the number grew to 275 and another 302 had visas but were still in transit. By the end of March 780 visas had been granted and estimates suggest that by late spring the number surpassed 1,000.

These numbers, despite the fact that they reflect increases, in no way satisfied those already unsatisfied with the Canadian government's policies. Indeed, the frustrations were compounded when in the summer of 1974 the Canadian government decreased the number of immigration personnel in Chile and neighboring countries where Chileans awaited visas for permanent asylum. A delegation of more than a dozen organizations advocating for the exiles presented demands to the Secretary of State for External Affairs and the Minister of Manpower and Immigration to make clear that Chileans and non-Chileans alike were in real danger. As a result, the coalition demanded that the Canadian government expand its Chilean refugee program to allow ten thousand persons to enter Canada under relaxed criteria. Dirks argues that evidence points to the Canadian government delaying any decision regarding treatment of the refugees until the pressure was sustained enough to indicate public concern for the problem (1977, 250). If the numbers are any indication, the government did eventually surrender to the pressure. By the end of 1984, at least 17,315 Chileans resided in Canada (Gilbert and Lee 1986, 123). What role did the Canadians in Vancouver have in bringing about these monumental changes in policy?

Protests and Sits-ins

In a press release dated October 31, 1973, the Chile Solidarity Committee and the Vancouver Area Council of the New Democratic Party (NDP, Canada's social democratic party) announced a protest scheduled for November 3, 1973, in response to an international call for a day of protest "to show support for the Chilean working class in battle of resistance against the military junta which seized power on September 11 of this year." The press release explained that "large demonstrations are planned throughout Europe, North America and in some Latin American countries. The largest are expected in Mexico City, where Mrs. Hortensia Allende will speak, and in Paris, where a particularly intensive mobilization is taking place" (Chile Solidarity Committee 1973e). The press release explained that protesters in Vancouver would be marching on the downtown courthouse, home to the Immigration Department, to demand that the Canadian government allow Chilean refugees to enter the country.

A week later, Friday, November 10, 1973, the Chile Solidarity Committee staged a sit-in at the passport office, demanding, among other things, that the Canadian government unconditionally let in all Chileans seeking asylum. According to Simon Fraser University's newspaper, *The Peak,* and at least two other Vancouver dailies, protesters numbered about twenty-five and stayed in the office for more than twenty-four hours (Bernard 1973, 3). Three additional demands included:

> 1) That the Canadian Government pressure, politically and economically the junta in Chile to grant safe conduct to the numerous refugees in the embassies of Santiago, to allow them out of Chile to Canada. 2) That the Canadian Government provide an airlift for the exiles and help facilitate their settlement in Canada. 3) That Ambassador Ross be immediately replaced in his post. (Bernard 1973, 3)[5]

Like most of the solidarity movement's activities, protests such as this one were coordinated throughout Canada (CSC 1974d, 1). The Vancouver action was originally scheduled to occur at the Immigration building but the protesters got word that the Canadian police were expecting them and they changed venues at the last minute (Bernard 1973, 3). Gary Cristall explained:

> [W]e had other sit-ins across the country and . . . we did them simultaneously. Later on we asked for a conference call to negotiate with the government. . . .

But the interesting thing about the first sit-in was we were supposed to occupy the Immigration building and the night before I got a phone call at my home, a guy said: "you don't know me, I'm a cop. They know that you are going to occupy the Immigration building tomorrow morning," he said, "I thought Salvador Allende was a really good guy" and he hung up. So we met at Spartacus Books, a left-wing book store and we sent a delegation down to check out the Immigration building and they walked in and there [were] like five bulls there reading the paper. . . . So we had our alternatives sites. It was really like out of the movies. We said to everybody there, "nobody here can use the phone, nobody can leave, we are not even going to say out loud where we are going" so we . . . wrote it down [and gave it] to each of the people with the cars and said: "go here," handed them pieces of paper and then we went and we occupied the building; we put up our banner on the wall and about ten minutes later the cops showed up and man were they pissed because they were waiting for us down at the other building.

While Canadian protesters were in their eighth-plus hour of the sit-in, Ana María Quiroz spoke to the New Democratic Party (NDP). The NDP let Ana María make a ten-minute presentation at their national convention about the situation in Chile. After her speech they unanimously passed two emergency resolutions supporting the Chilean cause and the protesters' four demands (Bernard 1973, 3).

In the meantime, the Canadians who refused to leave the passport office until their demands were met spent the night there. Though some officials were willing to engage with the protesters, none of the exchanges were to the satisfaction of the protesters and thus they refused to leave. The next morning, nearly twenty-four hours after arriving in the office, and with support from the NDP, the protesters again confronted the passport director, E. H. Woodyard, who finally agreed to coordinate a meeting between the Chilean Solidarity Committee and an official from External Affairs. The meeting happened six days later and because they were forbidden from inviting the press to attend, the protesters held a press conference immediately following the meeting (Bernard 1973, 3). Actions like this continued in Vancouver and throughout Canada until the Canadian government started to make concrete and noticeable changes in their policy toward Chilean exiles. By 1974 there were several thousand Chileans in Canada and the numbers continued to increase. Not only did they increase but refugees went from being treated entirely unfavorably to being offered free temporary housing and language classes upon arrival (CSC 1974f, 4). However, even when the protesters' actions changed, that is no sit-ins directed at the passport or immigration offices, their rhetoric supporting the refugees was fairly consistent.

Economic Strategies

Once Canadians began to feel like they were making headway regarding asylum for Chileans they began to shift their tactics toward more economic ones, namely boycotts. The solidarity movement throughout the world organized major boycotts of Chilean products, from grapes to copper, in an attempt to economically and politically isolate and thus embarrass the junta. In the Chile Solidarity Committee's winter 1974–1975 newsletter they write:

> Those of us in Canada are living in a country where the federal government, the banks and the businesses have shown themselves to be some of the Junta's closest friends. If we hope to assist the resistance in Chile, surely, above all, we should attempt to stop the flow of Canadian capital to Chile and maintaining in power one of the most barbarious [*sic*] governments in the world. (1974–75, 2)

The boycotts were both commodity-specific, around things like grapes and wine where supermarkets were targeted, as well as nationally nonspecified, which included boycotts by longshoremen with respect to unloading any Chilean products. That is, preventing them from ever reaching the shelves where consumers would have the option to purchase them. Vancouver was a particularly important city in this international campaign given its ports. While Canadians did help orchestrate meetings between local unions and Chilean activists, and pressured local politicians to respect the boycotts, Canadians should not be given the sole credit for such boycotts (CSC 1974a). For such actions to be successful they needed to be massive and transnational, and thus all sorts of coalitions were born. Additionally, not only did the calls for the boycotts come from Chile but also the campaigns themselves were largely the result of the efforts of exiles. The Revolutionary Marxist Group acknowledges this in their "Chile Fraction Report" submitted July 12, 1974.

Related to the longshoremen's boycott was the protest against "The Goodship 'Esmeralda.'" According to the CSC's July 1974 bulletin of news, the visit of the Chilean naval flagship Esmeralda was a complete debacle for the junta:

> The visit of the Chilean naval flagship, the Esmeralda, to Vancouver's harbour has been cancelled—the ship has been rerouted to the Hawaian [*sic*] Islands. The ship left Chile over a month ago on a goodwill tour with a crew of Army, Navy and Air Force troops aboard.
>
> A "goodwill tour" of this ship is particularly repugnant because of its role as a prison and torture ship by the junta last September. The Esmeralda was able to dock in Brasil but was met by mass demonstrations in the Dominican Republic, Panama and Guayaquil, Ecuador.
>
> When this "Flying Dutchman" representing the Junta, sailed into the San Francisco Bay area, the dockworkers of the International Longshore Workers

Union refused to tie up the ship. Instead the ship docked at the Alameda Navy
Air Station some distance away, and was placed under tight security. Due to the
large protest of other San Francisco people which met the ship, the "open house"
aboard ship was cancelled. . . . The huge amount of public pressure during the
Esmeralda's visit forced Sen. Tunney (D. California) and other local officials to
send Henry Kissinger a telegram objecting to its presence. . . .[6]

The "goodwill" tour has been a failure for the junta and the cancellating [*sic*] of
its visit to Vancouver is something we can clearly see is due to the junta's knowledge that the solidarity movement in Vancouver would not allow the Esmeralda to
have a nice relaxing visit here, if it managed to dock at all. (CSC 1974f, 5)

In other words, this action was transnational and successful. Additionally,
some of the union activists who intended to prevent the ship from docking in
Vancouver were the same ones who also refused to unload cargo from Chilean ships, thus supporting the boycott.

Finally, Canadians also worked to raise material aid for the Chilean resistance in the interior. They did this through their various educational campaigns,
for example touring Salvador Allende's widow, Hortensia Bussi Soto, showing
films, and the like. It is not entirely clear if the activities were more effective
because of their educational component or because of the amount of money
they raised. For example, the former First Lady's tour, a very successful event
in Vancouver, drew about three thousand people in total and raised several
thousand dollars, which eventually found its way back to Chile (CSC 1974c, 1).
(This of course was after much bickering about which organization and/or party
would receive what percentage of the monies.) As Gary Cristall explained:

We did some fund-raising for one thing or another but it was propaganda work
to do the fund-raising. . . . The money we raised was peanuts. I mean the Socialist International or the Cubans or the Soviets or the Bulgarians or anybody or the
East Germans for Christ sake! Could write a check tomorrow for more money
than the entire solidarity movement in every country of the world, squared,
could come up with.

Perhaps Gary is understating the material importance of their fundraising efforts; certainly they played some role, or all of the activists, Canadians and
Chileans alike, would not have attempted to raise funds above and beyond
what were necessary to pay their own bills. From my conversations with the
Chilean women, they certainly placed a lot of value in the fundraising efforts
of the movement.

In sum, first and foremost Canadians in Vancouver organized to call attention
to the situation in Chile and the role of the Canadian government in perpetuating
it. They did this in part through educational events, films, newsletters, conferences, and the like, as well as their focused campaigns. They coordinated their

efforts nationally and transnationally with other solidarity organizations to demand asylum for all those affected by the coup (Chileans and non-Chileans alike), organized economic boycotts against the junta, and provided material assistance to the resistance in the interior. Eventually, Chilean exiles started pouring into Vancouver and the coalitions and party politics took on a slightly different character. I turn now to the role of Chileans in the solidarity movement.

Structure, Goals, and Tactics: Chileans

In this section I will discuss the structure of the movement, including the place of party politics, and then look at the various types of projects Chileans organized, which more or less fall into the following categories: social support for new exiles, political economic tactics, media campaigns, and cultural events and fundraising. I take these up in turn. However, I must preface this by noting that there is much overlap between the categories. For example, some of the social services exiles organized ultimately proved to serve as cultural anchors for the community, namely the Chilean Housing Cooperative. Similarly, economic tactics like the boycotts also served as media campaigns. Regardless of the slipperiness between categories I have chosen to organize the discussion this way, as it adequately reflects the themes that emerged in my interviews and from looking at the movement's literature. I should also note that the movement organized a variety of women-only projects, most of which I will not discuss in this chapter but save for the next one when I take up the issue of gender in the movement.

As we know, the solidarity movement was largely started by Canadians given the absence of a critical mass of Chilean leftists in Vancouver at the time of the coup. There was at least one clear exception, however: Ana María Quiroz. Ana María was involved in the movement from the very beginning and offered me a lot of insight regarding the origins and structure of the movement. The Vancouver Chilean Association (VCA) was the first organization founded by Chileans. Ana María was one of its founders and the first president. She explained that in the beginning the VCA served as an umbrella organization, hence the word "association," for any Chilean interested in opposing the dictatorship and supporting the resistance in Chile. However, as time passed and more Chileans started arriving with their defined party allegiances, the VCA was plagued with sectarian battles. In retrospect Ana María and her colleagues found the sectarianism comical. Ana María explained:

> The Chilean Association had everybody, at the beginning, we had one organization when we started. . . . This was right after the coup and . . . it took some time for the parties to get organized. At first nobody knew the ground [Canada],

who was who, . . . you had to be checked out. . . . It was chaos when you look back! . . . So after a while the parties became organized but I would say . . . it took a few months of recognizing who was who and from what party and for the parties to start regrouping.[7]

So I was President of the Association . . . I kind of helped organize it and that went until about maybe '74 or '75 and then it was time for somebody who had come from Chile to take on the leadership and that is when Carmen [Rodríguez] took the leadership. At the time I was connected to the Socialist Party but the Socialist Party had about three different groupings and it was a mess, you know? Somebody would come, and we would meet, and there were documents. They would read us the "line" and then another one would come do the same thing; they would open their briefcases, pull out the documents, and say "this is the line from the interior" [laughs].

In our focus group discussion I spoke with Ana María Quiroz, Carmen Rodríguez (the first two presidents of the VCA), Isabel López (the first secretary of the VCA), and Magaly Varas, an early member and long-time activist with the VCA. They all were also involved in the women's band *Cormorán* and Carmen and Magaly were both founders of the feminist magazine collective *Aquelarre*. In other words, these four women had tremendous personal and political history together. In the course of our discussion much time was spent laughing at the past—the fun, the mistakes, and the absurdity of the sectarianism. For example, they spoke about how the Socialist Party originally reflected three main tendencies but that the splits never ceased and by the end it seemed as if there were about seventeen different factions. Once the parties were fully reconstituted the organizations started reflecting the party alliances, at which point the VCA dissolved. Ana María explained during our discussion:

I think once things got organized according to the parties, [things] changed; that was a different story . . . and then there were different positions and different approaches and everybody was having struggles and leaders [in Chile] were put in jail. . . . But usually when there were violations of human rights everybody across the [party] lines would support [each other] regardless of whether [he/she] was [from] the Communist Party or the MIR. . . . Struggles were inside [the parties], little petty things; the front was, I think, very united; we were seen as a group of Chileans.

The fact that Ana María felt the movement projected a unified position is significant because she was definitely one of the most cynical women I spoke to with respect to party politicking and sectarianism.

Sectarianism was obvious in the movement not just from hearing about it from nearly every person I interviewed but also from reading the movement's literature. For example, in a statement put out by the MAPU and Socialist Parties, vis-à-vis the VCA in July 1977, the leaders speak of their political open-mindedness while belittling the tactics and efforts of other Chileans.

> It must be clear that in Vancouver the Assoc. fully supports the Revolutionary alternative even though we don't claim ownership over the Revolution as others have done. People must understand who's who in the Vancouver situation and clarify any possible confusion over the issue.
>
> It is a fact that in Vancouver the reformist project of the Popular Unity does not have any organic manifestation.
>
> As for the MIR, this organization has forgotten the revolutionary positions that the late Compañero Miguel Henríquez [founder of the MIR] put forward and has taken an opportunist stand. Today the MIR works a "tactical Alliance" with the Popular Unity creating joint "Informational Offices" outside Chile. . . .
>
> In other words, they are looking for a "tactical Alliance" that doesn't have anything to do with and therefore is contradictory to the strategic objectives of a Socialist Chile. (MAPU and Socialist Party 1977, 3)

The animosity between the organizations is explicit and indeed confusing. This memo dismisses the importance of the Popular Unity (UP) to exile politics. However, the Socialist Party, when in Chile, was the biggest party in the UP coalition. Similarly, the word *opportunism* with respect to the MIR is also peculiar. The MIR in Chile was an armed resistance group. I met many women who left their relatively comfortable and very safe lives in Vancouver to return to South America to join this armed struggle during the dictatorship. (Not all went to Chile; some went to Argentina or Bolivia, for example.) They risked their own and their families' lives and, in some cases, did permanent damage to their personal relationships because of their commitment to, in the words of the MAPU and Socialist Party, the "revolutionary alternative." In other words, the actions of the *MIRistas* I met appear anything but "opportunistic." Many of the women I spoke to faulted the men in the parties for the persistent, and, as Ana María said, "petty," squabbles. I will take this up further in the next chapter.

Youth activists in Latin America have always been central to revolutionary politics and often directly connected to political parties. High school and university students have played historic roles in Latin American social movements, and most leftist political parties have their own youth sector. The same can be said for the exiles' movement as well. In the course of my interviews I spoke with a handful of women who participated in varying capacities in the youth movement, some as leaders. The youth sector was comprised of young adults organized as arms of their respective political parties. According to Andrea Diaz, who at seventeen was leader of the Vancouver chapter of the

Communist Party youth sector, members of these groups were typically in their late twenties, particularly the leaders. As she said, "I was one of the cute kids," meaning she was significantly younger than the other activists. From Andrea's perspective the youth sector was less plagued by sectarianism than their adult counterparts and in some senses they had an easier time organizing. The youth tended to learn English much more quickly than the adults and thus understood Canadian culture better as well. Both of these strengths expedited their efficacy as a subsector of the movement. Despite the umpteen splits within individual parties, the cross-party and cross-generational tensions, and the animosity this all generated, the Chileans were able to accomplish quite a lot in their movement to support exiles in Vancouver and the resistance movement in Chile.

Social Support for Exiles

One of the first things Chileans did was to provide ad hoc social services and support networks to the exiles who poured into Vancouver. Several women explained how they used to go to the airport and meet the planes arriving from Chile to help provide, if nothing else, emotional support for Chileans like themselves who were forced from their country. The activists knew the schedule of the Chilean airline and would be there to greet the exiles when they disembarked from the plane. They went for no one in particular but rather to welcome people like themselves who they knew were traumatized politically, emotionally, and often physically. Patricia Gomberoff explained:

> At the beginning all we wanted to do was help. . . . There were people that were in bad shape, terribly bad shape, not just economically but psychologically, uuff, terrible shape. So yeah, it was very amateur, I would say very amateur, but you did what you could.

Similarly, Ana María explained,

> [In] the very beginning . . . we had to do work, getting people settled, getting doctors, getting [help for] people that had been tortured, getting jobs. It was mainly that sort of assistance and at the same time trying to find out what was going on in Chile.

Once the government started providing temporary housing for exiles in a hotel, members of the solidarity movement would visit newly arrived Chileans there and provide booklets of information and "orientations" about things to help make the transition easier.[8] Magaly Varas recalls:

> We went down there [to the hotel] to meet them and talk to them and tell them about housing, food, frozen food [since] it was cheaper, stuff like that. And espe-

cially [things like] health clinics and the medical plan because they had children. And I remember something about abortion.[9]

Many of the women I spoke with recalled these welcomes, mostly with fondness and appreciation for what they were offered. One woman, Patricia Andrade, who had a particularly difficult transition in Vancouver due mostly to her two sons' depression, recalled: "It was like you need something, you call them [the Chileans] and you have it there immediately. Like I said, many times I did not have food in my house and they would come with a brown bag full of food."

Another woman I interviewed, Andrea Diaz, however, remembered the airport greetings and was very put off by them. Andrea was only fifteen when she arrived in Winnipeg (her family's first stop before moving to Vancouver). Her father was a militant in the Communist Party and was more or less forced from Chile. She was angry at having to leave Chile and angry at the Left for what she believed created the conditions that led to his expulsion. (Andrea eventually became very active in the youth sector of the Communist Party in Vancouver and a national leader in the solidarity movement.) She recalls the airport greeting:

> The first thing after we got off the plane was all of these people greeting us, Chileans, and calling my dad "compañero" or whatever else and I thought: "Oh God! Here they are" (laughs)! And I was just resentful, I figured, this is why we are here now. I am going . . . to have to put up with these people again . . . I was very resentful at the time; I was very angry having left Chile; I felt ripped off I guess.

It is safe to say that Andrea's age had much to do with her resentment toward the Chileans greeting her at the airport. In retrospect she felt it was a good thing, particularly for her parents. What her story does reveal, similar to all of the other ones women shared with me, is that leaving Chile and arriving in Canada led to an emotional earthquake for which no one was prepared. Members of the solidarity movement, most of whom had gone through this themselves, sought to ease the transition and did this initially at the airport, government-sponsored hotels, and even peoples' homes. This work was done predominantly by women, a theme I take up in the next chapter.

Perhaps the most concrete manifestation of Chileans creating social support for future exiles was the establishment of a housing cooperative that still exists. It has been around so long that at the time of my first interviews, the mortgage was nearly paid off. Cecilia Tagle, one of the earliest members of the co-op, explained its history. In 1981 she and her now-ex-husband, an architect, left Toronto for Vancouver. While in Toronto they were involved in a similar project to create housing for Chileans. Cecilia explained:

> Once we came here [Vancouver] we became involved with the group that moved
> to this housing complex, [with] this project. The group that came to live here
> was involved from the very, very beginning by looking for a site, by working
> together with the architects who were also Chileans, and by trying to stay within
> . . . the budget, to kind of accommodate what was really needed. And I think
> for us, it was family oriented. At that time when we first moved in here there
> were sixty-four children; we [Chileans] had impacted the school so they had to
> hire more teachers because [our kids] were all going to elementary school at
> that time!

(At the time of this interview Cecilia still lived at the co-op; she just recently
moved out.) It is made up of thirty-seven townhouse units of various sizes,
from one to four bedrooms. Of those, four are wheelchair accessible.

In addition to housing Chileans at a fairly affordable rate the co-op also
provided the space for *peñas* and countless other political events, including
speeches by people like Nobel Peace Prize–winner Rigoberta Menchú. Indeed,
an explicit objective was to guarantee a space for such cultural events and
meetings. Additionally, the founders of the co-op were incredibly dedicated to
raising their children in a "Chilean" atmosphere—helping them to keep their
Spanish, and living collectively among what came to be an extended family.
The extended family is central to the social structure of Chileans. However, being removed from their homeland, the exile community needed to create their
own extended family. Mothers were especially committed to this goal since
their children were separated from their families at a very young age. Cecilia
believes these aspects of the co-op were its unquestionable strengths:

> [Living in the co-op was a good way to] teach the kids to share and that was
> excellent; I think it was a value that we gave the kids. The other was the lan-
> guage. Our kids, the ones that grew up here, in a way have sustained the Span-
> ish language because they were forced to speak to old people who did not learn
> English. Also, for my kids, I do not have family in Canada so this is like family.
> They call everybody uncle, aunt, and the older people were the grandfather and
> grandmother figures.

Ursula Andrade's mother was pregnant with her when she arrived in Canada. She lived in the co-op since she was a young girl and credits it with her
current connection to her Chilean heritage. She explained that the co-op was
central in the maintenance of her Chilean identity. Ursula was so shaped by
the experience that she recently began a documentary project about Chilean
children raised in the co-op. Similarly, María Jose Valenzuela (Cecilia Tagle's
daughter) lived in the co-op from the age of thirteen until she got married at
twenty-eight. She left Chile with her parents when she was only three years
old. She credits the co-op with saving her Spanish and cultivating a Chilean

identity that she knows is lacking in other Chileans her age who were not raised in the co-op. Chilean culture was so central to the fabric of the co-op that when María Jose traveled to Chile she expected to find a world parallel to the co-op. She explained,

> I think when you go back to Chile it is like "wow this is another world!" so different, it was not anything like what I was expecting. I was expecting a world similar to the co-op . . . but in a bigger way and . . . people very active in solidarity. . . . Probably there were pockets of it that I never got to see because it was not open at the time [during the dictatorship].

Cecilia also believed that the co-op has some negative aspects, particularly for older people:

> The negative part is it is too closed and I know people here that never learned the English language. But I think that is a combination of many things. I think that many Chileans living here were . . . taken from a prison to the plane and then on the plane they met their family and then they arrived here emotionally [destroyed]; for these people, this is prison and I think they refused to learn the language in a very rebellious way, but not seeing that is affecting them, nobody else. So it is like living in two worlds. It is very difficult but on the other hand, this is what many people feel is home.

Many Chilean exiles experienced the co-op as one of the main centers of the movement and the Chilean community in Vancouver—they constantly had meetings, peñas, parties, exercise classes, dance classes for children, among other things there. It is not surprising then that the Chilean youth who grew up in the co-op believed it was a "mini Chile," while the older people were able to use it to buffer themselves from the non-Chilean world. The co-op is both a social service of sorts as well as a physical embodiment of Chilean culture in Vancouver. Currently it houses three generations of Chileans. It certainly does not play the same political role now as it did during the 1980s when Pinochet was still in power, but it remains emblematic of the Chilean diaspora and the leftist politics of the exiles who were central in conceiving and building it.

Political Economic Tactics

As we know, political economic tactics, namely boycotts and divestment campaigns, were also central to the solidarity movement. According to the Vancouver Chilean Association Newsletter number two:

> The objective of the VCA . . . is to struggle for the full restoration of Human Rights for the people of Chile and all Latin American countries. To this end the

> VCA works to inform the Canadian public about the Latin American reality,
> and to raise support for our struggle. In particular, our main task is to organize
> and carry on a boycott of food imports, wines, manufactured products, and raw
> materials from Chile, and of Canadian investment in Chile. (1978a, 2)

Boycotting Chilean commodities was so central to the exiles' tactics that
the VCA established a Boycott Research Committee. Among other things, the
committee produced an eighteen-page document (including appendices) entitled "Canadian Trade with Chile" (1978b). The report is highly detailed and
written in grammatically correct English. It includes data regarding Canada-
Chile trade relations, followed by an analysis of the statistics and data provided. It also includes organizational strategies applicable to the interior,
transnationally, and Vancouver more specifically. Additionally the authors
added a call and rationale for Canadian solidarity, and a series of appendices
with information regarding vendors to boycott, Canadian investment in Chile,
and Balances of Trade with South America. In other words, the document was
extremely detailed, which reflected the seriousness that the movement placed
on political economic protest tactics.

Similarly, in the VCA's second newsletter they include an overview entitled "Why to Boycott the Chilean Junta." In it they provide political context, offering numbers of murdered, tortured, and/or disappeared Chileans
as well as an update on the current economic state of the Chilean economy.
They note: "at the time of the coup unemployment was only 3.1%, today
[1978] it is 30–40%. And in 1974 inflation was 376%, 1975: 341%, 1976:
174%, and in 1977 it was over 100%"[10] (VCA 1978a, 5). The newsletter
continues: "In Santiago alone 30,000 children receive their main, or only,
meal each day in the soup kitchens of the Church and other charity institutions. And paradoxically while malnutrition has been increasing inside
Chile since Sep't [*sic*] '73, we see food stuffs from Chile . . . on sale in our
local supermarkets" (VCA 1978a, 6). From the VCA's perspective these
new imports were available in Canada because "the Chilean people can no
longer afford to buy the food that they produce. So long as there is a market in the rest of the world this is not seen as a problem as profits can be
maintained" (VCA 1978a, 6).

The newsletter concludes that the profits generated from exports and Canadian investment do not make it back to average Chileans and thus a boycott
hurts the Chilean elite, not the marginalized sectors of society. To quell the
apprehensions that some Canadians may have about reducing cash flow into
an already depressed economy, the VCA argues: "The best reason tp [*sic*]
support the boycott of Chilean products and investment is that the people
inside Chile themselves have asked the world for this support" (1978a, 6).

They then include the translation of a leaflet that an Italian dockworker found when unloading a cargo of fish meal from Chile:

> *We are profoundly grateful for every act of solidarity and support which is carried out on behalf of the people of Chile to help us overthrow once and for all the fascist military dictatorship which rules our country. With your help and our efforts we are absolutely sure that we will emerge victorious and defeat those who staged the coup. LONG LIVE INTERNATIONAL SOLIDARITY!* ¡*venceremos!* (1978a, 6, emphasis in original)

In other words, the assumption on the part of Chileans in the interior was that any dockworker, in any country (in this case Italy) would be aware of the boycott against Chilean goods because one of the main points of action were attempts to prevent the commodities from making it to the supermarkets in the first place and this task in part fell to longshoremen. Presumably the dockworker who came upon this note was aware of the boycott and perhaps participating in it or s/he would not have known how to contact solidarity organizations that eventually sent a copy of this note to at least groups in Vancouver and likely all over the world. Once again, we see the transnational linkages in this movement, between Chileans in the interior and solidarity movements outside of the country and cross-national coordination among exiles. The boycott was perhaps the most illustrative example of such a campaign.

Vancouver labor activists were specifically called upon to participate in the boycott. For example, in an open letter to Vancouver longshoremen Hernan Ortega, President of the Industrial Belts of Santiago Workers councils, and coordinator of the Chilean Left in exile, asks the workers to cease loading and unloading boats coming or going to Chile:

> We wish to reaffirm what wasexpressed [*sic*] during our first trip with Mrs. Hortensia Allende about the importance of international solidarity with the Chilean workers. We are grateful for what you have done so far in this regard and wish to request collaboration once again from you and all the members of your unionin [*sic*] order to bring about a boycott at a political and economic level to the fascist military Junta.
>
>   We directly ask you to make possible a boycott of the loading and unloading of boats coming from and going to Chile. This has been done by Longshoremen of Europe, Australia, and on several occasions by your fellow workers in the U.S. Moreover, English workers have refused to construct ships for the dictatorship or repair engines of airplanes belonging to the Chilean Air Forces.
>
>   We also wish to inform you that, like most labour leaders in Chile, a large number of longshoremen leaders have been assassinated, imprisoned, and tortured by the fascist military junta.

We are certain that you our brothers here in Vancouver, who pledged some time ago to safeguard human and trade union rights in Chile, will not, after receiving this information, continue loading or unloading ships for the government and capitalists who are repressing and assassinating the working class of Chile.

The military Junta in Chile declared publicly that the Longshoremen of Vancouver had rejected the petition for a boycott made by Mrs. Hortensia Allende. But we hope today you will give your answer to fascism.

Long live proletarian internationalism.

Long live international solidarity.

Long live the working class. (Ortega, n.d.)[11]

As we might recall in the summer of 1974 Pinochet rerouted the "Esmeralda" scheduled to dock in Vancouver to Hawaii. Just as the ship was protested in the California Bay Area the junta expected it would be in Vancouver because of the solidarity longshoremen had already demonstrated for the Chilean resistance in the interior. In other words, the junta's public declaration that the longshoremen of Vancouver rejected the former first lady's call for the boycott apparently eventually no longer rang true.

As we know, on Ms. Bussi Soto de Allende's stop in Vancouver she asked the solidarity activists "to boycott the junta in every way possible" (in Griffin 1973, 12). Exiles clearly took this to heart and, in addition to working with longshoremen and other unions to interrupt the actual flow of goods, activists performed what might be considered "commodity sabotage" to discourage Canadians from purchasing Chilean products, namely wine. (One woman I interviewed remains so disgusted with the political situation in Chile she still will not buy Chilean wine.) One way they discouraged the public from buying wine was to destroy the labels on the bottles and leave behind stickers that urged customers not to purchase it. Angélica Gutiérrez was active with the youth sector in Canada during the dictatorship. She recalls:

For many years in Vancouver and in Canada, everywhere in the world, there was a boycott . . . of Chilean products, Chilean wine, and that was another political activity we used to do. . . . [W]e used to go to the liquor store and there was a wine called "Gato Negro" [Black Cat] and it had a little cat [on the bottle] . . . it was a little present, so what we used [do was] . . . go to the liquor store and pull the cats off and rip the things off the bottles so that they would not be bought.

Angélica went on to explain that the activists also left behind stickers that explained the situation in Chile and the need for the boycott.

Also along these economic lines, exiles pressured Canadian universities to divest from Chile. For example, Carmen Rodríguez was a graduate student at the University of British Columbia (UBC) during part of the dictatorship. She recalls a series of events that culminated with UBC withdrawing its investments from Chile:

> There was a meeting . . . [with] the university Senate or . . . Board of Directors.
> . . . One of the points of discussion was the shares [invested in the mining company] Noranda. So we got to . . . speak at the meeting. This was all done months
> ahead of time. We had to ask [for] space to sit [and] they granted it so that week
> [of the meeting] we did a "Chile Week." We did all kind of events; every day
> we did things. We painted . . . Chilean flags on cardboard and we put them . . .
> [at] the entrance to UBC. . . . We put them everywhere. . . . We were students
> and [we had] a . . . different event every day. We sang, we were showing mov-
> ies, we were [selling] *empanadas*, and finally the day of the meeting [came] and
> we all went. We had a spokesperson; we had everything prepared. . . . [F]irst he
> presented the whole thing why UBC should not be investing in Chile and they
> should pull their shares from Noranda . . . and we all spoke and it happened! At
> UBC the Board of Directors decided to withdraw [the money from Noranda]!

Recall there had already been Canada-wide protests against Noranda investment in Chile and this action represents a sector-specific (university), local example of the national campaign.

Media Campaigns

All of the aforementioned campaigns and events were accompanied with press releases and at times press conferences. In addition to trying to bring attention to specific events organized by the solidarity movement the exiles also stayed in touch with the media in a more general way in a relentless attempt to keep them abreast of the developments in Chile. As one woman noted, when Chileans first arrived in Canada it felt like no one knew where Chile was, or as she put it, "Some Canadians thought that Chile was part of Mexico." Use of the media was a very conscious strategy to challenge this sort of ignorance and engender a sense of concern among Canadians for the fate of Chilean exiles and their compañero/as in the interior. As Isabel López explained:

> I remember [we would say] . . . "there hasn't been anything in the paper so let's
> call this journalist and maybe we could give him an interview with our family
> and we can show them whatever we are doing." Something! All we would say is:
> "Look are you interested? We are doing this and that. . . . Or if you want, [we will]
> tell a story about [our lives]?" . . . and then it would be in The [Vancouver] Sun!

Related to the use of the media, in 1978 some members of the solidarity movement in Vancouver started a radio program called "*América Latina al Día.*" The Vancouver Chilean Association's second newsletter advertised the

Spanish-language program as one that "features music, news, and interviews about the Latin American reality," sponsored by the Committee for the Defense of Human Rights in Chile (1978a, 10), the solidarity organization of the MIR. Though it was an effort of both women and men, for many years it was produced by four women. Significantly, the program still runs today. Additionally the different committees that made up the movement (Chilean and Canadian) published and circulated their own newsletters, including "Venceremos," from the Vancouver Chilean Association. The youth sector did what might be considered nontraditional media work; they did graffiti art around the city denouncing the dictatorship, painting slogans like "*¡Chile Si, Junta No!*" Angélica Gutiérrez explained:

> One thing that I remember doing when we were more active [in the] youth [sector], we used to go, and . . . this was cool because I thought this is what it must be in Chile, but you know under a lot different circumstances and conditions, but we used to go to the construction sites and spray paint "¡Chile Si, Junta No!" here in Vancouver. So in the middle of the night, at three o'clock in the morning, when there was no one around we used to spray paint some of the construction sites . . . you know sometimes construction sites are kind of covered outside . . . [with] wooden boards, and they were bare so . . . we used to spray paint in the middle of downtown which . . . at least we raised a little bit of awareness.[12]

The movement also organized parallel demonstrations to show their solidarity with the Chileans struggling back home while also bringing international attention to their efforts. For example, in 1978 Chileans in Vancouver organized a twelve-day hunger strike at the same time that the families of the disappeared in Chile did. The hunger strike happened in Chile in five different cities on May 22, 1978. The strikers in Chile demanded the release of all political prisoners and the return of the disappeared (Power 2009). This was an extremely pivotal moment in the movement against Pinochet inside Chile as it served as a public catalyst to additional protests against Pinochet (Shayne 2004, Chapter Four). The international attention that the exile communities were able to bring to the event was decisive in spreading the word, as the Chilean media was quick to suppress the news of the strike. Carmen Rodríguez participated in the strike in Vancouver and recalls:

> We had a hunger strike here for twelve days.
> *[I asked: Where were you?]*
> In a church; we had very close allies in churches here and there was one in particular . . . a priest . . . [and] he was part of the hunger strike too and we had it [at] the church on Burrard and 16th avenue. We got a lot of [media] coverage. The press would come and we would, I remember these calls that we would

make [every] couple of days to Chile, we would talk to the different people that were on strike there. And that was a successful strike. . . . Even though the [Chilean] press . . . suppressed the news, there was some kind of reaction.

In other words, exiles organized this parallel demonstration to guarantee some sort of media coverage for the Chileans on strike in the interior. [13]

Cultural Events and Fundraising

Another central goal of the movement was to raise money for the political prisoners and activists in Chile. One of the main ways this was accomplished was through organizing peñas. As I have explained the peñas always had music, often live bands, dancing, typical Chilean food, namely empanadas, dance performances by the children of exiles, political speeches, and of course, non-Chilean wine. The events and food were not free so the money raised went to support Chileans in Chile. They took a tremendous amount of effort to organize, particularly cooking all of the empanadas. As Ana María Quiroz recalled:

[We women] worked like crazy, making empanadas and doing the music like a poor circus! We did it all while the guys were discussing the politics. And then we would make maybe fifteen hundred [or] one thousand dollars after working the whole week and with all these kids running around. So we felt great; we got the money and we [would] deposit it in this account in Luxemburg which we never knew much about!

The account was actually a centralized account where exile committees from all over the world deposited the money from their fundraising events, which was eventually sent back to Chile to support the Chileans and the re-sistance movement there.[14] The exiles were gratified to learn that their monies actually made it to the hands of individual Chilean women and bought them a certain amount of security otherwise lacking under the dictatorship. For example, Magaly Varas, an activist in the movement, explained to the other three Chilean exiles and me during our focus group that two years ago when she was in Chile she met a woman who told her:

She got money every single month [from our efforts] . . . she was getting money every single month and thanks to the [money] she could take the bus. . . . I heard from somebody else [that without the money] they would have had to walk [everywhere] and that would [have looked very] suspicious.

I am not suggesting that the peñas organized in Vancouver put the bus fare in the pocket of the woman Magaly spoke with in Chile. However, it is accurate to suggest that the collaborative efforts of the exile communities, and indeed, the peñas that were organized everywhere, did work to protect and support the activists who remained in the interior. These women put a much higher value on their fundraising efforts than did Gary Cristall, who, as I discussed earlier, felt the money the movement raised was virtually irrelevant in comparison to what Socialist countries were able to provide Chileans in the interior.

Despite the festive atmosphere of the peñas, the political position of the organizers was conveyed through speeches, banners that hung in the venues, and the radical lyrics of the music (translated into English for the Canadians in the audience). Indeed, much of the political spirit of the peñas was embodied by the music. During this period five Chilean women (including Magaly Varas, Ana María Quiroz, Carmen Rodríguez, and Isabel López) formed a band called Cormorán. (A cormorán is a type of bird.) Carmen Rodríguez recalled, "We were five women and . . . none of us had sung publicly before. But it was just this urge to tell people what had happened and why we were here [Canada]. [To encourage] people to join the solidarity movement [we did] whatever we needed to do." Isabel López, another member of the group, remembers it this way: "I can't sing, I wish I could sing. . . . But I did it . . . because it was needed." In other words, they did what they felt would be most effective and for everyone I interviewed, Chileans and Canadians alike, music was an extremely effective political tactic for a variety of reasons.

Music, and by extension the peñas, served as a tool to communicate the situation in Chile to non-Chileans while also serving as a way to keep Chileans attached to the movement. For many women I spoke to the music and peñas created a therapeutic environment they so desperately needed after experiencing the trauma of the coup and exile. Nina Vaca, a supporter of the MIR in exile, explained, "The guitar and the musical instruments . . . [were] tools for us [to] express . . . to the Canadian society or anybody what happened in Chile."[15] Or, as Lorena Jara explained, "I think . . . it [music/peñas] helped both to make people [non-Chileans] interested in the culture, and then the politics, and also it was for therapy and connection [to] our country; it was very important."

The political and emotional importance of the peñas was not lost on Canadians. Gary Cristall explained:

> One of the things that endured was the peñas. The beauty of the peñas was that they combined social activity with political activity. . . . You would go, there would be speeches, there would be tables with all kind of stuff [including *arpilleras* for sale], there would be food, there would be wine, and there would be music. . . . So these things really were a combination and they were quite brilliant in that sense because one, for the Chileans who were here I am sure it was as close to home as they were going to come. And the kids were there, you know? You know, North Americas, "get a baby sister, leave the kids." There

were a million rug rats. I see those kids, some of them the children of friends
. . . who are now nine-feet tall and . . . with their own kids, but they are always
going to be the little rug rats who were racing around. They would run across
the stage in the middle of the music. . . . And then the big brothers taking care of
little sisters and . . . the whole nine yards. It was lovely and it was also a place
[where] the Canadians and Chileans and various others interacted. So those
things were very, very enduring.

In addition to running across the stage while the bands performed, children
also took center stage to perform traditional Chilean folk dances or plays that
they learned in their folk music and theater groups. Like the music and peñas
more broadly, these performances also served a dual purpose. On the one
hand they served to share Chilean culture with non-Chileans and thus inspire
a deeper sense of connection to the solidarity movement. And second, they
fostered a sense of cultural connection to Chile within children who could
have easily felt more Canadian than Chilean. For example, a children's dance
troupe was formed in the co-op called The *Araucanitos*. *"Arauco"* refers to
Mapuche land, and "Araucanos" to the indigenous people from the south of
Chile. Thus, Araucanitos, refers to young ("itos") indigenous peoples (personal interview, Cecilia Tagle, 2004). The dance group was started by adults
but later taken over by the older children (i.e., eighteen year olds). Adults
also helped design and sew the costumes that the children wore in their performances. María José Valenzuela was one of the participants in the dance
group. She explained:

[The group] started at the co-op . . . it was part of the identity thing; we [the
youth] just wanted to learn about our culture, or our heritage, and just keep
passing [it] down to the generations. I was probably like . . . thirteen, fourteen.
. . . A lot of us had grown up here or were even born here, we had just seen it
[the dance] on videos so they [the adults] had to teach us how to do it. . . . We
performed everywhere; we tried to go to different festivals across the country,
or at least in the West; in Vancouver at all the festivals at schools, whatever we
could. . . . The leaders would . . . say "this [dance] is from the [indigenous] in
the North or from the South."

In other words, the kids did the performances wherever they were welcome. They explained the dances to their audiences, particularly the Canadian
audiences, and thus fostered a sense of solidarity from the spectators while
cultivating a Chilean identity among themselves. There was also a Children's
choir organized by the adults. Magaly Varas was instrumental in that en-
deavor and they performed similarly to the way the dance troupe did, that
is, wherever they were welcome. Children also organized theater groups and
did performances that in part conveyed their experiences with exile (personal

interview, Irene Policzer, 2004). All of these activities at various times were fused into the peñas as well as performed independent of them. They all served to further announce and explain Chileans to Canadians, why they were in Vancouver in the first place, while cultivating a collective identity that sustained the community through very tumultuous times.

The solidarity movement also used cultural production to raise money and awareness by selling arpilleras. Recall, arpilleras are tapestries women made from scraps of fabric. Each arpillera conveyed the woman's interpretation of life under the dictatorship, including the permanent loss of their children and loved ones. The arpilleras were then smuggled out of Chile and sold abroad by Chilean exiles, who used the folk art to articulate life under the dictatorship while raising funds to support the anti-Pinochet movement in Chile (Adams 2001; 2002; Agosín 1987; Sepúlveda 1996; Moya-Raggio 1984). Cecilia Tagle explained how in 1978 she returned to Chile from Canada. As she said, "I was not living emotionally" and needed to return, if only for a few months. While in Chile, a human rights activist asked her to take fifty kilos of arpilleras back to Toronto (where she was living at the time). She was terrified because during that period photos would appear in the Chilean newspapers of boxes of confiscated arpilleras at the post office. But the woman would not take no for an answer—she showed Cecilia a room full of items collected from and created by political prisoners—things like crafts, notes, and arpilleras. Cecilia was so moved, she sat on the floor surrounded by the items and cried. Her own father had been a prisoner for two months. When he was finally released he came home to his family and showed them his tortured body. No doubt those images came back to her while surrounded by the creations of others like him. She decided to put her fear aside and bring the arpilleras back to Toronto. She hid them in her suitcases among her and her children's clothes. Upon returning to Toronto she was able to get Amnesty International to organize an exhibition of the arpilleras. According to Cecilia, arpilleras were "a way for many Chileans inside Chile or outside Chile to express and denounce what was happening. . . . [T]he beauty of the arpilleras is [they were] one of the . . . strong[est] artistic expressions [that] could be done. . . . [They] were done in a group; it was kind therapeutic [for the women who made them]."

The final example of the fusion of fundraising and cultural production was the café *La Quena* Coffee House. (A quena is a pre-Columbian wooden flute.) La Quena was a café/peña formed by Chileans and Canadians. It was founded around 1983 and lasted until about 2003; (no one could quite remember for sure). The La Quena collective rented a space in East Vancouver (the predominantly Latino area of the city) that they ran like a peña. During the day it functioned as a restaurant and every weekend there would be some sort of solidarity activities. Amanda explained that La Quena "was used by everybody in town as the place for political activities. At the beginning it was mostly . . . Chileans . . . but then in the '80s it was . . . [used to help] all the different causes, . . . Guatemala, El Salvador."[16] Dale Fuller, American ex-patriot-turned-Canadian, was on the Board of La Quena. She recalls:

> There was one paid person as the coordinator and he or she, it changed at different times . . . had a salary. We got different grants sometimes [from] the government to put out little publications. . . . We made most of the money serving food and drink [not alcohol]. . . . There were educational things there; there was some music, and we had speakers. It went on for a long, long time; . . . [it] was amazing! It [lasted] for twenty years!

Yet again, another activist marvels at the longevity of their activities.

In sum, Chileans organized down party lines. They projected a unified movement to non-Chileans though at times the sectarianism became too much for activists to handle. Their strategies can be divided into social support, political economic tactics, media campaigns, and cultural production and fundraising. We have also seen that there is much overlap between these categories, as every event was a potential media story, while some social services ultimately ended up being cultural institutions. We also saw that most of what Chileans did in Vancouver was intimately connected to Chileans in the interior as well as other exile solidarity organizations throughout Canada and the rest of the world. In some cases the events were consciously coordinated, for example the former First Lady's tour, or commodity boycotts, while in other cases the parallel tactics were more a product of history than strategy, for example, La Quena in Vancouver and La Peña in Berkeley. In many senses Vancouver was a mirror image of the countless cities around the world where Chilean exiles settled and subsequently organized.

The Movement's Impact

According to Wright and Oñate the ousting of Pinochet "can be attributed, in no small measure, to the efforts of the exiles" (1998, 151).[17] Many of the women interviewed for this project absolutely concur with this sentiment. I spoke with many of the Chileans about the movement's impact. Certainly, asking the protagonists themselves is not the most objective way to approach this question; however, I do find their insights useful in illuminating some accomplishments that are confirmed by media coverage as well as treatment of the activists themselves. (I return to this point later.)

Perhaps the most significant accomplishment of the solidarity movement was forcing the Canadian government to change its policy toward Chilean refugees. According to Gary Cristall,

the solidarity movement mattered in the sense that . . . we forced the government
to let in a bunch of people that they would not otherwise have let in. . . . We
raised a lot of peoples' consciousness . . . but the one clear thing we did was we
forced the Canadian government . . . to let in people they had no plan to let in.

I asked Gary if he thought the government would have let the exiles in
without the pressure of the solidarity movement, and he responded:

No! I think they would have let in a few, they would have had to one way or
another but I think they let in far more than they wanted to. [There] is a lovely
quote [from] . . . one of the aids to the Immigration Minister saying: "well, we
are certainly not going to let in five thousand Chileans leftists," but they did!

As we know, the Canadian government's initial policy toward the junta
and refugees was entirely unacceptable to the movement; the government
formally recognized Pinochet (Allen 1973b; CP 1973; Mallory 1973; Winsor 1973) and put up significant barriers to refugees attempting to enter the
country (Gilbert and Lee 1986, 124–25). Through ongoing protests, sleep-
ins, press conferences, and pressure from political, religious, union, student,
and Chilean organizations the policies eventually changed. The government
provided legal entry and status, as well as housing and social services, to the
exiles who arrived in Canada.

There was also general consensus among the interviewees that the movement was significant for its ability to raise awareness about Chilean politics.
As we know media campaigns were central to the solidarity movement. Ana
María Quiroz explained: "We really got the point across; we really created an
awareness of Chile; we kept everyone informed, every chance of somebody
[a Chilean] coming [to town], we . . . did press conferences. We got the media, we got the radio, so it was a constant." Indeed, because Chileans were so
relentless about keeping the media abreast of the situation eventually articles
in the newspapers stopped explaining who Allende was or how the coup came
about, because it had been covered so regularly it was assumed to be common knowledge to those who followed the news. For example, in an article
in the *Trail Times* dated February 10, 1976, about a musical performance
by the women's folk music group Cormorán the author wrote: "a group of
Chilean women who have been living out an exile in Vancouver since the fall
of the Allende government, sang" (Jardine 1976, 5). Two and half years after
the coup this journalist believed her readers needed no more detail than that
provided above to understand why exiles lived in Vancouver.

Ana María Quiroz also believes that one of the movement's greatest accomplishments was "isolating the junta in terms of doing business with
them." As we know the solidarity movement organized everything from boy-

cotts of Chilean wine to divestment from Chilean corporations. As Carmen Rodríguez explained, their efforts were successful at least with respect to the University of British Columbia. Though it is virtually impossible to measure the real effects of a commodity boycott, if nothing else, the sabotage of labels and political messages left behind certainly alerted consumers to the political turmoil in the nation.

The movement's impact was also felt inside of Chile. For example, as I noted just two and a half months after the coup Salvador Allende's widow traveled internationally to ask for the support of Chileans and non-Chileans abroad (Griffin 1973, 12). Were the solidarity movement's efforts not useful in pressuring the junta and supporting those who remained in Chile, it is unlikely she would have asked for their continued support. Similarly, the Chilean longshoremen offered a blanket thank you to the world's dockworkers for their support of the boycotts. We also know that some money generated through small fundraising events went back to Chile and supported individuals and groups fighting against the junta. As Gary Cristall explained, the amounts were miniscule compared to what Eastern European governments were able to send, but they were in no way irrelevant, as the story Magaly Varas shared about providing bus fare and safety suggest.

Perhaps the most concrete way to understand the significance of the movement is from the perspective of the junta. For example, Ana María Quiroz was not even in Chile at the time of the coup; she left in 1968 prior to the election of Allende and thus had nothing to do with his election or his government while he was in power. However, when she tried to go back to Chile before the end of the dictatorship she was denied a passport and told her citizenship was revoked:

> I was not [in Chile] at the time of the coup but because of my involvement here [Vancouver] and my speaking up against the government . . . when I went to get a passport they would not renew it so I did not have a citizenship for a while. Then I applied for Canadian [citizenship] and then I tried to get back into Chile and they told me no. . . . I was allowed back in '84 [when my name appeared] on the list [published in the newspaper] that came out in December '83.[18]

In other words, the activities of the exiles were so well known and threatening to the junta that living legally in a country as safe as Canada could not guarantee that they remained outside of Pinochet's political radar. For example, in September 1977 "Chile News," a newsletter published by Canadians for Democracy in Chile, included what appears to be excerpts from an article in the Canadian Tribune dated August 29, 1977.[19] According to Chile News and/or the Canadian Tribune:

Toronto—There is evidence that the Chilean secret police, DINA, are active in
Canada, a spokesman for the Toronto Chilean Association told a news Conference [*sic*] here August 24th. Threatening phone calls and anonymous letters
have been received by Chilean exiles, he said, and the automobiles of leaders
of the Chilean community have been attacked in Edmonton and Calgary. . . . In
a rally following the press conference speakers denounced the actions of DINA
abroad and the new tactic of the Pinochet regime in kidnapping persons at home
and spiriting them to unknown jails where they are tortured and killed. (in Canadians for Democracy in Chile, September 5, 1977)

According to John Dinges, professor of journalism, who has written ex-
tensively about the junta's transnational repression, "An entire generation of
political exiles [was] forced to look over their shoulder wherever they were in
the world" (2004, 229). Chilean exiles who felt they were being pursued by the
DINA felt psychologically and/or physically limited to move about freely.

As we know, on October 5, 1988, the Chilean people, with the help of the
exiles, voted Pinochet out of power. Begrudgingly, Pinochet stepped down
and in December of 1989 the first democratic elections since the dictatorship occurred. Patricio Aylwin, a Christian Democrat with solid support from
the Left, including the Communists, who were prevented from running, was
victorious and in 1990 assumed the presidency. By this point the movement
in Vancouver had all but ended. Canadians had moved on to other causes,
namely the wars in Central America; some Chileans returned to Chile; many
felt their job was done now that Pinochet was out; and others felt defeated
by what they believed was a permanent manipulation of Chilean democracy,
compounded by the global collapse of socialism, while others were simply
burned out and tired of party politics (personal interviews 2004; 2005; Espinoza and Arvay 2004, 97). In other words, once the urgency of ousting
Pinochet was eliminated, so too was the solidarity movement.

How Did All This Happen?

What accounts for the emergence of a movement strong enough to contribute
to ending a seventeen-year dictatorship? Why weren't Chileans in Vancouver
(and elsewhere) entirely demobilized by their political, emotional, and physical pain? What answers might sociologists provide for this question? Did opportunities in the structural sense that political process theorists posit present
themselves (McAdam 1982; Tarrow 1988; 1995)? There were notable political openings in Vancouver yet from my perspective they were not sufficient to
cause the movement. As I have noted the outpouring of international solidarity certainly played some part in the rapid emergence of the movement; however, I maintain the movement would have emerged even in its absence; what

solidarity did impact was the efficacy of the exiles' efforts, particularly in the formal sphere of politics. Was it the opportunity provided by the Canadian government's eventually welcoming position toward Chileans? In my estimation though this political hospitality aided the Chileans, it was not responsible for the emergence of their movement, particularly given that the movement emerged prior to the welcoming policies. Indeed, it was the political hostility of the Canadian government that in part served as the initial organizing strategy of the movement, particularly for Canadians; their earliest lobbying call was for the Canadian government to grant unconditional asylum to all Chileans seeking it. This goal provided a concrete organizational anchor for the movement from September 11, 1973, onward. Similarly, the United States government was anything but welcoming to Chileans and similar movements emerged there as well (Eastmond 1997; Power 2009).

What about the political opportunity created by Canada's open democracy? Freedom of association, particularly in contrast to what the exiles left behind, created the political space to organize, but that space, in and of itself, was not a sufficient pre-condition for the movement's emergence. Recall, Chileans in the interior eventually began to publicly protest the dictatorship even while freedom of association remained categorically illegal. Was it their pre-existing networks, political parties, and the like that Chileans brought with them? The political parties and the networks they fostered helped facilitate the development and expansiveness of the movement but cannot explain why people, particularly women, were motivated to invest time and effort into it. I suspect that the place of political parties in mobilizing women in the movement, at least the ones I spoke with, was less than that of men. Recall that most of the women left Chile due to their husband's party affiliations, not their own activism. But many joined the movement on their own accord, particularly after their marriages ended. The networks definitely played a role in the movement's strength but cannot fully explain its emergence. After all, networks or not, the exiles were politically and physically safe; why not just bask in the comforts of democracy?

As I discussed in the introduction to this book, I find other theories more helpful in explaining the emergence of the movement. Specifically, I draw on social and new social movement theories of emotions (Jasper and Poulsen 1995; Nepstad and Smith 2001; Wood 2001) and symbolic resources (Fine 1995; Foran 1992; 1997; Reed and Foran 2000) to explain why exiles and Canadians organized the solidarity movement. In short, I argue Chilean exiles were motivated to form, join, and stick with the movement as a result of emotional and cultural factors. Their anger and indignation over the coup and Pinochet's assault on their political dream, compounded by the exiles' sense of moral and political obligation to confront and hopefully overturn the dictatorship, combined with the symbolic/cultural resources they had at their disposal, help explain why the movement came about in the first place. This section is meant to further connect the theories I reviewed in the introduction to the specific case discussed in this chapter.

Emotions

I begin with emotions. We might recall that moral shocks (Jasper and Poulsen 1995; Jasper 1997; 1998) and moral outrage (Nepstad and Smith 2001) help explain why emotions, specifically anger, propel some to join and even lead social movements. Anger was a feeling shared by many of the women I interviewed. Where did this anger come from? The anger was both politically and personally inspired. As I explained in Chapter One, Chileans, particularly those exiled, poured their political hearts and souls into the UP's agendas. They felt they were on the path to full-blown social transformation, which would ultimately culminate in economic and political justice and equality. The coup violently undid their accomplishments and derailed their idealistic visions for a socialist future, which was beginning to feel attainable. This political assault inspired an unstoppable anger. The anger was also personally motivated as the exiles watched their friends, family members, and compatriots be tortured, disappeared, and murdered. Take Amanada; she explained, "The rage and the hatred that I feel for Pinochet is so huge that it is embarrassing . . . the damage that he produced to so many people to so many generations, he can rot in hell for an eternity."

Some women spoke of an explicit connection between these emotions and deciding to organize, for example, Isabel López. Recall Isabel's story. She arrived via bus in Santiago the night of September 11th. A few months later, at the age of nineteen, Isabel left Chile alone. She arrived in Vancouver in February 1974 while her brother was still being held in a makeshift concentration camp. Isabel had many visual, familial, and even physical emotions in response to the coup, all of which she brought into exile. When I asked her how she got involved in the movement and eventually went on to play a leading role, she explained:

> I think that in my case . . . I was compelled to do something. I was not that [politically] involved in Chile. I was fairly shy, . . . I did not have a lot of experience, I did not know a lot of politics, . . . I did not understand what exactly had happened. I had to . . . just make sense [of everything] but I . . . have never studied politics. I think we were compelled because it was . . . so terrible what was happening; people being imprisoned, tortured, and killed. It was just like we had to [organize], we were just compelled. . . . I think a few of us women . . . did many things that we would not have done otherwise if we were just living a normal life. We had to find a way to get people to hear us, to help.

Emotions are very much at play in Isabel's testimony. She never explicitly speaks of "moral outrage" or even anger, but there is a noticeable urgency to her feelings, likely the result of what she personally experienced (her brother's incarceration) and witnessed (dead bodies in the streets of Santiago). Emotions compelled her and others like her to mobilize; emotions overpowered her shyness, political inexperience, and social conditioning to be a "well-behaved" young woman. Indeed, even though Isabel was younger than most of the activists she eventually played a leading role in the solidarity movement.

Similarly, Wood (2001) argues that pride and pleasure are also factors that propel individuals to mobilize. She maintains that when alienated sectors of society organize themselves politically, the process transforms individual feelings of alienation to collective experiences of pride and even pleasure. In the case of the solidarity movement I argue that many Chilean women did get and/or stay involved for similar reasons. They were politically and emotionally devastated from the coup and exile, and attending the events provided a collective space for healing, which eventually translated into hope and thus momentum to continue organizing. Many of the women I spoke to conveyed these experiences to me, mostly with respect to the peñas and other cultural events organized by the exiles. For example, Carla Gutierrez explained to me why the movement had so many cultural events:

> When you get to a country that does not speak your language, the culture is different, the weather is different, the food is different, and you [cannot] relate [to anything], and on top of that very few people [even] know where Chile is, then you start feeling very little, [very] insignificant. So for us to bring our music, our culture here was sort of mandatory. Not only to contribute to the mental health of our own people by saying: "Here is this group who was singing along with us all [through the] years of Allende, . . . [they are] here again, and [they] bring [back] a lot of memories;" but also to say to rest of the [non-Chilean] community: "We are offering you this group that is good quality musicians, and songs that [mean] a lot to us [to] sort of to say . . . [w]e are equal[s]. And we are capable of having good musicians and we wanted to share [this] with you." So [it] was sort of two things: To contribute to the culture of the community and also to vindicate ourselves [by] saying: "We are normal human beings with the same aspirations that everybody else has and . . . this is part of who we are."

In other words, the concerts and peñas that exiles organized helped mediate the deep sense of alienation many felt upon arriving in Canada. As Carla said, everything from the weather to the language created a sense of isolation among exiles. This pain was further compounded by the fact that many Canadians were completely ignorant about Chile; as she told me later, beyond human rights and leftist activists, "The majority [of Canadians] thought that Chile was part of Mexico!" As a result, some Chileans felt compelled to organize the cultural events to counter the naïve and even xenophobic images and reclaim their culturally rich collective identities. The processes, as Wood suggests, turned the alienation into hope and thus fueled mobilization.

Other women explained to me that they continued to go to and organize the peñas because it helped mediate the pain by creating a familiar atmosphere. As a result, the exiles started feeling more settled in Vancouver and were able to mobilize more effectively. They also felt that implicit in their events was a call for justice. That demand proved empowering to the exiles and also fueled their ability and desire to keep organizing. Amanda explained:

> At the emotional level [I felt like] . . . I need to do this, I need to be there [at the events]. It was a need for [a] connection. And aside, the political [message] is all one and the same because it is all about justice, right? So that is what makes our trauma so different. Political trauma is about justice, whether they are Chileans, Salvadorans, or whoever . . . So it [their activism] was about . . . denouncing what is happening and telling the world and the society; it is about getting a sense of justice, at least the idea that someone is listening to your story, someone who is from outside your community.

Again, we see Amanda conveying a sentiment extremely similar to Carla. That is, the deep sense of alienation and political frustration led many Chileans to mobilize and transform negative and demobilizing emotions into those of hope and triumph. The exiles had a sense that they were part of a larger political community and larger struggle that transcended their own individual needs and desires. The movement itself, moreover, reinforced and reproduced their political beliefs and this sense of community, solidarity, friendship, sorority (among the women), etc., through its collective rituals and activities. In other words, Chileans turned political and social isolation into pride and even pleasure, precisely what Wood describes with respect to guerrilla activists in El Salvador. Such emotional transformations propel individuals to collectively mobilize, thus another cause for the birth of the solidarity movement.

It is important to note, however, that some Chileans explicitly warned of surrendering political analysis to emotional reaction. That is, they feared the solidarity movement would be driven by emotions rather than politics. In 1974 the MAPU in Canada started a newsletter called *Resistencia*. After a disclaimer that reads, "Please excuse our errors in translation. We have few resources at our disposition. We will try to improve the quality of the translation in our next issues," the newsletter includes an editorial that attempts to explain the purpose of this issue.[20] Their goal is to provide a political analysis of the cause of the coup and political developments one year later. It reads:

"[W]e have the duty to give an integral proyection, rich in ideological and political contents, to the events happened September 11th. In order to avoid at any rate that solidarity towards Chili changes in a mere emotional and subject analysis of facts" (1974a, 3) [errors in original]. In other words, the core party activists of the MAPU felt activists should be inspired by facts, not feelings.

Symbolic Resources

The other catalyst in the emergence of the solidarity movement was the availability of resources; or more accurately, symbolic resources. Here I borrow from Fine's (1995) reinterpretation of Zurcher and Snow (1981). Zurcher and Snow attempt to fuse symbolic analysis with resource mobilization theory to explain the place of ideology as a tool "that functions in a symbolic fashion and that is importantly related to a movement's mobilization efforts and organizational viability" (cited in Fine 1995, 132). Fine reinterprets their contention by replacing "ideology" with "culture." That is, "culture" becomes a resource from which potential activists draw. This is similar to Foran (1992; 1997) and Reed and Foran's (2002) argument about political cultures of opposition. We might recall that for Foran and Reed political cultures of opposition draw from and are reflected in a variety of cultural productions, including ideology and historical experience. Collective memories, experiences, and ideologies all function as potential resources in the mobilization of political cultures, which, from Foran and Reed's perspective, need be present for a revolutionary movement to triumph. Together Fine, Foran, and Reed argue that potential activists need resources from which to draw, but resources can be as abstract as collective memory, history, culture, and/or ideology.

The case of Chilean exiles very much confirms their arguments. In addition to their political parties and networks, exiles came armed with leftist ideologies, histories, and cultural training, which they used as resources to mobilize against Pinochet. This is not to say that all of the women who got involved were activists in Chile; many were not for a variety of reasons, not the least of which being the male-dominated structure of party politics. However, even without direct organizational experience the exiles had come of age politically in a Chile alive with leftist political culture, namely the New Song movement and Popular Unity in general. They brought those memories into the diaspora in the form of symbolic organizational resources. Many of the women I spoke to explained this phenomenon to me. For example, Cecilia Bosier talked about the impact the Popular Unity era had on her and other Chileans:

> I guess what happened to me, well to many of us actually, through the process, through this very deep experience of the *Unidad Popular*, and how we were growing into that . . . politics and life became one thing. You know, for mystics

for example, religion and life is the same. And today, art and life is the same to
me. There is no separation anymore. So it was impossible to conceive any activity, any life, everyday, without politics. We were absolutely immersed in it.

In other words, living through the politically vibrant era of the UP, regardless of one's explicit party affiliation, fostered a political spirit and conviction
that could not be squelched, not even by political trauma and exile. Recall
the UP's ambitious agenda (discussed in Chapter One). Being submerged in
a political culture that was successfully working to transform an economy
designed to fully empower the working and peasant classes through control
of their workplaces and land left an indelible mark on all those even remotely
connected to the project. Landolt and Goldring make a similar argument
based on their research about Chilean exiles in Toronto: "[The] distinct repertoires of immigrant political practice . . . is a result of the historically and
cultural [*sic*] specific experiences and resources that a group brings with it,
including political culture and organizing repertoires" (2006, 28–29).

Isabel López also talked about the exiles drawing from the organizational
resources they amassed before and during the UP. She explained that the
reason the exiles mobilized and eventually used cultural tactics was the result
of their histories:

> I think [we organized this way] because of our experience back in Chile. . . . We
> always had singing . . . throughout all the years. . . . I remember when I was a
> kid, my cousins played guitar, somebody sang, [there] was . . . culture all over
> the place. The kids learned to sing . . . and I was always quite shy but I was
> involved in some plays at school. So . . . I think . . . we brought . . . that with us;
> we just thought that was the easiest way to reach people.

The political tools leftists shared with each other, including their children and
young relatives, were symbolic and indeed portable (i.e., songs and musical
instruments) and exiles brought them into the diaspora and promptly used them
to organize against the junta. Rather than feel threatened by an entirely new
political landscape, the exiles marshaled the resource with which they were
most familiar, political culture. In the case of the solidarity movement, political
cultures were both a cause of its emergence, particularly as manifest in collective histories and ideology, and ultimately an embodiment of its strength.

In sum, from the exiles' perspective, the movement was inevitable and even
spontaneous. Here I have applied a sociological lens in an attempt to make
sense of their assessment. As I have attempted to demonstrate, the impetus behind the solidarity movement in Vancouver were strong emotions and a powerful sense of commitment (moral outrage and obligation) that arose from the
political beliefs, sense of community, and cultural history of its protagonists.

These emotions, coupled with the political histories and resources of the exiles, fused to inspire their organizing.[21] Their political beliefs and cultural resources preceded the movement to some extent, but were also reproduced by it and of course diffused to new people. We also know that international solidarity, Canada's ultimately welcoming immigration policies, and freedom to associate in Canada's open democracy all provided organizational opportunities to the exiles. Preexisting political networks also contributed to the movement's efficacy and reach, but none of these necessary conditions were sufficient to bring about the movement and thus do not explain why exiles organized. As I have argued, such opportunities and networks served to strengthen the movement rather than entirely explain its existence.

CONCLUSION

Forcing leftists out of the country was a deliberate and effective tactic that permitted Pinochet to rapidly consolidate power (Angell and Carstairs 1987, 157). As we know this tactic partially backfired given that the exiles formed countless organizations in the more than one hundred countries where they fled. The committees worked transnationally to influence world opinion by publicizing the dictatorship's human rights abuses, crimes that may have remained under the media's radar were exiles not spreading the word. Wright argues that such activities were fundamental in preventing the junta from gaining international legitimacy and "fueled repeated condemnations of Pinochet and his policies by the United Nations, the Organization of American States, the World Court, and other international bodies" (1995, 199). The Canadian case of Vancouver certainly lends credence to his argument. The Canadian government initially recognized Pinochet as the official leader of Chile but, in response to pressure from the solidarity movement, was eventually forced to change its position, open its doors, and provide safety and social services to thousands of Chilean leftists.

As I have demonstrated in this chapter, culture was central to birthing, structuring, and sustaining the solidarity movement. Shared histories and memories spawned political cultures of opposition, which served as the manifestation of the solidarity movements. Chileans organized in a variety of ways; most of their tactics centered one way or another around culture: peñas, music, food, art, movies, children's dance troupes, and the housing co-op. We also saw that emotions were central to the solidarity movement. They helped motivate activists to organize and kept them connected and inspired to keep devoting countless hours to attending and organizing the events. The exiles in Vancouver coordinated with Canadians, other exiles around the world, and

Chileans in the interior. Exile committees everywhere organized peñas and deposited their funds into accounts like the ubiquitous one in Luxemburg. The monies eventually made their way back to Chile, supporting individual activists and their resistance movement more broadly. According to some, the movements were ultimately successful as measured by the ousting of Pinochet. Many, however, have an entirely different interpretation of Chilean politics. They were happy to see Pinochet forced down but completely unsatisfied with how it happened and the legacy he left behind. In the next chapter I look at the movement and its efficacy using a gendered lens.

NOTES

1. Historian Thomas Wright shared this information with me based on his and Rody Oñate's extensive research on the Chilean diaspora (personal communication 2006).

2. In some of the organization's literature they refer to themselves as the "Chile" Solidarity Committee and in others the "Chilean" Solidarity Committee.

3. Information in this section regarding Canada's immigration policies toward Chileans comes from Gerald E. Dirks, (1977), *Canada's Refugee Policy: Indifference of Opportunism?* (Montreal and London: McGill-Queen's University Press), 244–50.

4. There were a significant number of non-Chileans living in Chile at the time of the coup, particularly from other parts of Latin America. This was due in part to tumultuous political situations in their own countries, namely Brazil, and also a desire to live in a country experiencing such an historical transformation. As a result, these non-Chilean leftists were also unsafe after the coup and returning to their countries of origin was not always an option.

5. Andrew Ross was ambassador to Chile at the time of the coup. In September 1973 confidential cables from Ambassador Ross to the external affairs department in Ottawa were leaked to the New Democratic Party. In them Ross made a series of remarks supportive of the junta and tolerant of its tactics. Additionally, information conveyed indicated a highly inaccurate assessment of the future and longevity of the dictatorship, thus providing the Canadian government with bad intelligence from which they were expected to design foreign policy (Lavoie 1973; Eayrs 1973b; LAWG 1973f).

6. Margaret Power calls the U.S. protest against the Esmeralda "one of the more successful and unifying national campaigns" (2009, n.p.) of the period. In addition to the information reported by the CSC she adds: "[A]ctivists hung a huge banner from the Golden Gate Bridge that proclaimed in large letters 'Junta No!' A flotilla of ten boats sailed out to meet, but not welcome, the Esmeralda and some five hundred people protested the presence of the boat in the Alameda Naval Yard." Margaret Power, (2009 [forthcoming]), "The U.S. Movement in Solidarity with Chile in the 1970s," *Latin American Perspectives*.

7. Carmen Rodríguez, also present in this focus group discussion, did not recall exactly but estimated that it took the parties in Vancouver between two and three years to truly reconstitute themselves. She arrived in Vancouver in August 1974.

8. The hotel used to be called The Court Motor Inn. Now it is a medium-end hotel called The English Bay, right near the water, in a prime tourist destination (personal interview, Carmen Rodríguez, 2004).

9. Magaly recalled providing information about access to abortion clinics and the like in part for women who had been raped either while incarcerated or as a result of intimate partner violence. She did not recall the details, however, regarding how exactly they conveyed this information in a nonalienating manner.

10. Lois Oppenheim reports a similar trend with slightly different statistics: Inflation was 505 percent in 1974. It decreased a bit to 375 percent in 1975 and 212 percent in 1976. Oppenheim concurs that unemployment was less than 5 percent pre-coup. She reports that by 1975 it rose to 14.5 percent and by 1976 it dropped slightly to 13 percent. However, in the Greater Santiago area, home to one-third of the nation's population, unemployment was almost 20 percent (1999, 121–22). Lois Hect Oppenheim, (1999), *Politics in Chile: Democracy, Authoritarianism, and the Search for Development* (Boulder: Westview Press).

11. This open letter is not dated. However the tour through Canada took place in December of 1973, and this letter was written not long after that, so I would guess it was circulated no later than February 1974.

12. The slogan "¡Chile Si, Junta No!" was not limited to Canada. On September 21, 1976, one of the most infamous attacks of the Pinochet dictatorship happened on U.S. soil. A car bomb was detonated in Washington D.C. that took the lives of Chilean diplomat Orlando Letelier and his twenty-six-year-old American colleague Ronni Karpen Moffit. According to Peter Kornbluh, "[T]he target was Orlando Letelier—at the time of his murder the most respected and effective spokesman in the international campaign to condemn and isolate the Pinochet dictatorship. A longtime friend of Salvador Allende, Letelier had been named the Popular Unity government's first ambassador to Washington" (2003, 341). Within days, solidarity activists in the U.S. organized protests all over the country. 5,000 people marched at the site where Letelier and Moffitt were murdered, wearing black armbands and chanting, "¡Chile Si, Junta No!" (Power 2009). Peter Kornbluh, (2003), *The Pinochet File: A Declassified Dossier on Atrocity and Accountability (A National Security Archive Book)* (New York: New Press); Power, "The U.S. Movement in Solidarity with Chile in the 1970s."

13. Vancouver was just one of many cities where these parallel demonstrations happened: "Nine hundred exiles in twenty-one different countries and seventy-three different cities in Europe, Latin America, and North America, backed by the solidarity movement, joined them [the strikers in Chile]" (*Chile Democrático*, June–July 1978, cited in Power, "The U.S. Movement in Solidarity with Chile in the 1970s.")

14. Recall, Ana María Quiroz returned to Chile in 1990 and currently works for the Chilean government. She is very institutionally plugged in and connected with many former exiles who were also activists in the solidarity movement. As she explained in our focus group discussion, "I still have not found anybody in Chile to tell me about that account in Luxemburg; they just laugh at it!"

15. Nina says "anybody" because Vancouver is a very internationally diverse city and many of the peñas' attendees were from outside of Chile and Canada.

16. Establishments like La Quena are common relics of the solidarity movement. Many, many cities populated by exiles created cafés such as this one. For example, in Berkeley, California, Chileans worked with other Latinos and North Americans and created a similar establishment called *La Peña*. It was formed in June 1975 and still exists today. Its history is somewhat similar to La Quena in that it started out predominantly hosting Chilean events but later branched out to include all sorts of political causes, especially the Central American solidarity movement in the 1980s. In Amanda Esteva's story "*¡Venceremos!* Words in Red Paint," she talks about the beauty of La Quena (the instrument) and the significance of La Peña in Berkeley. Amanda Esteva, (2006), "¡Venceremos! Words in Red Paint," in *Homelands: Women's Journeys Across Race, Place, and Time*, ed. Patricia Justine Tumang and Jenesha De Rivera (Emeryville, Calif: Seal Press), 63–75.

17. For an assessment of the efficacy of the movement in the United States, see Power, "The U.S. Movement in Solidarity with Chile in the 1970s."

18. In an attempt to quell international pressure and demonstrate that repression was subsiding in Chile, the junta published lists of exiles who had formerly been banished from the country and were now allowed to return. Family members in Chile looked for their relatives' names in the newspapers and in 1984 there was a massive return of exiles. Alan Angell and Susan Carstairs, (1987), "The Exile Question in Chilean Politics," *Third World Quarterly* 9(1): 155; Thomas Wright, (1995), "Legacy of Dictatorship: Works on the Chilean Diaspora," *Latin American Research Review* 30(3): 199.

19. The newsletter includes one-half page of typed text at the end; it says, "-Canadian Tribune, August 29, 1977."

20. I have not noted with "[*sic*]" every grammatical, spelling, or translation-related error in either excerpt I share here.

21. Margaret Power offers a somewhat different analysis of the emergence of the solidarity movement in the United States. In my estimation our differences serve to complement and reinforce one another's analysis. Power argues that three factors led to the movement's emergence:

> (1) the reality of Chilean politics, which includes the vision and practice of the UP government, the violence of the military coup that overthrew it, and the repressive character of the military dictatorship; (2) the time period and political context in which the UP came to power and was overthrown (1970–1973); (3) the political impact that Chileans who supported the UP government had on North Americans, both in Chile during the UP period and in the United States after the 1973 coup. (2009, n.p.)

I argue that implicit in Power's analysis are emotions and symbolic resources that are central to the movement's emergence. For example, the violent nature of the coup (Power's number 1) and the political impact of leftist Chileans on North Americans (Power's number 3) inspired an emotional response that propelled activists to mobilize. Similarly, the time period and political context (Power's number 2) provided a set of symbolic resources and collective memories from which activists drew. Power, "The U.S. Movement in Solidarity with Chile in the 1970s."

Chapter Five

Gender, Emotions, and Culture in the Solidarity Movement

There was a difference between our public lives, how we presented our-selves in public activities such as the peñas, and our private lives, family lives, and our own meetings. My perception is that if you went to a peña, for example, you would see men and women in the kitchen, on stage, selling tickets. But if you attended one of our meetings, chances are that women would be cooking and men would be carrying [out] the meeting.

—Irene Policzer

INTRODUCTION

Gender is an important variable in understanding and shaping all social phenomena. The term *gender* refers to sociocultural expectations of behav-ior based on one's biological sex. Lorber maintains that gender "establishes patterns of expectations for individuals, orders the social processes of everyday life, is built into the major social organizations of society, such as the economy, ideology, the family, and politics, and is also an entity in and of itself" (1994, 1). In other words, gender functions at an individual, group, and societal level, and is thus central to all activities, social move-ments included. Gender permeates all processes and interactions, from behavioral expectations to access to resources. That is, gender, as assigned by one's sex, influences what men and women should, can, and ultimately do on a daily basis. Gendered expectations and behaviors are not limited to the domestic sphere, as popular imagination may assume. Rather, gendered expectations saturate all social, political, and economic interactions, public and private alike.

Social movements and their actors are not immune from assigned norms established by gender. Using gender to study social movements helps one understand the convergence of behavioral expectations and available resources, which ultimately sheds light on how social movement actors create and sustain their movement. For example, are women expected to be leaders or followers? How do social movements encourage or discourage women to transgress from those expectations? Are women presumed competent enough to have access to formal political and financial resources? If not, how do women subvert these restrictions? The solidarity movement and Chilean women's participation in it will show that despite unspoken and often very uncompromising behavioral prescriptions that privilege men over women, women held the movement together with their emotional and cultural labor. In this book's conclusion I will argue that using gender to ground my analytic and methodological approach in this study has greatly enhanced our understanding of the Chilean solidarity movement. This chapter is meant to begin that discussion.

As of late, the place of gender in social movements has received a great deal of attention. Scholars discuss women-only and mixed (or so-called "gender neutral") organizations from empirical, typically single-case, and theoretical angles. A variety of themes repeat themselves in the literature including gender differences in activist experience, movement participation and recruitment, division of labor, emotions, and efficacy. Rather than restate the existing literature I point the reader to these comprehensive sources: Einwohner et al. (2000); Kuumba (2001); and *Gender & Society*'s special issues on gender and social movements (1998; 1999). This book, specifically this chapter, helps to further illuminate the place of gender in social movements, particularly with respect to the division of leftist labor, and culture and emotions work.

I begin this chapter with a brief overview of previous scholarship about Latin American women's political mobilization and the gendered division of labor. Next, I discuss this division in the Chilean solidarity movement, specifically the different types of tasks that women did and did not do. I then discuss the place of gender and emotions in mobilizing culture. Finally, I conclude with an analysis of the interplay between gender, culture, and resistance in the solidarity movement. I will argue that emotions, particularly sorrow, were central to the exiles' use of culture in the solidarity movement. Emotions also help explain women's sustained involvement in the movement, particularly given their very limited time. We will also see that cultural events and institutions served the movement and Chilean exiles in very distinct ways: They created free spaces that bred more mobilization and they served as a form of political resistance in that they forcefully conveyed that despite the dictatorship's goals, the Chilean Left was alive and artfully thriving. Together these arguments will help demonstrate that Chilean women exiles played the role of mothers of the movement by managing the community's pain and sustaining the cultural face of the movement. In other words, we will see that gender, emotions, and culture fused to sustain and grow the movement, in large part due to the efforts of Chilean women.

LATIN AMERICAN WOMEN ORGANIZE

It has been well documented that leftist movements in Latin America are organized around and even reinforce the same gendered division of labor as the mainstream societies they are often fighting against (see Chinchilla 1993; Craske 1999; 2003; Jaquette 1973; Kampwirth 2002; Lobao 1990; Luciak 2001; Miller 1990; Shayne 2004). What do we mean by gendered division, also referred to as the patriarchal or sexual division of labor? Dorothy Smith argues that such a division mandates that women do the labor that falls in "the bodily mode," tending to the "immediate and concrete world," whereas men's work lies in the "abstracted conceptual mode," or the "ruling mode in industrial society" (cited in Jaggar 1988, 372). At its most basic level the patriarchal division of labor mandates that women are responsible for the often unrecognized and undervalued daily maintenance of family and by extension society, whereas men are responsible for the seemingly grander tasks that have monetary, political, and thus social value attached to them. One political implication of this arrangement is the time constraint placed upon women due to the ongoing nature of their expected tasks. For example, the gendered division of labor in its most traditional sense mandates that women are responsible for feeding their families. If a woman is expected to be at home around dinner time she is unable to attend political meetings which often happen after men finish their work days. If this expected division of labor is adhered to then women's work does not end at the end of a traditional work day (Hochschild 2003). These time constraints have very real implications for women's political involvement and in part translate to a gendered division of leftist labor.

Time constraints and social expectations aside, women have always been part of the leftist politics and movements that define Latin American history. As we know, late-twentieth-century Latin America was dominated by military rule (thus exile) and opposition movements. The organizations that make up these movements fall into a variety of often overlapping categories, including human rights, Christian base communities, labor, urban, and armed. The growing historical record shows that despite social and structural barriers women consistently participate in these movements, though typically in lesser numbers, in seemingly less important roles, and often with less support and acknowledgment of their efforts. Despite this, women have participated and continue to participate in leftist politics in all of the aforementioned sectors, and many that have emerged since the transitions to democracy in the region. Serena Cosgrove argues:

> Women in Latin America are uniquely positioned to contribute solutions to the major problems threatening their societies because their culturally ascribed roles as caretakers in the home and in the community, as well as their activism and volunteerism during periods of economic and political crisis, often translate into having developed skills like networking, cooperation, and listening across difference. (Forthcoming, 9)

Leftist women even hold executive positions of power, specifically Chilean president Michelle Bachelet, a former exile herself.[1] In other words, history has demonstrated that Latin American women's collective political skills are formidable enough to erode social structural barriers such that a leftist woman, who comfortably uses feminist discourse, was elected president of Chile in 2006.

Latin American women's organizational competence is perhaps most illustrative in the human rights movements, namely, the families of the disappeared that organized in at least Argentina, Chile, El Salvador, and Guatemala. As the region was entrenched in military rule disappearing suspected "subversives" was often the military's tactic of choice. Military and paramilitary organizations relied on this tactic as a means to terrorize the population and discourage them from protesting against physical, political, and psychological injustices. However, as women lost their loved ones, particularly their children, the opposite occurred and previously apolitical women joined together to denounce military rulers for their systematic human rights violations. In many cases women were the first members of society to publicly oppose dictatorships, which paved the way for more explicitly political organizations to follow suit. This was certainly the case in Pinochet's Chile, as I discussed in Chapter One.

Women also organize as union and student activists, two sectors extremely important to opposition movements in general. In both cases, particularly in labor unions, women's roles were seen as peripheral, at best. Many women eventually left mixed labor unions to form their own women's sectors as they saw their gender-specific demands and potential political contributions undermined. There are exceptions, of course, particularly in women-dominated fields, like teaching, but in general women labor activists have yet to be fully included in and represented by unions or the union movement. Student movements have always been central to the Latin American Left. Women did/do participate in student groups but typically in support roles. This is partly due to sexist assumptions outside of the university, which have unofficially restricted women's access to colleges, thus reducing the real numbers of women available to participate. Fortunately, there is a consistently growing female student body at colleges and universities in Latin America. Student movements are quite illustrative of the place of social class in enabling women to claim leadership positions in the Left. By virtue of experiencing university life, women (and men) are exposed to cultural capital that the working poor and peasant classes are not. The cultural capital often translates into access to leadership positions. Similarly, access to university is reserved for wealthier members of society who can afford tuition while in many cases not even working in paid jobs. University students tend to have a reserve of time not available to poorer women, who typically work in and outside of the home to survive. In other words, the social class of women activists in university movements has in part buffered them from the patriarchal division of labor present in other sectors of the Left.

Latin American women have also participated in the Left through their involvement with Christian Base Communities (CBCs). CBCs are organized around the premise of liberation theology, which fuses Marxism and Catholicism. Liberation theologians maintain that poverty and human suffering are in direct contradiction to Catholicism. CBCs organize educational, consciousness-raising groups to explore the causes of exploitation of the poor in order to develop concrete and permanent ways to challenge it. Their teachings are firmly grounded in the Bible and have proven both radical and highly inviting to women looking to register their social opposition.

Interestingly, many women who started their activism in Christian Base Communities went on to join guerrilla movements. In the past twenty or so years the numbers of women have increased significantly in Latin American guerrilla struggles. For example, approximately 30 percent of the Salvadoran guerrillas, who fought their war in the 1980s, were women, whereas during the Cuban insurrection in the 1950s, only 5 percent of the guerrillas were women (Shayne 2004). Political changes beyond the borders of Latin America, not the least of which was the rise of an international feminist movement, are in part responsible for creating a climate that facilitated such an increase (Luciak 2001, 2). Karen Kampwirth (2002) argues that the numbers have risen in part due to the prolonged nature of guerrilla struggle, changes in the economy (which have pushed women into the public sphere), and the increased participation of women in liberation theology. Women play a variety of roles in these movements, most of which run parallel to the gendered division of labor in nonrevolutionary society. For example, women cook and sew for guerrilla armies; they tend to the wounded as nurses and medics; they perform so-called logistical tasks like delivering messages and weapons; they operate rebel radio stations and propaganda campaigns. In other words, women play what are typically considered support roles. As the aforementioned numbers suggest in many cases women also serve as armed combatants and members of the urban underground movements but for the most part in rank-and-file rather than leadership positions. Similar to student movements, women who do rise into leadership positions are typically members of the upper/educated class and have the financial resources to circumvent rigid gender prescriptions that exclude women from political power, leftist or otherwise (Shayne 2004).

In short, Latin American women have participated in all sorts of leftist organizations. There has been a steady increase in the numbers of women activists yet women typically remain in support rather than leadership positions. Elevated social class has opened the leadership door to some women leftists while leaving it locked for others. Despite the often low sociopolitical value attached to women's political labor, their contributions are often fundamental to keeping movements alive. Indeed, the same can be said of women's unpaid and often invisible labor that ultimately keeps society functioning. In the next section I discuss how this division of labor played out in the solidarity movement, particularly given that Chilean exiles were organizing at the same time as their compañeras inside of Chile (the interior), where the aforementioned trends have been well documented. The obstacles and lower value attached to their political involvement have not soured all women on political participation, as their overwhelming leadership in civil society and even executive power demonstrates.

DIVISION OF LABOR IN THE SOLIDARITY MOVEMENT

No single position emerged about the roles and status of Chilean women in the solidarity movement. I asked all of the women what types of tasks they did as well as those they saw other women doing. There was an underlying message that many of the patterns present in mixed social movements in Latin America were also evident in the diaspora. Just as the exiles brought their party sectarianism with them so too did they bring a sexist division of political labor. I suspect that if the same sort of systematic studies of exile solidarity movements were conducted as those about the Left in Latin America the similarities or differences would be more obvious. However, given the lack of research, rather than offer a definitive conclusion, my goal here is to share the impressions of the women I interviewed about political labor and gender in the exiles' solidarity movement. Categorical conclusions aside, there was an implied consensus that women were more often found performing the emotional and cultural labor of the movement; or, as was the case inside Latin America, the seemingly less political tasks.

According to the interviewees women did a variety of tasks; everything from cooking *empanadas* for the *peñas*, to greeting exiles at the airport, to returning to Chile to join the underground movement against Pinochet. Carla Gutiérrez was active in the solidarity movement in Edmonton and then returned to Chile to fight with the Movement for the Revolutionary Left (MIR) in the underground armed movement against Pinochet before coming to Vancouver. Carla recalls:

> I think in any movement [there] are different levels of participation and all of them are very valid. Some women were ready to participate [by] making empanadas and some other women were happier doing a radio . . . show denouncing the government. Other women . . . talk[ed] to Canadian politicians [and] explain[ed] what was going on in Chile. And some other women went back to Chile and work[ed in the] underground against Pinochet. . . . [It was] very hard to do it because men are not willing to release that amount of power. But fortunately among the left-wing parties, and because of the values and ideas they are promoting, they cannot say no to us; they cannot push us aside. So we had experiences and opportunities to do all these things. . . . It has not been easy in a sense that [it] also conflict[ed] with our own nature.

Some women I spoke with felt they were on completely even footing with the men in the organizations, while others were too intimidated to even share their opinions at meetings and instead asked their husbands to speak on their behalf. For the most part, however, the women I spoke with fell some place in the middle of this continuum and as time passed many women found themselves getting more politically involved and less patient with sexist compañeros and/or partners.[2] Rebeca Jimenez recalls fondly:

> Actually, we were so wonderful; I learned so much and our [male] compañeros, they were very respectful. [The] decisions were respect[ed]. . . . [S]ay for instance, I was in charge of the activity [on a] particular night. . . . I took the responsibility. Every complaint, every decision, it needed to be made [by me] and they [the men] respected that.

Irene Policzer, supporter of the solidarity movement and leading figure in the feminist magazine *Aquelarre* collective, had different experiences in the movement than Rebeca. She recalls:

Even when there was a group having a meeting in somebody's living room and there would be a mix of men and women, discussing whatever you want, it tend[ed] to be men who did most of the talking and women would just [be] sitting [there]; even if you had a very strong opinion about something. . . . We did not have the preparation; we did not have the habit you know? . . . If I want[ed] to talk in a meeting I . . . would have the tendency to say: "Adam [her husband] this is what I want to say, you go and say it."

Patricia Gomberoff had a similar interpretation. She got involved with the solidarity movement early on and played what she considered to be support roles. She recalls:

Of course the ones who spoke were men. There were maybe two or three women [who] would speak and organize; . . . they were always in the shadow and men were the big ones. . . . Women participated yes, but not as many women [as] men participated in these activities. And the . . . women of those men that participated . . . were in their homes, or working . . . but they did not participate politically . . . You know, you just bring your baggage with you [laughs] and you try to do better and you do better but you cannot get rid of it. It will take many generations and then who knows?

Some women felt that men were in the kitchen just as much as women, while others remember women as the domestic leaders. Another interesting observation shared by some women is that they felt that if women did not take on leadership positions it was because they chose not to, not due to men dominating the organizations. Isabel López, the first Secretary of the Vancouver Chilean Association (recall, the first organization formed in Vancouver after the coup) and member of the all-woman singing group *Cormorán* recalls:

Everybody was participating in our group and we had other people that helped . . . we . . . got all the people involved . . . educated, I mean. We read a lot; we learned a lot; we discussed documents. We all had that opportunity, whoever wanted to. . . . Some women maybe just helped, they were not interested but they had the opportunity; some older women maybe just wanted to come and help just do the cooking or something but I think . . . everybody . . . had an opportunity to. It was endless though, endless meetings [laughs].

On the other hand, some women pointed out that women's personal domestic labor prevented them from fully participating and thus inevitably limited their political options. Lorena Jara arrived in Vancouver in 1977. She was active in the solidarity movement and to a lesser degree the feminist projects. She recalls about her compañeras with children:

I remember many times . . . raising the issue, "what time are we going to have the meetings?" And men would say, "oh let's have [it] at 7:00 at night." And I said "well you have no problem because you are not looking after your kids but there are women here who are single mothers; they have to think about daycare; can they do it? Or should we do it at their homes?" So that debate started happening, at least in the party I was working with. . . . [These] were issues that were often very important in my mind because women could not participate because they were mothers.

Perhaps most interesting about these seemingly conflicting opinions is that many of the women had multiple interpretations of the period. For example, in a general sense they would say that men were in the kitchen as much as women but then later recall the one or two exceptional men who did help out or, more typically, the man who refused to help because chopping onions for empanadas burned his eyes too much.

Despite these different recollections, there were several themes that came up in nearly every discussion of this topic: All of the roles were important, even the most visible women—with some exceptions—were not leaders per se, and no matter how involved women were in the movement they still were the main (and often sole) caretakers of their families. In other words, they worked extremely hard on paid, domestic, and political labor, in many cases with them entirely intertwined. Cecilia Tagle, activist in both the solidarity and feminist movements, explains:

[Women] multitasked; you have to be a mom, to [have] your dinner ready, and then go to the meeting. And make sure you do the poster, make sure you make decisions: what is going to be the program? And make sure that the kitchen schedule is taken care of; that is what I remember. Who is going to [work] the door? Who is going to . . . give [the] prizes? Who is going to do the introductions, the speech, who spoke better English?

Magaly Varas sees herself as supportive yet peripheral to the solidarity movement. She was a member of the musical group Cormorán and very active in the Aquelarre collective. Magaly recalls with frustration the fact that women always remained in charge of the home front: "We had to do the cooking and leave everything ready for our husband and then take the children with us to rehearsal. And clean the house; everything before, so, do our thing at home and then we could [go]."

Many women reflected on these years astounded with themselves; I often heard things like, "I do not know how we did it all." They also expressed a deep sense of pride when recalling their accomplishments. Cecila Tagle recalls:

Women I think in general, in my group that I worked with, were very well organized. The level of organization we had, Gosh! Unbelievable! *Un-be-liev-able*!
I do not know if we would ever do it again but we organized to send clothes
to Chile once and we had trucks coming from Alberta, you know those trailer
trucks full of clothes. We had the underground parking lot full of clothes and
we had [arranged] for free, two containers, in those days Canadian Pacific airline. . . . So we had, Oh my God! So much clothes! But the way we organized it
[all]: how to check all the clothes, how to put [them] together in boxes, and then
take [them] to the airport, and you would do this, and you would do that, bla . . .
bla . . . bla. [I]t was unbelievable *Un-be-liev-able*. (Cecilia's emphasis)

These sorts of tasks, the "social service work" of the movement, tended to
fall to the women. Recall, women met planes at the airport, delivered food to
the exiles, and provided leads regarding employment, schools, and health care.
For the most part, as a result of the tasks assigned to Chilean women vis-à-vis
the gendered division of labor, they were ultimately responsible for the well
being of the community and movement. In the next sections I look at emotional
and cultural labor and how women were involved in both of these.

EMOTIONS, GENDER, AND MOBILIZATION

As I discussed in Chapter Four, emotions in part explain the emergence of the
solidarity movement. In this section I will further explore the place of emotions in the solidarity movement, specifically focusing on how they shaped
the tactical decisions Chilean exiles made in organizing their movement. I
will also discuss how, for many of the women I spoke to, emotions played a
major role in sustaining the movement.

Moving Politically through the Stages of Exile

According to Ana Vásquez and Ana María Araujo (1990) the exile experience
passes through three distinct phases. Stage one involves "trauma and grieving," and the recovery from persecution, alienation, and disorientation, or
what they call "living with the suitcases packed" syndrome. This stage of exile is marked by much self-blame, believing, for example, "I am alive because
another died in my place" (in Wright 1995, 205). The second stage of exile,
according to Vásquez and Araujo, is "transculturation" (in Wright 1995, 205)
and includes adapting to the various ongoing obstacles presented by exile,
namely, living in a reduced social space, learning (or not) a new language,
and the forced reorganization of one's daily life routines. Together these experiences lead to "an exaggerated reverence for the symbols and rituals" (in

Wright 1995, 205) of the homeland. The third and final stage, "the collapse of myths," involves the adjustment to living in limbo and acknowledgment that there is no fixed or clear end of exile (in Wright 1995, 205). The women I spoke with all had experiences that fit into at least one of these stages.[3]

When we analyze some of the solidarity movement's tactics in conjunction with this emotional framework we can see these three stages at play. I argue that the first phase of exile, trauma and grieving, played a role in inspiring exiles to organize peñas as a place partially able to manage the pain and enable some sort of collective healing. This is not to say that the organizers consciously decided to organize peñas as a therapeutic tactic. As I explained in Chapter Four the peñas were largely the result of the shared political and cultural experiences the exiles had in Chile, namely the New Song movement. What I am suggesting is that the ability of peñas to lessen the emotional sting of exile for some of the attendees inspired them to keep coming back and helping out with everything from the exceedingly arduous task of making empanadas, to selling tickets, to performing on stage. In my focus group discussion with the members of the women's musical group Cormorán the women repeatedly expressed their self-amazement at how hard they worked during the solidarity movement. They all organized around the clock, had paid jobs, were raising children, often alone, and at different times were university students. But they still found/made time to start a band. This meant finding time to rehearse and tour, not just perform in Vancouver. But as Ana María explained, with clear consensus from the other three women: "It [Cormorán] was a therapy for us . . . we just enjoyed singing; we got a lot from each others' voices, the instruments, getting the music ready, [everything]."[4]

The second stage of exile, transculturation, leads the diasporic community to an extreme longing for national identity and rituals. Again, we see this in the peñas and other cultural events, especially those related to children. Children dancing traditional and indigenous Chilean dances very much conveyed a sort of national reverence and the peñas were the perfect space to express that sentiment. The emotional need to work through this second phase of exile and the longing for national identity and rituals propelled many women to work with the children of exiles to develop dance, theater, and singing groups. Nearly all of the women I interviewed were mothers. Many brought children with them, while others had their babies in Canada, or other stops along the way. Regardless of where their children were born, all of the women explained to me that keeping Chilean culture alive in their children's individual and collective psyche was of the utmost importance. Magaly Varas even bemoaned the movement's success in this respect as her adult daughter recently moved back to Chile with her husband and had their first baby. Magaly said she wished her daughter felt more Canadian rather than Chilean so she would not have left Vancouver in the first place; she longed to live near her daughter and granddaughter. In my discussion with these women it became clear that it was the mothers who took on the responsibility of cultivating the Chilean identity in their children. They were the ones who ran the Spanish schools, who taught the kids to sing, who sewed their traditional Chilean outfits for their dance performances, and so forth. In this sense, women became the mothers of the movement, safeguarding Chilean culture in a response to the larger exile community's "longing for national identity and rituals."

The national idealization fueled a commitment to attend the events that in part allowed the Chileans to at least mentally travel back to Chile. The music also served this purpose. Cecilia Tagle recalls attending a *Quilapayún* concert in Toronto:

> I remember the first time in Toronto when I went to see Quilapayún which was a [Chilean] group that was also in exile in Europe. During the whole concert we were all singing all of the songs and crying . . . it was great [that] we had the chance to [do that], because before having to come here and during Allende that was what we did; we were on the street singing with those groups, at all the marches in support of Allende, that is what it was, and the feeling was, "it is not just yourself, we are all in it [together]."

Later Cecilia explained how the peñas also bred that same energy:

> It was so beautiful; *so beautiful*. It lasted many years and in Vancouver, there were always peñas everywhere; everywhere and the same thing: somebody would have a guitar and start to sing songs of Silvio Rodríguez, Pablo Milanés, and Inti-Illimani. I think it was part of our healing process; I think so because that was the only collective expression that we had. (Cecilia's emphasis)

The music, childrens' performances, and the peñas more generally allowed the exiles to bring Chile to Vancouver, which was one of the most concrete and immediate ways to deal with the separation.

Finally, the third phase of exile, "the collapse of myths," where exiles acknowledge the permanence of exile, led to the erection of cultural institutions like the housing cooperative and *La Quena* Coffee House. In some cases, it was also this phase that propelled many women to finally learn English. For example, one woman explained to me that she did not learn English for several years after arriving because she always thought she would return to Chile. Once it became clear that she was in Vancouver indefinitely she decided it was time to learn English. The feminist magazine *Aquelarre* is another manifestation of acknowledging the permanence of exile. As we will see in the next chapter, the intellectual, cultural, and logistical effort women poured into that magazine was in part a way of culturally claiming some of the proverbial feminist airwaves. Acknowledging the permanence of exile was thus reflected in physical space, linguistic shifts, and cultural articulations. (I take up this permanence further in the book's conclusion.)

Shared Emotions

When Vásquez and Araujo's observations are combined with Jasper's concept of shared emotions (1997; 1998), and Taylor (1995) and Taylor and Whittier's (1995) about rituals, we get an even clearer sense of how such experiences and the emotions attached to them shaped the decisions exiles ultimately made regarding organizational strategies in their movement, namely the use of cultural production. This is particularly so with respect to stages one and two of exile: trauma and grieving, and transculturation, respectively.

As I discussed in the introduction of this book, Jasper argues that shared emotions are those that are collectively, consciously, and simultaneously held by a group. He maintains that experiencing emotions collectively allows a group to generate or articulate anger while creating a level of trust for certain individuals and institutions and mistrust toward others. Jasper asserts that the power of shared emotions results from collective expression and thus recognizing and proclaiming that they are shared (1997, 187). I argue that Jasper's conclusion regarding the mobilizing potential of emotions is similar to Vásquez and Araujo's characterization of the first phase of exile, trauma and grieving, and the way I have suggested it influenced the solidarity movement's cultural tactics. For example, the peñas provided the space for exiles to collectively experience and claim their anger while clearly fostering a level of trust. Because the emotions were shared, much of the pain was left unsaid, which in and of itself was healing for many exiles. This cyclic process encouraged exiles to keep attending and organizing the peñas. As Amanda explained about the peñas,

> I think at some level you need a connection. It was healing. . . . It was not "ok let's have a session here" but just the fact that you have belonging, that you go to a place where you do not need . . . to worry about your accent, [where you can say] . . . "ok, I can be myself now, I can cry if I want to, eat my empanadas, listen to the music and sing, I can get angry because I am not happy about what is going on in Chile."

Patricia Andrade conveyed the same sentiment regarding the strength she believed Chileans received from attending the peñas and being surrounded with hundreds of people who had experienced things entirely similar to each other:

> I think [this] is what it is: When you come . . . you find these people and they think like you, and all of the sudden they start talking, and he went through

exactly the same thing. Some of them left good jobs [or others] they did not work
ever. Others [now] have bad jobs, [and] they were displaced, just like me.

That is, the peñas allowed the exiles to collectively process the trauma of
exile and in part begin to heal from it.

Rituals

In the introduction to this book I also discussed Taylor and Whittier's assertion that rituals serve as cultural mechanisms in which subordinate groups
transform and express emotions that are the result of repression. Additionally,
they argue that rituals provide the space for actors to redefine dominant feelings to express more positive individual self-conceptions and group solidarity. Taylor and Whittier maintain that certain types of activities, for example,
films, plays, and musical events, enable rituals to be used as a way to express
emotion and communicate injustice (1995, 178). In other words, rituals help
transform potentially demobilizing and individually experienced emotions to
those replete with mobilizing potential.

Their arguments complement my interpretation of Vásquez and Araujo's
stage two of exile, or transculturation, and its impact on the solidarity movement. I argue that phase two was in large part responsible for the proliferation
of children's dance, theater, and singing groups. These are the types of rituals that Taylor and Whittier maintain have the potential to express injustice,
thereby transforming demobilizing emotions into proaction. Nina Vaca's
interpretation of the importance of the peñas and music to the movement
very much supports Taylor and Whittier's assertion: "They kept us closer
to our country, with the music, and the liberation of what you feel inside.
It was like [it all] came together [through] practicing our music; it was like
being in Chile." "Being in Chile" for Nina and, in her assessment, for other
exiles meant transforming the pain of separation and exile into a space, as she
says, of liberation and empowerment. These feelings sustained activists and
inspired them to keep coming back and volunteering their time to the events.
In sum, emotions not only help explain why the solidarity movement came
about—recall moral shocks (Jasper and Poulsen 1995; Jasper 1997; 1998)
moral outrage (Nepstad and Smith 2001), and pride and pleasure (Wood
2001)—but also why activists chose the tactics they did and were able to
sustain their movement through very difficult times.

Emotional Service and Sustenance

For many of the movement's participants, especially the women I spoke to,
the emotional component was in some senses palpable. In my estimation

emotions in part suggest some reasons for women's sustained involvement in the movement even when structural and social barriers remained formidable. I do not intend to suggest that women's convictions were in any way less political than their male compañeros, but rather wish to offer some explanation for the place of emotions and gender in this culturally rooted movement. First, for some women, emotions served as a pull factor into the movement. As I explained, most of the women I interviewed were eventually single mothers and thus worked in and outside of the home with very little, if any, time to get involved in politics. The lack of time, however, did not minimize their will to protest or to join the movement. In some cases, women got involved with the peñas as a way to meet the emotional needs of their children and, by extension, themselves.

The extended family is tremendously important in Chilean culture. However, exile split families, in some cases permanently. Overnight women lost their support network of other women relatives, often their own mothers, and were forced to raise their children alone (often even when still married) in an entirely foreign atmosphere. This shift in and of itself, trauma of exile aside, was exceedingly difficult for many of the women exiles. (See also Kay 1987, Chapter Six, for a similar discussion.) As a result many women turned to the movement, particularly the peñas and other cultural events, to keep their children submerged in Chilean culture and provide a surrogate extended family. Additionally, the nature of the peñas allowed women to remain active in politics while also meeting their families' needs. That is, children were entirely welcome at the peñas, indeed even literally took center stage. As a result, women could attend, know their children were fed and entertained, while also sustaining relationships with other Chilean children and adults who would ultimately serve the place of their extended families who either remained in Chile or ended up in different parts of the world.

Additionally, I argue that emotions and gender played a role in the movement's commitment to social services. Recall that women were instrumental in making sure that newly arriving refugees had the basic social services and emotional support they were capable of providing. Similarly, women exiles felt a need to do whatever they could for the Chileans who remained in the interior, including collecting and delivering truckloads of clothes. Rather than feel paralyzed by the reality of material and psychological deprivation, women exiles transformed that frustration into arranging for basic necessities. Their actions served in part to sustain the exile community in Vancouver in a literal sense while also feeding the political spirit of older and newer members alike. Additionally, organizing to provide clothes and the like for Chileans in the interior created a sense of accomplishment rather than paralysis, which is crucial in sustaining the political will of individuals and communities to organize.

Does all of this then suggest that women are born more emotional than men and this is why they perform these sorts of political tasks? No. We know that the social construction of gender approach argues, simply put, that males and females learn to be men and women, that biology only effects gendered expectations, and it does not determine behavior. Thus, the social characteristics we typically associate with boys/men and girls/women are acquired and sustained over time through one's interactions with and responses to the micro and macro social world. We might also recall that all social structures help reinforce the status-quo assumptions about appropriate behavior for men and women. Social movements, like all structures, have the potential to mandate and reinforce gendered behavior (Lorber 1994). Similarly, as we have seen, the patriarchal division of leftist labor tends to place women activists in the so-called support and thus seemingly less important roles. In the case of the solidarity movement, providing social services, cooking at peñas, and teaching children to sing and dance were seen by some as less political than, say, organizing a boycott. Though women participated in those sorts of campaigns as well, my research suggests that women dominated these more "emotional" projects rather than the so-called political ones. What this suggests, as does the research on the leftist division of labor in Latin America, is that what we consider "doing politics" needs to be expanded to properly account for women's political contributions to social movements such as this one. I turn now to the importance of culture to the solidarity movement and the place of women in this realm.

GENDER, CULTURE, AND THE SOLIDARITY MOVEMENT

In this section I take a closer look at the relationship between culture and resistance in the solidarity movement. Specifically: What is the political significance of culture to the solidarity movement and how do Chilean women exiles embody the political intersection of gender, culture, and resistance? As I discussed in the book's introduction, I work from Jofré's conception of culture. In short, he argues that culture "is the whole set of signifying practices and products that convey meaning to a total society" (1989, 71) while also serving as the "collective self of a community" (1989, 70). Bearing this definition in mind, I use the solidarity movement to help demonstrate Duncombe's (2002) three assertions about the political place of culture in social movements: First, cultural events serve as "free-spaces"; next, cultural events serve as "first-steps" to other forms of political activism; and finally, cultural events and material culture are in and of themselves forms of resistance. The discussion that follows is meant to demonstrate that the women were fundamental in transforming culture from "signifying practices and products" into political defiance of Pinochet.

Political Culture and Free Spaces

Duncombe argues that political culture has the potential to create a "free space" to generate ideas and practices. Free spaces, as Polletta suggests, "seem to provide [an] institutional anchor for the cultural challenge that explodes structural arrangements" (1999, 1). That is, free spaces provide alternative spaces for movements to organize, strategize, and foster networks among participants. Conceptually, the notion of free spaces points to the inherent strength in subaltern groups to form and maintain identities that engender mobilization (Polletta 1999, 3). In my estimation the social movement theory concept of free space is more limiting than I interpret Duncombe's to be.[5] That is, I argue a free space in the solidarity movement was one where the actors felt politically, emotionally, and psychologically safe to advance their agenda of forcing Pinochet from power.

Why is "safety" necessary if the Chileans were legally in Canada and thousands, and thousands of miles from Pinochet and his military? Was not the entire nation of Canada a safe space? Ana María Quiroz's story about temporarily losing her Chilean citizenship as a result of her political activities in Canada implies that the junta was indeed watching the activists. (See Chapter Four.) Certainly the exiles did not live in the same sort of fear that their compañeros and compañeras in Chile did but they did not feel entirely safe either. This was particularly true for those Chileans who experienced repression while in Chile before arriving in Canada. For example, Nina Vaca explained that her now-ex-husband was captured and held as a political prisoner not long after the coup. He was eventually released and confined to house arrest for a year. Throughout that year she recalled that the military would pound on their door in the middle of the night demanding her ex-husband "confess." They would apprehend him and he would disappear for a few days at a time, come back, skinny, and visibly tortured. Arriving in Canada did not erase those experiences and that deeply imbedded sense of insecurity. Nina and her family lived in Pinochet's Chile for five years, with this sort of regular terror, before she came to Canada. Intellectually she knew she was safe once she got to Canada but she explained that psychologically "it takes about one year to get used to not having the door [pounded on at] 3:00 in the morning. Sometimes I felt like it was going to happen . . . [but] of course we were protected."

Additionally, from the perspective of the activists, it was not only their safety at stake but that of their families and compañeros in Chile. I met many activists who used pseudonyms during the dictatorship while in Canada. As we know, there was a lot of communication back and forth between the exile communities and Chileans in the interior. Each group needed to keep the other abreast of political strategies and the like. But phones were tapped and mail often opened so both in and outside of Chile activists created codes to communicate with one another while offering as little detail as possible. Again, no one would argue that the Chileans in Canada faced daily threats comparable to those in Chile but for some they never felt entirely safe either. Indeed, three women I interviewed were left with such a permanent state of insecurity they were not comfortable using their real names when interviewed for this project. This was particularly the case for those who went back to Chile to work with the resistance movement before the dictatorship ended. Thus, real or imagined fears were often temporarily appeased when Chileans felt protected by the cultural events and institutions that made up their movement. I argue that both the peñas and the Chilean housing co-op served as free and safe spaces. In addition to providing psychological safety, both venues were entirely fertile for the ongoing proliferation of progressive ideas and agendas. The peñas and co-op served as the physical political heart and soul of the movement and embodied these free spaces.

Cultural Events as Step One

Duncombe and other social movement theorists further assert that cultural events have the potential to serve as the first step in more explicit political activity. That is, cultural events actually serve as a method for mobilizing protest (Duncombe 2002; Eyerman and Jamison 1998; Garofalo 1992; Denisoff 1983; Pratt 1992). Eyerman (2002) makes a similar argument using music as an example. He maintains that recordings provide a listener the "initial psychological and social contact with a wider group" which allows for "participation without apparent commitment" (2002, 450). Eyerman's data suggests that individual listeners were later compelled to attend concerts by the same performers, which in turn fostered "emotional attachment and collective identity formation" (2002, 450) to a given cause. My analysis of the solidarity movement supports his contention. This process was noticeable with respect to recruitment of activists. For example, an exile may see a flyer for a movie or peña and attend knowing very little about the exile community in Vancouver. More established organizers looked for these newer attendees and later recruited them to become active players in the movement. For example, Magaly Varas explained that while in Chile she was not very political or progressive. Once in Vancouver she and her now-ex-husband saw a flyer for a Chilean film scheduled to be shown on the first anniversary of the coup. She explained: "So we went and we met all these Chilean people we did not know they were here, [we had] no idea, . . . no idea there was a movement here." From that film she and her ex-husband were then invited to a peña, and from there Magaly was recruited as a regular supporter of the movement. Eventually she joined Cormorán and became a very active supporter of the movement. In other words, the cultural events that formed the foundation of the movement lent themselves to networking and recruiting potential activists like Magaly.

Additionally, the peñas and music served to motivate and inspire non-Chileans, namely Canadians, to demonstrate their solidarity with the exiles by pressuring their own government to denounce the Pinochet dictatorship. In the words of one Canadian journalist who saw Cormorán perform at a Canadian folk music festival: "It was a moving performance, fervid, passionately patriotic. They struck an especially patriotic chord amongst the women of the audience with their strength and dignity" (Jardine 1976, 5).[6] In this case, the exiles reached out to Canadians through music rather than political speeches and the like. They translated all of their songs and offered the historical context necessary but the Canadians in the audience likely went to the festival for music not politics. From the journalist's perspective it sounds as if she was pleasantly surprised and moved when she ultimately received both. Certainly working with the support of Canadian citizens was fundamental to offering institutional power to the movement. Sympathetic Canadians served as conduits between exiles and elected Canadians. Exiles and Canadian activists together pressured the Canadian government to join them in denouncing Pinochet's assault on human rights, which added further credibility to their movement.

The peñas and the co-op also served as places where the children of exiles acquired their political literacy by learning radical political ideology in an accessible manner, namely through cultural representation. Many children who grew up in that atmosphere became politically active in the solidarity movement to varying degrees. I spoke to several who started by performing in the youth dance troupes at the co-op and peñas and later became the architects of activities like the label sabotage, which was an important component to the wine boycotts. Cecilia Tagle explained that her daughter grew up around political meetings and later, instead of playing with dolls as is typical for girls her age, she and her friends pretended to have similar meetings and sat in circles with their pads of paper and pens in hand. At the time of our interview her daughter was thirty-one and a social activist with the Latin American community in Vancouver. Carmen Aguirre, another daughter of a political leader in the movement, went even further; after she graduated from high school in Vancouver she went to South America to join the armed resistance movement, which at that time was plotting to assassinate Pinochet (see appendix). Certainly, many factors encouraged these young women to make their respective decisions, not just political exposure at peñas and the co-op, but I argue that communicating political ideology through cultural events made it significantly less alienating for the noninitiated, young, old, Chilean, or non-Chilean alike.[7] In other words, for some the cultural events served as the first step in what became long-term and often quite militant political commitments.

Culture as Resistance

Finally, Duncombe argues, and this relates to what I argued in the book's introduction regarding Jofré's and Gramsci's ideas about the inherent political nature of culture, cultural production in and of itself may actually serve as political resistance. If we understand politics as another form of cultural discourse, radical cultural production also reflects politics. I argue that the peñas, the music, artwork, fiction, poetry, dance performances, the arpilleras, and various other forms of cultural production most certainly served as resistance.

In a quite literal sense the goal of Pinochet was to physically, politically, and permanently eliminate the Left. The junta disappeared leftists; they declared their organizations and political parties illegal; they murdered and tortured their members in order to destroy their will to organize and intimidate others from following suit. Recall, according to Stern a reasonable estimate for deaths and disappearances during the dictatorship is 3,500–4,500, with political detentions between 150,000–200,000, and torture estimates surpassing 100,000. And, in the case of the exiles, the junta kicked hundreds of thousands of them out of their country. As a result, any proclamation that the Left was alive, either in or outside of Chile, that the dictatorship was unsuccessful in eliminating it, was a statement of defiance and even triumph. Landolt and Goldring make a similar argument: "If Pinochet's project was to rid the country of its leftist history, then Chilean exiles had not only to safeguard this history but had to forever plan to re-establish that institutional and historical presence in their country of origin" (2006, 21). In other words, survival was resistance and leftist cultural artifacts were concrete representations of that survival.

Take the case of the arpilleras. As we know, the arpilleras were made by women in Santiago with an express purpose of articulating life under the dictatorship. The women made these fully intending to smuggle them out of Chile to serve as a tool to denounce Pinochet and garner material support for the opposition within the country. The exiles played a central role in disseminating the arpilleras outside of Chile. The fact that the junta regularly confiscated arpilleras at airports and from the mail is an indication that this tactic was a threat to the dictatorship. Indeed, when Pinochet banished the exiles he expected their "subversive" activities would cease and no longer play a role in the politics of the country. He could not have been more wrong and the material culture created and distributed in the diaspora was a concrete reminder of his gross political miscalculation. Furthermore, the cultural productions and events of the solidarity movement served to feed the spirit of the Left, thus keeping it alive, which further undermined the dictatorship's goal of elimination.

CULTURAL AMBASSADORS AND REPRODUCERS

In my estimation Chilean women exiles enabled and represented the political intersection of culture and resistance in the solidarity movement. How did this happen? First, women offered logistical contributions toward articulating resistance vis-à-vis culture. That is, in a very basic sense we know that women were central in organizing the peñas, which served as the free spaces, and political cultural centers of the movement. They did everything from chop the onions, to translate the songs, to publicize the events, to work the door. As I have suggested, much of what women did for the peñas was mandated by the gendered division of labor and further motivated by an emotional need to create extended families and the like. However, reasons aside, women were ultimately fundamental to creating these cultural outlets that served as free spaces that protected and cultivated further political action. In other words, arguably the peñas could not have happened without women's contributions and without the peñas the solidarity movement would have lacked what some experienced as its political and cultural anchor. Second, women further contributed to fusing culture with resistance by serving as cultural ambassadors of the movement. That is, women formed their own folk music group, Cormorán, and sang at any event and folk music festival that made room for them. The exiles' compañeras inside of Chile made the arpilleras for the exiles, in many cases women, to smuggle out and circulate among the international community. Chilean women exiles organized exhibits of them in Canada, showcasing a political art designed specifically to convey resistance. Finally, women fused cultural expression with political resistance by teaching their children the music, dance, and folklore of Chileans in the interior. That is, as the mothers in and of the movement, women implicitly took the responsibility for keeping the collective identity of the exile community alive by ensuring their children's attachment to and promotion of Chilean culture.

Chilean exiles are not the only women activists to consciously and unconsciously mobilize culture in this manner to advance an agenda of political resistance. Bahati Kuumba documents similar patterns in her study of women's participation in the U.S. civil rights and South African anti-apartheid movements (2001). She explains how activists in the anti-apartheid and civil rights movements used alternative educational venues as consciousness-raising centers for their children. In South Africa they were even called "culture clubs." The gendered division of labor, leftist or otherwise, places women in the role of educators. As a result, women were typically the ones in the position to teach the youth about political issues and events important to their respective communities. In the case of the exiles, these alternative educational venues were the cultural stages in the peñas and co-op.[8] Mothers taught their children Chilean history through dance, music, and theater. Additionally, and similar to what I argued above, Kuumba maintains that "the very maintenance of a particular 'way of life' in face of attempted cultural genocide and assimilation is, in and of itself, resistance" (2001, 112). She goes on to explain how South African and African diaspora women played the role of the cultural carriers of their communities vis-à-vis producing traditional products, beer in the case of South Africa and music in the U.S. South, both of which articulated and represented resistance in these particular historical moments. The Chilean exiles were not threatened with an ethnocultural genocide in the same manner as Black South Africans or African Americans in the U.S. but the attempt to wipe out the Left was far reaching in its own political context. For Pinochet, leftists were an ethnicity of sorts. In a genocidal sense, they were a marginalized group targeted for extermination, and his goal was absolutely to eliminate them from Chile's sociocultural mosaic. Women in all three cases were instrumental in thwarting the process of political or ethnic genocide by creating and circulating cultural manifestations of their racial, ethnic, and/or political communities. In other words, as cultural educators and ambassadors, Chilean women produced, reproduced, and represented the resistance to the dictatorship that the exiles were collectively attempting to communicate.

CONCLUSION

In sum, gender, emotions, and culture were all central to the solidarity movement. In the last chapter I argued that emotions were key in catalyzing the movement in the first place and played a special role in recruiting women. I also argued that leftist cultural histories were key to the movement's emergence. Here I have attempted to take that argument a bit further by demonstrating that emotions were in part responsible for Chileans anchoring their main tactics in the cultural realm. In part, the exiles organized things like peñas and started musical bands as a way to lessen their community's pain. We also saw that Chileans' collective longing for their homeland propelled them, especially women, to teach their children traditional Chilean dances and songs. Emotions also organizationally influenced the movement by pushing women to organize social services for newly arriving Chileans. Woven throughout all of this was the unwavering sense that emotions sustained women's participation in the movement. The events, the children, the home-delivered food, and the impromptu extended family that resulted from all of this sustained women's spirits in the face of deep psychological obstacles.

I have also attempted to demonstrate that the cultural events and productions, born of emotions and history, were politically powerful in their ability to nurture the Chilean political and personal spirit, recruit new members, and exemplify resistance in and of themselves. The peñas and the like created the free spaces that allowed Chileans to charge their political batteries while creating a safety that was surprisingly absent. We also saw that the cultural events were politically important for their ability to recruit new activists—Chileans and non-Chileans alike. Finally, I argued that the cultural productions—be it children's dance, arpilleras, music, or peñas—were a form of political resistance to the dictatorship as they boldly asserted to Pinochet that the Left was indeed still alive and even thriving. Women's efforts in all of this were the result of both the traditional gendered division of labor as well as their personal and political aspirations. Their contributions large and small were all fundamental to sustaining the spirit of the movement and its children. In the next chapter I look at the more explicit relationship between gender and politics through the case of exile feminism.

NOTES

1. The current president of Argentina, Cristina Fernández de Kirchner, is also a woman but she is not considered a leftist.

2. See Kay (1987, Chapter Six), where she discusses similar trends in the Scottish manifestation of the solidarity movement. In Kay's study she explicitly talked to the women she interviewed about things like divorce and concluded that many marriages end as a result of women becoming much less tolerant of sexism once they arrived in Great Britain. Diana Kay, (1987), *Chileans in Exile: Private Struggles, Public Lives* (Wolfeboro, N.H.: Longwood Academic). As I have mentioned, most of the women I interviewed have long since divorced their husbands and, though we rarely discussed it directly, it was implied that many left them due to their sexism.

3. See Marcela Cornejo, (2008), "Political Exile and the Construction of Identity: A Life Stories Approach," *Journal of Community & Applied Social Psychology* 18(4): 333–48, for a psychological analysis of exiles' experiences.

4. Patricia Chuchryk identifies a similar process with the Association of the Relatives of the Detained and Disappeared, which operated in Chile during these same years. In 1978 fourteen members of the Association formed a folk group that was designed in part to articulate protest but also to provide therapy for its members. Patricia Chuchryk, (1989), "Subversive Mothers: The Women's Opposition to the Military Regime in Chile," in *Surviving Beyond Fear: Women, Children and Human Rights in Latin America*, ed. Marjorie Agosín (New York: White Pine Press), 91.

5. See Franesca Polletta, (1999), "'Free Spaces' in Collective Action," *Theory and Society* 28(1): 1–38, for further details.

6. Margaret Power reports a journalist having a similar response, albeit more cynical, to a concert by Chileans in the United States: "[T]he music was so powerful, and the program so well done, that the somewhat jaded Chicago Sun-Times reporter who covered it noted, 'the event was disconcertingly well organized for a political affair,'" quoted in Margaret Power, (2009 [forthcoming]), "The U.S. Movement in Solidarity with Chile in the 1970s," *Latin American Perspectives.*

7. It was definitely not the case that all children of exiles entered politics as a result of being exposed to the Left through their parents. In some cases all of the political activity alienated exiles' children from politics. Take the example of Alejandra Aguirre, Carmen Aguirre's sister. Both are Carmen Rodríguez's daughters and Carmen was extremely active in the solidarity and feminist movements. She went to South America with her young children to work with the armed movement against Pinochet (see Chapter Two). Alejandra remains angry with her mother for risking her and her sister and brother's lives in the name of the movement. Overall, her parents' organizing eventually pushed Alejandra away from politics. She explained to me:

> I guess in a way, I am just trying to be . . . selfish. . . . I am not involved in any [politics]. . . . I sponsor a child, in Chile actually. We used to sponsor two, one in India and one in [Chile]. . . . I just do not want to know any more; I am just tired of . . . seeing. . . . [W]e would go to films . . . and . . . I remember my mom coming up to us and [saying] 'Oh well, you guys better go outside because this is not appropriate for kids.' You know, after we had already seen it.

Both Alejandra and her sister Carmen's testimonies are in the appendix.

8. See Carolina Palacios, (2009), "Social Movements as Learning Sites: Knowledge Production, Chilean Exiles and the Solidarity Movement" (Ph.D. diss., The University of British Columbia, work in progress), for a detailed discussion of collective learning practices, knowledge production, and the educational role of the solidarity movement in Vancouver.

Chapter Six

Exile and Feminism

Chilean women are tremendous; you have to tie them down to keep them
from organizing.

— María Elena Carrera (quoted in Wright and Oñate 1998, 159)

INTRODUCTION

Feminists look at the world through gendered lenses. Some argue that the
gendered division of labor (discussed in the last chapter) unfairly positions
women with respect to men in cultural, political, and social spaces. As I demonstrated in the last chapter, if a woman's work day has no clear beginning
or end then she has significantly less time to invest in anything else, be it
painting, political mobilization, or a career. For some feminists, this assumed
and imposed division of labor gives men a categorical advantage over women
and is the primary explanation for men and women's power differential in
any given situation or society. Some feminists are concerned with systems of
power like classism, heterosexism, racism, and xenophobia, particularly when
they intersect with sexism. They might ask, for example: how are social structures that privilege whiteness and heterosexuality experienced more acutely
by women? Or, what similarities do racist and sexist institutions share, and
how might challenging racism inherently undermine sexism and vice versa?
Some feminists are most concerned with women's personal and physical autonomy, meaning a woman must have the final say about and legal protection
for her own reproductive and sexual decisions. Or, that all women have an
inalienable right to live free from violence, and if it does occur, they can be
confident that perpetrators will be criminally punished. Some feminists might

be most concerned with things like collective autonomy or equal representation in political and educational institutions. In short, feminists are concerned with power inequities in all social spheres—from their own bodies to institutional politics—and strive for the full and equal participation of all women, in all sociopolitical and economic structures. That said, there is no universal definition of feminism nor does fighting for women's rights automatically translate to being called a feminist. When I conduct my own research I attempt to never impose these or any other definitions of feminism upon the women I interview. Rather, the women work from their own interpretations, definitions, histories, and experiences, which ultimately impact the way I understand and expand my own definitions of feminism.

Chilean women exiles' feminist and women-focused activism followed a similar historical trajectory to their *compañeras* inside of Chile (the interior). In both cases women started organizing in women-only spaces during the revolutionary and anti-dictatorship movements and as those movements wound down their efforts became more explicitly feminist. In this chapter I look at the projects of Chilean exile feminists in Vancouver organized both during and after the Pinochet dictatorship. I begin with a brief overview of Latin American and transnational feminisms. Latin American women and their compañeras around the globe have been organizing for women's rights for decades and this section is meant to provide context for understanding Vancouver's exile feminist movement. Next, I share some of the exiles' reflections on feminism, particularly how they came to be (or not be) feminists. This section is meant to further introduce the reader to the exiles and provide definitions based on their own specific memories and experiences. The majority of this chapter focuses on the specific projects organized by exile feminists and their supporters in Vancouver: Conferences, International Women's Day celebrations, and their flagship project, the magazine *Aquelarre*.

LATIN AMERICAN AND TRANSNATIONAL FEMINISMS

Regional Coordination

Latin American women have long been competent activists with respect to moving their agendas into regional and national arenas, as evidenced by their contributions to the inter-American conferences held between 1880 and 1948 (Miller 1990, 11). Since 1981, this regional coordination has been virtually institutionalized with the birth of the first Latin American Feminist *Encuentro*[1] (Alvarez et al., 2003; Sternbach et al., 1992). The Encuentros began in July of 1981, with two hundred women from fifty organizations convening in Bogotá, Colombia. For the past two and a half decades women attendees have represented a plethora of types of organizations: women union activists, guerrillas/ex-guerrillas, lesbians, women of color, indigenous women, leftist party members, religious organizations, members of autonomous feminist organizations, nongovernmental organizations (NGOs), and human rights organizations.

According to Alvarez and colleagues these meetings have inspired "numerous intraregional issue- and identity-specific networks as well as advocacy coalitions on a range of issues such as women's health and sexual and reproductive rights, violence against women, and women's political representation" (2003, 539). Such networks were often the result of contentious and prolonged debates. For example, one of the earlier conflicts was the tension between women who identify as *políticas* (women of leftist parties) and the *feministas* (feminists). Políticas argue that the goal of women's liberation can only be achieved by women working within their leftist parties. Feministas on the other hand argue that the parties are too restrictive with respect to the realization of feminist goals and even politically hostile to women, therefore autonomous organizations are necessary. Put another way, some women, the políticas, felt the need to prioritize national liberation, which for them inherently included women's rights. While others, the feministas, argued women need to fight for their rights independent of national liberation movements to guarantee their goals are not trumped by the so-called "real" revolution. Many women, however, took another approach by embracing what they call *doble militancia* (double militancy), thereby prioritizing neither their commitments to feminism nor their leftist parties. These debates were largely the result of women participating in left politics in the 1980s when revolutionary movements consumed the region. Once the revolutionary movements ceased and transitions to democracy were firmly underway the division shifted to a split between institutional and autonomous feminists. Institutional feminists believe that women should work within the new democratic structures, particularly since many of them were the result of women's efforts during the dictatorships and revolutionary movements. Autonomous feminists, on the other hand, are unsatisfied with the new governments and their lack of commitment to women's demands; they maintain that feminists need to carve out a space in civil society separate from the government (Alvarez et al., 2003).

Though the demographics of the attendees have diversified significantly, conflicts surrounding the hegemony of white/*mestiza*, heterosexual, middle-class, and Spanish-speaking women continue to percolate. Despite these conflicts, the exchange of, and exposure to each other's revolutionary, feminist, and other political experiences have served to strengthen regional and local feminisms. This is in part due to women moving between the different positions as political and economic factors shifted, and their personal lives, commitments, and professional paths unfolded.

Since the 1980s most Latin American and Caribbean feminist dialogue has occurred in the Encuentros. Interestingly, it has only been recently that Latinas outside of Latin America began participating in these meetings (Alvarez et al. 2003, 569). However, some exile feminists were aware of the Encuentros, though my sense is few attended them. Issue 6 (October/ November/December 1990) of *Aquelarre* includes an article by Carmen Rodríguez, one of the founders of the magazine and leaders of the feminist movement in Vancouver. It is titled "Fifth Feminist Conference of Latin America and the Caribbean: A Bet on the Future," and is about the 1990 gathering in San Bernardo, Argentina. The article definitely reads as though Carmen attended the conference, though we never discussed it. In the article Carmen speaks to the importance of the conferences in articulating and developing transnational feminist action and analyses:

> At times, it was difficult and chaotic, but the event succeeded in providing feminists from all over the continent with a space for reflection, communication, debate and networking. Latin American and Caribbean women living in the United States, Canada and Europe were also present, as well as many nationals from those countries. . . . One thing became clear: the feminist movement is growing within broad and diverse parameters. However, there is still a long way to go in order to successfully resolve the problem of dispersion. . . . Latin American and Caribbean women have been giving birth to important work which has contributed to bettering the life conditions of thousands of women in the continent. . . . Ten years of feminist conferences have contributed and will continue to contribute to the articulation of this movement (1990, 34).

Carmen's reflections on the 1990 conference speak to the tensions and successes of such a monumental event. The Canadian equivalent of the Encuentros were similarly replete with friction and accomplishments, as I will discuss below.

Transnational Coordination

Just as Latin American women have been regionally coordinated for some time now, feminist and women's movements more broadly have been transnational in focus long before the terms "transnational" and "globalization" became standard academic discourse (see also Ferree and Mueller 2004, 584–87). For example, the end of the nineteenth and beginning of the twentieth centuries bore witness to three major transnational women's organizations: the International Council of Women, the International Woman Suffrage Alliance (later International Alliance of Women), and the Women's International League for Peace and Freedom (Rupp 1997; Rupp and Taylor 1999).[2] Latin American feminisms regionally, and transnational feminisms globally, experienced a boom in the 1970s and 1980s due in part to the United Nations declaration of the Decade for Women from 1975 to 1985. The goals for the decade included: "the eradication of underdevelopment, the quest for peace, and the pursuit of equality for women in all forms of political, economic, and social life" (Çagatay, Grown, Santiago 1986, 401). In 1975 and 1980 the United Nations hosted two world congresses on women, in Mexico City and Copenhagen, respectively. These first two conferences were quite contentious, particularly with splits between women of the global South (Third World) and global North (First World) with respect to what "real" feminist agendas include. Third World women were far more inclined to include issues of poverty and war, for example, in their feminist agendas, whereas First World women felt reproductive rights and violence against women should be prioritized. We will see later in this chapter that exile feminists represent a unique convergence of these two different positions. For many women the divisions resulted in political demobilization rather than feminist empowerment.

The third conference in Nairobi, Kenya, in 1985 was a pivotal point in the decade (Çagatay, Grown, Santiago 1986; Moghadam 2005; Basu 1995). The conference was the largest world gathering of women ever, with an estimated 13,500 attendees, lasting ten days. Agendas were packed with intense dialogue, cultural events, and celebration. Çagatay, Grown, and Santiago argue that the Nairobi conference was significantly more productive than the prior two. The first reason Nairobi was less divisive than the prior, particularly Copenhagen, is due to the fact that women were determined not to repeat the same mistakes and prepared intensively for the conference. For example, many feminists of the North consciously incorporated an integrative analysis to sexism, which included race, class, and nation. In other words, they started to unpack the ways women experience racism, classism, and imperialism differently than men. Northern feminists also began to understand that poverty and war are rampant problems in the Third World (particularly in the 1980s) and are intimately connected to Southern women's secondary social and political status. Working from this broadened point of departure allowed women from the North to understand how Third World women's battles for peace and economic survival must unequivocally be part of any feminist agenda. Additionally, the conference was held in an African nation, which gave many First World women the chance to observe first hand, and often for the first time, the social and economic conditions under which much of the world's women live. Finally, by 1985 (the beginning of Ronald Reagan's second term) social, political, and economic conditions in the world were seriously deteriorating, so much so that First World women, particularly from the United States, were feeling the negative effects of military spending taking precedence over social spending. As a result, many women in the United States were achieving a sense of solidarity with women in the global South in a way no one could have anticipated (Çagatay, Grown, Santiago 1986, 403–4). Despite the increased harmony, Çagatay, Grown, and Santiago do not suggest that the meeting was tension free. Indeed, heated debate is inevitable when nearly 14,000 political activists join forces in an attempt to define the most urgent issues for over half of the world's people.

Needless to say, the ambitious goals of feminists and women-centered activists worldwide were not all realized by the end of the UN-sponsored decade. Not surprisingly, transnational networks persist and continue to grow stronger. Ten years later the UN sponsored another world conference on women, this time in Beijing, China. A nongovernmental forum preceded the main conference and lasted nine days. There were approximately 30,000 attendees, general public and press combined. The governmental forum was eleven days long with representatives of 189 governments in attendance. These UN-sponsored gatherings were by far the biggest to date.

As of late, more and more attention has been given to transnational feminisms (e.g., Ferree and Tripp 2006; Moghadam 2005; Naples and Desai 2002). In one of the most recent and comprehensive studies of transnational feminism, Valentine Moghadam (2005) argues that globalization, particularly the neoliberal mantra of minimal state-provided social services, balanced budgets, and restrictive monetary policies, is one leading cause of the recent boom in transnational feminist networks.[3] There is a rapidly growing global consensus, at least among feminists, that the current period of globalization has intensified the feminization of poverty, increased women's paid and unpaid workloads, and thus exacerbated women's subordinate social, economic, and political status. In other words, poverty remains and is becoming a more urgent feminist issue worldwide. Moghadam also argues that the rise of religious fundamentalism, namely Islam in Muslim countries and Hindu in India, is in part responsible for an increase in transnational feminist organizing. As these fundamentalist movements gained in power, they pressured governments to mandate traditional patriarchal norms, which thus tightened controls over women. These developments disturbed and thus mobilized feminists in both the North and South. Finally, developments in information and communication exchange have also played a pivotal role in allowing feminists to organize transnationally. As we will see when we analyze the case of Chilean exile feminism in the diaspora, Moghadam's arguments are partially applicable. Chilean exiles started organizing as feminists at the very beginning of the phase that Moghadam focuses upon in her analysis. They certainly responded to the feminization of poverty in and outside of Latin America, and arguably were in part motivated to mobilize because of it. And even without the internet, compounded by the lack of political freedom within Chile, they were able to stay remarkably networked. For the most part, Chilean exiles in Canada were outside of transnational feminist networks, yet the aforementioned histories and developments help us understand the regional and global political contexts in which exile feminism in Vancouver emerged.

Chilean feminists in the diaspora fit into the two aforementioned categories, "Latin American" and "transnational" feminists. Chilean exile feminists are Latin American and, as we will see, their activities are inherently transnational since their projects were the quintessential embodiment of transnationalism, individuals of one national heritage living in another nation state. This later point is particularly true when we think about the period when feminist mobilization started in the Chilean diaspora. Much of their activities began in the mid- to late-1980s. (The same time feminist activism was flourishing in Chile and globally.) By that point, many exiles had been in Canada for at least ten years, which meant they were fluent in English and their level of comfort with all things and people Canadian was quite established. As a result, their dual, or transnational identity was significantly pronounced once feminists started organizing in the diaspora.

However, regardless of how well these labels fit Chilean exile feminists, they are also wholly inadequate. "Latin American feminists" generally refers to Latinas residing in Latin America, clearly not the case of exiles. Additionally, "transnational" feminist movements suggest movements whose participants, agendas, and tactics cross national borders. Specifically, Valentine Moghadam defines transnational feminist networks as "structures organized above the national level that unite women from three or more countries around a common agenda" (2005, 4). Chilean feminists in exile were connected to issues and feminists in Latin America but the transnational component of their movement was, in a sense, more coincidental than intentional. That is, their overlapping agendas were more the result of shared national identity and loyalty than a pre-determined strategy to link agendas across national borders. I offer these qualifiers not to suggest that both histories are inadequate for explaining feminism in the Chilean diaspora. Rather, I hope to highlight the difficulty in theorizing movements in diasporas given the current limitations in the literature. Ultimately, "in each time and place, feminism reflects its history and prior developments, as well as present opportunities and constraints" (Ferree and Martin 1995, 2). This is not to say that feminist movements emerge in a vacuum from one another; rather, they highlight the specific sociohistorical processes and events that lead feminists to mobilize.

SOCCER, SYNAGOGUES, AND SIBLINGS

I spoke to most of the women I interviewed about feminism. We talked about the different feminist projects they organized—like conferences and magazines—as well as the personal experiences that led them to identify, or not, as feminists. Most of the women who now call themselves feminists recall the seeds being planted long before leaving Chile, often before they got involved in anything political, and typically long before they were even familiar with the word feminism. It was often the women's relatives, namely strong mothers, grandmothers, and aunts, who served as role models to the future feminists. In some cases, women saw their options limited in ways quite distinct from the boys and men around them. They felt restricted in a variety of subcultures, everything from religion to sports. Similarly, some women felt frustrated that their labor, particularly their unpaid labor, had a social value significantly lower than that of the men in their lives. These experiences often contributed to women's understandings of what the word *feminism* means. Others found feminism once in exile and often as the result of abusive relationships with their partners. Interestingly, in many cases the same women who consciously revered the strong women in their lives and resented the men who controlled their every life decision rejected the term *feminism*. Many rejected the term because they felt it was simply a label and for them feminism was more about one's actions. In other words, there are a variety of reasons Chilean women either accept or reject the term *feminist*: what feminism means to them and what influenced them to come to their conclusions. This variety is not limited to Latin American women in the diaspora. Indeed, women in Latin America also have differing opinions on what feminism does and does not mean to them (see Shayne 2004, Chapters Two, Four, and Six). In this section I will share some of the women's interpretations regarding feminism and the development of feminist consciousness.

Many of the women I interviewed see feminism as a way to challenge the unequal social value assigned to men's and women's labor. Irene Policzer, an architect, believes feminism should erode the social hierarchy between paid and unpaid labor. She explains:

> I think for me [feminism] is a matter of values. I want . . . knitting to be as important in society in terms of payment, respectability, status, the whole thing. . . . That for me is the important thing; it is the job itself that women do that has to have status, not the woman. . . . So the thing is to change the perception of the value of the different jobs. . . . [A]ll the issues of equal pay [and] all that, I don't think they go far enough in that regard. . . . It took me five years [of schooling] and then one year of practice to . . . be allowed by society to design a house. What does society require from me to raise a child? One book, Dr. Spock at my

time. . . . I have done both and I find the child much more difficult than a house quite frankly. . . . That is the kind of thing that is not equal right now . . . I can live in a . . . rotten house but we cannot live as a society with rotten children . . . The values are wrong.

Magaly Varas considers herself "150 percent feminist." She sees feminism similarly to Irene:

To me, it means equal rights, but I am not talking about [paid] work, no. . . . It . . . is so obvious that women can do the same or better [than men]; I am not interested in that. . . . I would love to have men in my kitchen. That is my revolution! That is my feminist point of view. . . . To me feminism is not being an executive or . . . a scientist . . . feminism to me [is in] . . . the kitchen, the bathroom.

For both of these women, and many of the others I spoke with, the gendered division of labor assigns social value to men's and women's traditional labor where women's contributions are significantly less valued than men's. Similarly, men are not expected to do the domestic labor, which places an unfair burden on women as indicated by Magaly's desire to have feminism in the kitchen and bathroom. In the last chapter we saw that this division of labor is not only in the family but also in the political world as well.

Many of the women I spoke to credited their strong women relatives for developing their feminist consciousness, often long before they had a word to attach to it. Ana María Quiroz believes Chilean families are shaped by both matriarchy and *machismo*[4]:

My mother was very strong . . . very strong for her age, for her times.[5] We were four women and my brother and I think too a lot of women in families in Chile are single moms and it is a matriarchal society. But it is a mixture because you see a lot of machismo on the surface but deep down the ones that are keeping everything going are women.

Magaly Varas was raised in a similar atmosphere:

I come from a matriarch[y]. My mother was a widow, and my grandmother was a widow. [W]e were . . . nine women at home and my brother. . . . And my mother was . . . a feminist . . . and she was a very strong woman, and my grandmother was too very, very, very, very strong.

Strong women relatives provided role models to many of the women I interviewed. The interviewees made it abundantly clear that the strength their mothers, grandmothers, and aunts exhibited provided them a vision that eventually inspired them to fight, implicitly or explicitly, for women's rights.

In addition to strong women relatives, some women explained how as young girls they saw their social options limited in contrast to the boys in their lives and those experiences also laid the foundation for feminist consciousness. Carmen Rodríguez explains how her desire to play soccer with her brothers was one of her earlier feminist moments:

There is a moment, I guess when I was about ten; my brothers were part of a soccer team. My oldest brother had founded it and [was] the president or . . . coach and this was [in the] neighborhood . . . we lived in Valparaíso. . . . Because I had two brothers . . . I was always surrounded by older boys. They took me everywhere. So they took me to their soccer games, their soccer practices, everything, and they would let me play with them and I was really good at left wing. So when we went to the soccer practices . . . I was left wing a lot of the time, and they had the games, and then when they played on the street . . . they needed two goalies at the bottom [laughs] because otherwise the ball would keep on [rolling.] So I used to be one of those goalies. . . . I had been part . . . of the Ferrari Futbol Club. (Ferrari was the name of our street.) . . . I thought . . . that "all I have to do is practice [and] when I am bigger I [will] be part of the team." And then one day, I do not know exactly what happened or what somebody said, I was about ten, I realized that no matter how good I was, no matter how big I was, I would never . . . never, never be part of the Ferrari Futbol Club and it was such a feeling of being ripped off, of injustice. I remember that feeling so clearly just because I am a girl it just seemed so absurd to me, right? So my feminism I think was brewing for a long time and I think I was feminist . . . since I was a kid.

From Carmen's perspective, this revelation provided her an insight into the gendered nature of cultural norms, in this case sports, and how they affect women/girls adversely. Patricia Gomberoff recalls similar feelings but in a much different world—Judaism. She explains:

I was sort of opening my eyes a bit and I thought it was not fair between men and women . . . in the religion, the Jewish religion. I started [seeing this] at a very young age, 12, 13, 14. I felt very segregated because my parents went [to temple] for the High Holidays [or] for whatever and . . . women sat on one side and men on the other; I could not give my hand to the Rabbi.

These women realized as young girls that they were living in a different world, with fewer opportunities, than the boys and men in their lives. Their memories never went away and eventually became the seeds to their political activism—feminist and otherwise.

Finally, some of the women I spoke with, regardless of their strong women relatives, limited experiences as girls, or even abusive ex-husbands as adults, decided they did not want to use the word *feminist* to describe themselves but rather feel that their actions are more important than how they identify. Rebeca Jimenez is one such example. Despite the fact that she works as a professional advocate for women—as a domestic violence counselor—she does not consider herself a feminist. This is in large part because she finds the term is more of a label than anything and she believes labels contribute to negative stereotypes. Similar to the women who embraced the term *feminist*, Rebeca credits her strong women relatives with fostering her own inner strength, which ultimately translated into her current profession working on behalf of abused women:

> I was born in a family of . . . seven children and my [parents] were separated when I was ten years old. They got separated and my mom took care of us and then . . . my older sister [did]. . . . I saw my father once in a while so I grew up in a female family. . . . [A]nd my grandmother from my mother's side, she was in the same situation. So I come from a family of women very much in power. . . . [T]hat is why [my mother and my grandmother] became my role models.

Sacha Rodríguez[6] was also less concerned with calling herself a feminist than acting like one. She explains, "In my family women always worked; they had power, you know? In my case, my husband, I left him. So I think my actions speak louder than my words. Because I think within every divorced woman there is a feminist." If divorcing one's husband makes one a feminist then the majority of the women in my sample, including the ones who rejected the term, are feminists. As we saw in Chapter Two many of the women left Chile because of their husbands. The decisions they made once in Canada were also the results of their husbands. Some women did not learn English or work or live where they wanted to until after they were divorced. Indeed, many divorced their husbands precisely to achieve the freedom to do those sorts of things. (Sacha is one such woman.) In other words, many of the same women who rejected the term *feminist*, either because they did not feel they knew enough about the concept to embrace it, or in some cases felt it is politically divisive, elitist, or both, were the same women who left their husbands because of psychological and/or physical abuse. In Sacha's mind, the women who made the decision to leave are feminists whether they know it or not, or claim or reject the term.

In short, the women who marched on International Women's Day, organized the feminist conferences, started the magazine *Aquelarre,* and the like became feminists at different points in their lives for a variety of reasons including religion, sports, and strong women relatives. Some identified as feminists before they left Chile and others not until they were exiled. Some of the women I spoke to initially shied away from the feminist movement but eventually became active for women's rights, including their own in their personal, namely marital, relationships. In other words, a variety of factors propelled Chilean exiles to organize (or not) as feminists just as is the case within Chile and the region more generally. I turn now to the organizational efforts of the exile feminists in Vancouver.

CHILEAN WOMEN MOBILIZE:
EXILES IN A TRANSNATIONAL CONTEXT

Women-Centered Activities

Latin American women and women in the Third World more generally have long organized in women-only spaces without identifying as feminists. As I have discussed in previous chapters, the classic Latin American example is the Mothers of the Disappeared.[7] The same can be said about women exiles in Vancouver. For example, women organized within their political parties to support women-centered groups in Chile. Chilean women in Canada also started a group called the "Chilean Women's Committee," which worked to support women's groups within Chile, namely the Association of Relatives of the Detained and Disappeared (*Agrupación de Familiares de Detenidos y Desaparecidos*, AFDD) and Women of Chile (*Mujeres de Chile*, MUDE-CHI) as well as organized programs for themselves in Vancouver. According to Cecilia Tagle, former president of the Chilean Women's Committee, the organization lasted from around 1984 until 1997. (Over ten years into the dictatorship and seven years after.) Cecilia was also active with a similar group in Toronto, her first stop after fleeing Chile. She explained the purpose of the Vancouver group:

> We did a lot of solidarity work, especially with the relatives of the disappeared in Chile and we collected material aid to send to Chile. I am talking about in the 1980s, late 1980s early 1990s. . . . We were [about] thirty[8] women, all ages, different backgrounds. The majority were women that were housewives and it was a very good experience to be [part of the organization]. . . . We [also] organized exercise classes in the common area [of the housing co-op] . . . late [at] night [and] in the summer we went for walks in the neighborhood; we did exercise and talked about a lot of things. Sometimes the family violence issue came up too.

In our focus group discussion the following summer Cecilia offered more detail:

> We did fundraising events; I remember *Cueca* [traditional Chilean dance] competitions [and we made] *empanadas* for the Peace March. I think . . . the best thing that we did was that we went through a process as a group of women to

see what we wanted to do here, to [plant] our two feet, for the first time, here
. . . in Canada. . . . I am very proud to say that many of those women studied
something. They had a career; they studied [and became] nurse aids. They
learned the language; some of them, their marriages broke down because of
[their experiences in the group].

The organization ultimately had a dual goal: (1) to politically and materially support the women activists in Chile while (2) empowering women
exiles in Vancouver. The Chilean Women's Committee provided a space to
acknowledge the difficult paid, unpaid, and political labors of women in their
Vancouver community. The Committee allowed these same women to focus
on themselves for a change. For example, the exercise classes and mutual
support sessions were designed around women's busy schedules, that is, late
at night, after work, and household chores are finally done. Even if all of the
members of the group were not feminists, nor part of any feminist movement,
their activities empowered women all the same, so much so that some women
were able to remove themselves from abusive, often violently so, relationships with their husbands.

Chilean women exiles also organized themselves within the Canadian Hispanic Congress. Irene Policzer explains:

There was a national organization called the Canadian Hispanic Congress, an
umbrella for a number of Latin American groups and organizations, created
in the late 1970s or early 1980s, in which I was involved sometime in the
late 1980s, I think.[9] At that time, they got funding from Heritage Canada to
organize a Latin American Women's conference (not the one we talked about
[see below]; this one was for women living in Canada only). I was part of the
group who organized the conference, which took place in Vancouver. One of the
resolutions passed in that Conference was that the Congress should have, I do
not remember the exact name—Women's Secretariat, I think. Shortly after the
conference, we created the Vancouver Sector of that Secretariat, expecting that
similar chapters would be created in other provinces. So I was the coordinator
of that Women's branch of the Congress, and started to invite different women
to form this Secretariat. As we started to meet regularly, it did not take us long
to realize that what we really wanted was an independent organization: our priorities were different from what the Congress expected from us, tensions arose,
and we decided we needed a "space of our own." That is how the BC Society of
Spanish Speaking Women was born.

Irene mentions the need for a separate and autonomous space for women
(feminists or not.) This issue of autonomy was one of many with which
Latin American feminists inside Latin America also grappled. From Irene's
perspective:

Women need a space in which they feel safe, unthreatened, unembarrassed; in which to share notes on everything, from daily experiences to larger issues; a place to develop skills and get prepared to participate in the society at large. We have been conditioned for so long to step aside and let men take the lead, that we will not be able to change roles until and unless we go through this process of finding out what our collective needs and aspirations are, and we need to do this by ourselves.

In short, the group started as a nonfeminist, women's wing of an umbrella organization. Eventually women found the women-only space empowering and some, including Irene, became active feminists even though the original conception of the group was entirely separate from feminism.

This development of political consciousness for the exiles is quite similar to patterns that existed within Latin America. History has shown that women-only, nonfeminist spaces have consistently led to feminist consciousness and eventually activism. These women-only spaces empowered women beyond just providing exercise classes and support groups, regardless of whether the women consider themselves feminists. As I discussed, some of the women I spoke with credited their strong women relatives for their feminist conscious-ness while others found that experiences within these women-only spaces provided the initial catalyst for feminist consciousness, while in other cases, women organized as and for other women but never embraced the term or ideology of feminism. In either case, women recognized their own political strength regardless of the identity they claimed.

Fifth Canadian Conference in Solidarity with Women of Latin America

Conferences, as the above overview of the Latin American Encuentros and UN-sponsored meetings suggests, are a staple to national, regional, and trans-national feminist mobilization. Ferree and Mueller argue that international feminist conferences are not only mobilizing structures but also manifestations of protest (2004, 594–95). Chilean exile feminists certainly corroborate their point. For example, Andrea Diaz, leader in the youth sector of the solidarity movement explained that International Women's Day (March 8) was marked annually by a day of celebrations, part of which was a conference. The celebra-tions involved both the adult and youth sectors of the solidarity movement and were not limited to Chilean exile feminists, though exiles played a major role in organizing the celebrations/protests. International Women's Day has always played a major role in feminist mobilization in Latin America and for many is used as a barometer for assessing a feminist presence (Shayne 2004, Chapter Four). Chilean exile feminists also organized national and transnational feminist conferences to articulate feminism more generally. Jackie Smith also notes the importance of conferences to political mobilization, specifically international conferences. In Smith's estimation global conferences foster an "international community by generating common understandings of problems and their causes and a shared set of objectives and commitments to address them" (2004, 322). While Smith's overall assessment is accurate, Latin American feminist history suggests she may be overstating the sense of common understandings while downplaying the often paralyzing political fissures. One international conference organized by exile feminists in Vancouver is a case in point.

Conference Overview

On February 27 through March 1, 1987, the "Fifth Canadian Conference in Solidarity with Women of Latin America" took place in Vancouver. The first of these five conferences happened in 1981 and then biannually until this last one in Vancouver. The Latin American Encuentros were on a similar schedule, though not all of the Chilean women, including conference organizers, I spoke to were aware of them, so it is hard to know if the overlap was coincidental or intentional.[10] While in Vancouver I spoke with many women involved with this conference at various levels: main organizers, supporters, activist participants, and new-to-feminism attendees. The different women, particularly as related to their previous level of feminist activism, had very different impressions of the conference and the benefit it offered Chilean exile and other Latina feminists in Vancouver. For some (namely the core organizers) the conference was fraught with divisiveness and tension, which completely trumped the accomplishments of the conference. For others (previously uninitiated feminists) the conference served as either a pivotal moment in the development of their own feminist consciousness or a confirmation that feminism was too polemic and thus politically uninviting. Others still (mostly the moderately involved) felt the conference reflected some combination of both, thus not enhancing nor minimizing their post-conference feminist activism. In this section I will discuss these and other details regarding the conference. I will begin by providing an overview of the organizational process that resulted in the conference and the political tensions that, for some, destroyed it. I then look at the different responses to the conference from some of the women attendees. I will close this discussion with a note on the long-term results of the conference for exile feminism in Vancouver.

Cecilia Tagle was one of the main organizers of the fifth conference and, in part, responsible for bringing it to Vancouver in the first place. She and other women from Vancouver attended the fourth conference in either Montreal or Toronto (she could not recall which) and "at the time of the resolutions I

[Cecilia] stood up [and said] 'We come from Vancouver and we would like to [have] the next conference [in] Vancouver' and everybody supported it." Thus began ten months of intense preparation for this international conference. The organizing committee was composed of eleven women representing different nationalities, including: Chilean exiles, Latina immigrant and exiles from elsewhere in the region, particularly Central America, as well as Canadians, including First Nation women. The conference was the result of all volunteer labor. Cecilia explains that they did everything:

> We did lots of fundraising and we brought women from every country [in Latin America]. [We] even brought Amparo Ochoa from Mexico.[11] . . . We sent letters to the unions, to women's groups, solidarity groups . . . [the] Peace movement, everywhere. We got a lot of support [and we were able to] pa[y for] all the [plane] tickets [for the women coming from Latin America]; we had everything; we had all the money that we needed. . . . We were very, very successful in terms of organizing; [with respect to fundraising], and in terms of [ethnic and National] representation.

Between 150 and 300 delegates attended the conference, depending on who one asks. The organizations represented many different countries and issues; for example, Irene Policzer recalls with joy the "Lesbian Nuns Association"! Conference organizers intended to address a variety of topics during the weekend. According to a bilingual (Spanish and English) registration form for the conference:

> The following themes were selected to reflect the reality experienced by Latin American women. Through these themes we will analyze the reasons why two thirds of the population lives in misery and who benefits from this situation. In this context women play a determining role in the social transformation of the Latin American people.
>
> 1. The economic crisis in Latin America.
> 2. The situation of women in Central America.
> 3. Critical analysis of Human Rights.
> 4. Native [sic] Women.
> 5. Psychological effects on immigrant women.
> 6. Women and the peace movement.
> 7. Political Development of women. (n.a. 1987)

To address these issues the organizations present at the conference represented a variety of sectors: union activists, guerrillas, human rights groups, feminists, etc. That is, the attendees represented groups quite similar to those who attended the Encuentros in Latin America. It is likely that many of the women who came from Latin America had attended the Encuentros as well. Not surprisingly, then, just as the Latin American Encuentros were plagued with tension, so too was the conference in Vancouver. In Vancouver the most divisive issue was the role of men.

The Man Question

What is the answer to "the man question" for Chilean exile feminists? Or, put another way, what role should men play in feminist mobilization? This question of course was not limited to Chilean exiles but is one debated by feminists in many different social and geographic locales. Unfortunately the man question was not answered via consensus on behalf of the organizers or attendees of the conference and as a result ruined it for many women involved. According to Cecilia, up until the very last minute the organizing committee agreed that men would attend the conference. In some sessions they would be permitted to speak and in others only allowed to listen and observe. Additionally, men were asked to offer their concrete support by doing child care and helping in the kitchen. From Cecilia's perspective women would benefit if men attended; they needed to understand the issues some women face: "We needed to have a space where we can discuss our issues and then also we need to educate ourselves, [and] especially men, you know?" For Cecilia, violence against women is a prime example. In our focus group discussion Irene Policzer recalled hearing the testimony of a woman who was physically abused by her husband. She said she began the conference feeling that men should be allowed to attend but after hearing that testimony she felt it made more sense for men to be excluded so that women would have a safe space to discuss these difficult issues. In this same focus group discussion, Cecilia pointed out that "men should [hear] those testimonies" as well.

Lorena Jara was another member of the organizing committee and she has a different interpretation of the situation. Lorena thought it was "ridiculous" to even consider allowing men to voice their opinions and vote during the conference. According to Lorena the women who concurred with this position

saw them [men] as supporting us in terms of . . . day care [and] logistical support but we did not see the reason to have them speaking up, [or] voting at the conference. . . . My position, and I think that some of us at that time, [felt] that there were a lot of women who were afraid to talk when men [were present]; we are talking about the 1980s [when] . . . it was very traditional. . . . So there was this huge debate about it and it took us many meetings, finally with my position, the position I represented . . . [prevailing]: no voice, no vote, for the men because this is a women's conference and we want men definitely to help us and they were welcome to support us.

The most frustrating part of this debate for Cecilia was the manner and timing in which Lorena's position ultimately triumphed. Cecilia explains that though the committee had previously agreed to allow men to participate in a limited way, and men were invited and planned to attend, at the last minute this decision was reversed:

> The day that we were opening the conference something changed. At this organizing committee meeting other women came into the meetings who [had] never [been] part of the organizing committee and they were saying that men should not be allowed in. . . . I did not agree with that because we . . . had already had that discussion. It was a very, very [heated] discussion and I left. I did not open the conference because . . . I believed in that [original] decision and I was very mistreated by some of the women.

According to Cecilia, her frustration with this process led her to have a breakdown and withdraw from the conference entirely. She ended up sick with shingles for six months, which she is convinced was brought on by the stress of the conference. As I discussed in Chapters Four and Five, the Chilean exile community was swimming in emotions brought on by dictatorship, exile, and destroyed families. It is impossible to know if the conference was the sole catalyst for Cecilia's breakdown and shingles. What is important, however, is that from her perspective it was. How did this debate and conference, more generally, affect other organizers and attendees?

Effect on Attendees

The conference politically affected women in different ways. Irene Policzer's experiences reflect that of some women like her who attended. At the time of the conference Irene was interested in women's issues but did not have a full sense of what feminism is and why it is necessary. She was aware of the debate about men's participation but completely unaware of the fact that the issue had supposedly been resolved prior to the conference. She thus experienced the debate as a deep learning process and was not personally betrayed by it as was Cecilia. Indeed, she did not understand its implications for the organizers, namely Cecilia, until some years later. For Irene, the conference was:

> The big turning point for me. . . . All of this is going on and I did not have any idea that it was happening. You know, all of the . . . different movements, and all the different organizations, and all the issues that are being discussed, and all this awareness. . . . We [Irene and Cecilia] were at totally different levels; for you [Cecilia] the conference was very frustrating; not for me, it was "WOW!" . . . I would not have dreamt of it! From Mexico; from Nicaragua; from Argentina; from all [over the place]; and the most incredible focuses of interest. So I said:

"all of that is going on in Latin America! . . . And all of this is going on right here
in Canada, with Latin American women too!" and I did not have a clue so [I] was
. . . parachute[ed into] these things; everything was knowledge for me!

By the end of the conference Irene was "parachuted" into a new level of
consciousness, which ultimately translated into a major commitment of her
time to women's issues.

In addition to Irene's excitement about the breadth of feminist mobilization, the conference also made her aware of different issues and the need for
women-only spaces. She explains:

I did not speak in that conference; I was still not used to speaking in public.
But I went with a friend, and my friend did! She was whispering to me "I think
this, I think that" and . . . at some point, she stood up. She went to the front, and
she spoke, and she said what she wanted [to say]. She was wonderful! [And]
. . . the glory she had in her face. And then she told me: "You know what? . . .
This is what I need. . . . [I]f my husband had been here I would have told him
to say that." . . . [F]or me, that was a very important point; just seeing that, and
hearing my friend say that, and I think that most of us went through that, . . .
this need for a space.

By 1987 many of the women who attended this conference had many,
many years of political experience. Exiles involved themselves in the solidarity movement as early as 1974. These same women thus had attended
countless meetings with their husbands. Rather than developing their own
voice and comfort with public speaking many women simply conveyed their
opinions to their husbands and asked them to relay them to the entire group.
For Irene and her friend it was this conference that made them aware of
that dynamic and the need to challenge it. The trajectory of participating in
leftist politics, while experiencing sexism from their compañeros, and subsequent development of feminist consciousness, is one very similar to that
experienced by women revolutionaries in Latin America. In Latin America,
feminism is often born in the wake of revolutionary movements, in part due
to the contradiction between struggling for political justice while experiencing personal injustice (Shayne 2004). Again, despite the extremely different
political terrains—guerrilla war versus exile politics—some patterns crossed
geopolitical borders and thus contributed to the growth of a vivacious transnational feminist movement.

In short, the excitement that Irene and women in positions similar to hers
felt about feminism and ultimately feminist mobilization after the conference
was the result of two main things: first, their newly discovered knowledge of
the transnational and thematic breadth and depth of feminist issues; and sec-

ond, a new sense of awareness regarding the subordinated status of women
and thus need for a space and movement of their own. This newfound consciousness translated into direct action. Indeed, after the conference Irene
and her friend were both central to starting the feminist magazine *Aquelarre*,
which I will discuss below.

While some women like Irene and her friend were catapulted into feminist activism as a result of the conference, others were completely put off by
it. Nina Vaca is a case in point. Prior to the conference Nina was involved
with the Vancouver incarnation of the Movement for the Revolutionary
Left (*Movimiento de Izquierda Revolucionario*, MIR). Within the MIR she
worked with other women to support the Chilean organization MUDECHI
(Women of Chile). MUDECHI was a women's federation formed in Chile
in the early 1980s. It was an explicitly nonfeminist organization because it
believed feminism is ideologically parallel to "anti-men," a position Nina
and some of her compañeras rejected. Rather, MUDECHI emerged in response to the political and economic crises brought on by the dictatorship
and saw their primary goal as ousting the junta. Despite its non-feminist
identity MUDECHI emphasized the importance of women taking on
public roles and participating with politics at a comparable level to men
(Chruchryk 1994, 76). Nina considers herself "a little feminist" (personal
interview 2005) and agreed with MUDECHI's approach to women's politics. Ultimately Nina felt frustrated by the conference, and feminism more
generally. Rather than experiencing the debate around "the man question"
as educational, as did Irene, to Nina it just represented divisions and bickering. From her vantage point some of the leftist political parties were attempting to push their own agendas vis-à-vis women. Rather than become
involved in those debates Nina opted to remain active with her own organizations and support women's issues in those forums, an environment she
saw as significantly more welcoming to women's issues. Nina feels that the
women members of the Vancouver MIR refused to let their male compañeros dictate the terms of women's political involvement and thus felt no need
for a women-only space or agenda. Given these differing sorts of responses
to the conference, what concretely came from it?

Conference's Results

What did the conference produce besides political frustration for some and
personal empowerment for others? Despite the tensions I would argue that the
conference produced quite a lot in the way of feminist activism. First of all,
the conference served as a manifestation of protest in the sense that Ferre and
Mueller argue (2004, 594–95). Additionally, it was an organizational starting

point that ultimately planted seeds and generated momentum for future feminist projects, namely the magazine *Aquelarre*. How did the conference serve as protest? Firstly, it took ten intense months to put it together, and in that process the pre-conference activities served as an articulate announcement to leftists in Vancouver, and beyond that women's movements and feminism were important issues to Chilean exiles and other Latina immigrants. One of the most concrete ways this happened was through fundraising. As Cecilia explained, the organizing committee contacted all sorts of leftist groups in order to drum up support. The committee was quite successful, as evidenced by their ability to fund all delegates' travel from Latin America. By the time the conference happened a whole cross-section of organizations in Vancouver was familiar and impressed enough with women's activism to offer material support to the cause. In addition to the ten months of pre-conference-generated discussion of feminism and women's issues, the conference itself certainly served that purpose to an even greater extent. That is, once the two-to-three hundred women were assembled in Vancouver, the statement about the need and presence of feminism was quite unmistakable and thus embodied a unique form of protest.

In addition to the conference itself embodying a particular form of protest, the event and its planning stages also generated a host of connections that previously had not existed. The networks eventually became a possible pool of support for post-conference feminist projects. For example, conference organizers arranged housing for all out-of-town guests and on-site day care for all attendees, local and non-locals alike. Indeed, the registration form asks if housing and/or day care are necessary and urged delegates to submit their requests by February 16, 1987, or ten days before the conference was to begin (n.a. 1987). Organizers needed reliable support in the community to feel confident guaranteeing all of their guests housing. Presumably the ties created through this sort of collaboration did not necessarily dissipate after the conference and were later available to support the activities of the *Aquelarre* collective and the like.

Networking among Latina activists and across the Left (i.e., with unions and government representatives) was important for post-conference activities, but from Cecilia Tagle's perspective the post-conference feminist potential was not close to fully realized. She explains:

> Everybody [the organizing committee] left [and we] never, ever met again. . . . Some people left very angry, and women disappointed, and it was sad because we lost touch with groups in Latin America that we could have continued to [work with], you know? That was the idea: [formalize] relationships with other women's groups, give them support, and [generate support] for us too.

The connections that did last were those between the attendees who were not necessarily part of the main organizing committee. At the conference, conversations began about how to keep this momentum moving and some recall tossing around the idea of a magazine. The idea eventually became a reality when a variety of other events also transpired.

In sum, an eleven-woman, cross-national committee worked together for ten intense months to organize the "Fifth Canadian Conference in Solidarity with Women of Latin America" in Vancouver. Between two and three hundred women attended from all over the Americas. Organizers raised enough money from the leftist community in Vancouver to cover travel expenses for women coming from Latin America with even some left over, which organizers talked about putting toward a publication of some sort. There was an intense debate about the place of men in the conference and thus in feminism more broadly, which served to educate and activate some women, while frustrating and burning out others. This and other debates at the conference were similar to those that transpired at the feminist Encuentros, which happened in Latin America and the Caribbean at the same time as this and the four preceding conferences in Canada. This conference served as a hub in the transnational feminist network of the Americas, which Chilean exiles were quite central in facilitating. Though the conference had the potential to create much more collaboration and activism in its aftermath than actually came to fruition, according to many of the women I spoke with, it was a success nonetheless. That is, the conference itself embodied feminist protest and the momentum was carried on by individual and informal networks of women who met at and were empowered by the conference. Even Cecilia, who was so disappointed with the conference that she remained sick for six months, remained involved with post-conference feminist politics as manifest in the *Aquelarre* collective, the subject of the next section.

Aquelarre Latin American Women's Cultural Society

Rebelliousness, resistance, and creativity have taken many forms in the history of the Latin American continent, but the beginning has always been a meeting, a gathering. Co-operation and organization are needed in order to do things. And as people meet and gather they start to create unions, musical groups, shanty-town organizations, publications, soup kitchens. People get together and remember, they speak, resist and struggle to change the world. They get together and make history, even if their names don't appear in books.

We are women from here and there, Latin American women. We are all present: those of us who never left, those who left and continue to be "Latinas" in far-away lands, those who left and then returned, and also those who, having been born in other parts of the world, share our love for Latin America.

We bring our voices, our pain, our banners, our ointments, our needles and brushes, our cooking pots, our handfuls of soil, our potions, our instruments, our brooms. We have come along different roads, but we are going in the same direction: we share a vision of a future where there is room for life, LIFE in capital letters.

We also share an increasing confidence in our capabilities as women and the conviction that together we can find new ways to advance and reach our destinations. We have power, we are witches. We will sweep away the fears and the hurdles and we will search our memories. We will recover the magical and silent work of the past and share our present efforts. We will start showing, speaking, discussing, fantasizing and inventing together. That's what brings us together in this magazine, which is one more space among the many that women have taken over. Let us all share it. We are all invited. Let us begin the AQUELARRE. (Aquelarre 1989a, 2)

These words appear on the first page, of the first issue, in the bilingual magazine *Aquelarre: A Magazine for Latin American Women/Revista de la Mujer Latinoamericana*. This first issue came out in July 1989, just before Pinochet officially relinquished power. The *Aquelarre* collective lasted for nearly ten years and produced twenty-one issues (sixteen individual magazines; some are double issues). Each issue used a variety of creative means to accomplish the goals implicit in the above statement. That is, the magazine strove to document the typically overlooked social, cultural, and political contributions of Latin American women. The collective also sought to create a space for the development and cultivation of feminist ideas and interpretations of a plethora of sociopolitical issues from human rights, to art, to globalization. The magazine is a remarkable accomplishment given the collective's limited resources and unlimited ambitions. In this section I will discuss the development of the magazine, including logistical and thematic concerns. I conclude by analyzing some of the more illustrative issues that best capture the goals the collective was attempting to achieve.

Aquelarre's *History*

In the course of this research I was fortunate to speak with five of the *Aquelarre* collective's original members. The collective was made up of about twelve core women and fifteen volunteers, both men and women. However, numbers varied from issue to issue. Most of the core members were Chilean exiles and the magazine was largely the result of their initiative, while others were from elsewhere in Latin America, including Argentina, Colombia, and Mexico, and a handful were from Canada.[12] I spoke to five of the founding members as well as some volunteers about the magazine's origins. There was some implicit agreement that the idea for a magazine was in the air, in part as a result of conversations and brainstorming sessions at the conference, but there were different interpretations regarding the prime catalyst for the magazine. I suspect that these differences are the result of what each woman remembers as the moment most important to her decision to commit herself to the magazine. Interestingly, the different stories I heard all revolve around cultural production.

Carmen Rodríguez was the Project Coordinator and Head of the Editorial Committee (Aquelarre Latin American Women's Cultural Society 1988e). For Carmen the magazine is in part the result of an art exhibit in Vancouver in 1987 organized by the Canadian feminist organization "Women in Focus." Two women from Chile attended and brought with them the work of thirteen other Chilean women. One of the Chilean women stayed with Carmen and was quite impressed with the work of the women in the solidarity movement. She suggested that the exiled Chileans create a magazine to share their accomplishments with other women, in and outside of Canada. Carmen then traveled to Chile (for the first time in fourteen years) and, among other things, did a bit of research about potential themes and stories for the magazine. Upon her return she and about nine other women from Chile, Argentina, Colombia, Canada, and the United States had their first brainstorming session. Carmen recalls it this way:

> We all talked about what we would like to see in a magazine. And from that very first session . . . the bilingual aspect came up; that it was important to be bilingual because we wanted to reach people here [Canada] as well as Central and Latin America. But not only because we wanted to reach people in Latin America but because it was a statement of who we are and where we come from. And we wanted it to be a political magazine, a feminist magazine. We wanted to cover all kinds of issues, political things to social things, to arts. Everything. We wanted it to look beautiful, and we wanted to write it collectively.

The final product definitely suggests that the collective met all of these goals.

Irene Policzer, another founding member, identifies a different catalyst for the magazine, also implicitly tied to art. Irene recalls receiving a call from a Chilean exile friend of hers who was working on her degree in photography. She explains:

> One day [she called me] and said: "I am desperate! I need to have [at least] twenty-five . . . photographs of Latin American women! Can you help me?!" So she came here [Vancouver] and we organized a tour. . . . Gena . . . had a particular style of taking the picture; she would ask the woman how she would like to appear in the picture . . . [and] everybody chose something that would

define her. . . . She asked me to go with her partly to introduce her to the different women but also to do the talking to keep the women sort of away from the camera. . . . So my job was that; . . . not distracting exactly but [something like that]. . . . [S]o those conversations happened [and] a lot of them [were] about the conference and . . . what had happened there. . . . It was some time . . . after the conference . . . [a]nd Gena had come with me to the conference . . . so she was aware of all those issues also, so it was kind of a natural [flow of events].

After the seeds were planted as a result of some conference attendees wanting to keep their voices out there, the "Women and Focus" exhibit, and Gena's photography project, a group of women met at Irene's for a brainstorming session. They decided to have an event at La Quena Coffee House to announce the idea and gather support and volunteers for the project. (Recall La Quena was a *peña* style café started by Chileans and Canadians.) One woman, Magaly Varas, recalls seeing an announcement for the event. She attended with great enthusiasm, feeling as though the project spoke to her personally and politically. Magaly explains at our focus group meeting:

I heard about [the magazine] . . . and I was typist, a secretary at that time. . . . I met you [Carmen] at La Quena and I met Margarita [another founder] for the first time. . . . I told them . . . "I am not a writer but . . . I want to join this project." . . . I was not involved in politics [at the time but] I have . . . always [been] involved with the Latin American community. For thirty years, I have never stopped doing that. So I wanted to do something with women and that project was the perfect one for me.

Magaly stayed with the magazine for ten years, from the beginning until the end. She eventually became the only paid staff member for the collective.

The women were very committed to a certain vision of *Aquelarre*; they wanted a cultural text that spoke to and reflected a diverse group of Latin American women. According to a grant application they submitted to the Canada Council:

We want to provide a concrete space for Latin American women living in Canada, Canadian women and Latin American women living in Latin America to carry out a cultural dialogue. We want to hear from and reach those women who, like many of us, have left Latin America and now live in some part of Canada. We want to show the cultural expressions of their experiences. At the same time, we want to hear from and reach those women who, like us, are from Latin America but, unlike us, never left their country of origin. We want to know in what ways our artistic expressions are still alike and how they have grown different. And finally, we want to hear from and reach Canadian women who have an interest in Latin American culture. . . . When women create their own spaces to express their cultural experiences or to take action, the results are quite distinct. AQUELARRE Magazine intends to provide such a space for these innovative artistic expressions. (Aquelarre Latin American Women's Cultural Society 1988e, 3, 9)

They immediately started to organize furiously, and not always harmoniously, in order to create the magazine that the collective envisioned.

Organizational Efforts

Cecilia Tagle was involved from the beginning. She shared a schedule of meetings with me (Aquelarre Latin American Women's Cultural Society, 1988a). According to the schedule the women met as often as every day but typically once every four days. The chronology starts with a meeting on April 13, 1988, and goes all the way until February 1989. It includes planning meetings, editorial meetings, fundraising peñas at La Quena, scheduled mailings, etc. In other words, it appears that from the beginning the women thought of everything. A grant proposal dated September 15, 1988, also reflects the organizational savvy of the collective. The application was submitted to the Exploration Program of the Canada Council and in it the collective requested $14,600Can to cover limited staff support and office supplies over a one-year period. According to the proposal it was one of many requests for support, some logistical, like office space, others for funding. The collective approached a cross-section of groups, local, national, and transnational, including: The Chilean Community Association of B.C., the Vancouver Status of Women (who eventually provided office space), Oxfam Canada, B.C. Women's Tour to Nicaragua, and El Salvador Information Office. According to the inside cover of the first issue their requests were successful: "Aquelarre is partially funded by the Explorations Program of the Canada Council. We also gratefully acknowledge the assistance of OXFAM-Canada, Vancouver Status of Women, Kinesis, La Quena Coffee House, Co-op Radio, and many others" (Aquelarre 1989a, i).

In our focus group discussion, Carmen and Magaly recalled with pride and amazement how hard they all worked in the ten years they dedicated to the magazine:

Carmen: You know, when I look back . . . I have no idea how . . . we did this; it was so much work!

Magaly: And when we had a deadline to publish, remember? We were [working] until three, four, five o'clock in the morning!

Carmen: [At] the office, or at somebody's house, my house, remember?

Magaly: . . . The first issue took us about nine months to publish. . . . And after that we had to write the final report, the budget, everything, so it was...

Carmen: it was exhausting, but it was great. . . . And it was such constant hard work; it was so all encompassing.

Magaly: And [by the end] we did not have any energy left.

Carmen: Yeah, we were drained.

Magaly: It was exhausting. . . . And in the mean time everybody had different jobs.

Carmen: Yeah, I worked full time.

Julie: And you were all mothers; are mothers.

Magaly: Oh yeah, single mothers.

One aspect of the magazine that was particularly time-consuming was fundraising. Each issue cost $5,000Can to print and required its own source of funding, which meant the collective had to research different funding sources, write grant proposals, and eventually write reports to funders after an issue was completed. Additionally, the collective did grassroots fundraising, like silent auctions, garage sales, and peñas in an ongoing way. Not only was the fundraising a constant job but also graphics and layout were exceedingly time-consuming as well. For the most part the magazine pre-dated simple desktop publishing computer programs; the women literally had to cut and paste articles and do the layouts by hand. Their graphics were surprisingly sophisticated given the technological limitations. Indeed, at least initially, the collective did not even have its own fax machine; rather they had to use one at one of the member's husband's office.

Attending meetings and making decisions about content and so forth was also time-consuming. In retrospect, some women felt they should have trusted one another more, which would have minimized the amount of time spent in meetings, but at the time everyone felt a need to be invested in all decisions, which led to very lengthy and often heated discussion. Cecilia Tagle explains:

We would discuss for each issue the theme, the pictures, and I guess we were so collective that we were all involved in *all* of the discussions, even [regarding] the color part, even in the little picture. And that was exhausting for many of us. We should have . . . delegated more and trust[ed] that the other [committees] were doing their parts, in the sense that the values and the objectives were present. . . . I think I should have been more patient but . . . I am *proud* of that magazine; what we did was incredible, and the first year, all the work that we did, it was very, very good . . . a lot of creativity. Incredible; it was excellent!

On top of the fundraising, brainstorming sessions, meetings, bickering, writing, translating, and page layouts, members of the collective spent time finding other artists, writers, poets, and activists to interview, and experts in given fields to also contribute to the magazine. In short, the women of the Aquelarre collective worked tirelessly for ten years and produced a professional-grade magazine with very limited resources.

How was this relatively small group of women able to produce sixteen magazines, all of which were thematically, graphically, and culturally rich, in their so-called spare time? In addition to political commitments to feminism the members of the collective brought together a variety of skills and experiences. According to The Canada Council grant:

> We are a group of Latin American and Canadian women determined to publish a bilingual (English-Spanish) cultural magazine by and for women. Although we come from different parts of the Americas, we have many things in common: . . .

> — Many of us practice some kind of cultural expression: writing, music, pottery, photography, drawing and painting, weaving, jewelry making, etc. Others have experience in publishing and printing.
> — We are established members of the Latin American, women's and/or cultural communities of Vancouver. We all have a history of involvement with other organizations that have successfully carried out and continue to carry out projects related to culture and/or women's issues. This has resulted in tremendous community support for AQUELARRE Magazine in terms of concrete donations, voluntary work, subscriptions, attendance to fund-raising events, free publicity and others (Aquelarre Latin American Women's Cultural Society, 1988(e)).

The qualifications the women described here illuminate patterns parallel to the development of feminism in Latin America. That is, all of the women involved in the collective had real political (and in this case cultural) tools already at their disposal, many of which were acquired by participating in other social movements, namely the solidarity movement. Similarly, the women also had networks from which to work, also resulting from their earlier political work. In other words, prior political involvement positioned the members of the collective to more successfully advance their ambitious project. The sociopolitical context of the Chilean diaspora in Vancouver is certainly different than that of revolutionary movements inside of Latin America. However, a commonality exists across borders with respect to women participating in leftist social movements and eventually taking their acquired skills and networks to organize feminist projects in the aftermath of leftists ones. By the time the women started *Aquelarre* (late 1987) many already had over ten years of political experience in Vancouver, so despite the tremendous work load, the transition from one social movement to another was relatively seamless.

The Audience

Who read *Aquelarre*? The issue of audience was tricky for the Aquelarre collective, as it often is for feminists. Striking a balance between "accessible" and "sophisticated" proved challenging. Some members of the collective were more satisfied with the group's ability to achieve this balance than were others. Some felt that despite the group's stated intention of producing a magazine relevant to a diverse cross-section of women, it ultimately ended up being elitist and exclusive. Others, however, felt the collective had concrete strategies to make the magazine appealing to more than just intellectuals. One concrete way they attempted to do this was to interview activists and other women who were not writers but whose stories made sense to include. Similarly, while some women felt the magazine only valued so-called "high" art, others felt just the opposite, and were quite proud of their ability to create an inclusive publication. Some felt the magazine truly represented the women's space they hoped to create, while others felt the magazine only spoke to the converted.

One way to get a sense of the magazine's readership is to look at the distribution strategy of the collective and the letters received. Additionally, during my focus group discussions and one-on-one interviews, I spoke to several members of the collective about this topic. In response to The Canada Council grant application's question, "How will the proposed work be presented to the public?" the collective wrote:

> AQUELARRE Magazine will be distributed to bookstores, Latin American groups, women's organizations and individuals, primarily throughout Canada but also in the United States and Latin America. Several bookstores and groups have already committed their assistance with distribution. . . . At the same time, a mailing list of hundreds of prospective subscribers has been compiled. These people will be re-contacted in order to consolidate their subscriptions. (Aquelarre Latin American Women's Cultural Society 1988e, 5)

According to the letters to the editors *Aquelarre*'s strategy was successful. In the front of the first fourteen issues, after a short introduction to the issue's central topic, was a section the editors called "Todas las voces, todas/all the voices."[13] There were anywhere between four and ten notes included, often from all over the place—including Canada, Latin America, the United States, and Europe. In reviewing the letters from every single issue I found readers in the following countries/states/cities: Argentina (Bariloche, Mendoza, and Paraná); Canada (Fredericton, Montreal, Nelson, Ontario, Ottawa, Rexdale,

Salt Spring Island, Saskatchewan, Telegraph Creek, Toronto, Vancouver, Vernon, and Victoria); Chile (Santiago); Colombia (Bogotá); the Dominican Republic (Santo Domingo); Ecuador (Quito); France (Lyon); Germany (Berlin); the Netherlands (Leeuwarden); Nicaragua (Matagalpa); Paraguay (Asunción); Peru (Lima); the United States (California, Massachusetts, and Oregon), and Uruguay (Montevideo). In other words, fourteen countries, and thirty cities/states/provinces. It is not clear how many readers there were per country, especially outside of Canada, but clearly this list suggests a transnational readership.

Despite this international interest in the magazine some in the collective remained unhappy with what they felt was a limited audience. The issue of accessibility, as I noted above, was tricky and another point that caused much friction within the collective. I spoke to Irene Policzer and Cecilia Tagle, both together and separately, at great length about the magazine. They were pleased with *Aquelarre*, at least initially, but eventually left the collective in large part because they felt the audience was too limited and did not reflect the original intentions of the collective. (Recall both Irene and Cecilia were involved from the very beginning.) Irene explains:

> At the beginning we [had] . . . this dream, this idea, this vision, and at the beginning it . . . seemed [we all had] . . . the same vision but as we started to work, no, it was not the same vision. Really there were two very distinct visions, [with respect to] what content? What is the philosophy? And so I wanted something accessible . . . more easy to understand, more chatty, more gossipy. I did not know about popular education at that time; had I known [about] it I would have said: "Yes! This is what I want!" . . . [S]omething that had to do with women's every day lives; cooking, recipes, or whatever. . . . [Issues] . . . that women talk about or are interested in and within that, yes, [you] have content a bit more than just cooking recipes, but not [in] . . . such a blatant [way]. . . . It [ended up being] . . . a magazine [that] pitched to the convinced. So that was the kind of tension that started to arise I think within the group not too long after [we started], the first year.

Irene continues, speaking more directly to the issue of language:

> Probably it is a magazine that looks much more attractive to . . . the academic community rather than to . . . the community in general because it has a lot of very innovative things, and has a lot of courage . . . and [shows] . . . a lot of resourcefulness to [accomplish]. . . . The language probably sounds very familiar and maybe even a bit naïve to academics because it is not really [a] very sophisticated language; it is a pretentious language [but] it is not sophisticated language, I think. It is an interesting phenomenon to study, I think, but for the community that we wanted to target, I do not think we reached them.

Irene is very educated. She and her husband are both architects and her son is a professor. She is concerned about the language being alienating to women less educated and familiar with academic rhetoric than is she. Irene rather hoped to create a magazine that reached women who were not as familiar with feminist and cultural discourse as was she and most of the founders.

On the other hand, Magaly Varas and Carmen Rodríguez, also involved from the beginning, felt the collective was quite effective in striking a balance between accessible and exclusive. They believe the collective achieved this balance by including a diversity of types of articles—fiction, interviews, political analysis, etc. Carmen, herself a writer, explains:

> I had this idea . . . that we could apply for some grants to have . . . writing workshops because we really wanted . . . a variety of voices; we did not just want writers, right? . . . The way that we got around that was with the interviews. . . . [T]hat was another debate that we would have; the level [of] the audience. . . . [T]here were people that would complain because there were articles, sometimes they were too elevated, right? And we said: 'That is ok. There is one of those but there is also one that is like a conversation . . . and there is another one that is a story, and there is another one that it is a [political] analysis . . . so that was the whole idea. . . . So we tried to incorporate everybody's voice but really incorporating voices of people that were not, that did not have experience writing, [was extremely challenging].

These different perspectives were more than just theoretical debates and thus led to lengthy and heated meetings. Indeed, certain themes addressed in the magazine offer concrete examples of the opposing positions.

The issue on violence against women (16/17) was quite illustrative of this tension. For example, Irene Policzer felt quite certain that the way the collective chose to articulate this important topic ultimately alienated the women who really needed to read it, that is, the sufferers and survivors of violence. On the other hand, Carmen Rodríguez and Magaly Varas felt that issue was one of the more appreciated ones because it was useful to social workers and the like. Irene explains one perspective:

> When we were producing [Aquelarre] one of the problems we had was "who would buy it?" It was very difficult to sell, so it survived based on the grants. [Y]ou should see the amount of issues that were . . . not distributed . . . because it was very difficult to distribute. . . . It looks intimidating; . . . even the issue of violence, looking at it now, if I did something today about [violence] that is not the way I would [do it]. The woman subjected to violence probably is not going to buy a magazine [that] says: "Violence against women" . . . on the cover; it has to . . . be in [a] more subdued way, [on the] inside but not so open. . . . [A woman might think:] "If I buy that . . . I am going to be seen as one of them.

If my husband sees it . . . on my night table or something, what is he going to think?" . . . So there is a way of talking about violence . . . and I think we did not do it right because we did not know; we did not know enough about the issue of violence at that time. . . . [The magazine was] not high-brow proper; [it] is not an intellectual magazine . . . but it tries to appear as something [that is].

From Irene's perspective the presentation of the magazine had such an intellectual feel to it that the practical gains an issue on violence could have provided to abused women was undermined by the alienation they experienced when seeing the magazine.

Once again, Carmen and Magaly had virtually opposite opinions about this issue. I asked both of them in our focus group discussion what they thought women not involved with *Aquelarre* felt about the magazine. They felt it was very well received; specifically, this same issue Irene felt was useless:

Julie: What do you think that women not involved with the magazine thought about it?

Carmen: They loved it. For example, the magazine about violence against women was used all throughout British Columbia by women's groups, by social workers, we went to workshops, [to Magaly] remember?

Magaly: And also I remember [we went to] . . . a Council of Women Counselors at Vancouver Family Services; Family Services of Vancouver . . . got quite a few [copies] of that issue.

Carmen: And the thing is, if people were not involved in the collective, they were involved in some way because we featured their stories, or their art, or their work, or because they volunteered to do whatever [we needed].

Magaly: We had tons of volunteers.

In other words, Carmen and Magaly feel the magazine was well read and appreciated because they got concrete feedback from women's advocacy groups to that effect. Additionally, the collective's commitment to featuring women of the community and what felt to them like an outpouring of volunteer support suggests the magazine involved and spoke to women beyond just the collective. Certainly any activist project that demanded this much intense, unpaid work, one where the goals of advocacy, education, and expression were at once tied together while also competing with one another, is likely to be fraught with tension. Additionally, the members of the collective all had their own personalities and personal issues that led to conflicts at the superficial level and ultimately translated into friction within the magazine. The tensions resulted in some members of the collective leaving rather than the entire project imploding. They did eventually stop producing magazines but at least from the perspective of

Carmen and Magaly, two of the women who stayed with it until the end, for no other reason than that they were exhausted and ran out of money.

Format

What did the magazine look like? What sort of articles did the editors include? What were some of the repeating themes? In this section I will address these and other related questions. I will start with a general overview of the magazines' content and then look at specific themes and issues. For the most part, *Aquelarre* was a very professional-looking publication, particularly given the limited budget and lack of access to computer graphic programs. Most of the covers were very colorful, and all text, including the dates of publication, was written in both Spanish and English. Nearly all of the covers include some sort of original art, including photography, paintings, drawings, and the like. Some have collages that appear to be made by the editors where things were literally cut and pasted and organized thematically (see figures 6.1–6.4).

Despite the covers, which, for the most part, looked relatively professional, there are a few inconsistencies that hint at the grassroots nature of the magazine. For example, some issues are identified by months, while others by seasons. Some issues are solo, for example "2," while others are combined, "7/8." Additionally, some issues have the English first and others the Spanish, and some have a price listed on the cover, while others do not. Interestingly, the price actually varied, sometimes as low as $3.50Can or as high as $5.00. The back of most issues bears the English and Spanish version of the following quote: "Aquelarre means 'illegal gathering of witches'. They used to call us witches. What do they call us now? Arpilleristas, weavers, union leaders, women in exile, political prisoners, mothers of the disappeared, artists" and what appears to be indigenous art portraying women in a circle. The magazine's standard graphics also speak to the theme of witchcraft. Most articles are concluded with what appears to be a small pot of "witch's brew" and the inside cover, which includes information about the collective and publishing details, typically includes a picture of a witch riding a fountain pen rather than a broom (see figure 6.5). Recall the title of this book: *They Used to Call Us Witches: Chilean Exiles, Culture, and Feminism*. Needless to say, the title was inspired by the magazine and its collective.

The content of each magazine is also somewhat standardized. After the table of contents, most issues begin with a page called "se abre el aquelarre/getting started."[14] This page includes an overview of the issue's theme. Typically, the next section is "todas las voces todas/all the voices" which includes the letters the collective has received presumably since the last issue. Most issues also have a "crítica/reviews" section. Reviews are generally of books and films.

The reviews, like everything in the magazine, appear in both Spanish and English, but the materials reviewed are typically one or the other. Additionally, most issues contain a list of resources and organizations often under the heading "otros aquelarres/other aquelarres." The majority of the issues also

Figure 6.1.   Cover of *Aquelarre*, Issue 1 (July/August/September 1989)

have a section called "noticias/news," and the stories are from Latin America and Canada. The editors also include cartoons in most issues, presumably to lend a bit of comic relief to often very serious subjects. For example, in the issue about immigrant women there are a few cartoons that depict some

Figure 6.2.   Cover of *Aquelarre*, Issue 2 (October/November/December 1989)

women immigrants' embarrassing moments upon arriving in Canada (issue number 3, 1990, 40–41). The cartoons also convey the grassroots nature of the magazine, since they are all handwritten (see figures 6.6 and 6.7).

Figure 6.3.   Cover of *Aquelarre*, Issue 5: "Alfabetización/Literacy" (July/August/September 1990)

Other sections include: "vamos al grano/getting to the point," the non-fiction articles; "palabra de mujer/woman's word," the fiction and poetry; "quehaceres/women do this," which includes stories about women's cultural and/or political activism; "manos a la obra/hands on" which are typically

Figure 6.4. Cover of *Aquelarre*, Issue 14: "¿Globalización de la Economía o de la Pobreza?/Globalization of the Economy or of Poverty?" (Spring 1994)

Used with permission of Carmen Rodríguez, *Revista Aquelarre.*

Figure 6.6.   "Wait, lady! That is not a mailbox! That is a garbage can!"
"My throat is so sore, doctor. I must be constipated." *(The English "to be constipated" translates into the literal Spanish "estar constipada", which means to have a cold.)*

Figure 6.7. "Can you come and pick me up? I think I got lost . . . "
"Can you tell me the name of the streets?"
"Let me see . . ."
"I'm at the corner of 'stop' and 'one way.'"

first-person narratives or interviews; and "así somos/as we are," which includes writings about identity. All issues include advertisements, most for
political organizations, including bookstores and groups doing solidarity
work in Latin America. Though most are local, some ads reflect a national
and international audience. And while some are very small establishments,
for example, La Quena Coffee House, which advertised in multiple issues,
there are also some big-name advertisers, like *Ms.* magazine.

Each issue (save two, 1 and 6) is organized topically. The common threads
to all of the magazines are women, feminism, and strength. It would take an
entire book to discuss each issue individually. Rather, I want to offer a sense
of what topics were important to the collective as reflected through the themes
upon which they focused. In analyzing the different issues I have found that
there are four overarching themes into which the different issues fit: identity
politics, cultural production, human rights, and sociopolitical issues. The following four issues fit into the category identity politics: Immigrant women
(3); Latin America & the Caribbean Feminism (7/8); First Nations Women
of the Americas: 500 Years of Resistance (10/11); and Ethnic and Cultural
Diversity (12/13). Three issues fit into the category cultural production:
Women and Art (4); Latin American Women Writers (9); and The Cultural
Work of Latin American Women in Canada (15). Three others fit under the
rubric human rights: Human Rights and the Rights of Women (2)[15]; Violence
Against Women: What Is To Be Done? (16/17); and When History Hurts (18).

The remaining four issues fit into the category sociopolitical issues: Literacy (5); Globalization of the Economy or of Poverty? (14); Labor/Globalization (19)[16]; and Popular Education: From and With Women (20/21). Without even looking at the details of each magazine one can see the potential for overlap. Indeed, poverty (issue 14) can be considered a form of violence (issue 16/17). Each issue is replete with examples of *Aquelarre*'s vision of feminist-inspired justice, but I have chosen only two issues to discuss in some detail: The inaugural issue (1) and their issue on feminism (7/8).

The Inaugural Issue

The editors of *Aquelarre* in part saw their tasks as documenting and inspiring the creative works of Latin American women; particularly those labors dedicated to social justice. From the collective's perspective social justice projects took many forms—from poetry to cartoons to feminist conferences. The first issue of *Aquelarre* was in July/August/September 1989 and it introduces the reader to the collective's vision of the interconnection between cultural production, women's voices, and political empowerment vis-à-vis a space of one's own. In this issue the collective begins the "quehaceres/women do this" section with an article entitled "Historias de Viajes Inesperados/I Wasn't Born Here," which centers on a theatrical piece written by, performed by, and about Latin American women living in Victoria, British Columbia. For the article, *Aquelarre* interviews Director Lina de Guevara (a Chilean exile) and some of the other actresses who collectively wrote about their own experiences as Latinas in Victoria.[17] *Aquelarre* asked the women: "What changes have you gone through since the beginning of the play?" Yolanda, a Chilean who has been in Canada since 1975, explained: "I now have more confidence in myself. I was coming out of a hole. I was really depressed; I couldn't speak. My teeth chattered. Then I decided to learn how to drive. Now I think I could even pilot an airplane" (quoted in *Aquelarre* 1989c, 6). Yolanda's words capture much of what *Aquelarre* was about: women's cultural production as an embodiment of strength and resistance. Toward the end of the interview Lina explains her vision for the type of theater she does:

> I want our theatre to be healing. This is the reason the play has had such a good reception. I think people feel that the play brings a message that heals wounds. We [Latina exiles and immigrants] have all experienced feeling attacked and injured from every side. Even though the play touches upon some very sad and tragic subjects, the outcome always shows that we are not alone (quoted in *Aquelarre* 1989c, 7).

Once again we see the women using cultural production politically while simultaneously nursing the emotional wounds caused by exile. *Aquelarre* very much supported that approach, as evidenced by the articles, stories, and images that filled their pages.

The *Aquelarre* project was fueled by passion. Indeed, the collective could not have survived so long, and done so much tedious and time-consuming work, for no pay, if the satisfaction of the end product was not worth something in and of itself. One article in the first issue that really captures their passion appears in the "así somos/as we are" section. It is a story about a Salvadoran refugee in Vancouver known as *"La Abuela"* (the grandmother). Included in this section is a poem written by La Abuela called "Yo Quiero/I Would Like:"

> I would like to be a messenger
> of love, work and well being.
> Let us struggle against war
> and love all that is life. . . .
> I would like our cry of protest
> to be heard in every corner of the world.
> We renounce war
> because we want to live. . . .
> I would like them [the warmongers] to abandon
> their ambition and resentment
> because in the third war
> there will be no winner. (in *Aquelarre* 1989c, 12)

This poem speaks to the explicit political convictions of the collective in its use of terms like *warmonger*. (*Warmonger* is La Abuela's word from an earlier sentence not included in this excerpt.) The editors' decision to include the poem alerts the readers that the magazine is about much more than Latinas in Canada; it is also about global social issues that are in part responsible for forcing the women from their homelands in the first place.

The final example from this first issue that speaks to their vision of documenting and supporting the varied efforts of Latinas toward social justice appears in the "crítica/reviews" section. It is a brief review of a book entitled *La Mujer Proletaria* written by Chilean Cecilia Salinas. The reviewer writes: "Researcher Cecilia Salinas takes on the difficult task of tracking down and following the until now invisible story of women's involvement in the Chilean working-class movement between 1880-1920. She satisfies a long overdue and ever urgent need, raising many questions and issues" (in *Aquelarre* 1989c, 28). Once again we see the collective's support and celebration of the work of Chilean women intellectuals in their task of documenting and disseminating the political history of women.[18] Similarly, reviewing a book by a Chilean author that was only published in Chile speaks to the collective's desire to stay linked with Latinas in the interior. The next to last section of the magazine, "otros aquelarres/other aquelarres," also speaks to their connections with Latinas and feminism inside of Latin America. It includes a brief notice about the upcoming regional Encuentro in Argentina, including contact information for more details. In other words, *Aquelarre* was one link in the transcontinental feminist movement that was flourishing in this post-dictatorship era.

The Feminism Issue

Aquelarre's issue 7/8 is called "América Latina & el Caribe Feminismo/Latin America & the Caribbean Feminism" and it came out Spring/Summer 1991. The "se abre el aquelarre/getting started" section of this issue is quite telling. The editors titled it "Una Semana en la Vida Feminista/A Week in the Life of a Feminist." It is a cut-and-pasted graphic of a detailed to-do list, handwritten, and meant to look like a page from a spiral-type notebook. The list conveys the full-time nature of the feminist's jobs and inserts humor apparently as a way to diffuse the stress brought on by the work load. A few choice entries include:

Monday 8:00—Take the kids to school and go to work
            10:15—Emergency union meeting
            12:00—Call the printer/organize meeting for Wed/check vegetable prices for festival end of week/schedule for volunteers/call teachers about Juanito's progress
            5:00—make supper
            7:00—editorial meeting. Café Roma ② *still exists in vancouver*
            8:30—collective meeting—discuss graphics policy
            10:00—pick up kids, put them to bed
            10:30—write and translate intro to poets' article
            1:00—bed/no dreams—how are we going to pay the printer?

Then skipping down to the weekend:

Saturday 6:00 [am]—load the truck/sell food all day at the festival/handout Aquelarre leaflets—other brujas [witches] are starting production of the magazine
Sunday   – same as Saturday
            midnight—take down the stand/load the truck, count the money
            2 am—Manuel wants to . . .
            I have a headache. . . . (*Aquelarre* 1991c, 2)

This section is telling for a variety of reasons. First, it very much concurs with the stories the women told me over and over regarding how busy they were with paid, domestic, and feminist labor. It hints of course at an inability to keep one's intimate relationships a priority in the face of the stress of the "week in the life of a feminist." The list also very much reflects the actual schedule of meetings that one of the women shared with me and the collective's propensity toward making all decisions cooperatively rather than delegating things out and thus minimizing everyone's workload. And finally, the format of this "getting started" section is in contrast to most of the other issues that tried to lay out a clear agenda and rationale for the topic at hand.

For example, in the "Women and Art/Mujer Y Arte" issue (4) the editors write:

> In the words of one of the artists we present, art is a subject as broad as life itself, so vast that in trying to describe it, [it] tends to slip away; it is hard to outline. But somehow we had to decide what to present, where to begin, and the first stroke we traced, for the sake of unity and space available, was to limit ourselves to visual art; an area, as many others, in which women have had to forge a way to express themselves and gain recognition. (*Aquelarre* 1990e, 2)

In this case, the editors set up the issue and the reader has a sense of its focus. In contrast, the feminism "getting started" section tells the reader about the feminist workload rather than the content of the magazine to follow. A commonality of both, however, is a sense of the collective celebration of women and feminists. The entry about art talks about women artists being forced to gain recognition, which implies battles and accomplishments, and the feminist one, albeit in an entirely different way, celebrates the hard work of feminists by acknowledging the behind-the-scenes tasks that remain hidden from nonactivists.

The predominant approach to feminism in this issue is that the feminist ideologies and projects are about much more than middle-class white women; they include positions of race, nation, ethnicity, class status, age, sexuality, and so forth. The editors attempt to present feminism as an inclusive rather than exclusive project. They do this in part by including articles and interviews with a variety of different women who talk abut feminism from their own social positions and challenge the hegemony of heterosexual, white, middle-class women in many feminist organizations. The issue starts with an overview of feminism in Latin America and the Caribbean based on reports from the fifth Encuentro in Argentina. The article is at once celebratory and cautious, ambitious and realistic. The article implies that feminism is about political economy and democracy as much as it is about women. The reader gets the sense that feminism in the region is on the verge of something, assessing the new post-dictatorship political context and attempting to insert a gendered analysis into it. Much the same was happening in the diaspora. The solidarity movement had ended years prior and this magazine helped

Chileans and other Latinas sort out their leftist pasts with their feminist futures. One commonality we see in both the solidarity and feminist movements is the place of cultural production in articulating politics.

Another entry that captures the ideological breadth of feminism is aptly called "¿Qué es el Feminismo? What is Feminism?" by Macarena Bernabei. It starts out:

> Hi! I'm Macarena. I'm 12 years old and in Grade 7. I'm going to tell you about how I came to interview feminist women.
>
> One day I heard that a lot of ladies, more precisely feminist women, were going to come here. So I asked my Mom why they were coming. She told me I should go and ask them.
>
> Curious as I am, I took some sheets of paper, a pen and I began to ask questions.
>
> The more questions I asked, the more I enjoyed it. . . . I managed to do 50, from all sorts of different countries.
>
> I took my work to school to show others. But everyone, even the teachers, treated me very badly. Maybe they were just jealous. But fortunately I didn't let that upset me, since in this way I had the satisfaction of meeting people from other countries, to learn about their customs, how they respond to different problems and above all else to know what feminism is in their countries. (Bernabei 1991, 14)

The article then goes on to include quotes from feminists from Argentina, Ecuador, Guatemala, Germany, Basque Country, Spain, Uruguay, Peru, and Paraguay. Macarena concludes her part of the article, as a highly sophisticated, passionate twelve-year-old:

> Well, I learned from doing these interviews that it is very nice of you to have come to defend us from men who think badly of women, for men to not be such machos in front of women and that you defend us a little so that the men don't think they own the whole world. . . . Thank you for everything. (Bernabei 1991, 17)

Here *Aquelarre* is simultaneously tackling accessibility and diversity. They attempt to show that if one wants to know about feminism, all one has to do is ask, like twelve-year-old Macarena did. For the "brujas" of *Aquelarre*, feminism is not meant to be exclusive and alienating but rather accessible and empowering, as evidenced by Macarena's response to her whole process.

That said, the Aquelarre collective was not naïve to the fact that feminism, particularly at this historical moment (early 1990s), has a history of being very closed to certain groups of women, namely women of color and lesbians. In the article "Hacia el Desarrollo de un Feminismo Incluyente/Towards the Development of an Inclusive Feminism," author Noga Gayle confronts the

issue of feminist racism head on, invoking African-American feminist think-
ers like bell hooks, Patricia Hill Collins, Audre Lorde, and Angela Davis to
support her arguments. The author writes:

> If the goal of feminism is transformation towards social justice for all women,
> then there must be a better understanding of the diversity of women's experience
> and concerns. The factors of class and race in feminist analysis must be given
> centrality. All women's experiences should be regarded as equally valuable. So
> far, this has not been the case. (Gayle 1991, 25)

The article speaks to the feminisms in the Americas—Canada, the United
States, Latin America, and the Caribbean—and articulates the way racism
crosses borders, is ideologically similar across nations, but operationalized
differently, particularly within feminist communities. The language is powerful and forces the reader to confront topics that, particularly at this time, were
extremely underacknowledged. *Aquelarre* unequivocally established that for
them, race and racism are feminist issues.

In a further attempt to present feminism as an inclusive project *Aquelarre*
also addresses the taboo issue of homosexuality, a topic that was conspicu-
ously overlooked by feminists in Latin America for a prolonged period (see
Alvarez et al. 2003; Sternbach et al. 1992). They include two separate pieces,
one, a first person testimony "Me Llamo Erika y Soy Lesbiana/My Name is
Erika and I am a Lesbian," and another, a more academic piece entitled "El
Continuum Lesbiano/The Lesbian Continuum." Both pieces attempt to break
the silence about sexuality, which in many cases is imbued with homophobia.
In Erika's testimony she boldly shares:

> We love like you do in your heterosexual relationships; we give flowers as gifts,
> we pamper each other, we make love with the same intensity as you; long kisses,
> impassioned embraces. And yes, we touch each other's vaginas, our breasts. We
> play with our tongues until we get tired. We dance together. Tell me, what do
> you know when you can barely handle this subject? Why are you silent? Why do
> you feel uncomfortable? Go ahead and tell me, ask me questions, even though
> they may be stupid. I don't want any more silences; I want to come out, liberate
> myself from that other self which I have carried for a long time because I was
> afraid of you. I don't blame you. (Espinoza 1991, 42)

Aquelarre's decision to include this essay as well as the other one about les-
bianism speaks to their commitment to break silences and document women's
lived experiences, even the painful aspects that reflect tensions, conflicts,
and prejudices among each other. *Aquelarre* was committed to creating and
maintaining a feminist dialogue across the Americas and this issue was a clear
example of that goal.

CONCLUSION

In this chapter I have outlined the political mobilization of Chilean women exiles in Vancouver. I have discussed how different women came to their feminist identities while others did not. We saw that the exiles organized women-only, nonfeminist projects as well as explicitly feminist ones. Some women felt connected to feminism, while others were alienated by it. Some women felt that men should participate in their projects, while others did not. Some women felt their male compañeros respected them and their political contributions; others felt politically dismissed. Once again, studying gender and feminism reminds us that women do not necessarily see eye to eye simply because of our shared biology.

Do the projects of the Chilean exiles constitute a transnational feminist movement? In my estimation, the answer is yes. A social movement is a grassroots, collectively organized series of actions that register opposition to a given set of circumstances or structures. The conference, *Aquelarre*, and all of the smaller projects that enabled both, constitute grassroots, collective action while also articulating feminist agendas relevant to Chilean exiles and other Latina immigrants in the Vancouver area. The conference and *Aquelarre* served as cultural and political embodiments of feminist opposition to patriarchal structures that erase women's political, social, and cultural contributions from the historical record. The conference embodied a collective statement of women's desires and abilities to participate in politics and *Aquelarre* served as a space to foster, articulate, and document their actions. In short, both projects were about locating and enhancing women's political power and voices. Arguably neither space was inherently political. However, feminist analyses of politics, particularly leftist politics in Latin America, has shown us that even some of the most seemingly apolitical women-only spaces are replete with political agency and power. That is, the conference was much more than a meeting and the magazine more than a cultural production.

How can a magazine or a single conference constitute a transnational feminist movement? According to Moghadam a transnational feminist network, and by extension, movement, is one organized above the national level and unites women from three or more countries around a common agenda (2005, 4). With respect to exile feminism, it is more accurate to argue "around" the national level in order to capture the truly nongovernmental and grassroots nature of both projects. The contributors, attendees, and organizers of both the conference and *Aquelarre* represent many more than three countries. Recall that both the Aquelarre collective and conference-organizing committee were made up of women from Chile, Argentina, Canada, the United States, Colombia, Mexico, and then some. Similarly, the women shared agendas: The conference organizers sought to create a collective space to enable networking among feminists across the Americas, and the *Aquelarre* collective sought to produce a magazine that spoke to the cultural, political, and social contributions of these same women. That is, both projects were about the political empowerment and collaboration of Latin American women, regardless of their current country of residence. Both projects sought to create dialogue between exiles and feminists in Latin America. Quantitatively we know that the conference in Vancouver was the fifth in Canada over a course of six years (1981–1987). Additionally, the Aquelarre collective lasted from 1987 until 1996.

In other words, these projects were far more than a single conference or magazine issue; rather, they were a series of transnational feminist events spear-headed by Chilean exiles in Canada that lasted from 1981 until 1996, or fifteen years, during and after the dictatorship. Qualitatively, the level of success of course depends on who one asks and how one measures it, particularly in the context of a feminist movement with such a ubiquitous agenda. Regardless, we do know that Chilean exile feminists in Vancouver organized across the Americas to declare, document, and direct women's experiences that might have otherwise remained hidden from history. Despite their efforts, many scholars and activists fail to identify exile feminism as an important link in transnational feminism. I hope this book contributes to a growing understanding of the place of diaspora in women's transnational politics.[19]

NOTES

1. "*Encuentro* (from the Spanish encontrar)—to meet or to find, oneself or another, to confront oneself or another. Also used in the reflexive, encontrarse—to find oneself, or to meet each other, as in coming together, to share. A meeting place where one exchanges ideas, expresses feelings, thoughts and emotions; listens and is listened to, agrees and disagrees, affirms and contradicts"). Nancy Saporta Sternbach et al., (1992), "Feminisms in Latin America: From Bogota to San Bernardo," in *The Making of Social Movements in Latin America: Identity, Strategy, and Democracy*, ed. Arturo Escobar and Sonia E. Alvarez (Boulder: Westview Press), 236–37.

2. See also Christine Bolt, (1993), *Women's Movements in the United States and Britain from the 1790s to the 1920s* (Amherst, Mass.: University of Massachusetts); Ellen Carol DuBois, (1991), "Woman Suffrage and the Left: An International Socialist-Feminist Perspective," *New Left Review* 186(March/April): 20–44; Richard J. Evans, (1977), *The Feminists: Women's Emancipation Movements in Europe, America and Australia, 1840–1920* (London: Croom Helm); Myra Marx Ferree and Carol McClurg Mueller, (2004), "Feminism and the Women's Movement: A Global Perspective," in *The Blackwell Companion to Social Movements*, ed. David A. Snow, Sarah A. Soule, and Hanspeter Kriesi (Malden, Mass.: Blackwell Publishing), 576–607; Sandra Stanley Holton, (1994), "'To Educate Women in Rebellion:' Elizabeth

Cady Stanton and the Creation of a Transatlantic Network of Radical Suffragists," *American Historical Review* 99(4): 1112–36; Jane Rendall, (1984), *The Origins of Modern Feminism: Women in Britain, France, and the United States, 1780–1860* (New York: Schocken); Leila Rupp, (1994), "Constructing Internationalism: The Case of Transnational Women's Organizations, 1888–1945," *American Historical Review* 99(5): 1571–1600; Clare Taylor, (1974), *British and American Abolitionists* (Edinburgh: University of Edinburgh Press).

3. See Valentine Moghadam, (2005), *Globalizing Women: Transnational Feminist Networks* (Baltimore: The Johns Hopkins University Press), 10–11, for a list of some of the most active networks. Her list includes thirty-six organizations based and comprised of members from all over the world, including Egypt, the United States, Canada, Kenya, Uganda, Poland, the United Kingdom, Nigeria, Pakistan, Malaysia, Bulgaria, Cyprus, Austria, Chile, The Netherlands, Japan, Fiji, and Belgium.

4. "Machismo is obviously a Latin American manifestation of global patriarchy, whereby males enjoy special privileges within society and within the family are considered superior to women." Ximena Bunster, (1993), "Surviving Beyond Fear: Women and Torture in Latin America," in *Surviving Beyond Fear: Women, Children and Human Rights in Latin America*, ed. Marjorie Agosín (New York: White Pine Press), 100.

5. Ana María is in her early sixties, as are many of the women I interviewed. Similarly, most of the women who talked about their strong women relatives noted that these women were significantly ahead of their times.

6. Sacha is a pseudonym.

7. Some examples outside Latin America include: the Self-Employed Women's Association in Gujarat, India, the Working Women's Forum, and the Tamil Nadu Women's Collective, both based in Tamil Nadu, India, and Ama Samuha, a Mother's Group in Nepal involved in social activism such as banning alcohol, fighting against violence, etc.

8. In our focus group discussion a year later Cecilia said there were about forty women in the group.

9. Irene was one of the women who repeatedly questioned her memory with respect to dates.

10. July 1981: Bogotá, Colombia; July 1983: Lima, Peru; July 1985: Bertioga, Brazil; October 1987: Taxco, Mexico; November 1990: San Bernardo, Argentina; October 1993: Costa del Sol, El Salvador; November 1996: Cartagena, Chile; November 1999: Juan Dolió, Dominican Republic; December 2002: Playa Tambor, Costa Rica; October 2005: Sao Paolo, Brazil; March 2009: Mexico City, Mexico.

11. Amparo Ochoa was a Mexican folklorist. Her most passionate songs reflect her concerns about poverty, and indigenous peoples' and women's rights. She passed away in February 1994.

12. One of the Canadian women was American born but left the United States for Canada during the Viet Nam war so her now-ex-husband would not be drafted.

13. For some reason the letters stopped appearing after issue number 14. It is not clear if the editors stopped receiving letters or ultimately chose to no longer include them.

14. All section headings are lower case.

15. This issue does not have a specific name.

16. This issue does not have a specific name.

17. I interviewed Lina for this book and discuss her work in the book's conclusion. Additionally, her testimony is included in the appendix.

18. I had the opportunity to interview Cecilia Salinas while in Chile. (She has since passed away.) Many of the other Chilean women I interviewed there pointed to Cecilia's book as an important contribution to the feminist historical record.

19. For further discussion of the place of diaspora in transnational feminisms, see Alena Heitlinger, ed., (1999), *Émigré Feminism: Transnational Perspectives* (Toronto: University of Toronto Press).

Conclusion

Gender and Permanence

For me, exile, it is like a puzzle . . . Like land cut up in little islands . . . Where each person lives with his own landscape, his own memories. Exile is not an immense territory shared among everyone. It is something very intimate.

—Ema Malig, Painter (in Guzmán 2004)

INTRODUCTION

On October 17, 2007, *Inti-Illimani* performed in North Vancouver. According to the flyer circulated by the brother of one of the Chilean women interviewed for this book:

> For four decades Inti-Illimani's music has intoxicated audiences around the globe. In 2007, Inti-Illimani celebrates its 40th anniversary and the release of *Pequeño Mundo*, its forty-third album. Wedded in traditional Latin American roots and playing on more than 30 wind, string and percussion instruments, Inti-Illimani's compositions are a treasure for the human spirit. Their mellifluous synthesis of instrumentals and vocals captures sacred places, people's carnivals, daily lives, loves and pains that weave an extraordinary cultural mural. (Flyer, received via LAVA email list, September 24, 2007)

Almost thirty-five years after Pinochet's coup the spirit of the Chilean Left continues to permeate the greater Vancouver area. Nearly every person I interviewed for this book, including the children who were raised in Vancouver, spoke of Inti-Illimani and their role in keeping Chile alive for them while in exile. Not surprisingly, Inti was welcomed back with open arms, ears, and likely tears.

As I have shown in this book music and tears were equally present in the exiles' solidarity movement and often it was women doing the singing and crying. We learned that at least a million Chileans left their homeland as a result of the dictatorship and that these exiles, in at least one hundred countries around the entire world, organized swiftly and transnationally to topple Pinochet and support their *compañeras/os* in the interior. Vancouver of course was no exception. I demonstrated that Chilean exiles were motivated to organize, join, and stick with the movement as a result of emotional and cultural factors. We saw that their outrage over the coup and Pinochet's attack on their socialist political aspirations and accomplishments, combined with the cultural histories they brought into exile help explain why the movement came about in the first place. That is, their political and emotional trauma fused with their leftist cultural roots to catapult activists into the movement and sustain them once there.

I also argued that the exiles' emotions, particularly women's, shaped the tactical decisions they made in organizing their movement and the sorts of events and institutions they prioritized, namely the culturally rooted ones. Related to this, we saw that for many of the women I spoke to, emotions played a major role in sustaining the movement, especially their own personal participation in it. Many women and their families were traumatized by exile and the abrupt and forced separation from not only their homeland but also their extended families. As a result the *peñas* and housing co-op offered them a "mini-Chile" and an impromptu extended family. So despite their extreme time pressures they still found ways to participate in the movement because it served to mediate their and their families' pain. One of the most concrete fusions of emotions with culture was embodied by the children. The exiles, again, particularly the mothers, taught their children to be Chilean and celebrate their Chileanness in dance, song, and theater. The children were partially responsible for keeping Chile in the exiles' personal and political worlds despite the fact that Canada and Chile were social and geographical hemispheres apart. We also saw that through the efforts of the Chilean exiles in Vancouver—men and women, adults and children alike—and their non-Chilean supporters, exiles in Canada, and elsewhere in the world, were a significant sector in ultimately forcing Pinochet from power and returning democracy to their beloved Chile.

I also argued that not only did women play key roles in the solidarity movement—everything from chopping onions, to starting New Song bands, to meeting with Canadian politicians, and speaking to the press—they also applied their activist skills to a feminist movement. And similar to the solidarity movement, cultural production was key to articulating their message of women's strength, pan-American solidarity, and ultimately contributing to the feminist archives of Latin American women's history. The story I shared in this book, particularly that specific to Vancouver, is told predominantly through the eyes of women from the solidarity and feminist movements. Much of what I shared I would have likely heard if I had spoken only to men, for example, the significance of peñas to the movement. But I would likely have heard more about the importance of the political parties in birthing the movement in contrast to the women mocking the parties, and their predominantly male leadership for spending more time discussing the "documents from the interior" and not chopping onions. In this conclusion I will discuss how using a gendered lens enhanced our understanding of the exiles' political experiences in Vancouver. I will close this chapter with a discussion of the permanence of exile, particularly with respect to women's cultural production.

THE GENDER LENS

What do I mean by a gendered lens?[1] Using a gendered lens means that one's starting point assumes, an assumption based on decades of research, that women experience and live in the world differently than men (and vice versa), especially where there exists a strong gendered division of labor. As a result women have ideas, perceptions, expectations, connections, and feelings that systematically differ from but potentially overlap with men's. It follows then that an analysis of the solidarity movement that did not begin from this assumption would have missed a lot. How exactly did I apply this gendered lens? First, I gave priority to the perspectives of women. I interviewed and re-interviewed women and I combed through their feminist archives.[2] That is, women were treated as the experts. Next, using a gendered lens effected the questions I asked and sought to answer. Centering women meant I wanted to hear and share their specific histories, and feminism is a fundamental part of many of the exiles' lives in Vancouver. Third, it influenced the theoretical and historical literature I drew from to help contextualize and interpret my research. My analysis of the women exiles' political experiences in Vancouver would have been less comprehensive had I not also previously researched (Shayne 2004) and read about women's political activism in Latin America and literature produced by other scholars using their own versions of a gender lens. Fourth, this approach meant I applied the gendered division of labor paradigm to understand the work women did in the movement and their feelings about it. Finally, in my estimation one reason to apply a gendered lens is to help archive women's untold stories. Sadly the old cliché that history is written by and about men is still quite viable. This is absolutely changing, as most bookstores, libraries, course catalogs, and journal titles will attest.

The only way to continue making progress toward this goal is to keep on our gendered lenses.

As I attempted to demonstrate throughout this book, two of the most prominent themes that emerged in my interviews were culture and emotions. I take these up in turn. As noted, I am quite confident that even if I only spoke with Chilean men I would have undoubtedly heard about the frequent peñas; they were such a staple and symbol of the movements all over the world it is unlikely anyone would overlook their existence. However, I believe by using a gendered lens and writing this social history from the perspective of women exiles, we have learned more than that peñas and cultural events were pillars of the movement. Rather, we were provided a window into why culture became so important to the movement—beyond the exiles' connections to the New Song movement. We saw that in many cases women attended and volunteered at them for the sense of security they received from being there and surrounded by other exiles. We also saw that women sang and performed because it made them feel better in the face of the trauma brought on by exile. As Ana María Quiroz shared in Chapter Five regarding their women's band *Cormorán,* "[it] was a therapy for us . . . we just enjoyed singing; we got a lot from each others' voices." That is, the women I interviewed taught us that the cultural events were more than just a product of history; they were an emotional need for and service to the exile community as well.

Related to this, since in many cases women were the cultural mothers and ambassadors of the movement—they started bands, taught their children Chilean dances and songs, made *arpilleras* in Chile and distributed them abroad—we saw the actual process that resulted in centering culture. Learning about the efforts undertaken to maintain a cultural component of the movement illuminated even further the amount of effort women put forth as a result of the sense of the urgency they attached to their cause. Exiles, men and women alike, worked tirelessly to denounce and dethrone Pinochet. Using a gender lens to look behind the scenes of the cultural events sheds light onto what it actually entailed to keep the music coming and the children dancing and singing. Women made time to teach themselves to sing and play instruments. They made time to sew the costumes the children needed to wear when doing the traditional Chilean dances. They made time to teach the children to sing the lyrics of songs they certainly were not learning at their neighborhood schools. And they did all of this and so much more while working paid jobs, taking care of their children, keeping their homes clean, and spouses fed—all in the absence of mothers and women relatives who would have significantly eased their burdens were they still in Chile. But they did it and they were proud of themselves. As I noted in Chapter Five the women said they grew tired just thinking about how hard they worked but given the chance they would do it all over again because they needed to force Pinochet from power.

Additionally, speaking specifically to women about the cultural components of the movements forces us to once again expand our definitions of "doing politics." As feminist scholars of Latin American social movements have consistently demonstrated, masculine definitions of politics tend to be entirely dismissive to women's realities and contributions. For example, if I asked a Chilean man active in the movement in Vancouver what sorts of tasks the activists did, I suspect he would not mention chopping onions or sewing children's costumes. On their face neither activity sounds political—cooking and sewing? But if we think about the activities in the context of the goals then they are most certainly political and deserve to be acknowledged as such. The women were not chopping onions because they were hungry or sewing clothes because their children had none. Rather, they needed to sell *empanadas* to raise money for their compañeros in the interior and dress their children in Chilean costumes to keep Chile alive while in exile while garnering solidarity for their cause. Their motivations were political and thus so too were the tasks. Expanding the definition of politics inevitably leads to capturing and celebrating a broader reality and subsequently creates historical archives more reflective of a given movement.

Emotions were also consistently woven into the women's personal testimonies and reflected in the collective face of the movement as well. I suspect there are several reasons the place of emotions in the movement became so pronounced to me, which would likely have not been the case if I removed my gender lens. On the one hand, social prescriptions for gendered behavior dictate that men behave "rationally" and women "emotionally." Though it is typically postulated as such, these potentially dichotomous behaviors are not a biological given but rather reinforced social expectations and performances. Because gendered expectations saturate everything—exile and exiles included—men and women's behavior typically reinforce the norms so much so as to make them look natural, or biological. As a result, it was acceptable for the women to open up to me emotionally without fear of me judging them. Men, however, are expected to be stoic and not carry their suffering with them. In the case of exile this is particularly unfair to men since in many cases they were the ones whose bodies were tortured and who experienced the physical and political assault more acutely. Also, because there was a certain sense of guilt on the part of the exiles that were able to get out while others stayed behind and were perhaps murdered, the men felt unable to acknowledge their pain. To do so would have implied not only personal weakness but also betrayal to their compañeros who were presumably suffering more.

Another reason I believe the gender lens allowed me to hear so much about emotions and their importance in the movement is related to the fact that women served as the managers of pain, particularly their children's pain. Just as men did, women also felt guilty for leaving Chile, particularly for separating their children from their grandparents. And as we learned many children of exiles were quite bitter they had to leave and did not hide their anger or depression from their parents. In the name of their children women then had to figure out ways to mediate their pain, and the solidarity movement and its cultural manifestations ultimately played a role in that process. For example, the exiles designed, funded, and built a housing cooperative in part so their children would have an extended family in the absence of the one they sorrowfully left behind. To be sure, men were very involved in that project, particularly as the architects. However, the women I spoke to about it talked about the co-op being much more than a physical space to house Chileans; it was partially meant to create an emotional space for their children, who felt plucked from their extended families in Chile.

Using a gendered lens, particularly the gendered division of labor, also elevated the place of emotions in this history because of the types of tasks women did in the movement. For example, recall women organized greetings at the airport to provide the newly arriving and traumatized exiles some form of emotional support. On the surface this does not sound like a particularly political project but when we think about why it was necessary and the coordination needed to accomplish it we see it as a branch of a larger social movement. I suspect if I asked Chilean men about the sorts of things they did in the movement I would not have learned about these greetings, as they sound beyond the bounds of the political. But similar to cooking and sewing, the women did not go to the airport to watch planes; they went because they were attempting to soften the pain caused by dictatorship and exile. Hearing the constant explicit and implicit reference to all things emotional pushed me to consult the social movement literature on emotions and in my mind ultimately helped me theorize more accurately where the movement came from. Without speaking to so many women I suspect my answer to that question would have left out the emotional component and thus been incomplete.

Related to this, the gender lens led me to deemphasize the place of political networks, namely parties, in birthing the movement. The limited scholarship that exists on the solidarity movement suggests that the movement was in a sense inevitable because of the political parties and networks the exiles brought with them when they fled. I do not deny that the parties and networks played an absolutely crucial role in facilitating and sustaining the movement. However, from the women's perspective, in many cases the parties and their persistent sectarianism often presented obstacles to the activists, not always opportunities. Similarly, many of the women were not involved in the parties because they are predominantly the domain of men. Though some of the women had party affiliations, often through their husbands at the time, it was not the parties that propelled them to organize, but oftentimes the pain and anger. As a result of deemphasizing the place of parties in the movement we ultimately see the place of agency ("the recognition of the ability to choose and the exercising of that choice") (Power 2002, 5). That is, the movement was started by people on the ground, not "documents from the interior." As I discussed in Chapter Three, the solidarity movement was highly networked across borders and continents. The parties absolutely made those networks more impenetrable but to keep them alive, particularly in the absence of the internet and open democracies, meant there had to be a lot of foot soldiers advancing the movement and sustaining the links. Speaking to the women allowed us to better connect with the foot soldiers.

We know that a gender lens determines who one turns to as experts and shapes the questions one asks. In the case of this book I wanted to know about feminism, which, if I was not thinking specifically about women, I would likely have missed entirely. Excluding the feminists, their organizations, accomplishments, and magazine from a story of Chilean exiles in Vancouver—women or men—would be historically imprecise. Feminism, particularly *Aquelarre*, represented more than hundreds of hours of unpaid labor, on top of paid work, and single motherhood. Rather, the feminists' efforts reflect the political skills of the exile community in general. *Aquelarre*, like the housing co-op and La Quena Coffee House, reflects the institutionalized nature of the exiles' community. Securing the funds and distributing the magazine took much more than ingenuity and hard work. The women needed things like grants, many from Canadian government agencies, which they were able to secure partly as the result of their long-standing positions in the community and familiarity with most things Canadian—including bureaucracy. In other words, the women would likely not have been able to produce *Aquelarre* so successfully if the Chilean exile community had not already fully established itself. Thus, the Aquelarre collective tells us about more than just women in Vancouver but Chilean exiles in general and their collective political efforts prior to the magazine.

In short, I believe using a gendered lens and writing this history from the women's perspectives led to a more complete picture of the movement than I would have been able to share had I not pursued the topic from this perspective. This book is motivated in part by the desire to archive an important node of a far reaching, vibrant, transnational movement. I still marvel at the exiles' solidarity movement—not just the Vancouver incarnation but everywhere. The ability to stay transnationally networked in the face of so many formidable structural, political, linguistic, and emotional obstacles absolutely warrants it a formal place in social movement history. This book was also motivated by a desire to contribute to the ever-growing archives of Latin American women's history, feminist and otherwise. Eventually the archives will catch up with history but in the mean time there is still much work to be done. This book is also meant to capture the cultural and historical footprint left by Chilean women exiles in Vancouver. In my estimation, using a gendered lens allowed me to more fruitfully meet those objectives.[3]

THE PERMANENCE OF EXILE

So (how) does this story end? How come the Chileans remain in Vancouver despite the return to democracy? Are they no longer exiles because they technically can return? Marcela Cornejo (2008) conducted a study with Chilean men and women who were exiled in Belgium during the dictatorship. She spoke to first- and second-generation exiles (as did I) as well as those who stayed in Belgium and those who returned to Chile.[4] Her research is largely psychological in focus and she was interested in issues of identity construction. Cornejo came upon many trends that were quite similar to those I bumped up against in my research. (I refer the reader to the article rather than list them here.) One, however, is worth noting in the context of this discussion. Cornejo concluded that all of the Chileans with whom she spoke, regardless of gender, generation, or current home country, felt that exile is forever. As she explains:

> All the narrators' life stories were stories of *exile after exile*, but the place of exile in an individual's life is always present; it never ends. Exiles are always looking for a place which they do not find here or there. Maybe that place does not exist, maybe it was destroyed forever. Or maybe it is the fact of having been displaced that condemned them forever not to have a place, to be in constant search. (2008, 342, emphasis in original)

In the course of my research I encountered a similar sentiment. Nearly every woman I interviewed spent the first many years of her exile expecting to someday return to Chile. Once that fantasy was squelched, often after returning to Chile to live and feeling they no longer belonged there, they did not surrender their exile status but rather accepted that their exile was most likely permanent. Some, however, did feel more at home in Vancouver after realizing they could not live in Chile, but in a sense that meant they turned into exiles in their own homeland. This sentiment is similar to Cornejo's observation that the exiles in Belgium were in constant search for a place that did not exist.

At first glance it seems rather ironic that Chileans in the movement did not rush back to the country to which they were so politically and emotionally attached and worked so passionately to change. Paradoxically, it was partly the result of their political work—directed at Chile, not Vancouver—that led the women to become more at home in Vancouver. Through their solidarity and feminist organizing they built new lives, new connections, and a new community for themselves in Vancouver to which they were eventually quite attached and could not easily abandon. The local connections and obligations were an unintended consequence of the movements that kept the women from going back to Chile. Some women I spoke with felt a certain relief at feeling at home in Vancouver, while others were bitter that they were "stuck" there. In either case, the new attachments reveal, albeit in a very different way, the power of culture and emotions.

Prior to conducting my interviews in British Columbia, I was introduced to the term "post-exile" by a Chilean woman who left Chile for reasons similar to the women I interviewed for this book. The term *post-exile* is meant to convey that one is no longer in exile because she now is legally entitled to return to her homeland. I asked many of the women about this term and received a variety of answers—some were adamant that exile could never end; the reasons one left the country are what defines an exile's status and those reasons will never change even though the Chilean government has. To these women the suggestion that one's exile status evolved into that of "post-exile" implied that their pain is a part of the past and no longer justified. For Patricia Andrade the pain is permanent regardless of the current political structure in Chile or her legal right to return. She unequivocally explained: "Never, never, never, never [can I get over it.] I still remember the things that I saw; I will never, never [forget]. . . . At night time I still cry; when I talk about it, I still [cry]. I am never, never, never going to forget. Never, never." On the other hand, there were women who felt the term *post-exile* accurately captured their lives; to them it did not suggest that they were no longer exiled but rather that their lives are significantly different than when they fled Chile. As Irene Policzer put it,

> [Post-exile] is not a bad term, I would call myself a post-exile. I am part of an ethnic community in Canada. . . . I still consider myself Chilean but I do not think I feel at home in Chile anymore. Chile has changed now; I have been away for too long; I do not feel comfortable there anymore. . . . The term post exile is good.

Debate around the term *post-exile* makes sense and I suspect there are many factors why different women either embrace or reject the term. If we move from academic discourse to political descriptors we might more accurately call the current era "post-Pinochet" rather than post-exile.

In this section I will speak to the permanence of exile as manifest in the cultural productions of Chilean women. I argue that exiles use cultural production, specifically popular theater, to continue to articulate and manage the emotions of exile and as a result have further entrenched Chileans into the cultural fabric of their formerly host, now home, country. During the dictatorship Chileans used art and cultural production to denounce the dictatorship and exile. In the post-Pinochet period they use it to claim the formerly transitional space as their own. I will focus specifically on the Theater of the Oppressed productions of Carmen Aguirre and Lina de Guevara.

Chilean women of the diaspora have used theater in the post-Pinochet period to keep their communities alive while also reflecting and documenting the past that brought them to Canada in the first place. Specifically, they use a Theater of the Oppressed approach. Theater of the Oppressed is a theatrical form developed in the 1960s by Brazilian director Augusto Boal (1985).[5] It arose in response to the military dictatorship's repression against theater companies that did not support the regime. The very basic premise of Theater of the Oppressed is to do theater based on the real experiences of disenfranchised people in order that they may find and rehearse strategies to overcome oppression. Boal created a model of working with a community, and through a series of games and exercises the playwright/director collects stories that eventually become the foundation of a play. In other words, a play emerges directly from the grassroots. While in B.C. I spoke to two Chilean women who started theater companies based on this model.

The younger of the two is Carmen Aguirre, the young woman we met in the first pages of this book whose house was raided by the Chilean military when she was six years old. At the time of our interview Carmen was thirty-six years old and already has an impressive career with theater. She has written or co-written fourteen plays and is working on two more. When I asked Carmen what made her realize that she wanted to use theater as a political tool she recalled a story of her time living in Lima, Peru, during the guerrilla war there, while working as an urban guerrilla for the anti-Pinochet movement; (see the appendix for more detail):

> I went to see this play which was three men and one woman. . . . And they did a play that was probably at least two hours; it might have been more, maybe three, with no intermission. And it was just them and they had one guitar but they had no props, they had nothing, [not even] texts. They basically told the history of Peru from the time of the conquest until that moment with their bodies and their voices but without text. And just to sit in that room at that time and to literally hear bombs going off as it was happening . . . with this group of people, and we were sitting in a circle, it was in the round, and I [thought] "Yeah! This is it; there is nothing more powerful than this; this is a political tool."

Carmen returned to Vancouver from South America in 1990 and went to theater school. By 1995 she started Vancouver's first Latino Theater Group (see also Habelle-Pallán 2002). She put out a call to the Latino community in Vancouver announcing that she was looking for Latinos interested in getting involved with theater. As a result, she founded the theater group and directed, wrote, produced, and acted in the play "Que Pasa con la Raza, eh?" As she explained to me,

> Basically what I did in the original theatre group and eventually what came out of it was the play "Que Pasa con La Raza" which was based on all these stories of these Latino youths living in Vancouver who came from, none of them were guerrillas as it were, right? but definitely children of guerrillas and children of disappeared people. So the whole play was about culture clash but it was based on their stories. And they performed that play even though they are not actors, which of course made it very strong. And that one was a big hit. I was with the group for [almost] ten years and it was very taxing . . . because I basically did everything; I wrote, directed, stage managed, produced, did the publicity; did everything and at the same time of course I did a whole bunch of other theatre with the professional theatre community in which I'm the only Latino person in the entire professional theatre community in Vancouver.

Carmen worked with this group of young people, late teens to early twenties, to help them articulate the experiences of Latino youth in Vancouver. She knew the story would not be told unless she facilitated it and politically she felt it needed to be done. Despite the fact that the group is no longer active (most of them learned or re-learned Spanish and subsequently returned to Latin America after working with Carmen) she still is working on a variety of other political plays, including one about the first group of Chileans that arrived in Vancouver in 1974 (Aguirre 2005). For Carmen, life is political and art is life; her plays will likely always engender the fusion of culture and politics as experienced through the eyes of a Chilean woman.

Lina de Guevara is the other Chilean playwright I met in B.C. Lina is seventy-one years old and her exile in Canada began in 1976. She and her husband were Allende supporters at the time of the coup but no longer active in politics. Despite their relatively low profiles in politics, she and her husband had lived in Cuba from 1961 through 1964, something that certainly put them on the junta's radar (see appendix for more details). Through contacts in Canada they were able to leave Chile for Toronto, where they lived for one year, and then went to Victoria, B.C., where they have lived ever since. She currently teaches theater at the University of Victoria. Like Carmen, Lina also works from Augusto Boal's Theater of the Oppressed model.[6] And like Carmen, she had a burning need to share her and other women immigrants' stories with the people she was meeting in Canada. She explained:

During those first years here I felt a growing need to explain myself to my new fellow citizens, because I had lost all my old connections. I was no longer living among people with whom I shared a past, a culture, a language, a history. I needed to tell my new fellow citizens who I was, where I came from. Because, especially when you come from a Third World country, we are known by our problems, not by our successes. What most people in Canada knew about Chile was that it had undergone a bloody military coup, and suffered under a cruel dictator: Pinochet. Few people knew that Chile had at least two great poets who were Nobel Prize winners; that we had great architects; that the University of Chile was an internationally respected institution; that our Social Security System had, at one time, been exemplary. . . . So I wanted to tell my story the way I saw it. I did not want to be looked down upon; I did not want to be pitied. I wanted to be known and respected on my own terms. And I found that these feelings were shared by all immigrants. Maybe expressed in different ways, but the need, the hunger to communicate our reality and our worth was acknowledged by all immigrants I talked to. (2001)[7]

In 1988 she applied for and received the support of the Canadian federal government in the form of the "Manpower and Immigration" grant. The objective of the grant was to provide professional training to people who would not otherwise be employable. With the grant she established PUENTE Theatre, which, as of summer 2009, still exists.

PUENTE's first play was called "I Wasn't Born Here: Stories of Unexpected Voyages." Lina recruited five other Latina immigrants and they did the research to write the play. Each one interviewed ten other women, working from a questionnaire that they designed to elicit images, feelings, and anecdotes that would later become the text of the play. They also confronted and overcame the language barriers and were able to present the play in such a way that even the women who spoke little English were also able to tell their stories. The company has gone on and continues to do many, many more plays, including one about domestic violence in the Latino community. Often the plays are interactive and call upon the audience to help solve the problems that the actors present, thus facilitating active listening rather than passive consumption. For Lina, like the other Chilean women artists I spoke to for this research, art is political. Theater, when used as a political tool, has the ability to empower those not typically given voice, in the case of Lina and Carmen's work, Latin Americans in Canada.

In the end, Chileans like Lina and Carmen continue to leave their mark in British Columbia, and indeed everywhere they ended up. Exiles left and inspired a trail of political culture: They left a housing cooperative; their children and grandchildren are in or graduated from the local schools; they have taught Canadians at the local universities; they have written fiction and poetry available in the local bookstores; they have performed and directed their plays in local theaters. And, as I noted in the opening of this chapter, they continue to bring their beloved Inti-Illimani to share with the peoples of Vancouver. Chileans left a political cultural footprint in many cases inspired and orchestrated by the women I had the fortune of meeting while writing this book. The Vancouver of September 10, 1973, was very different from what it is thirty-six years later, and that is in great part due to Chilean women exiles.

NOTES

1. The discussion that follows is not meant to analyze the gender dynamics in the movement but rather to think about what we learned as a result of using a gendered lens. I point the reader to Diana Kay, (1987), *Chileans in Exile: Private Struggles, Public Lives* (Wolfeboro, N.H.: Longwood Academic); Diana Kay, (1988), "The Politics of Gender in Exile," *Sociology* 22(1): 1–21, for a comprehensive study of gender dynamics in a Chilean exile community in Great Britain.

2. Most of the material I received specific to the solidarity movement came from the one man (a Canadian) that I interviewed.

3. See also Bahati Kuumba, (2001), *Gender and Social Movements* (Walnut Creek, Calif.: AltaMira Press), for a similar argument about the efficacy of a gender lens in studying social movements.

4. During my research in Vancouver I interviewed one woman who had permanently returned to Chile but happened to be visiting Vancouver at the time of my research. I spoke to another woman who was about to return to Chile for what she hoped would be for good. Another woman was making plans to spend half of the year in Chile and half in Vancouver because her daughter, who was raised in Vancouver, had recently returned to Chile and had a baby there. About half of the women I interviewed had returned for some extended period of time, many hoping they could move back home but later realizing they were no longer comfortable in Chile and returning to Vancouver. While conducting my research in Chile most of the women I interviewed were exiled for some duration of the dictatorship, often many years, and eventually returned to Chile.

5. Theater of the Oppressed, just as it sounds, is the theatrical version of Paulo Freire's theories regarding popular education. Paulo Freire, (1993), *Pedagogy of the Oppressed, 2d ed.* (New York: Continuum).

6. Once I arrived in Vancouver I found out that Lina had actually been a mentor to Carmen but I had located them independent of one another. I recently accessed Lina's theater company's webpage (http://www.puentetheatre.ca/) and saw that she is in the process of producing one of Carmen's plays.

7. This text comes from a keynote speech she gave at a conference at the University of Victoria in March of 2001.

Appendix
More Testimonies

Along the years it [exile] was really, it was extremely beneficial. . . . After all the suffering, and all the problems, and homelessness, and the times of precariousness, and all kinds of . . . pain, in the long run, there is a lot to be gained from that process because it has been constantly a process of change.

—Cecilia Boisier

Here I share the remaining testimonies. Two women's stories are not included, as I did not have enough detail to do their experiences justice. The testimonies appear in the order the women left Chile.

THE CHILEANS

Carmen Aguirre

Carmen is Carmen Rodríguez's eldest child. At the time of our interview she was thirty-six. Recall her story with which I opened this book—memories of watching her parents sob as they listened to Allende's last speech; memories of her home being ransacked by the military while she, her sister, and their nanny were psychologically terrorized, and memories of leaving Chile with her very anxious parents. Carmen and her family grew up in student housing at the University of British Columbia (UBC) while her parents re-validated their degrees. Carmen recalls living in what felt like two worlds:

Because my parents were key figures in the solidarity movement our house was always full of Chileans; there were always people sleeping on the floor. It

221

seemed to me like . . . we were surrounded by Chile, or what I thought Chile
was, of course. . . . I really literally did live in two worlds; in the world of Chile,
which is actually very specific, Chileans in exile in Vancouver, Canada, [laughs]
. . . and the world of Canada. The school, the elementary school/high school at
UBC is incredible so we were also lucky that we got to [attend it] . . . [it] is full
of international students' children . . . and it was an alternative school, . . . probably the most alternative school in Vancouver at that time.

At twelve Carmen and her sister traveled back to Chile for the first time.
They stayed with their grandparents and reunited with other relatives. Her
mother did not go with them because she was on the blacklist and could not
reenter Chile. Not long after, Carmen and her sister started "commuting"
between South America (Bolivia and Argentina) and Vancouver, where their
father was. (Recall Carmen's mother and partner Bob decided to return to
South America to join the resistance movement there.) Carmen had some
sense of the nature of her mother and Bob's work, if nothing else, that it was
entirely secretive, but did not realize until much later how much danger she
was actually in. Though politically she understands why her mother brought
them with her she feels it was an irresponsible decision and that she and her
sister would have been better off with their grandparents in Chile.

However, Carmen's interpretation of the past did not sour her to guerrilla
politics. After she graduated high school in Vancouver, at the age of eighteen,
independent of her family, she returned to South America to join the MIR
herself. She started in Argentina and was sent to Lima, Peru. She explains:

I was sent to Lima to go to a meeting during the Shining Path [guerrillas] near
take-over of Lima. There I was, having to go to these meetings in cafés, and
literally bombs going off around us. . . . I met with two men who were . . . much
older than me of course . . . so I met with them about ten times . . . during those
days in Lima. . . . I [told] them . . . that I wanted to go to Santiago, hopefully
to a marginal neighborhood, and work there . . . [as] an urban guerrilla; . . . I
wanted to be trained to be an urban guerrilla. . . . So they said that they had too
many people in Chile, that they had a lot of people doing that and they needed
rearguard and very specifically they needed somebody to learn how to fly planes
from the Andes. . . . They basically said you have to go to some Patagonia town
in Argentina and . . . sign up at a flying club and pretend you are some bourgeoi-
sie woman wanting to [learn to] fly.

Carmen was particularly disappointed with these orders and debated whether
to leave the movement entirely. She decided to stay involved and did things
like transport bombs across borders, nearly getting caught on multiple occa-
sions. She went to South America hoping to live inside one world but found
herself, once again, straddling two different universes:

I taught English about forty hours a week, full teaching [with] standing in front of a group of people teaching, and that is not counting the lesson plans and exams and everything, and I had to have a normal life, so I had a group of friends that I would have to go to coffee with . . . who were all either apolitical or right-wing. My roommate in Argentina was another English teacher, a young woman whose father was a big military man in Argentina; she was completely right-wing. So I had to have this whole façade . . . I had to dress very fashionably and the whole thing; it had to make sense that I joined a flying club; "Oh she's just an adventuresome kind of yuppie."

After living that life for four years, spending much of the time sick from stress, sleep deprivation, and fear, Carmen returned to Vancouver in 1990 at the age of twenty-two. She then enrolled in theater school to pursue an art form that for her very much lent itself to political expression. She is now a mother, accomplished actress, playwright, and producer who creates plays that strike deeply political chords.

Alejandra Aguirre

Alejandra is Carmen Aguirre's younger sister, by one year. In general Alejandra's memories are far less detailed than her sister's. She also has a different relationship to politics. In some senses she is grateful to have lived in Bolivia and Argentina and has very fond memories of that part of her childhood. As she explained, living in the Third World exposed her to another social, economic, and political reality she would not have seen if she stayed in Vancouver her whole life. And, as a teenager, she enjoyed feeling "popular" once in Bolivia and Argentina. She recalls:

The funny thing is in a way it was some of the happiest times because we have always been pretty poor, when we were here [Vancouver], and when we lived in Bolivia Bob was the president at Digital Computers and my mom was the Director of this English Institute and so they had some money for once and we lived in a big house with three bedrooms and an upstairs and downstairs. We used to have all these boys come over and Bob would make these big spreads and hot dogs and it was just so nice in that way. And I remember, if we needed some clothes we could just buy [them] and that was really nice. And then we were popular.

Despite some of the happier feelings Alejandra does feel deeply traumatized by her experiences there. Alejandra remembers she and her sister being trained in methods of clandestine collaboration:

We were trained when I was eleven by some friends of mom. They were a couple and they would take us out. We had to wear sunglasses and close our eyes and they would take us somewhere, I do not know where. This was all part of the training. We had to learn to close our eyes and not try to figure out where we were in case we were caught and tortured. We were always told that we could be caught and tortured so when they tortured us we would not say where we were.

Neither Alenjandra nor Carmen were ever caught or physically harmed. Nonetheless, they were in many compromising and frightening situations, many of which still haunt Alejandra while others she has blocked entirely from her memory.

Alejandra remains fairly distanced from politics and feels she is entitled to be "selfish" with her time. But she recalls hearing the news about Pinochet's arrest and feeling quite vindicated: "I was really surprised when they arrested Pinochet. I was really emotional about that. I was soooo happy, I was crying. They came on the news [and] I was crying. I was absolutely elated. It just kind of gave the whole thing validity in a way I guess."[1] Alejandra feels more Canadian than Chilean. She is married to a Canadian and they have one son together. She went to college in Vancouver and earned a certificate in small-business, which has allowed her to be self-employed. In addition to being a mother, she is a photographer and fitness instructor. She is thirty-five years old, happy in Vancouver, but deeply scarred by the past and the compromising positions families found themselves in as a result of exile and the dictatorship.

Marilyn Gutiérrez-Diaz

Marilyn left Chile in 1974 when she was nineteen years old, with her now-ex-husband. They left for entirely personal reasons not connected to the coup. Her family did not like her ex-husband so she and her ex decided they would rather not stay in Chile. Originally they wanted to go to the United States but were denied entry so they got tourist visas for Canada, went straight to Vancouver, and eventually acquired papers to stay legally. Marilyn comes from a humble background. Both of her parents were from working-poor backgrounds, especially her mother. Growing up, her mother and mother's siblings were malnourished. Her mother ended up being a Pinochet supporter, which Marilyn always found a bit ironic.

Marilyn feels like she lived a very sheltered and privileged life before leaving Chile. She was a university student at the time of the coup, studying economics and statistics, and was more concerned about clothes and being popular than anything academic or political. She describes herself as comfortably selfish and unaware of the structural differences that offered some people choices while not others. It was not until 1988 when she received counseling for being in a physically abusive relationship for nearly fifteen years that she started to gain a different perspective on the world. She had kept herself isolated from everyone, especially women, while she was still married to her ex-husband and remained entirely dependent upon him. As she says, she felt like a "baby." Such isolation led her to further close her eyes to structural injustices. She also stayed away from the solidarity movement because she resented the assumptions people made about her and her background and never felt she could really discuss things honestly. The movement made her feel ashamed of her family for not being supporters of Allende and she was already steeped in shame and isolation as a result of living in an abusive relationship. Rather than compound those feelings she chose to avoid the movement and even Chileans as much as possible.

Marilyn never received a college degree in Chile or Vancouver but after leaving her ex-husband she went back to school and earned a certificate as a substance abuse counselor. She currently works as a domestic family violence worker and counsels and advocates for women who were in situations much like her own. She has two sons, both in their mid-twenties, and though they both live in Vancouver she feels she does not see them nearly enough. At the time of our interview in 2005 Marilyn was fifty-one years old and an entirely different woman than the nineteen-year-old that left Chile with her abusive ex-husband in 1974.

Cecilia Boisier

Cecilia is the younger sister of Irene Policzer. Cecilia is an artist and educator. As she explains: "I guess I was born a painter and I always had to paint like other people have to breath, or jump, or dance. . . . [This] is my resource; this is my life." At the time of the coup Cecilia was thirty years old, and married, with two boys ages five and six. She and her now-ex-husband were both politically active during the UP government. She explains:

> My husband and I . . . were not . . . different [from] most Chileans who were involved in Allende's process. He [my husband] was a very involved writer and journalist. . . . He was a militant of one of the parties, MAPU . . . and I was beginning as an assistant teacher at the University, assisting with the professor teaching art to women who study early child education. And I was also involved in the Party and I did a lot of work with propaganda. . . . It was mainly developing flyers, and talking to people, calling people to meetings in order to promote the ideas. It was agitation actually, it was mostly an agitatory [*sic*] activity. [I was] not in a leading role, but I was really very active and really very passionate about it. . . . The Party at the time commanded my husband before the situation got worse. . . . He was never a prisoner . . . but he decided that we should take off because it would become dangerous. He was too much of a public figure in the field of communications, and defending Allende.

At the time of the coup Cecilia's husband (Antonio) was involved in a project with a German filmmaker who arranged for Antonio to receive a development grant for artists in Berlin, so Cecilia and her family were granted safe passage out of Chile. On their way to Germany she explains they "stayed one year in Buenos Aires because there was still work . . . for him [to do.] . . . So we were in Buenos Aires and then we stopped for a while in Portugal and in Belize because there was also work to be done." Finally, in 1975 she and her family ended up in Berlin.

Once in Berlin she and her husband both got involved in political cultural work with other exiles. She explains:

> We built a cultural center, Antonio and I, in Berlin, a Chilean Cultural Center. And we [made] contact with galleries, and [did] readings. So we did sort of cultural-intellectual work within the context of the *Unidad Popular*, but in Berlin; . . . political cultural work. And . . . practically exactly the same [thing was] happening in Amsterdam, and in Paris. They were all friends of ours that were here and there doing the same thing, [including] . . . Ariel Dorfman.[2]

After spending seventeen years in Berlin, in 1992 Cecilia moved to Vancouver to be close to her sister. Her two sons are now adults and both live in Berlin. At the time of our interview in 2004, at sixty-one, Cecilia was preparing to travel to Germany for an art exhibit and speaking tour. Her trip was originally scheduled for one month but while there she decided she wanted to move back and has since left Vancouver.

María José Valenzuela

María is Cecilia Tagle's daughter. (Recall Cecilia was very active in the solidarity and feminist movements.) She arrived in Toronto with her family in February of 1976 and the next month turned four years old. María has very few memories from her first three-plus years in Chile other than of her daycare. She explains: "I remember the women that worked with me that were very sweet and that I was extremely shy." Getting adjusted in Canada was a bit challenging due to language barriers and her shyness but María felt at home there relatively quickly. In 1978 she, her younger brother, and mother all traveled back to Chile for the first time. The trip highlighted for María the geographic and cultural differences between herself and her family in Chile, a family of which she had virtually no recollection. She explains:

> My mom, my brother, and I went back in 1978 so I guess that would be the first time that I realized that my family is really far away and that I was kind of different because I was learning another language [and] my language sounded

funny. I remember my mom's youngest brother who is only like three years older than me, he would make fun of me, [as did] lots of other friends that I had grown up with while I was in Chile would also look at me kind of funny because of my English-Spanish, Spanglish.

María did keep her Spanish and feels that is in large part due to her parents' efforts. She explains they always spoke to her and her brother in Spanish and they were also surrounded by Chileans and other Latinos since they grew up in the co-op.

As I explained, María's mother got involved with the solidarity movement not long after arriving in Canada. I asked María how she felt about her parents' activism. She explains:

My mom was really active, much more than my dad. My mom got involved with the movement so I was proud, you know? Proud of them. My mom and I have a very close relationship so I always looked up to her; I always wanted to be involved with her, in what she was doing.

Not surprisingly María eventually got involved in the movement herself. She explains:

There was a few of us [Chilean kids] that became more involved than others. We kind of tried to follow in the footsteps of our parents. . . . There was a handful of us, and then there were a bunch more that did not really get involved, even my brother was not interested. . . . But I wanted to know about everything. I read a lot, and I asked a lot, and I just went to a lot. I observed. . . . And we did a lot of events at the co-op . . . even [bringing] musical groups . . . [like] *Inti-Illimani,* . . . that was really exciting. Rigoberta Menchú even came once. So that was kind of like, "Wow! This is important."[3]

At about age fourteen the impact of all of these sorts of events translated into María's desire and ability to organize with other children of exiles. She explains:

I was about fourteen . . . when I really started becoming more conscious of it, in what I was doing, and learning. . . . [W]e [the youth] just met and talk[ed] and . . . present[ed] our own activities, like [showing] videos [about Chile] or we also tried to do a theatre group. We tried to incorporate the cultural as well; we had a dance group.

In other words, some children of exiles followed the lead of their parents and organized similar events but in the youth sector.

In 1991, María traveled back to Chile. After high school, María explains, "I worked for six months, I saved up money, and I went [back to Chile] by myself. I was eighteen [and] some people would have thought I was crazy, and I probably was. I went all on my own even though I ha[d] my whole family there at the time." Just like many of the children of exiles, María felt the need to travel to Chile and explore her roots. She did eventually return to Vancouver, where she studied at Simon Fraser University and earned a BA in psychology. She is currently married to a Colombian man who works as a financial analyst. María works as a family support worker with a local nongovernmental agency. Her organization works a lot with new immigrants, setting up things like English classes and family programs. Her duties are a combination of advocacy, training, social work, and even a bit of counseling. At the time of our interview in 2005 she was thirty-three years old, living in Vancouver, and very close to her mother.

Angélica Gutíerrez

Angélica is Rebeca Jimenez's daughter. She was twelve years old when they left Chile and her brother was nine. Angélica's father's side of the family was much more educated than her mother's. All of the men in her father's family, save her father, received post-secondary education. Two of her uncles (father's brothers) are engineers. Angélica and her brother were the first in her immediate family to receive a college education. She remembers her life in Chile after the coup as one marked by political, emotional, and economic instability.

> The instability . . . that I remember was the economic instability because my dad lost his job in the port, so he was working two jobs, and my dad is an alcoholic. So you know, the pressure, and the family violence. . . . I think that it was all coupled, everything was just meshed. . . . The political [in]stability of the country, the insecurity [of] military on the street. . . . For the first two months . . . we could hear gun shots . . . in the neighborhood.

In addition to the general sense of instability resultant from the dictatorship, Angélica also remembers burning documents and papers that, were they found by the junta, would have put her family at greater risk.

> We lived in a house in Chile where . . . there was an empty house next door . . . to us and we had access to it. It . . . was empty and the kitchen had a . . . ceramic floor so it was not wood because most of the floors are wooden. . . . . But this is like cement. . . . So my parents went into that kitchen, that empty kitchen, and put . . . wood boards on the windows and burned everything in there! We could have been asphyxiated in there because of the smoke . . . with all the paper and books and things that were burned because we lived in a neighborhood [that] was not politically active, or . . . they were right-wing, or at least opposed to the [Allende] government. So . . . my parents had these parties for the campaign of

Allende [and the neighbors] knew . . . that my [family] were "*UPientos;*" we were from the UP, so we feared that they could tell [the military] and in any moment they [would] come . . . because everybody would . . . spill the beans.

In other words, Angélica's family expected to be "turned in" by their neighbors. (Recall, Angélica's mother Rebeca was surprised and relieved that never happened.)

Despite the fear and instability that surrounded Angélica's life in Chile under Pinochet she remembers not wanting to leave. To challenge this sentiment her father tried to entice her and her brother with the prospect of visiting Niagara Falls:

My dad called us into the house and said that we got the visas and that we were leaving, we were going to Canada. . . . I remember saying "No! We cannot leave; I do not want to leave this home!" I knew right away that it would mean something very drastic, traumatic. . . . My dad tried to convince us that . . . we are going to Canada [and] that is where the Niagara Falls are, so that was the consolation!

Given that she and her brother had never heard of Niagara Falls it did not prove much of a consolation. Angélica also explained that she only saw Niagara Falls many years after arriving as a result of her own political efforts that took her all over Canada, and she is fairly certain her parents have yet to see it.

Eighth grade was Angélica's first year of school in Canada. Because she was in Quebec she took her first class in French. In 1978, just a couple of years later, her family moved to Vancouver, where they had to learn English. She was just about to turn fifteen when they moved, and not long after arriving she got very involved in the solidarity movement. She visited Chile in 1989, right after the plebiscite, and has not been back since. She has little faith in the future of democracy in that nation given that Pinochet's constitution and other residual effects of the dictatorship still shape the country. She is currently married to a Mexican and the two of them hope and plan to live in Mexico sometime in the future but they cannot imagine living in Chile.

Her passion lies with social justice and at times she has been able to shape her paid career around her political goals. She explains:

I work for the provincial government and . . . for the last three years I was doing anti-racism and multiculturalism work . . . [by] trying to work with public institutions and implementing multiculturalism programs. . . . [T]hen my position got cut last year so now I am back and doing clerical work which I hate, I just hate. But . . . I have been doing community development . . . since I was a teenager, working with community, understanding what the community is about, . . . working [in the] solidarity movement. But I never got paid for it until I got the other job and now I do not do that anymore.

Given Angélica's insatiable hunger for social justice I suspect it is only a matter of time until she is able to locate another paid position that reflects her political goals and ambitions.

Lina de Guevara

Lina is a seventy-one-year-old actress and theater director whose father was a painter. She and her husband lived in Cuba for three years from 1961 to 1964 because they were interested in seeing a Revolution in action. (Castro's revolutionary movement triumphed and took power on January 1, 1959, not long before Lina arrived.) Though the experience and Cuba was amazing, she and her husband came back to Chile a bit soured on leftist politics due to what they saw as an uncompromising dogmatism, lack of self-criticism, and generally inflexible ideologies.

In 1970 they moved to Canada for a couple of years while her husband attended the University of Toronto between 1970 and 1972. As a result, they missed much of Allende's presidency and upon return to Chile in 1972 they decided they needed a life-style change and wanted to move from Santiago to a much smaller city. Lina's husband got a job at the Technical University and she got one teaching theater at the Austral University, both in Valdivia in the south of Chile, so they decided to move there.

At the time of the coup her husband had just accepted a job with the government to oversee a small shipyard in Valdivia. As Lina recalls, fortunately the position had not yet begun when the coup happened. Not only was it a government job but the position potentially included military strategizing and would have certainly brought her husband to the military's attention. Additionally it was no secret that the two of them spent time in Cuba, which of course was literally another red flag. Because they no longer lived in Santiago they were removed from their previous political contacts, which, according to Lina, was quite fortunate. She explains: "Immediately after the coup we realized that we had to get out of there. . . . People with exactly the same background [as us were] put in jail, or sent into camps immediately. But because we were in Valdivia and we were so disconnected we lasted longer. But we could see the writing on the wall."

After a lengthy immigration process they finally left Chile in 1976 for Toronto. They stayed there for a year and then moved to Victoria, Vancouver Island, where her husband got a job teaching engineering at Camosun College. They love Victoria because physically it reminds them very much of the south of Chile. Lina has taught in Victoria as well but never felt completely satisfied with her work until she founded PUENTE Theatre to

> express my own experience as an immigrant from Latin America. . . . I had th[e] idea that I wanted to do something with women, to tell women's stories . . . and

then I got the support of a theatre company in Victoria which . . . once I created the project, they took on the administration of the project, the financial administration, and I got a very good grant from the federal government.

Lina still runs PUENTE Theatre and works with Latina immigrants using Augusto Boal's (1985) "Theater of the Oppressed" model of political/theatrical expression.

Nina Vaca

Nina comes from a family with mixed educational opportunities. Her father's family is educated; he was an accountant, but her mother's side was not nearly as fortunate. Nina believes her mother achieved a maximum of a sixth grade education but was not entirely sure. She explains: "[She was a] very smart woman but with very bad luck. She lost her family [when she was] very young." Specifically, Nina's grandmother died of cancer when her mother was only six years old and her death spawned her grandfather's alcoholism. Her mom was ultimately raised by various aunts and uncles, moving frequently. Nina is the oldest of six children. All except for Nina remained in Chile during the dictatorship. And all except for Nina are at least right-leaning if not Pinochet supporters. Of the six children, four are college educated with professional degrees and the other two have a high school education. Nina completed three years of college in Antofagasta but was unable to finish after the coup happened.

Her now-ex-husband was arrested not long after the coup. He was confined to house arrest and banished from his home city for a year and a half. Nina went with him, forfeiting her own education. Nina got pregnant with her daughter while she was away from the University and Antofagasta, which made it even harder to return to her studies. She was just six months shy of finishing her degree in early childhood education.

At the time of the coup Nina feels like she was politically very naïve. Her husband, however, was involved with the MIR. It turns out she was actually clandestinely collaborating with the MIR both before and after the coup but she would not find that out until she and her family were safely in Canada. Even after serving his time as a political prisoner, her ex-husband was frequently disappeared for a few days at a time. Despite her and her husband's desire to remain in Chile they found it impossible to live there. She explains:

That was not a life [any more]. So my father one day called me and he said: . . . "You should go; I am so sorry to say it, but you should go." . . . [During] those four years after the dictatorship, we did not have a life, not at all. I was so nervous and sick; he got ulcers; I got ulcers. We [would] . . . walk on the streets with a lot [of dis]comfort [and] repression. We would see specific cars, like [a] white truck, [and] I was like: "Oh, this is following me." Sometimes it was true, sometimes it was my imagination. It was not a [proper] life and my daughter, she was so young, she was getting that from us. . . . So we just . . . decided . . . to leave with the idea of coming back soon.

That was in 1978, when Nina was twenty-one, her husband twenty-two, and their daughter a year and a half. They left Chile for Canada and like most other exiles expected eventually to return to Chile. Almost thirty years later, they all remain in Canada. She recalls: "[O]ne of the most terrible days I can remember [was] when I had to say good-bye to [my family]."

Upon arriving in Brandon, Manitoba, in the dead of winter, Nina was very, very depressed. She explains, she felt

like a robot, everyday day [the] same thing. [It was] . . . my daughter that made [me] feel more alive, but it was really hard because everything changed. Everything changed. I missed my family so much because I was very attached to my mother, to my family; it was a good family, good bonds. . . . Finally we thought of moving to Calgary where it is a little . . . warm[er].

One thing that did make her feel a bit more grounded was participating in the solidarity movement. She and her husband got involved almost immediately, particularly with the cultural aspects.

Once her daughter started kindergarten Nina started to learn English and started feeling a bit better. Like most of the other women, she too had a series of unpleasant jobs, including hotel cleaning and sewing in a factory. She finally decided she had to work around children and would not let her Chilean education go to waste. She contacted a private daycare close to her house and told them she would do anything, including cleaning the facility, just so she could be around children. The woman who ran the place looked at Nina's records and decided to give her a chance. She started taking care of the children in a very limited capacity but eventually became a regular employee. However, her ex-husband then lost his job, became very depressed, and decided they had to leave Calgary for Vancouver. Nina did not want to leave Calgary since she finally had a good job and was learning English. Her husband made her feel she had no choice so they left Calgary together and she has lived in Vancouver for twenty-two years.

She and her ex-husband divorced seven years ago. She did not go into detail but did explain that her twenty-eight-year-old daughter, an accountant who also lives in Vancouver, no longer speaks to her father. Nina also has a seventeen-year-old son who lives with her. Nina works as a child care worker again and feels satisfied with her work. However, because her children are so rooted in Canada and she is not willing to move back to Chile without them, she feels trapped in Vancouver. She explains: "I am stuck here; completely stuck. I do not want my mother dying and I cannot go [to her funeral] . . . like what happened with my father." Exile has the ability to separate families in a uniquely permanent way.

THE CANADIANS

Gary Cristall
Gary was born in Toronto, Ontario, in 1950. He grew up in, as he says, "a Communist Party household" with his parents and one sister. Gary left school when he was fifteen "and went and had adventures and traveled around, lived in the streets or one thing or another." His political activism began in 1965 when he participated in a solidarity movement with civil rights activists in Selma, Alabama, which Gary describes as his "real education." He got more involved in various leftist projects affiliated with 1960s youth politics but never found what he was looking for until he discovered European Trotskyism, at which point he became a Trotskyist and remains one today.

In his quest for the political ideology and movement that best suited his ideals, Gary threw himself into all sorts of causes and read a lot. It was at this same time that he went to a solidarity event where some people had just returned from Chile and discussed life under Allende. He and his girlfriend at the time had saved money to travel to Europe but after hearing the talk decided to go to Latin America instead. So in 1971, at the age of twenty-one, he was off to South America. Gary explains that he and his ex-girlfriend assumed:

> We [would] go for three months or something and ended up staying for a year and a half and I was not planning on leaving. . . . It was an amazing time to be there [Chile], and experience to go through, and . . . I just said: "well I am not leaving this" so I figured out how to cobble together between photo journalism and some journalism and various activities enough . . . to make a living.

After living in Chile for a year and a half he decided to return to Canada for a visit. So he came to Vancouver during the Canadian summer (Chilean winter) of 1973 and was scheduled to return to Chile on September 11th. Despite the violence and chaos in Chile he wanted to go back. He explains: "I was going to go back. I managed to get through on the phone in the afternoon to a friend but he said: 'Hey they are shooting everybody,' he said, 'don't come back!'" So Gary stayed in Vancouver and was one of the founders of the Canadian end of the solidarity movement. It was upon return from Chile that he resumed his formal schooling, at which point he was admitted into Simon Fraser University as a "mature student." He earned a BA in Latin American history and intended to pursue a Ph.D. but eventually realized his political heart and intellect did not belong in academia.

Gary considers himself an internationalist. He explains:

> I was a revolutionary militant and an internationalist. I was happy to do work, which I did, in solidarity with Guinea Bissau against the Portuguese, with [the] Namibians, Chileans, Vietnamese. We were activists . . . who believe[d] in internationalism and we were not too choosy. It happened to be that I had a particular thing for Chile because I lived there but I went there as a revolutionary and I came back as a revolutionary and a number of us, it was the same people, were involved in other things.

In 1978 Gary started organizing folk music festivals. He devoted a significant amount of his organizational energies to bringing revolutionary bands and musicians from Central and South America to Vancouver. He also supported the solidarity movement by letting them set up information tables and the like. He still organizes these festivals and finds music and cultural events very effective political tools. He remains politically active and explains that he is

> still a member of a small Trotskyist organization after all these years. I am . . . involved in the . . . election here with the campaign called "Left Turn" to run an independent socialist candidate. Now I am actually getting involved a little bit, there is going be a World Peace Forum here again. I have been asked to do some of the coordination of the cultural stuff about that and then those kinds of . . . things that leftists do.

At the time of our interview Gary was fifty-five years old and married to a woman who works as an elementary school teacher. As Gary proudly explains, "She is God's gift to the eight year olds!"

Dale Fuller

Dale was born in California and, like many of the Chilean women I interviewed, a convergence of political factors brought her to British Columbia and ultimately Vancouver. She comes from a leftist, working-class family. Both of her parents were teachers, her father at a high school and mother at an elementary school. Her mother and father were always active in union and community organizing, including during the McCarthy era. Her parents eventually grew frightened by the hostile political climate in the United States and feared being targeted so decided to leave the country. In 1967 they moved up to the Sunshine Coast of British Columbia, got jobs as teachers, and lived there the rest of their lives. They remained active in left politics in their teachers' unions, the anti-war movement, and the like. Dale never finished her college degree. She studied architecture in both Oregon and California but after a year and a half withdrew from school to travel. She did reenroll in Vancouver and did quite well but never finished her degree. Dale has two sisters and one brother, all younger than she, all of whom live in British Columbia.

Given her parents' political histories Dale feels it was somewhat inevitable that she became active in politics. When she was a teenager and still living in San Jose in the Northern California Bay Area she got involved with the civil rights movement and from there the anti-war movement. She did not move to Canada with her parents but political reasons brought her there as well. Dale had been traveling in Europe where she met her first husband, a Spaniard. In the middle of the Viet Nam war they moved to California together and got married. When he went to deal with his immigration papers he found out that immigrants needed to register for a draft lottery so his name was entered. Dale and her now-ex-husband were planning on moving to Canada anyway rather than risk him being drafted, but they left before that happened, and she has lived in British Columbia ever since. Dale was pregnant at the time and given their lack of health insurance the Canadian health care system was another draw. They divorced about five years later and in 1975 Dale moved from the Sunshine Coast to Vancouver.

Once in Vancouver she became quite active in the Chilean solidarity movement. She had always been interested in Latin American politics and culture. She explains: "I . . . already sort of considered myself not Latina obviously . . . but I have always considered that I have some roots in that culture . . . because . . . the friends [I grew up with] and . . . my parents were politically active with the Mexican-American community." So she followed the election and tenure of Allende closely and was very interested in what was happening in Chile. But when the coup happened she was not yet living in Vancouver and had no political contacts there. Not long after the coup Salvador Allende's widow went on a speaking tour through Canada. Dale went to Vancouver for the event and learned of the solidarity movement. When she moved there in 1975 she started looking to get politically involved and immediately gravitated toward the solidarity movement. She eventually became very active in the Aquelarre collective.

At the time of our interview Dale was fifty-nine years old. She is married to her second husband, a Chilean architect. She has one son and two stepsons. Dale has held all sorts of jobs in her lifetime, including working on a university alumni magazine, as a freelance graphic artist, and as T-shirt silk-screener. Right now she does not work and is hoping to write a novel. She has been active in politics on and off for the majority of her adult life.

236   *Appendix*

NOTES

1. For an interesting study of Chilean exiles' responses to the news regarding Pinochet's arrest, see Adriana E. Espinoza and Marla J. Arvay, (2004), "Re-Constructing Political Identities: Post-dictatorship Narratives of Chileans in Exile," *Constructivism in the Human Sciences* 9(1): 91–110.

2. Ariel Dorfman was a cultural advisor to Allende. Starting with the UP and continuing to this day he is a very prominent cultural intellectual in Chilean politics. Currently he is a professor at Duke University and author of many books and articles, fiction and nonfiction, about Chilean life, politics, and exile.

3. Rigoberta Menchú is a Mayan Indian from Guatemala. She has spent her life fighting for indigenous peoples' human rights and won the Noble Peace Prize in 1992.

Bibliography

SECONDARY SOURCES

Print

Acker, Joan. 1990. "Hierarchies, Jobs, Bodies: A Theory of Gendered Organizations." *Gender & Society* 4(2): 139–58.

Acosta, Mariclaire. 1993. "The Comadres of El Salvador: A Case Study." Pp. 126–39 in *Surviving Beyond Fear: Women, Children, and Human Rights in Latin America*, edited by Marjorie Agosín. New York: White Pine Press.

Adams, Jacqueline. 2000. "Movement Socialization in Art Workshops: A Case from Pinochet's Chile." *The Sociological Quarterly* 41(4): 615–38.

———. 2001. "Art in Social Movements: Shantytown Women's Protest in Pinochet's Chile." *Sociological Forum* 17(1): 21–56.

———. 2002. "The Makings of Political Art." *Qualitative Sociology* 24(3): 311–48.

Afkhami, Mahnaz, ed. 1994. *Women in Exile*. Charlottesville: University of Virginia Press.

Agarwal, Bina. 1992. "The Gender and Environment Debate: Lessons from India." *Feminist Studies* 18(1): 119–58.

Agosín, Marjorie. 1987. *Scraps of Life: The Chilean Arpillera*. Toronto: Williams-Wallace Publishers.

Agosín, Marjorie, and Emma Sepúlveda. 2001. *Amigas: Letters of Friendship and Exile*. Austin: University of Texas Press.

Aguirre, Carmen. 2005. *The Refugee Hotel (sixth draft)*. Los Angeles, Calif.: New Work Festival, The Center Theatre Group.

Alarcón, Norma, Caren Kaplan, and Minoo Moallem. 1999. "Introduction: Between Woman and Nation." Pp. 1–16 in *Between Woman and Nation: Nationalisms, Transnational Feminisms, and the State*, edited by Caren Kaplan, Norma Alarcón, and Minoo Moallem. Durham, N.C.: Duke University Press.

237

Almeida, Paul, and Rubén Urbizagástegui. 1999. "Cutumay Camones: Popular Music in El Salvador's National Liberation Movement." *Latin American Perspectives* 105, 26(2): 13–42.

Alvarez, Sonia. 1990. *Engendering Democracy in Brazil: Women's Movements in Transition Politics.* Princeton, N.J.: Princeton University Press.

Alvarez, Sonia E., Elisabeth Jay Friedman, Erika Beckman, Maylei Blackwell, Norma Stoltz Chinchilla, Nathalie Lebon, Marysa Navarro, and Marcela Ríos Tobar. 2003. "Encountering Latin American and Caribbean Feminisms." *Signs: Journal of Women in Culture and Society* 28(2): 537–79.

Alvarez, Sonia, Evelina Dagnino, and Arturo Escobar, eds. 1998. *Cultures of Politics, Politics of Cultures: Re–Visioning Latin American Social Movements.* Boulder: Westview Press.

———. 1998. "Introduction: The Cultural and Political in Latin American Social Movements." Pp. 1–29 in *Cultures of Politics, Politics of Cultures: Re-Visioning Latin American Social Movements,* edited by Sonia Alvarez, Evelina Dagnino, and Arturo Escobar. Boulder: Westview Press.

Aman, Kenneth. 1991. "Introduction: Placing Chile's Popular Culture in Context." Pp. 1–10 in *Popular Culture in Chile: Resistance and Survival,* edited by Kenneth Aman and Christián Parker. Boulder: Westview Press.

Ameringer, Charles D. 1974. *The Democratic Left in Exile: The Antidictatorial Struggle in the Caribbean, 1945–1959.* Coral Gables, Fla.: University of Miami Press.

Aminzade, Ron, and Doug McAdam. 2001. "Emotions and Contentious Politics." Pp. 14–50 in *Silence and Voice in the Study of Contentious Politics,* edited by Ronald R. Aminzade, Jack A. Goldstone, Doug McAdam, Elizabeth J. Perry, William Sewell, Jr., Sidney Tarrow, and Charles Tilly. Cambridge: Cambridge University Press.

Anderson, Benedict. 1991. *Imagined Communities: Reflections on the Origin and Spread of Nationalism.* New York: Verso.

Andreas, Carol. 1977. "The Chilean Woman: Reform, Reaction, and Resistance." *Latin American Perspectives* 4(4): 121–25.

Angell, Alan. 2001. "International Support for Chilean Opposition, 1973–1989: Political Parties and the Role of Exiles." Pp. 146–74 in *The International Dimensions of Democratization: Europe and the Americas,* edited by Laurence Whitehead. Oxford: Oxford University Press.

Angell, Alan, and Susan Carstairs. 1987. "The Exile Question in Chilean Politics." *Third World Quarterly* 9(1): 148–67.

Arditti, Rita. 1999. *Searching for Life: The Grandmothers of the Plaza de Mayo and the Disappeared Children of Argentina.* Berkeley: University of California Press.

Aronoff, Myron. 1983. "Conceptualizing the Role of Culture in Political Change." Pp. 1–18 in *Culture and Political Change,* edited by Myron Aronoff. New Brunswick, N.J.: Transaction Books.

Arrate, Jorge. 1987. *Exilio: Textos de Denuncia y Esperanza.* Santiago: Documentas.

Arriaza, Bernardo T. 2005. "The Chileans." Pp. 289–302 in *The Peoples of Las Vegas: One City, Many Faces,* edited by Jerry L. Simich and Thomas C. Wright. Las Vegas: University of Nevada Press.

Atria, Rodrigo, Eugenio Ahumada, Javier Luis Egaña, Augusto Góngora, Carmen Quesney, Gustavo Saball, and Gustavo Villalobos. 1989. *Chile: La Memoria Prohibida: La Violaciones A Los Derechos Humanos, 1973–1983.* Santiago, Chile: Pehuén.

Baldez, Lisa. 2002. *Why Women Protest: Women's Movements in Chile.* Cambridge: Cambridge University Press.

Barkan, Elazar, and Marie-Denise Shelton. 1998. *Borders, Exiles, Diasporas.* Stanford: Stanford University Press.

Barsamian, David. 2003. *Culture and Resistance: Conversations with Edward W. Said.* Cambridge, Mass.: South End Press.

Barudy, Jorge. 1988. "The Therapeutic Value of Solidarity and Hope." Pp. 135–52 in *Refugees – The Trauma of Exile: The Humanitarian Role of Red Cross and Red Crescent,* edited by Diana Miserez. Boston: Martinus Nijhoff Publishers.

Basu, Amrita. 1995. "Introduction." Pp.1–21 in *The Challenge of Local Feminisms: Women's Movements in Global Perspective,* edited by Amrita Basu. Boulder: Westview Press.

Benford, Robert D. 1993. "Frame Disputers Within the Nuclear Disarmament Movement." *Social Forces* 71(3): 677–701.

Berdichewsky, Bernardo. 1994, December 1. "The Hispanic Community in British Columbia." Conference proceedings from Multi-Cultural Marketing Symposium, Vancouver, B.C., Canada.

———. 1999. *Hispanic Integration's Process Into Canadian Pluralistic Society in British Columbia.* Vancouver, B.C., Canada: Canadian Hispanic Congress.

Blaine, Patrick. 2009. "Recovering Democratic Transitions in Postdictatorial Chilean Fiction and Film." Ph.D diss., University of Washington, Seattle [work in progress].

Boal, Augusto. 1985. *Theatre of the Oppressed.* New York: Theatre Communication Group.

Bobel, Chris. 2005. "'I've never defined myself as an activist, though I've done a lot of it': Doing Activism, Being Activist and the Gendered 'Perfect Standard' in a Contemporary Movement." Paper presented at the American Sociological Association conference, Philadelphia, Pa., August 13–16.

Bolt, Christine. 1993. *Women's Movements in the United States and Britain from the 1790s to the 1920s.* Amherst, Mass.: University of Massachusetts.

Boorstein, Edward. 1977. *Allende's Chile: An Inside View.* New York: International Publishers.

Bouvard, Margarite Guzmán. 1994. *Revolutionizing Motherhood: The Mothers of the Plaza de Mayo.* Wilmington, Del.: Scholarly Resources Inc.

Boyarin, Daniel, and Jonathan Boyarin. 1993. "Diaspora: Generational Ground of Jewish Identity." *Critical Inquiry* 19(4); 693–725.

Bravo, Alejandra, Evelyn Encalada Grez, Lorena Gajardo, and Magaly San Martín, interviewed by Jorge Ginieniewicz and Daniel Schugurensky. 2007. "Generation 1.5, Identity and Politics: A Conversation with Chilean-Canadian Women." Pp. 336–360 in *Ruptures, Continuities and Re–Learning: The political participation of Latin Americans in Canada, 2d ed.,* edited by Jorge Ginieniewicz and Daniel Schugurensky. Toronto, ON: Transformative Learning Centre, OISE/UT.

Braziel, Jana Evans, and Anita Mannur. 2003. "Nation, Migration, Globalization: Points of Contention in Diaspora Studies." Pp. 1–22 in *Theorizing Diaspora: A Reader*, edited by Jana Braziel and Anita Mannur. Malden, Mass.: Blackwell Publishing.

———, eds. 2003. *Theorizing Diaspora: A Reader*. Malden, Mass.: Blackwell Publishing.

Broughton, Simon, and Mark Ellingham, eds. 2000. *World Music, volume 2*. London, England: Rough Guides Ltd.

Broyles-González, Yolanda. 1994. *El Teatro Campesino: Theater in the Chicano Movement*. Austin: University of Texas Press.

Buijs, Gina, ed. 1996. *Migrant Women: Crossing Boundaries and Changing Identities, 2d ed*. Washington, D.C: Berg.

Bunster, Ximena. 1993. "Surviving Beyond Fear: Women and Torture in Latin America." Pp. 98–125 in *Surviving Beyond Fear: Women, Children and Human Rights in Latin America*, edited by Marjorie Agosín. New York: White Pine Press.

Burawoy, Michael. 1991. "The Extended Case Method." Pp. 271–87 in *Ethnography Unbound: Power and Resistance in the Modern Metropolis*. By Michael Burawoy, Alice Burton, Ann Arnett Ferguson, Kathryn J. Fox, Joshua Gamson, Nadine Gartrell, Leslie Hurst, Charles Kurzman, Leslie Salzinger, Josepha Schiffman, and Shiori Ui. Berkeley: University of California Press.

Burgos, Raúl. 2002. "The Gramscian Intervention in the Theoretical and Political Production of the Latin American Left." *Latin American Perspectives* 122, 29(1): 9–37.

Butler, Kim. 2001. "Defining Diaspora, Refining a Discourse." *Diaspora: A Journal of Transnational Studies* 10(2): 189–219.

Buttigieg, Joseph A. 2002. "On Gramsci." *Daedalus* 131(3): 67–70.

Bystdzienski, Jill, and Joti Sekhon. 1999. *Democratization and Women's Grassroots Movements*. Bloomington, Ind.: Indiana University Press.

Çagatay, Nilüfer, Caren Grown, and Aida Santiago. 1986. "The Nairobi Women's Conference: Toward a Global Feminism?" *Feminist Studies* 12(2): 401–12.

Campbell, Sue. 1989. "Being Dismissed: The Politics of Emotional Expression." *Hypatia* 9(3): 46–65.

Cantor, Paul. 2008. "Who Killed Víctor Jara?" *NACLA: Report on the Americas* 41(5): 4–5.

Cariola, Patricia, and Josefina Rossetti. 1984. *Inserción Laboral Para el Retorno: El Caso de los Exiliados Chilenos*. Santiago: Center for Research and Development in Education (CIDE).

Carr, Paul. 2007. "In Exile." Pp. 217–21 in *Ruptures, Continuities and Re-Learning: The Political Participation of Latin Americans in Canada, 2d ed.*, edited by Jorge Ginieniewicz and Daniel Schugurensky. Toronto, ON: Transformative Learning Centre, OISE/UT.

Carrasco Pirard, Eduardo. 1982. "The Nueva Canción in Latin America." *International Social Science Journal* 3(4): 599–623.

Carstairs, Susan. 1988. "Review of *Chileans in Exile, Private Struggles Public Lives*." *Journal of Latin American Studies* 20(1): 268–69.

Cassidy, Sheila. 1978. *Audacity to Believe, 2d ed.* Cleveland, Ohio: Collins World.

Castillo-Feliú. 2000. *Culture and Customs of Chile.* Westport, Conn.: Greenwood Press.

Cavallo Castro, Ascanio, Manuel Salazar Salvo, and Oscar Sepúlveda Pacheco. 1989. *Chile, 1973–1988: la historia oculta del régimen militar.* Santiago: Editorial Antártica.

Celedón, María Angélica, and Luz María Opazo. 1987. *Volver a Empezar.* Santiago: Peguen.

Chafetz, Janet Saltzman, and Anthony Gary Dworkin. 1986. *Female Revolt: Women's Movements in World and Historical Perspective.* Totowa, N.J.: Rowman & Allanheld.

Chaney, Elsa M. 1974. "The Mobilization of Women in Allende's Chile." Pp. 267–80 in *Women in Politics*, edited by Jane Jaquette. New York: John Wiley and Sons.

Chelech, Faride Zerán. 1991. *O El Asilo Contra La Opresión: 23 Historias Para Recordar.* Santiago: Paradoz.

Chinchilla, Norma. 1992. "Marxism, Feminism, and the Struggle for Democracy in Latin America." Pp. 38–49 in *The Making of Social Movements in Latin America*, edited by Arturo Escobar and Sonia Alvarez. Boulder: Westview Press.

———. 1993. "Gender and National Politics: Issues and Trends in Women's Participation in Latin American Movements." Pp. 37–54 in *Researching Women in Latin America and the Caribbean*, edited by Edna Acosta-Belén and Christine E. Bose. Boulder: Westview Press.

Chuchryk, Patricia. 1984. "Protest, Politics and Personal Life: The Emergence of Feminism in a Military Dictatorship, Chile 1973–1983." Ph.D. diss., York University, Toronto.

———. 1989a. "Feminist Anti-Authoritarian Politics: The Role of Women's Organizations in the Chilean Transition to Democracy." Pp. 149–84 in *The Women's Movement in Latin America: Feminism and the Transition to Democracy*, edited by Jane Jaquette. Boston: Unwin Hyman.

———. 1989b. "Subversive Mothers: The Women's Opposition to the Military Regime in Chile." Pp. 86–97 in *Surviving Beyond Fear: Women, Children and Human Rights in Latin America*, edited by Marjorie Agosín. New York: White Pine Press.

———. 1994. "From Dictatorship to Democracy: The Women's Movement in Chile." Pp. 65–107 in *The Women's Movement In Latin America: Participation and Democracy*, edited by Jane Jaquette. Boulder: Westview Press.

Clifford, James. 1992. "Traveling Cultures." Pp. 96–116 in *Cultural Studies*, edited by Lawrence Grossberg, Cary Nelson, and Paula Treichler. New York: Routledge.

———. 1994. "Diasporas." *Cultural Anthropology* 9(3): 302–38.

Cobos, Ana María, and Ana Lya Sater. 1986. "Chilean Folk Music in Exile/Nueva Canción Chilena en el Exilio." Pp. 295–339 in *Intellectual Migrations: Transcultural Contributions of European and Latin American Émigrés.* Papers of the Thirty-First Annual Meeting of the Seminar on the Acquisition of Latin American Library Materials, edited by Iliana L. Sonntag. Madison: Memorial Library, University of Wisconsin.

Cockcroft, Eva, John Pitman Weber, and James Cockcroft. 1998. *Toward a People's Art: The Contemporary Mural Movement, 2d ed.* Albuquerque: University of New Mexico Press.

Cockcroft, James D., ed. 2000. *The Salvador Allende Reader: Chile's Voice of Democracy.* Melbourne, Australia: Ocean Press.

Cohen, Jean L. 1985. "Strategy or Identity: New Theoretical Paradigms and Contemporary Social Movements." *Social Research* 52(4): 663–716.

Cohen, Robin. 1997. *Global Diasporas: An Introduction.* Seattle: University of Washington Press.

Collier, Simon, and William F. Sater. 2004. *A History of Chile, 1808–2002, 2d ed.* Cambridge: Cambridge University Press.

Collins, Randall. 1990. "Stratification, Emotional Energy, and the Transient Emotions." Pp. 27–57 in *Research Agendas in the Sociology of Emotions,* edited by Theodore D. Kemper. Albany, N.Y.: State University of New York Press.

Constable, Pamela, and Arturo Valenzuela. 1991. *Chile Under Pinochet: A Nation of Enemies.* New York: W.W. Norton.

Cooper, Marc. 2002. *Pinochet and Me: A Chilean Anti–Memoir, 2d ed.* New York: Verso.

Corbin, Juliet, and Anslem Strauss. 1990. "Grounded Theory Method: Procedures, Canons, and Evaluative Criteria." *Qualitative Sociology* 13(1): 3–21.

Cornejo, Marcela. 2008. "Political Exile and the Construction of Identity: A Life Stories Approach." *Journal of Community & Applied Social Psychology* 18(4): 333–348.

Cosgrove, Serena. Forthcoming. *Leadership from the Margins: Women and Civil Society Organizations in Argentina, Chile, and El Salvador.* New Brunswick, N.J.: Rutgers University Press.

Craske, Nikki. 1999. *Women and Politics in Latin America.* New Brunswick, N.J.: Rutgers University Press.

———. 2003. "Gender, Poverty and Social Movements." Pp. 46–70 in *Gender in Latin America,* by Sylvia Chant with Nikki Craske. New Brunswick, N.J.: Rutgers University Press.

Da, Wei Wei. 2002. "Chileans in Canada: Contexts of Departure and Arrival." Prepared for Latin American Research Group. Toronto: York University.

Darnovsky, Marcy, Barbara Epstein, and Richard Flacks. 1995. "Introduction." Pp. vii–xxiii in *Cultural Politics and Social Movements,* edited by Marcy Darnovsky, Barbara Epstein, and Richard Flacks. Philadelphia: Temple University Press.

Debray, Régis. 1971. *The Chilean Revolution: Conversations with Allende.* New York: Pantheon Books.

Denisoff, R. Serge. 1983. *Sing a Song of Social Significance.* Bowling Green, Ohio: Bowling Green State University Popular Press.

Diaz, Harry. 1999. "Chileans." Pp 347–55 in *Encyclopedia of Canada's Peoples,* edited by Paul Robert Magocsi. Toronto: University of Toronto Press.

Díaz, Jorge. 1970. "Reflections on the Chilean Theater." *TDR/The Drama Review* 14(2): 84–86.

Dinges, John. 2004. *The Condor Years: How Pinochet and His Allies Brought Terrorism to Three Continents.* New York: New Press.

Dirks, Gerald E. 1977. *Canada's Refugee Policy: Indifference or Opportunism?* Montreal and London: McGill-Queen's University Press.

Dominguez, Rosario. 1984. "Psicoterapia de un niño Chileno exiliado y retornado." Pp. 116–30 in *Psicoterapia y Represión Política,* edited by Elizabeth Lira, Eugenia Weinstein, Rosario Dominguez, Juana Kovalskys, Adriana Maggi, Eliana Morales, and Fanny Pollarolo. Mexico City: Siglo Veintiuno Editores.

Dorfman, Ariel. 1998. *Heading South, Looking North: A Bilingual Journey.* New York: Farrar, Straus and Giroux.

Dorfman, Ariel, Salvador Allende, Pablo Neruda, Joan Jara, Beatriz Allende. 2003. *Chile: The Other September 11.* Melbourne, Australia: Ocean Press.

Drake, Paul W., and Iván Jaksić, eds. 1995. *The Struggle for Democracy in Chile, rev. ed.* Lincoln, Nebr.: University of Nebraska Press.

DuBois, Ellen Carol. 1991. "Woman Suffrage and the Left: An International Socialist-Feminist Perspective." *New Left Review* 186 (March/April): 20–44.

Duncombe, Stephen. 2002. "Introduction." Pp. 1–15 in *Cultural Resistance Reader,* edited by Stephen Duncombe. New York: Verso.

Dunn, Jennifer L. 2005. "'Victims' and 'Survivors': Emerging Vocabularies of Motive for 'Battered Women Who Stay.'" *Sociological Inquiry* 75(1): 1–30.

Durán, Marcela. 1980. "Life in Exile: Chileans in Canada." *Multiculturalism* 3(4): 13–16.

Eastmond, Marita. 1993. "Reconstructing Life: Chilean Refugee Women and the Dilemmas of Exile." Pp. 35–53 in *Migrant Women: Crossing Boundaries and Changing Identities,* edited by Gina Buijs. Oxford, Washington, D.C.: Berg.

———. 1996. "*Luchar y Sufrir* – Stories of Life and Exile: Reflexions on the Ethnographic Process." *Ethnos* 61(3–4): 231–50.

———. 1997. *The Dilemmas of Exile: Chilean Refugees in the U.S.A.* Göteborg, Sweden: ACTA Universitatis Gothoburgensis.

Eder, Donna, Lori Sudderth, and Suzanne Staggenborg. 1995. "A National Women's Music Festival: Collective Identity and Diversity in a Lesbian-Feminist Community." *Journal of Contemporary Ethnography* 23(4): 485–515.

Einwohner, Rachel L., Jocelyn A. Hollander, and Toska Olson. 2000. "Engendering Social Movements: Cultural Images and Movement Dynamics." *Gender & Society* 14(5): 679–99.

Elam Jr., Harry J. 1997. *Taking It to the Streets: The Social Protest Theater of Luis Valdez and Amiri Baraka.* Ann Arbor: University of Michigan Press.

Ember, Carol R., Melvin Ember, and Ian A Skoggard, eds. 2004. *Encyclopedia of Diasporas: Immigrant and Refugee Cultures Around the World.* New York: Kluwer Academic/Plenum.

Emirbayer, Mustafa, and Ann Mische. 1998. "What is Agency?" *American Journal of Sociology* 103(4): 962–1023.

Ensalaco, Mark. 2000. *Chile under Pinochet: Recovering the Truth.* Philadelphia: University of Pennsylvania Press.

Escobar, Monica. 2000. "Exile and National Identity: Chilean Women in Canada." Ph.D. diss., University of Toronto. Toronto, Canada.

―――. 2007. "Nation and Gender Views from Chilean-Canadian Women in Post Exile." Pp. 166–78 in *Ruptures, Continuities and Re-Learning: The Political Participation of Latin Americans in Canada*, 2d ed., edited by Jorge Ginieniewicz and Daniel Schugurensky. Toronto, ON: Transformative Learning Centre, OISE/UT.

Espinoza, Adriana E. 2002. "The Collective Trauma Story: Personal Meaning and the Recollection of Traumatic Memories in Vancouver's Chilean Community." Master's thesis, University of British Columbia. Vancouver, Canada.

―――. 2004. "Trials and Tribulations for Social Justice." Pp. 73–87 in *Public Acts: Disruptive Readings on Making Curriculum Public*, edited by Francisco Ibáñez–Carrasco and Eric R. Meiners. New York: RoutledgeFalmer.

Espinoza, Adriana E., and Marla J. Arvay. 2004. "Re-Constructing Political Identities: Post-dictatorship Narratives of Chileans in Exile." *Constructivism in the Human Sciences* 9(1): 91–110.

Esteva, Amanda. 2006. "¡Venceremos! Words in Red Paint." Pp. 63–75 in *Homelands: Women's Journeys Across Race, Place, and Time*, edited by Patricia Justine Tumang and Jenesha De Rivera. Emeryville, Calif: Seal Press.

Evans, Richard J. 1977. *The Feminists: Women's Emancipation Movements in Europe, America and Australia, 1840–1920*. London: Croom Helm.

Evans, Sara. 1979. *Personal Politics: The Roots of Women's Liberation in the Civil Rights Movement and the New Left*. New York: Knoft.

Evans, Sara, and Harry Boyte. 1986. *Free Spaces: The Sources of Democratic Change in America*. New York: Harper and Row.

Eyerman, Ron. 2002. "Music in Movement: Cultural Politics and Old and New Social Movements." *Qualitative Sociology* 25(3): 443–58.

Eyerman, Ron, and Andrew Jamison. 1998. *Music and Social Movements: Mobilizing Traditions in the Twentieth Century*. Cambridge: Cambridge University Press.

Fagen, Patricia Weiss. 1973. *Exiles and Citizens: Spanish Republicans in Mexico*. Latin American Monographs No. 29. Austin: The University of Texas Press.

Fairley, Jan. 1985. "Annotated Bibliography of Latin-American Popular Music with Particular Reference to Chile and to Nueva Canción." *Popular Music* 5: 305–56.

Fantasia, Rick, and Eric L. Hirsch. 1995. "Culture in Rebellion: The Appropriation and Transformation of the Veil in the Algerian Revolution." Pp. 144–62 in *Social Movements and Culture*, edited by Hank Johnston and Bert K. Klandermans. Minneapolis: University of Minnesota Press.

Feinberg, Richard E. 1972. *The Triumph of Allende: Chile's Legal Revolution*: New York: Mentor Books.

Femia, Joseph V. 1981. *Gramsci's Political Thought: Hegemony, Consciousness, and the Revolutionary Process*. Oxford: Clarendon Press.

Ferree, Myra Marx. 1992. "The Political Context of Rationality: Rational Choice Theory and Resource Mobilization." Pp. 29–52 in *Frontiers in Social Movement Theory*, edited by Aldon D. Morris and Carol McClurg Mueller. New Haven, Conn.: Yale University Press.

Ferree, Myra Marx, and Aili Mari Tripp. 2006. *Global Feminism: Women's Transnational Organizations, Activism and Human Rights.* New York: New York University Press.

Ferree, Myra Marx, and Carol McClurg Mueller. 2004. "Feminism and the Women's Movement: A Global Perspective." Pp. 576–607 in *The Blackwell Companion to Social Movements,* edited by David A. Snow, Sarah A. Soule, and Hanspeter Kriesi. Malden, Mass.: Blackwell Publishing.

Ferree, Myra Marx, and Patricia Yancey Martin. eds. 1995. *Feminist Organizations: Harvest of the New Women's Movement.* Philadelphia: Temple University Press.

Fine, Gary Alan. 1995. "Public Narration and Group Culture: Discerning Discourse in Social Movements." Pp. 127–43 in *Social Movements and Culture,* edited by Hank Johnston and Burt Klandermans. Minneapolis: University of Minnesota Press.

Fisher, Jo. 1993. *Out of the Shadows: Women, Resistance, and Politics in South America.* London: Latin American Bureau.

Flam, Helen, and Debra King. 2005. *Emotions and Social Movements.* New York: Routledge.

Foran, John. 1992. "A Theory of Third World Social Revolutions: Iran, Nicaragua, and El Salvador Compared." *Critical Sociology* 19: 3–27.

———. 1993. *Fragile Resistance: Social Transformation in Iran from 1500 to the Revolution.* Boulder: Westview Press.

———. 1997. "Discourses and Social Forces: The Role of Culture and Cultural Studies in Understanding Revolutions." Pp. 203–26 in *Theorizing Revolutions,* edited by John Foran. New York: Routledge.

Forgacs, David, and Geoffrey Nowell–Smith, eds. 1985. *Antonio Gramsci: Selections from Cultural Writings.* Cambridge, Mass.: Harvard University Press.

Franceschet, Susan. 2005. *Women and Politics in Chile.* Boulder: Lynne Rienner Publishers.

Fraser, Arvonne. 1987. *The U.N. Decade for Women: Documents and Dialogue.* Boulder: Westview Special Studies on Women in Contemporary Studies.

Freire, Paulo. 1993. *Pedagogy of the Oppressed, 2d ed.* New York: Continuum.

Friedmann, John. 1986. "The World City Hypothesis." *Development and Change* 17: 69–83.

Frohmann, Alicia, and Teresa Valdés. 1995. "Democracy in the Country and in the Home: The Women's Movement in Chile." Pp. 276–301 in *The Challenges of Local Feminisms: Women's Movements in Global Perspective,* edited by Amrita Basu. Boulder: Westview Press.

Frye, Marilyn. 1983. "A Note on Anger." Pp. 84–94 in *The Politics of Reality: Essays in Feminist Theory.* Trumansburg, N.Y.: The Crossing Press.

Futrell, Robert, and Pete Simi. 2004. "Free Spaces, Collective Identity, and the Persistence of U.S. White Power Activism." *Social Problems* 51(1): 16–42.

Galeano, Eduardo. 1998. *Upside Down: A Primer for the Looking-Glass World.* New York: Picador.

Gamson, William A. 1990. *The Strategy of Social Protest, 2d ed.* Belmont, Calif.: Wadsworth.

———. 1991. "Commitment and Agency in Social Movements." *Sociological Forum* 6(1): 27–50.

———. 1992a. *Talking Politics.* Cambridge: Cambridge University Press.

———. 1992b. "The Social Psychology of Collective Action." Pp. 53–76 in *Frontiers in Social Movement Theory*, edited by Aldon D. Morris and Carol McClurg Mueller. New Haven, Conn.: Yale University Press.

———. 1996. "Safe Spaces and Social Movements." *Perspectives on Social Problems* 8: 27–38.

Gamson, William A., Bruce Fireman, and Steven Rytina. 1982. *Encounters with Unjust Authority.* Homewood, Ill.: Dorsey Press.

Garofalo, Reebee. 1992 "Popular Music and the Civil Rights Movement." Pp. 231–40 in *Rockin' The Boat: Mass Music and Mass Movements*, edited by Rebee Garofalo. Boston: South End Press.

Garretón, Manuel Antonio. 1995. "The Political Opposition and the Party System under the Military Regime." Pp. 211–50 in *The Struggle for Democracy in Chile*, edited by Paul W. Drake and Iván Jaksić. Lincoln, Nebr.: University of Nebraska Press.

Gaviola, Edda, Eliana Largo, and Sandra Palestro. 1994. *Una Historia Necesaria: Mujeres En Chile: 1973–1990.* Santiago: ASDI, Suecia.

Geertz, Clifford. 1973. *The Interpretation of Cultures.* New York: Basic Books.

Gender & Society. 1998. "Special Issue: Gender and Social Movements, Part 1." 12(6): 617–784.

———. 1999. "Special Issue: Gender and Social Movements, Part 2." 13(1): 1–152.

Gilbert, Jorge, and Mario Lee. 1986. *The Bridge Between Canada and Latin America.* Coquitlam, B.C., Canada: Two Thirds Editions.

Gilroy, Paul. 1987. *There Ain't No Black in the Union Jack: The Cultural Politics of Race and Nation.* London: Hutchinson.

———. 1993. *The Black Atlantic: Double Consciousness and Modernity.* Cambridge: Harvard University Press.

Ginieniewicz, Jorge, and Daniel Schugurensky, eds. 2007. *Ruptures, Continuities and Re-Learning: The Political Participation of Latin Americans in Canada, 2d ed.* Toronto, ON: Transformative Learning Centre, OISE/UT.

Giugni, Marco G. 1998. "Structure and Culture in Social Movement Theory." *Sociological Forum* 13(2): 365–75.

Glaser, Barney, and Anslem Strauss. 1967. *The Discovery of Grounded Theory: Strategies for Qualitative Research.* Chicago: Aldine.

Goldring, Luin. 2006. "Latin American Transnationalism in Canada: Does it Exist, What Forms Does It Take, and Where Is It Going?" Pp. 180–201 in *Transnational Identities and Practices in Canada*, edited by Vic Satzewich and Lloyd Wong. Vancouver: University of British Columbia Press.

Gómez, Ines. 1998. "The Metaphoric Language of Suffering of Latina Refugee Women." *Curare* 21(2): 137–39.

———. 1999. "A Space for Remembering: Home Pedagogy and Exilic Latina Women's Identities." Pp. 200–17 in *Engendering Forced Migration: Theory and Practice*, edited by Doreen Marie Indra. New York: Berghahn Books.

Gómez-Barris, Macarena. 2005. "Two 9/11s in a Lifetime: Chilean Art, Terror and

Displacement." *Latino Studies* 1(3): 97–112.

Gonzalez, Mike. 1976. "Ideology and Culture Under Popular Unity." Pp. 106–27 in *Allende's Chile*, edited by Philip O'Brien. New York: Praeger Publishers.

González, Mónica, and Héctor Contreras. 1991. *Los secretos del Comando Conjunto*. Santiago, Chile: Ediciones del Ornitorrinco.

Goodwin, Jeff. 1997. "The Libidinal Constitution of a High–Risk Social Movement: Affectual Ties and Solidarity in the Huk Rebellion, 1946 to 1954." *American Sociological Review* 62(1): 53–69.

Goodwin, Jeff, James M. Jasper, and Francesca Polletta. 2000. "The Return of the Repressed: The Fall and Rise of Emotions in Social Movement Theory." *Mobilization* 5(1): 65–84.

———, eds. 2001. *Passionate Politics: Emotions and Social Movements*. Chicago: The University of Chicago Press.

———. 2001. "Why Emotions Matter." Pp. 1–24 in *Passionate Politics: Emotions and Social Movements*, edited by Jeff Goodwin, James Jasper, and Francessca Polletta. Chicago: The University of Chicago Press.

Gordon, Steven. 1981. "The Sociology of Sentiments and Emotion." Pp. 562–92 in *Social Psychology, Social Perspectives*, edited by Morris Rosenberg and Ralph Turner. New York: Basic Books.

Gormley, Louise (Luisa). 2007. "A Man Called Pablo: Popular Theatre and Latin American-Canadian Grassroots Political Participation." Pp. 132–37 in *Ruptures, Continuities and Re-earning: The Political Participation of Latin Americans in Canada, 2d ed.*, edited by Jorge Ginieniewicz and Daniel Schugurensky. Toronto, ON: Transformative Learning Centre, OISE/UT.

Gramsci, Antonio. 1971. *Prison Notebooks*, edited and translated Quintin Hoare and Geoffrey Nowel Smith. New York: International Publishers.

Guevara, Che. 1962. *On Guerrilla Warfare*. New York: Frederick A. Praeger, Inc.

de Guevara, Lina. 2001. "Telling Stories." Keynote speech at the "Untold Stories of British Columbia" conference. University of Victoria. March.

———. 2003. "Telling Stories: PUENTE Theatre and the Immigrant Experience." Pp. 87–93 in *Untold Stories of British Columbia*, edited by Paul Wood. Humanities Centre: University of Victoria.

Gupta, Akhil, and James Ferguson. 1992. "Beyond 'Culture': Space, Identity, and the Politics of Difference." *Cultural Anthropology* 7(1): 6–23.

Gutierrez y Muhs, Gabriella. 2006. *Communal Feminisms: Chicanas, Chilenas, and Cultural Exile: Theorizing the Space of Exile, Class, and Identity*. Lanham, Md.: Lexington Books.

Habelle-Pallán, Michelle. 2002. "'Don't Call Us Hispanic': Popular Latino Theater in Vancouver." Pp. 174–89 in *Latino/a Popular Culture*, edited by Michelle Habell-Pallán and Mary Romero. New York: New York University Press.

Hale, Sondra. 1993. *Gender Politics in Sudan: Islamism, Socialism, and the State*. Boulder: Westview Press.

Hall, Stuart. 2003. "Cultural Identity and Diaspora." Pp. 233–46 in *Theorizing Diaspora: A Reader*, edited by Jana Braziel and Anita Mannur. Malden, Mass.: Blackwell Publishing.

Hanff, George. 1979. "Decision-Making Under Pressure: A Study of the Admittance of Chilean Refugees by Canada." *NorthSouth* 4(8): 116–35.

Heitlinger, Alena, ed. 1999a. *Émigré Feminism: Transnational Perspectives.* Toronto: University of Toronto Press.

———. 1999b. "Émigré Feminism: An Introduction." Pp. 3–16 in *Émigré Feminism: Transnational Perspectives,* edited by Alena Heitlinger. Toronto: University of Toronto Press.

Hercus, Cheryl. 1999. "Identity, Emotion, and Feminist Collective Action." *Gender & Society* 13(1): 34–55.

Hirsch, Eric. 1990. *Urban Revolt: Ethnic Politics in the Nineteenth Century Labor Movement.* Berkeley: University of California Press.

Hite, Katherine. 2000. *When the Romance Ended: Leaders of the Chilean Left, 1968–1998.* New York: Columbia University Press.

Hochschild, Arlie Russell. 1975. "The Sociology of Feeling and Emotions: Selected Possibilities." Pp. 280–307 in *Another Voice: Feminist Perspectives on Social Life and the Social Sciences,* edited by Marcia Millman and Rosabeth Moss Kanter. Garden City, N.Y.: Anchor Books.

———. 1979. "Emotion Work, Feeling Rules, and Social Structure." *American Journal of Sociology* 85(3): 551–75.

———. 1990. "Ideology and Emotion Management: A Perspective and Path for Future Research." Pp. 117–42 in *Research Agendas in the Sociology of Emotions,* edited by Theodore D. Kemper. Albany, N.Y.: State University of New York Press.

———. 2003. *The Second Shift, 2d ed.* New York: Penguin Books.

Hoff, Lee Ann. 1990. *Battered Women as Survivors.* London: Routledge.

Holton, Sandra Stanley. 1994. "'To Educate Women in Rebellion:' Elizabeth Cady Stanton and the Creation of a Transatlantic Network of Radical Suffragists." *American Historical Review* 99(4): 1112–36.

Hunt, Lynn. 1984. *Politics, Culture, and Class in the French Revolution.* Berkeley: University of California Press.

Hunt, Scott, and Robert Benford. 2004. "Collective Identity, Solidarity and Commitment." Pp. 433–57 in *The Blackwell Companion to Social Movements,* edited by David Snow, Sarah Soule, and Hanspeter Kriesi. Malden, Mass.: Blackwell Publishing Ltd.

Hunt, Scott, Robert Benford, and David Snow. 1994. "Identity Fields: Framing Processes and the Social Construction of Movement Identities." Pp. 185–208 in *New Social Movements: From Ideology to Identity,* edited by Enrique Laraña, Hank Johnston, and Joseph R. Gusfield. Philadelphia: Temple University Press.

Jaggar, Alison. 1988. *Feminist Politics and Human Nature.* Totowa, N.J.: Rowman & Littlefield Publishers, Inc.

———. 1989. "Love and Knowledge: Emotion in Feminist Epistemology." *Inquiry* 32(2): 151–76.

Jaquette, Jane S. 1973. "Women in Revolutionary Movements in Latin America." *Journal of Marriage and the Family* 35(2): 344–54.

Jara, Joan. 1998. *Victor: An Unfinished Song, 2d ed.* London: Bloomsbury Publishing.

Jasper, James M. 1997. *The Art of Moral Protest: Culture, Biography, and Creativity in Social Movements.* Chicago: The University of Chicago Press.

———. 1998. "The Emotions of Protest; Affective and Reactive Emotions In and Around Social Movements." *Sociological Forum* 13(3): 397–424.

Jasper, James M., and Francesca Polletta. 2001. "Collective Identity in Social Movements." *Annual Review of Sociology* 27: 283–305.

Jasper, James M, and Jane D. Poulsen. 1995. "Recruiting Strangers and Friends: Moral Shocks and Social Networks in Animal Rights and Anti-Nuclear Protests." *Social Problems* 42(4): 493–512.

Jay, Nancy. 1991. "Gender and Dichotomy." Pp. 89–113 in *A Reader in Feminist Knowledge,* edited by Sneja Gunew. New York: Routledge.

Jellin, Elizabeth. 1994. "The Politics of Memory: The Human Rights Movement and the Construction of Democracy in Argentina." *Latin American Perspectives* 81, (21)2: 38–58.

Jenkins, J. Craig, and Bert Klandermans, eds. 1995. *The Politics of Social Protest: Comparative Perspectives on States and Social Movements.* Minneapolis: University of Minnesota Press.

Jenkins, J. Craig, and Charles Perrow. 1977. "Insurgency of the Powerless: Farm Worker Movements (1946–1972)." *American Sociological Review* 42(2): 249–68.

Jenkins, Pamela J. 1996. "Contested Knowledge: Battered Women as Agents and Victims." Pp. 93–111 in *Witnessing for Sociology: Sociologists in Court,* edited by Pamela Jenkins and Steve Kroll-Smith. Westport, Conn.: Praeger.

Jofré, Manuel Alcides. 1989. "Culture, Art, and Literature in Chile: 1973–1985." *Latin American Perspectives* 61, 16(2): 70–95.

Johnson, Stuart D., and Cornelia B. Johnson. 1982. "Institutional Origins in the Chilean Refugee Community in Winnipeg." *Prairie Forum* 7(2): 227–35.

Johnston, Hank, and Bert K. Klandermans, eds. 1995. *Social Movements and Culture.* Minneapolis: University of Minnesota Press.

———. 1995. "The Cultural Analysis of Social Movements." Pp. 3–24 in *Social Movements and Culture,* edited by Hank Johnston and Bert K. Klandermans. Minneapolis: University of Minnesota Press.

Johnston, Hank, Enrique Laraña, and Joseph R. Gusfield. 1994. "Identities, Grievances, and New Social Movements." Pp. 3–35 in *New Social Movements: From Ideology to Identity,* edited by Enrique Laraña, Hank Johnston, and Joseph R. Gusfield. Philadelphia: Temple University Press.

Kampwirth, Karen. 2002. *Women and Guerrilla Movements: Nicaragua, El Salvador, Chiapas, Cuba.* University Park, Pa.: Pennsylvania State University Press.

———. 2004. *Feminism and the Legacy of Revolution: Nicaragua, El Salvador, Chiapas.* Athens, Ohio: Ohio University Press.

Kaplan, Caren, and Inderpal Grewal. 1999. "Transnational Feminist Cultural Studies: Beyond the Marxism/Poststructruralism/Feminism Divides." Pp. 349–363 in *Between Woman and Nation: Nationalisms, Transnational Feminisms, and the State,* edited by Caren Kaplan, Norma Alarcón, and Minoo Moallem. Durham, N.C.: Duke University Press.

Kaplan, Temma. 1982. "Female Consciousness and Collective Action: The Case of Barcelona, 1910–1918." *Signs: Journal of Women in Culture and Society* 7(3): 545–60.

———. 1992. *Red City, Blue Period: Social Movements in Picasso's Barcelona.* Berkeley: University of California Press.

Karpinski, Eva C. 1999. "Choosing Feminism, Choosing Exile: Towards the Development of a Transnational Feminist Consciousness." Pp. 17–29 in *Émigré Feminism: Transnational Perspectives,* edited by Alena Heitlinger. Toronto: University of Toronto Press.

Katz, Jane, ed. 1983. *Artists in Exile.* New York: Stein and Day Publishers.

Kay, Diana. 1987. *Chileans in Exile: Private Struggles, Public Lives.* Wolfeboro, N.H.: Longwood Academic.

———. 1988. "The Politics of Gender in Exile." *Sociology* 22(1): 1–21.

Keck, Margaret E., and Kathryn Sikkink. 1998. *Activists Beyond Borders: Advocacy Networks in International Politics.* Ithaca, N.Y.: Cornell University Press.

Kemper, Theodore. 1978. *A Social Interactional Theory of Emotions.* New York: Wiley.

———, ed. 1990. *Research Agendas in the Sociology of Emotions.* Albany, N.Y.: State University of New York Press.

Kim, Hyojoung. 2000. "Shame, Anger, and Love in Collective Action: Emotional Consequences of Suicide Protest in South Korea, 1970–1997." Paper presented at the Social Science History Association conference, Pittsburgh, Pa., October 26–29.

Kirchheimer, Donna Wilson. 1973. "Songs of Revolution by the People's Musicians of Chile." *Sing Out* 22(5): 6–14. New York: People's Artists.

Kleinman, Sheryl. 1996. *Opposing Ambitions.* Chicago: University of Chicago Press.

Kornbluh, Peter. 1998, December 21. "Prisoner Pinochet: The Dictator and the Quest for Justice." *The Nation* 267(21): 11–26.

———. 2003. *The Pinochet File: A Declassified Dossier on Atrocity and Accountability (A National Security Archive Book).* New York: New Press.

———. 2004, September 27. "Pinochet, Stripped." *The Nation* 279(9): 5–6.

———. 2005, January 31. "Letter From Chile." *The Nation* 280(4): 22–24.

Kriesberg, Louis. 1997. "Social Movements and Global Transformation." Pp. 3–18 in *Transnational Social Movements and Global Politics: Solidarity Beyond the State,* edited by Jackie Smith, Charles Chatfield, and Ron Pagnucco. Syracuse, N.Y.: Syracuse University Press.

Kuumba, Bahati. 2001. *Gender and Social Movements.* Walnut Creek, Calif.: AltaMira Press.

Lamb, Sharon, ed. 1999. *New Versions of Victims: Feminist Struggles with the Concept.* New York: New York University Press.

Landolt, Patricia. 1993. "Chilean Immigration to Canada: 1973–1990." Prepared for Alan Simmons of York University, Centre for Refugee Studies. Toronto, Canada.

Landolt, Patricia, and Luin Goldring. 2006. "Activist Dialogues and the Production of Refugee Political Transnationalism: Chileans, Colombians and Non–Migrant Civil

Society in Canada." Paper presented at Second International Colloquium of the International Network on Migration and Development. Cocoyoc, Morelos, Mexico.

Lavie, Smadar, and Ted Swedenburg. 1996a. "Introduction: Displacement, Diaspora, and Geographies of Identity." Pp. 1–25 in *Displacement, Diaspora, and Geographies of Identity,* edited by Smadar Lavie and Ted Swedenburg. Durham, N.C.: Duke University Press.

———, eds. 1996b. *Displacement, Diaspora, and Geographies of Identity.* Durham, N.C.: Duke University Press.

Lewis, Paul. 1965. *The Politics of Exile.* Chapel Hill, N.C.: The University of North Carolina Press.

Lind, Amy. 1992. "Power, Gender, and Development: Popular Women's Organizations and the Politics of Needs in Ecuador." Pp. 134–49 in *The Making of Social Movements in Latin America,* edited by Arturo Escobar and Sonia Alvarez. Boulder: Westview Press.

Linn, Karen. 1984. "Chilena Nueva Canción: A Political Popular Music Genre." *Pacific Review of Ethnomusicology* 1: 57–64.

Lobao, Linda. 1990. "Women in Revolutionary Movements: Changing Patterns of Latin American Guerrilla Struggle." Pp. 180–204 in *Women and Social Protest,* edited by Guida West and Rhoda Lois Blumberg. Oxford: Oxford University Press.

Lofland, John. 1995. "Charting Degrees of Movement Culture: Tasks of the Cultural Cartographer." Pp. 188–216 in *Social Movements and Culture,* edited by Hank Johnston and Bert Klandermans. Minneapolis: University of Minnesota Press.

Lopez-Calvo, Ignacio. 2001. *Written in Exile: Chilean Fiction from 1973–Present.* New York: Routledge.

Lorber, Judith. 1994. *Paradoxes of Gender.* New Haven, Conn.: Yale University Press.

Loveman, Brian. 2001. *Chile: The Legacy of Hispanic Capitalism, Third Edition.* New York: Oxford University Press.

Lowden, Pamela. 1996. *Moral Opposition to Authoritarian Rule in Chile, 1973–1990.* New York: St. Martin's Press.

Luciak, Ilja A. 2001. *After the Revolution: Gender and Democracy in El Salvador, Nicaragua, and Guatemala.* Baltimore: Johns Hopkins University Press.

Magocsi, Paul Robert, ed. 1999. *Encyclopedia of Canada's Peoples.* Toronto: University of Toronto Press.

Margolis, Diane Rothbard. 1993. "Women's Movements Around the World: Cross-Cultural Comparisons." *Gender & Society* 7(3): 379–99.

Márquez, Gabriel García. 1987. *Clandestine in Chile: The Adventures of Miguel Littín, 2d ed.* New York: Henry Holt and Company.

Martz, John. 1975. "Latin America's Exile Politics." *Latin American Research Review* 10(1): 193–201.

Mata, Fernando G. 1985. "Latin American Immigration to Canada: Some Reflections on the Immigration Statistics." *Canadian Journal of Latin American and Caribbean Studies* 10(20): 27–42.

Matear, Ann. 1997. "'*Desde La Protesta a La Propuesta*': The Institutionalization of the Women's Movement in Chile." Pp. 84–100 in *Gender Politics in Latin*

America: Debates in Theory and Practice, edited by Elizabeth Dore. New York: Monthly Review Press.

Matta, Fernando Reyes. 1988. "The 'New Song' and Its Confrontation in Latin America." Pp. 447–60 in *Marxism and the Interpretation of Culture*, edited by Cary Nelson and Lawrence Grossberg. Urbana, Ill.: University of Illinois Press.

Mattern. Mark. 1997. "Popular Music and Redemocratization in Santiago, Chile 1973–1989." *Studies in Latin American Popular Culture* 16: 101–13.

McAdam, Doug. 1982. *Political Processes and the Development of the Black Insurgency, 1930–1970*. Chicago: University of Chicago Press.

———. 1984. "Culture and Social Movements." Pp. 36–57 in *New Social Movements: From Ideology to Identity*, edited by Enrique Laraña, Hank Johnston, and Joseph R. Gusfield. Philadelphia: Temple University Press.

———. 1992. "Gender as a Mediator of the Activist Experience: The Case of Freedom Summer." *American Journal of Sociology* 97(5): 1211–40.

McAdam, Doug, John D. McCarthy, and Mayer N. Zald, eds. 1996. *Comparative Perspectives on Social Movements, Political Opportunities, Mobilizing Structures, and Cultural Framings*. Cambridge: Cambridge University Press.

McCarthy, John D., and Mayer N. Zald. 1973. *The Trend of Social Movements in America: Professionalization and Resource Mobilization*. Morristown, N.J.: General Learning Press.

———. 1977. "Resource Mobilization and Social Movements: A Partial Theory." *American Journal of Sociology* 82: 1212–41.

McLuhan, Elizabeth, ed. 1995. *Safe Haven: The Refugee Experience of Five Families*. North York, Ontario: University of Toronto Press.

McSherry, J. Patrice. 1998. "The Emergence of 'Guardian Democracy'." *NACLA: Report on the Americas* 22(3): 16–24.

Melucci, Albert. 1989. *Nomads of the Present: Social Movements and Individual Needs in Contemporary Society*. Philadelphia: Temple University Press.

———. 1995. "The Process of Collective Identity." Pp. 41–63 in *Social Movements and Culture*, edited by Hank Johnston and Bert Klandermans. Minneapolis: University of Minnesota Press.

———. 1996. *Challenging Codes: Collective Action in the Information Age*. Cambridge: Cambridge University Press.

Mercer, Kobena. 1988. "Diaspora Culture and Dialogic Imagination." Pp. 50–61 in *Blackframes: Celebration of Black Cinema*, edited by Mbye Cham and Claire Andrade-Watkins. Cambridge, Mass.: MIT Press.

Meyer, Julie. 1994. "Breaking Many Taboos: Women in Solidarity." *Crossroads* 40: 11–14.

Miller, Francesca. 1990. "Latin American Feminism and the Transnational Arena." Pp. 10–26 in *Women, Culture, and Politics in Latin America: Seminar on Feminism and Culture in Latin America*, edited by Emile Bergmann, Janet Greenberg, Gwen Kirkpatrick, Francine Masiello, Francesca Miller, Marta Morello-Frosch, Kathleen Newman, and Mary Louise Pratt. Berkeley: University of California Press.

———. 1991. *Latin American Women and the Search for Social Justice*. Hanover, N.H.: University Press of New England.

Moghadam, Valentine M. 1997. "Gender and Revolutions." Pp. 137–67 in *Theorizing Revolutions*, edited by John Foran. New York: Routledge.

———. 2005. *Globalizing Women: Transnational Feminist Networks*. Baltimore: The Johns Hopkins University Press.

Mohanty, Chandra Talpade. 1988. "Under Western Eyes: Feminist Scholarship and Colonial Discourses." *Feminist Review* 30: 61–88.

Molyneux, Maxine. 1985. "Mobilization without Emancipation? Women's Interests, the State, and Revolution in Nicaragua." *Feminist Studies* 11: 227–54.

Montupil, Fernando, ed. 1993. *Exilio, Derechos Humanos y Democracia: El Exilio Chileno en Europa*. Santiago: Casa de América Latina y Servicios Gráficos Caupolicán.

Morgan, Scott, and Elizabeth Colson, eds. 1987. *People in Upheaval*. New York: Center for Migration Studies.

Morris, Aldon D. 1984. *The Origins of the Civil Rights Movement: Black Communities Organizing for Change*. New York: Free Press.

Morris, Aldon D., and Carol McClurg Mueller, eds. 1992. *Frontiers in Social Movement Theory*. New Haven, Conn.: Yale University Press.

Morris, David J. 1973. *We Must Make Haste—Slowly: The Process of Revolution in Chile*. New York: Vintage Books.

Morris, Nancy. 1986. "Canto Porque es Necesario Cantar: The New Song Movement in Chile, 1973–1983." *Latin American Research Review* 21(2): 117–36.

Moulián, Tomás. 1991. "Political Movements and Popular Culture." Pp. 69–79 in *Popular Culture in Chile: Resistance and Survival*, edited by Kenneth Aman and Christián Parker. Boulder: Westview Press.

Moya, Jose C. 1998. *Cousins and Strangers: Spanish Immigrants in Buenos Aires, 1850–1930*. Berkeley: University of California Press.

———. 2004. "Diaspora Studies: New Concepts, Approaches, and Realities?" Paper presented at Social Science History Association Meeting. Chicago, Ill, November 18–21.

Moya-Raggio, Eliana. 1984. "*Arpilleras*: Chilean Culture of Resistance." *Feminist Studies* 10(2): 277–90.

Mueller, Carolyn McClurg. 1994. "Conflict Networks and the Origins of Women's Liberation." Pp. 234–263 in *New Social Movements: From Ideology to Identity*, edited by Enrique Larana, Hank Johnston, and Joseph Gusfield. Philadelphia: Temple University Press.

Multiculturalism Directorate, Department of the Secretary of State. 1979. *The Canadian Family Tree: Canada's Peoples*. Don Mills, Ontario: Corpus Information Services Limited.

Munck, Gerardo. 1995. "Actor Formation, Social Co-Ordination, and Political Strategy: Some Conceptual Problems in the Study of Social Movements." *Sociology* 29(4): 667–85.

Muñoz, Heraldo. 2008. *The Dictator's Shadow: Life Under Augusto Pinochet*. New York: Basic Books.

Naficy, Hamid, ed. 1999. *Home, Exile, Homeland: Film, Media, and the Politics of Place*. New York: Routledge.

Naples, Nancy, and Manisha Desai, eds. 2002. *Women's Activism and Globalization: Linking Local Struggles and Transnational Politics.* New York: Routledge.

Navarro, Marysa. 1989. "The Personal is Political: Las Madres de Plaza de Mayo." Pp. 241–58 in *Power and Popular Protest: Latin American Social Movements,* edited by Susan Eckstein. Berkeley: University of California Press.

Nepstad, Sharon Erickson. 2004. "Persistent Resistance: Commitment and Community in the Plowshares Movement." *Social Problems* 51(1): 43–60.

Nepstad, Sharon Erickson, and Christian Smith. 2001. "The Social Structure of Moral Outrage in Recruitment to the U.S. Central American Peace Movement." Pp. 158–74 in *Passionate Politics: Emotions and Social Movements,* edited by Jeff Goodwin, James Jasper, and Francessca Polletta. Chicago: The University of Chicago Press.

Neustadter, Roger. 1992. "Political Generations and Protest: The Old Left and the New Left." *Critical Sociology* 19: 37–55.

Neves-Xavier de Brito, Angela. 1986. "Brazilian Women in Exile: The Quest for an Identity." *Latin American Perspectives* 13(2): 58–80.

Noonan, Rita K. 1997. "Women against the State: Political Opportunities and Collective Action Frames in Chile's Transition to Democracy." Pp. 252–67 in *Social Movements: Readings on Their Emergence, Mobilization, and Dynamics,* edited by Doug McAdam and David A. Snow. Los Angeles: Roxbury.

North American Congress on Latin America (NACLA) Chile Project. 1973. *New Chile, 2d ed.* Berkeley: Waller Press.

Oboler, Suzanne. 2005. "Introduction: Los Que Llegaron: 50 Years of South American Immigration (1950–2000)—An Overview." *Latino Studies* 3(1): 42–52.

Ochsenius, Carlos. 1991. "Popular Theater and Popular Movements." Pp. 173–88 in *Popular Culture in Chile: Resistance and Survival,* edited by Kenneth Aman and Christián Parker. Boulder: Westview Press.

Oppenheim, Lois Hect. 1999. *Politics in Chile: Democracy, Authoritarianism, and the Search for Development.* Boulder: Westview Press.

Oral History Project. 2002. Conference proceedings from "Immigration and Identity: Life Experiences of Latin American Immigrant and Refugee Women Residents of the Lower Mainland of B.C." Sponsored by the Heritage Trust of British Columbia and Family Services of Greater Vancouver, October 3.

Orellana, Patricio, and Elizabeth Quay Hutchinson. 1991. *El Movimiento de Derechos Humanos en Chile, 1973–1990.* Santiago: Centro de Estudios Políticos Latinoamericanos Simón Bolívar (CEPAL).

Oxhorn, Philip D., and Graciela Ducatenzeller, eds. 1998. *What Kind of Democracy? What Kind of Market? Latin America in the Age of Neoliberalism.* University Park, Pa.: Pennsylvania State University Press.

Pagnucco, Ron. 1987. "The Transnational Strategies of the Service for Peace and Justice in Latin America." Pp. 123–38 in *Transnational Social Movements and Global Politics: Solidarity Beyond the State,* edited by Jackie Smith, Charles Chatfield, and Ron Pagnucco. Syracuse, N.Y.: Syracuse University Press.

Palacios, Carolina. 2008. "The Political Struggles of Chilean Exiles: Social Movement Learning and Redemocratization in Chile." Pp. 273–79 in Online Proceedings of the Canadian Association for the Study of Adult Education (CASAE): "Thinking Beyond Borders: Global Ideas, Global Values," 27th National Conference. Edited by Janet Groen and Shibao Guo. The University of British Columbia, Vancouver, British Columbia.

———. 2009. "Social Movements as Learning Sites: Knowledge Production, Chilean Exiles and the Solidarity Movement." PhD diss., The University of British Columbia. Vancouver: Canada [work in progress].

Palestro, Sandra. 1991. *Mujeres en Movimiento 1973–1989*. Santiago: Facultad Latinoamericana de Ciencias Sociales.

Partnoy, Alicia, ed. 1988. *You Can't Drown the Fire: Latin American Women Writing in Exile*. Pittsburgh: Cleis Press.

Patterson, Sheila. 1977. "The Poles: An Exile Community in Britain." Pp. 214–41 in *Between Two Cultures: Migrants and Minorities in Britain*, edited by James L. Watson. Oxford: Blackwell.

Picart, Caroline Joan S. 2003. "Rhetorically Reconfiguring Victimhood and Agency: The Violence Against Women Act's Civil Rights Clause." *Rhetoric and Public Affairs* 6(1): 97–126.

Policzer, Pablo. 2009. *The Rise and Fall of Repression in Chile under Pinochet: Organization and Information in Authoritarian Regimes*. Notre Dame, Ind.: University of Notre Dame Press.

Politzer, Patricia. 2001. *Fear in Chile: Lives Under Pinochet, rev. ed.* Translated by Diane Wachtell. New York: Pantheon Books.

Polletta, Francesca. 1999. "'Free Spaces' in Collective Action." *Theory and Society* 28(1): 1–38.

Polletta, Francesca, and Edwin Amenta. 2001. "Second that Emotion? Lessons from Once-Novel Concepts in Social Movement Research." Pp. 303–16 in *Passionate Politics: Emotions and Social Movements*, edited by Jeff Goodwin, James Jasper, and Francesca Polletta. Chicago: The University of Chicago Press.

Polletta, Francesca, and James M. Jasper. 2001. "Collective Identity in Social Movements." *Annual Review of Sociology* 27: 283–305.

Pottlitzer, Joanne. 2000. "Arts Abroad: A Long-Deferred Museum in Honor of Allende." Arts section of *The New York Times*, January 6.

———. 2001a. "Under the Music: Signs of Resistance Under Pinochet, parts 1 and 2." *Crimes of War Magazine: The Cultural Supplement*. Accessed on August 10, 2005, from www.crimesofwar.org/cultural/music.

———. 2001b. "The Game of Expression Under Pinochet." In *Theater* (Summer): 3–33.

———. 2002a. "Tres Marías y una Rosa (Three Marias and a Rose)." In *Censorship: An International Encyclopedia*, edited by Derek Jones. London: Fitzroy Dearborn Publishers.

———. 2002b. "Colectivo de Acciones de Arte (CADA; Arts Action Collective)." In *Censorship: An International Encyclopedia*, edited by Derek Jones. London: Fitzroy Dearborn Publishers.

———. 2002c. "Hojas de Parra (Parra's Pages)." In *Censorship: An International Encyclopedia*, edited by Derek Jones. London: Fitzroy Dearborn Publishers.

————. 2002d. "Literature: A Censorship Trial." In *Censorship: An International Encyclopedia*, edited by Derek Jones. London: Fitzroy Dearborn Publishers.

Power, Margaret. 2002. *Right-Wing Women in Chile: Feminine Power and the Struggle Against Allende 1964–1973*. University Park, Pa.: Pennsylvania State University Press.

————. 2008. "The Engendering of Anticommunism and Fear in Chile's 1964 Presidential Election." *Diplomatic History* 32(5): 931–53.

————. 2009 [forthcoming]. "The U.S. Movement in Solidarity with Chile in the 1970s." *Latin American Perspectives*.

Pratt, Ray. 1992. *Rhythm and Resistance: Explorations in the Political Uses of Popular Music*. New York: Praeger.

Prokopy, Joshua, and Christian Smith. 1999. "Introduction." Pp. 1–16 in *Latin American Religion in Motion*, edited by Christian Smith and Joshua Prokopy. New York: Routledge.

Qureshi, Lubna Z. 2009. *Nixon, Kissinger, and Allende: U.S. Involvement in the 1973 Coup in Chile*. Lanham, Md.: Lexington Books.

Ray, Raka. 1999. *Fields of Protest: Women's Movements in India*. Minneapolis: University of Minnesota Press.

Ray, Raka, and Anna C. Korteweg. 1999. "Women's Movements in the Third World: Identity, Mobilization, and Autonomy." *Annual Review of Sociology* 25: 47–71.

Reed, Jean–Pierre, and John Foran. 2002. "Political Cultures of Opposition: Exploring Idioms, Ideologies, and Revolutionary Agency in the Case of Nicaragua." *Critical Sociology* 28(3): 335–70.

Reilly, Charles. 1983. "Cultural Movements in Latin America: Sources of Political Change and Surrogates for Participation." Pp. 127–53 in *Culture and Political Change*, edited by Myron Aronoff. New Brunswick, N.J.: Transaction Books.

Rendall, Jane. 1984. *The Origins of Modern Feminism: Women in Britain, France, and the United States, 1780–1860*. New York: Schocken.

Rettig Guissen, Raúl, Jaime Castillo Velasco, José Luis Cea Egaña, Mónica Kiménez de la Jara, Ricardo Martin Díaz, Laura Novoa Vásquez, Gonzalo Vial Correa, and José Zalaquett Daher. 1992. *Summary of the Truth and Reconciliation Commission Report*. Santiago, Chile: Chilean Human Rights Commission/Centro IDEAS Ministry of Foreign Affairs of Chile.

————. 1993a. *Report of the Chilean National Commission on Truth and Reconciliation, Vol. 1*. Notre Dame, Ind.: Center for Civil and Human Rights, Notre Dame Law School.

————. 1993b. *Report of the Chilean National Commission on Truth and Reconciliation, Vol. 2*. Notre Dame, Ind.: Center for Civil and Human Rights, Notre Dame Law School.

Roberts, Kenneth M. 1998. *Deepening Democracy? The Modern Left and Social Movements in Chile and Peru*. Stanford: Stanford University Press.

Rochlin, James. 1994. *Discovering the Americas: The Evolution of Canadian Foreign Policy Towards Latin America*. Vancouver: University of British Columbia Press.

Rodríguez, Carmen. 1992. *Guerra Prolongada, Protracted War*. Toronto: Women's Press.

————. 1997. *And A Body to Remember With*. Vancouver: Arsenal Press.

Rodríguez, Lilia. 1994. "Barrio Women: Between the Urban and the Feminist Movement." *Latin American Perspectives* 21(3): 32–48.

Roniger, Luis, and James N. Green, eds. 2007a. *Latin American Perspectives: Special Issue: Exile and the Politics of Exclusion in Latin America* 155, 34(4).

————. 2007b. "Introduction: Exile and the Politics of Exclusion in Latin America." *Latin American Perspectives* 155, 34(4): 3–6.

————. 2007e. "Concluding Remarks: Exile and the Setting of Future Research Agendas." *Latin American Perspectives* 155, 34(4): 106–8.

Rorty, Amelie. 1980. *Explaining Emotions*. Berkeley: University of California Press.

Rosaldo, Michelle Z. 1984. "Toward an Anthropology of Self and Feeling." Pp. 137–57 in *Culture Theory: Essays on Mind, Self, and Emotion*, edited by Richard A. Shweder and Robert A. Levine. New York: Cambridge University Press.

Roscigno, Vincent J., William F. Danaher, and Erika Summers-Effler. 2002. "Music, Culture and Social Movements: Song and Southern Textile Worker Mobilization, 1929–1934." *International Journal of Sociology and Social Policy* 22(1): 141–74.

Rowe, William, and Vivian Schelling. 1991. *Memory and Modernity: Popular Culture in Latin America*. London: Verso.

Rupp, Leila. 1994. "Constructing Internationalism: The Case of Transnational Women's Organizations, 1888–1945." *American Historical Review* 99(5): 1571–1600.

————. 1997. *Worlds of Women: The Making of an International Movement*. Princeton, N.J.: Princeton University Press.

Rupp, Leila J., and Verta Taylor. 1999. "Forging Feminist Identity in an International Movement: A Collective Identity Approach to Twentieth-Century Feminism." *Signs: Journal of Women in Culture and Society* 24(2): 365–86.

Ruprecht, Alvina, ed., and Cecilia Taiana, assoc. ed. 1995. *The Reordering of Culture: Latin America, the Caribbean and Canada In the Hood*. Carleton: Carleton University Press.

Safran, William. 1991. "Diasporas in Modern Societies: Myths of Homeland and Return." *Diaspora: A Journal of Transnational Studies* 1(1): 83–99.

Sagastizábal, Patricia. 2001. *A Secret For Julia*. New York: W.W. Norton & Company, Inc.

Said, Edward. 2000. *Reflections on Exile and Other Essays*. Cambridge, Mass.: Harvard University Press.

Salinas, Maximiliano. 1991. "Love and Rural Popular Culture." Pp. 141–54 in *Popular Culture in Chile: Resistance and Survival*, edited by Kenneth Aman and Christián Parker. Boulder: Westview Press.

San Martín, Magaly. 2007. "The Sisterhood Was Not Us." Pp. 124–31 in *Ruptures, Continuities and Re-Learning: The Political Participation of Latin Americans in Canada, 2d ed.*, edited by Jorge Ginieniewicz and Daniel Schugurensky. Toronto, ON: Transformative Learning Centre, OISE/UT.

Satzewich, Vic, and Lloyd Wong, eds. 2006. *Transnational Identities and Practices in Canada*. Vancouver: University of British Columbia Press.

Scalena, Matthew. 2005. ""I don't get out without a fight": Exploring the Life Histories of Chilean Exiles." Master's thesis, Simon Fraser University. Burnaby: Canada.

Scheman, Naomi. 1980. "Anger and the Politics of Naming." Pp. 174–87 in *Women and Language in Literature and Society,* edited by Sally McConnell Ginet, R. Borker, and Nelly Foreman. New York: Praeger.

Schild, Veronica. 1999. "Transnational Links in the Making of Latin American Feminisms: A View from the Margins." Pp. 67–94 in *Émigré Feminism: Transnational Perspectives,* edited by Alena Heitlinger. Toronto: University of Toronto Press.

Schirmer, Jennifer. 1993. "The Seeking of Truth and the Gendering of Consciousness: The COMADRES of El Salvador and the CONAVIGUA Widows of Guatemala." Pp. 30–64 in *"Viva": Women and Popular Protest in Latin America,* edited by Sarah A. Radcliffe and Sallie Westwood. New York: Routledge.

Schutzman, Mady. 1990. "Activism, Therapy, or Nostalgia? Theatre of the Oppressed in NYC." *The Drama Review* 34(3): 77–83.

Scott, James. 1990. *Domination and the Arts of Resistance: Hidden Transcripts.* New Haven, Conn.: Yale University Press.

Sewell, Jr., William H. 2001. "Space in Contentious Politics." Pp. 51–88 in *Silence and Voice in the Study of Contentious Politics,* edited by Ronald R. Aminzade, Jack A. Goldstone, Doug McAdam, Elizabeth J. Perry, William Sewell, Jr., Sidney Tarrow, and Charles Tilly. Cambridge: Cambridge University Press.

Selbin, Eric. 1997. "Revolution in the Real World: Bringing Agency Back In." Pp. 123–36 in *Theorizing Revolutions,* edited by John Foran. New York: Routledge.

Sepúlveda, Emma, ed. 1996. *We, Chile: Personal Testimonies of the Chilean Arpilleristas.* Falls Church, Va.: Azul Editions.

Shain, Yossi. 1989. *The Frontier of Loyalty: Political Exiles in the Age of the Nation State.* Middletown, Conn.: Wesleyan University Press.

Shayne, Julie. 1999. "Gendered Revolutionary Bridges: Women in the Salvadoran Resistance Movement, 1979–1992." *Latin American Perspectives* 26(3): 85–102.

———. 2004. *The Revolution Question: Feminisms in El Salvador, Chile, and Cuba.* New Brunswick, N.J.: Rutgers University Press. [© 2004 by Julie D. Shayne. Parts used with permission of Rutgers University Press.]

Shayne, Julie, and Girija Sankaranarayanan. 2005. "¡*Chile Si, Junta No!* Culture and Resistance in the Chilean Diaspora." Paper presented at the Social Science History Association. Portland, Oregon, November 3–6.

Slaney, Erin. 1990. "The Chilean Community in Vancouver." Unpublished paper for Sociology/Anthropology 400 course with Professor Lomas at Simon Fraser University, B.C., Canada.

Slater, David. 1992. "On the Borders of Social Theory: Learning from Other Regions." *Environment and Planning D: Society and Space* 10: 307–27.

———. 1994. "Power and Social Movements in the Other Occident: Latin America in an International Context." *Latin American Perspectives* 81, 21(2): 11–37.

———. 1998. "Rethinking the Spacialities of Social Movements: Questions of (B)orders, Culture, and Politics in Global Times." Pp. 380–401 in *Cultures of Politics, Politics of Cultures: Re-Visioning Latin American Social Movements,* edited by Sonia Alvarez, Evelina Dagnino, and Arturo Escobar. Boulder: Westview Press.

Smith, Jackie. 2004. "Transnational Processes and Movements." Pp. 311–35 in *The Blackwell Companion to Social Movements,* edited by David A. Snow, Sarah A. Soule, and Hanspeter Kriesi. Malden, Mass.: Blackwell Publishing.

Smith, Jackie, Charles Chatfield, and Ron Pagnucco, eds. 1997. *Transnational Social Movements and Global Politics: Solidarity Beyond the State.* Syracuse, N.Y.: Syracuse University Press.

Smith, Jackie, Ron Pagnucco, and Charles Chatfield. 1997. "Social Movements and World Politics: A Theoretical Framework." Pp. 59–77 in *Transnational Social Movements and Global Politics: Solidarity Beyond the State,* edited by Jackie Smith, Charles Chatfield, and Ron Pagnucco. Syracuse, N.Y.: Syracuse University Press.

Snow, David A., E. Burke Rochford Jr., Steven K. Worden, and Robert Benford. 1986. "Frame Alignment Processes, Micromobilization and Movement Participation." *American Sociological Review* 51: 456–81.

Snow, David A., and Robert D. Benford. 1988. "Ideology, Frame Resonance, and Participant Mobilization." *International Social Movement Research* 1: 197–217.

———. 1992. "Master Frames and Cycles of Protest." Pp. 133–55 in *Frontiers in Social Movement Theory,* edited by Aldon D. Morris and Carol McClurg Mueller. New Haven, Conn.: Yale University Press.

Spooner, Mary Helen. 1999. *Soldiers in a Narrow Land: The Pinochet Regime in Chile.* Berkeley: University of California Press.

Stasiulis, Daiva K. 1999. "Relational Personalities of Nationalisms, Racisms, and Feminisms." Pp. 182–218 in *Between Woman and Nation: Nationalisms, Transnational Feminisms, and the State,* edited by Caren Kaplan, Norma Alarcón, and Minoo Moallem. Durham, N.C.: Duke University Press.

Steadman, Ian. 1994. "Toward Popular Theater in South Africa." Pp. 11–34 in *Politics and Performance: Theater, Poetry, and Song in Southern Africa,* edited by Liz Gunner. Johannesburg: Witwatersrand University Press.

Stefranko, Jacqueline. 1996. "New Ways of Telling: Latinas' Narratives of Exile and Return." *Frontiers* 17(2): 50–69.

Stephen, Lynn, ed. 1994. *Hear My Testimony: María Teresa Tula, Human Rights Activist of El Salvador.* Boston: South End Press.

———. 1997. *Women and Social Movements in Latin America: Power from Below.* Austin: University of Texas Press.

Stern, Steve J. 2004. *Remembering Pinochet's Chile: On the Eve of London 1998.* Durham, N.C.: Duke University Press.

Sternbach, Nancy Saporta, Marysa Navarro-Aranguren, Patricia Chuchryk, and Sonia E. Alvarez. 1992. "Feminisms in Latin America: From Bogota to San Bernardo." Pp. 207–39 in *The Making of Social Movements in Latin America: Identity, Strategy, and Democracy,* edited by Arturo Escobar and Sonia E. Alvarez. Boulder: Westview Press.

Stienstra, Deborah. 1994. *Women's Movements and International Organizations.* London: St. Martin's.

Strauss, Anslem, and Juliet Corbin. 1990. *Basics of Qualitative Research: Grounded Theory Procedures and Techniques.* Newbury Park, Calif.: Sage Publications.

———. 1994. "Grounded Theory Methodology: An Overview." Pp. 273–85 in *Handbook of Qualitative Research,* edited by Norman K. Denzin and Yvonna S. Lincoln. Thousand Oaks, Calif.: Sage Publications.

Swidler, Ann. 1986. "Culture in Action: Symbols and Strategies." *American Sociological Review* 51(2): 273–86.

———. 1995. "Cultural Power and Social Movements." Pp. 25–40 in *Social Movements and Culture,* edited by Hank Johnston and Bert K. Klandermans. Minneapolis: University of Minnesota Press.

Sznajder, Mario, and Luis Roniger. 2007. "Political Exile in Latin America." *Latin American Perspectives* 155, 34(4): 7–30.

Taffet, Jeffrey. 1997. "'My Guitar is Not for the Rich': The New Chilean Song Movement and the Politics of Culture." *Journal of American Culture* 20(2): 91–103.

Tarrow, Sidney. 1988. "National Politics and Collective Action: Recent Theory and Research in Western Europe and the United States." *Annual Review of Sociology* 14: 421–40.

———. 1992. "Mentalities, Political Cultures, and Collective Action Frames: Constructing Meanings through Action." Pp. 174–202 in *Frontiers in Social Movement Theory,* edited by Aldon D. Morris and Carol McClurg Mueller. New Haven, Conn.: Yale University Press.

———. 1995. *Power in Movement: Social Movements, Collective Action and Politics.* New York: Cambridge University Press.

Taylor, Clare. 1974. *British and American Abolitionists.* Edinburgh: University of Edinburgh Press.

Taylor, Verta. 1989. "Social Movement Continuity." *American Sociological Review* 54(5): 761–75.

———. 1995. "Watching for Vibes: Bringing Emotions Into the Study of Feminist organizations." Pp. 223–233 in *Feminist Organizations: Harvest of the New Women's Movement,* edited by Myra Marx Ferree and Patricia Yancey Martin. Philadelphia: Temple University Press.

———. 1996. *Rock-A-Bye Baby: Feminism, Self Help, and Postpartum Depression.* New York: Routledge.

———. 1999. "Gender and Social Movements: Gender Processes in Women's Self–Help Movements." *Gender & Society* 13(1): 8–33.

Taylor, Verta, and Nancy Whittier. 1992. "Collective Identity in Social Movement Communities." Pp. 104–29 in *Frontiers in Social Movement Theory,* edited by Aldon D. Morris and Carol McClurg Mueller. New Haven, Conn.: Yale University Press.

———. 1995. "Analytical Approaches to Social Movement Culture: The Culture of the Women's Movement." Pp. 163–87 in *Social Movements and Culture,* edited by Hank Johnston and Bert K. Klandermans. Minneapolis: University of Minnesota Press.

Ternar, Yeshim. 1999. "My Journey as a Woman across Continents." Pp. 208–18 in *Émigré Feminism: Transnational Perspectives,* edited by Alena Heitlinger. Toronto: University of Toronto Press.

Tetreault, Mary Ann. 1993. "Civil Society in Kuwait: Protected Spaces and Women's Rights." *Middle East Journal* 47(2): 275–91.

Thiele, Beverly. 1986. "Vanishing Acts in Social and Political Thought: Tricks of the Trade." Pp. 30–43 in *Feminist Challenges: Social and Political Theory*, edited by Carole Pateman and Elizabeth Gross. Boston: Northeastern University Press.

Thoits, Peggy A. 1990. "Emotional Deviance: Research Agendas." Pp. 180–203 in *Research Agendas in the Sociology of Emotions*, edited by Theodore D. Kemper. Albany, N.Y.: State University of New York Press.

Tilly, Charles. 1978. *From Mobilization to Revolution*. Reading, Mass.: Addison–Wesley.

Tölölian, Khachig. 1991. "The Nation State and its Others: In Lieu of a Preface." *Diaspora: A Journal of Transnational Studies* 1(1): 3–7.

Touraine, Alain. 1981. *The Voice and the Eye: An Analysis of Social Movements*. New York: Cambridge University Books.

Tyyskä, Vappu. 1999. "Western Feminism? Problems of Categorizing Women's Movements in Cross-national Research." Pp. 252–66 in *Émigré Feminism: Transnational Perspectives*, edited by Alena Heitlinger. Toronto: University of Toronto Press.

Unidad Popular (Popular Unity, UP). 1970. "Popular Unity Program." Reprinted in *The Salvador Allende Reader: Chile's Voice of Democracy*, edited by James D. Cockcroft. Melbourne: Ocean Press, 2000.

Valdés, Teresa, and Marisa Weinstein. 1993. *Mujeres que Sueñan: Las Organizaciones De Pobladoras En Chile: 1973–1989*. Santiago: Facultad Latinoamericana de Ciencias Sociales.

Valenzuela, Arturo. 1978. *The Breakdown of Democratic Regimes: Chile*. Baltimore: Johns Hopkins University Press.

Valenzuela, Arturo, and J. Samuel Valenzuela. 1975. "Visions of Chile." *Latin American Research Review* 10(3): 155–75.

Vásquez, Ana, and Ana María Araujo. 1990. *La Maldición de Ulises: Repercusion Psicológicas del Exilio*. Santiago: Sudamericana.

Vergottini, Tomaso de. 1991. *Miguel Claro 1359: Recuerdos de un Diplomático Italiano en Chile (1973–1975)*. Santiago: Atena.

Vidal, Hernán. 1996. *Dar la vida por la vida: Agrupación Chilena de Familiares de Detenidos Desaparecidos*. Santiago, Chile: Mosquito Editores.

Villouta, Mili Rodríguez. 1990. *Ya Nunca Me Veras Como Me Vieras: Doce Testimonios Vivos del Exilio*. Santiago: Ornitorrinco.

Walsh, Edward. 1981. "Resource Mobilization and Citizen Protest in Communities around Three Mile Island." *Social Problems* 29(1): 1–21.

West, Lois A. 1999. "The United Nations Women's Conferences and Feminist Politics." Pp. 177–93 in *Gender Politics in Global Governance*, edited by Mary K. Meyer and Elisabeth Prügl. Lanham, Md.: Rowman & Littlefield.

Wieringa, Saskia. 1992. *The Perfumed Nightmare: Some Notes on the Indonesian Women's Movement*. The Hague: The Institute for Social Studies.

Wilde, Alexander. 1999. "Irruptions of Memory: Expressive Politics in Chile's Transition to Democracy." *Journal of Latin American Studies* 31(2): 473–500.

Williams, Raymond. 1977. *Marxism and Literature*. Oxford: Oxford University Press.

———. 1981a. *Culture*. Glasgow: Fontana.

———. 1981b. *The Sociology of Culture*. New York: Schocken Books.

———. 1983a. *Culture and Society, 1780–1950, 2d ed.* New York: Columbia University Press.

———. 1983b. *Keywords: A Vocabulary of Culture and Society (Revised edition)*. New York: Oxford University Press.

Wood, Elisabeth Jean. 2001. "The Emotional Benefits of Insurgency in El Salvador." Pp. 267–81 in *Passionate Politics: Emotions and Social Movements*, edited by Jeff Goodwin, James Jasper, and Francessca Polletta. Chicago: The University of Chicago Press.

Wright, Thomas. 1991. *Latin America in the Era of the Cuban Revolution*. Westport, Conn.: Praeger Publishers.

———. 1995. "Legacy of Dictatorship: Works on the Chilean Diaspora." *Latin American Research Review* 30(3): 198–209.

———. 2007. *State Terrorism in Latin America: Chile, Argentina, and International Human Rights*. Lanham, Md.: Rowman & Littlefield Publishers.

Wright, Thomas, and Rody Oñate. 1998. *Flight from Chile: Voices of Exile*. Albuquerque: University of New Mexico Press.

———. 2007. "Chilean Political Exile." *Latin American Perspectives* 155, 34(4): 31–49.

Wuthnow, Robert. 1987. *Meaning and Moral Order: Explanations in Cultural Analysis*. Berkeley: University of California Press.

Zammit, J. Ann, ed. 1973. *The Chilean Road to Socialism*. Brighton, England: The Kensington Press.

Zurcher, Louis Jr., and David A. Snow. 1981. "Collective Behavior: Social Movements." Pp. 447–82 in *Social Psychology: Sociological Perspectives*, edited by Ralph H. Turner and Morris Rosenberg. New York: Basic Books.

Films

Barrera, Verónica. 2008. *Lo que Me Tocó Vivir—The Life I Got to Live*. Seattle: Luchadora Productions.

Cruz, Quique, and Marilyn Mulford. 2008. "Archeology of Memory: Villa Grimaldi." San Francisco: Quique Cruz Productions.

Farnsworth, Elizabeth, and Patricio Lanfranco. 2008. *The Judge and the General*. New York: The Cinema Guild.

Field, Rachel, and Juan Mandelbaum. 1993. *In Women's Hands: The Changing Roles of Women*. Part of the Americas television series. South Burlington, Vt.: Annenberg/Corporation for Public Broadcasting.

Guzmán, Patricio. 2004. *Salvador Allende*. Brooklyn, N.Y.: First Run/Icarus Films.

Jamison, Gayla. 1991. *Scraps of Life*. New York: Lightfoot films.

Mallet, Marilú. 2003. *La Cueca Sola*. Les films de l'atalante in co-production with the National Film Board of Canada. New York: Women Make Movies.

Muñoz, Susana, and Lourdes Portillo. 1986. *Las Madres: The Mothers of the Plaza de Mayo*. Los Angeles: Direct Cinema.

Paez, Claudia. 2003. *This Is Also My Home: Chileans in Vancouver, 30 Years Later*. Vancouver: The Chilean Cultural Institute of Canada.

Parot, Carmen Luz. 1999. *El derecho de vivir en paz/The right to live in peace*. Santiago, Chile: Fundación Víctor Jara.

Shaffer. Deborah. 1989. *Dance of hope*. New York: First Run/Icarus Films.

Wood, Andres. 2004. *Machuca*. Barcelona, Spain: Cameo Media.

Websites

http://chile.exilio.free.fr/index.htm

http://www.collectionscanada.ca/proyecto–adrienne/index–e.html

http://www.puentetheatre.ca/

http://reel.utsc.utoronto.ca/relac/index.html

http://www.siemprechilenos.com/

http://www.vcn.bc.ca/alad/index.php

PRIMARY DOCUMENTS

Periodicals

Allen, Glen. 1973a. "Fists and Flowers. Neruda—Poet to the Americas." In *The Montreal Gazette*. September 29. Montreal, Canada.

———. 1973b. "Canada's Recognition of Chile a Weak Move, at Best." In *The Montreal Gazette*. October 2. Montreal, Canada.

Associated Press (AP). 1973. "Chile Sentences 12 Women." In the *Vancouver Sun*. December 28.

Associated Press and Reuter News Agency. 1973. "Junta Chief May Declare War Against Allende's Followers." In *The Globe and Mail*. September 20. Toronto, Canada.

Bernard, Mike. 1973. "Sit-in Wrests Concession from Government." In *The Peak (Simon Fraser University)*. November 15, No. 10: 1 and 3.

Bruce, Marian. 1973. "Mrs. Allende Confident: 'Chilean Resistance Growing.'" In *The Vancouver Sun*. Wednesday, December 5.

Burns, E. Bradford. 1973. "True Verdict on Allende." In *The Nation*. October 29.

Canadian News Synthesis Project (CNSP). 1973. "Chile and the Canadian Press." Toronto, ON: Canada.

The Canadian Press (CP). 1973. "Canada Recognizes Junta as Government of Chile." In *Globe and Mail*. October 1. Toronto, Canada.

Coppard, Patricia. 2004. "La Quena 20-Year Reunion Sure Bet to Be Politically Correct." Accessed from *The Vancouver Courrier.com* on January 13, 2006. http://www.vancourier.com/issues03/103203/opinion/103203op2.html

Eayrs, James. 1973a. "Envoy Missed the Action: Bad Advice from Santiago?" In *The Ottawa Citizen*. October 1. Ottawa, Canada.

———. 1973b. "From Our Man in Santiago: The Edsel of Dispatches: Opinion." In *The Toronto Star*. November. Toronto, Canada.

Eisendrath, Charles. 1973. "The Coup: The View from the Carrera." In *Time Magazine*. September 24. Montreal, Canada.

Giniger, Henry. 1973. "Madrid Bans Death Notices of Allende." In *The New York Times*. September 23. New York.

Goodsell, James Nelson. 1973. "Junta Grabs Legendary Pepe." In *The Christian Science Monitor*. September 25. Boston.

Griffin, Sean. 1973. "Mrs. Allende Appeal: 'Allow Chile Refugees to Enter Canada Freely.'" In *Pacific Tribune*. December 7, Vol 34, No. 49: 1 and 12.

Haverstock, Nathan A. 1973. "Before the Chilean Coup." In *The Winnipeg Free Press*. September 25. Winnipeg, Canada.

Hendrickson, Bob. 1973. "Help for Chile Refugees Asked at Passport Sit–in." In a daily newspaper in Vancouver, not clear which one. November.

Jardine, D. 1976. "Kootenay Valley Folk Festival '76." *Trail Times*. February 10: 4–5.

Kandell, Jonathan. 1973. "After the Coup Chile Settles Down As the Junta Settles In." In *The New York Times*. September 23. New York.

Labreveux, Philippe. 1973. "Chile after the Coup: The Repression Goes On." In *Globe and Mail*. October 2. Toronto, Canada.

Lavoie, Michael. 1973. "Envoy's Secret Cables Leaked." In *The Toronto Star*. November 6. Pg A15. Toronto, Canada.

Mallory, J. R. 1973. "Too Hasty Recognition?" In *The Montreal Gazette*. October 2. Montreal, Canada.

Martin, Everett G. 1973. "Chile's Rulers Face Huge Economic Woes, Make Some Progress." In *The Wall Street Journal*. September 18. New York.

N/A. 1973a. "After the Coup. Chile Not by Nature Rightist." In *The Toronto Star*. September 12. Toronto, Canada.

———. 1973b. "Breadlines and Inflation. 'We Just Cannot Go On.'" In *The Toronto Star*. September 12. Toronto, Canada.

———. 1973c. "Allende Vowed to Leave Office 'in a Pine Box.'" In *The Toronto Star*. September 12. Toronto, Canada.

———. 1973d. "Protesters Stage Sleep-in At Passport Office." In *The Vancouver Sun*. November N/D. Vancouver, Canada.

———. 1973e. "Bodies Carted off in Trucks, Canadian Woman in Chile Says." In *The Globe and Mail*. September 18. Toronto, Canada.

———. 1973f. "Junta 'Tours' Depict Allende as Traitor to Peasants." In *The Toronto Star*. September 21. Toronto, Canada.

———. 1973g. "The Fighting's Not Over Yet." In *The Economist*. September 22. London, England.

———. 1973h. "Lessons of Chile." In *The Guardian*. September 26. New York.

———. 1973i. "Canada's Ambassador Backs Army Coup in Chile." In *The Toronto Star*. September 26. Toronto, Canada.

———. 1973j. "Rootless Outsiders." In *The Economist*. September 29. London, England.

———. 1973k. "Unification Through Intimidation." In *The New York Times*. September 30. New York.

————. 1973l. "Facing Facts in Chile." In *The Ottawa Citizen*. October 1. Ottawa, Canada.

————. 1973m. "19 Refugees Seeking Asylum Complicated Diplomatic Talks." In *The Globe and Mail*. Toronto, Canada.

————. 1973n. "Chile's No Place for a Monolith." In *The Economist*. October 5. London, England.

————. 1973o. "Chile: A Strange Return to Normalcy." In *Time Magazine*. October 8. Montreal, Canada.

————. 1979. "Music, Poetry and Memorials 'For a Free Chile.'" In the *Chicago Sun-Times*. February 26.

New York Times Service. 1973a. "Widow Believes Allende Did Not Commit Suicide." In *The Globe & Mail*. September 12. Toronto, Canada.

————. 1973b. "Witnesses Contend Thousands of Foreigners Are Being Held, Ill–Treated by Chilean Junta." In *The Globe & Mail*. September 12. Toronto, Canada.

O'Shaughnessy, Hugh. 1973. "Champagne and Death in Santiago." In *The Observer*. September 16. London, England.

Reuter. 1973. "Charged in Violence, Allende Foes Freed." In *The Globe & Mail*. September 14. Toronto, Canada.

Reuter-UPI. 1973. "Allende Found Dead after Coup in Chile." In *The Toronto Star*. September 12. Toronto, Canada.

Rubin, Barry. 1973. "Fascist Coup Topples Allende in Chile." In *The Guardian*. September 19. New York.

Simmons, Jean, and Alan Simmons. 1973. "Chile's Class Conflict Destroyed Allende, Toronto Couple Says." In *The Toronto Star*. September 20. Toronto, Canada.

Stern, Laurence. 1973. "U.S. Applied Economic Pressure to Topple Allende." In *The Ottawa Citizen*. September 21. Ottawa, Canada.

UPI–Special. 1973. "Death's Stench Lingers on in Santiago." In *The Toronto Star*. September 20. Toronto, Canada.

Velasco, Eugenio. 1977. "Chile: The New Mask of Repression." In *The Vancouver Sun*. October 1.

Winsor, Hugh. 1973. "Canada's Concern for a $5 Million Deal Cited as Factor in Recognition of Chile." In *The Globe and Mail*. October 2. Toronto, Canada.

Zuniga, Jose. n.d. "Coup Set Last Year, Chile's Leader Says." In the *Vancouver Sun*

Solidarity Movement Documents[1]

Ad Hoc Chilean Solidarity Committee. 1973a. Flyer, "Protest the Military Coup in Chile." September 15. Vancouver, BC: Canada

————. 1973b. First leaflet distributed on the street at the first demonstration against the coup. September 15. Vancouver, BC: Canada.

————. 1973c. Second leaflet distributed on the street at the first demonstration against the coup. September 15. Vancouver, BC: Canada.

Ad Hoc Committee to Establish Solidarity With Resistance in Chile. 1977. "Resistance in Chile: Speaking and Fund Raising Tour Across Canada by A Representative of the People's Front of Chile." Organizational leaflet and schedule. October 29–December 10. Montreal, Quebec: Canada.

Agencia Noticiosa Chilena Antifascista (A.N.CH.A.). 1978. "Editada Por El Frente Del Pueblo En El Exterior." No. 29, February.

Bussi Soto de Allende, Mercedes Hortensia. 1973. "An Open Letter to the People of Canada." November.

Canadians for Democracy in Chile. 1977a. "Chile News: Solidarity with Chile." Vol. 1, No. 1. June. Vancouver, BC: Canada.

———. 1977b. "Chile News: Solidarity With Chile." September. Vancouver, BC: Canada.

———. 1977c. "Chile News: Solidarity With Chile." Vol. 1, No. 4. October. Vancouver, BC: Canada.

Carroll, William. 1974. "The Response of the Canadian Academic Community to the Chilean Crisis." *Bulletin of the Canadian Association of University Teachers.* 23(2/October): 1.

Chile Solidarity Committee (CSC). 1973a. Flyer for "Panel discussion on Chile." September 18. Vancouver, BC: Canada.

———. 1973b. Letter to potential activists. September 29. Vancouver, BC: Canada.

———. 1973c. "Newsletter No. 1." October. Vancouver, BC: Canada.

———. 1973d. "Resolution," regarding granting refugee status to all Chileans. Announcement for Teach-in. November 3.

———. 1973e. "Press Release" regarding demonstration scheduled for November 3. October 31. Vancouver, BC: Canada.

———. 1973f. Flyer for picket and rally at Simon Fraser University and University of British Columbia "to demand Asylum in Canada for Refugees From Chile." November. Vancouver, BC: Canada.

———. 1973g. Flyer for protest against Prime Minister Trudeau. November. Vancouver, BC: Canada.

———. 1974a. "Support the Chilean Resistance." Flyer distributed at NDP convention regarding Chilean wine boycott and support of Chilean opposition. Vancouver, BC: Canada.

———. 1974b. Announcement for Cinema Solidaridad. Vancouver, BC: Canada.

———. 1974c. "Bulletin of News & Political Views on the Struggle in Chile." Number 2, January. Vancouver, BC: Canada.

———. 1974d. "Bulletin of News & Political Views on the Struggle in Chile." Number 3, March. Vancouver, BC: Canada.

———. 1974e. Flyer for the film "Chile with Poems and Guns." April. Vancouver, BC: Canada.

———. 1974f. "Bulletin of News & Political Views on the Struggle in Chile." Number 4, July. Vancouver, BC: Canada.

———. 1974g. Flyer for Solidarity Week commemorating first anniversary of the coup. September. Vancouver, BC: Canada.

———. 1974h. Leaflet for Solidarity Week commemorating first anniversary of the coup. September. Vancouver, BC: Canada.

———. 1974i. "Support the Chilean Resistance." Flyer regarding the work of the Chile Solidarity Committee. September. Vancouver, BC: Canada.

————. 1974j. "Support the Chilean Resistance." Flyer directed toward union activists regarding the work of the Chile Solidarity Committee. Vancouver, BC: Canada.

————. 1974–1975. "Newsletter." Winter. Vancouver, BC: Canada.

————. 1975a. Educational Series Committee. Agenda and suggested readings for first Chile Solidarity Committee Educational. Vancouver, BC: Canada.

————. 1975b. "Chile Solidarity Newsletter." Vancouver, BC: Canada.

Chile Canada Solidarity Newsletter (CCSN). n.d. Newsletter, no issue number. Toronto, ON: Canada.

————. 1973a. Newsletter, Issue 4. October 9. Toronto, ON: Canada.

————. 1973b. Newsletter, Issue 6. October 29. Toronto, ON: Canada.

————. 1973c. Newsletter, Issue 7. "Immigration." November 25. Toronto, ON: Canada.

————. 1974. Newsletter, Issue 8. January 21. Toronto, ON: Canada.

Chile Democrático. 1978. "Chile y el mundo entero exigen la verdad sobre los desaparecidos." Edición Española. June–July: 1, 5.

Comités de Solidarité-Chile-Solidarity Committees. 1973. "Visite Hortensia Allende Visit." Contact information.

Cortes, Osvaldo. n.d. An Urgent Appeal from the Central Única de Trabajadores de Chile, Comisión Exterior. Toronto, ON: Canada.

Cram, George, T. E. Floyd Honey, Antonio Urello, Romeo Maione, Yvon Préfontaine, Albert Dumont, Clotilde Bertrand, Lionel Vallée, Michel Chartrand, Murray Thompson, John Zimmerman, Hilda Creswick, Ronald Levesque, Donald MacDonald, Ricardo Hill. Michael O'Kane, Robert Smith, Robert Quevillon, Suzanne Chartrand, M. Michel Blondin, Susan Vander Voet, John Foster, and George Tillman. 1974. "Canadian Policy Toward Chile / Politique Canadienne Envers Le Chili." Brief presented to The Honourable Allan J. Maceachen, Secretary of State for External Affairs and The Honourable Robert K. Andras, Minister of Manpower and Immigration. October 9.

Foster, John W. 1974. Memo to Solidarity Committees on behalf of The United Church of Canada. (Includes "General Information About Immigration to Canada" from the Canadian Embassy in Santiago, dated March 1974.) April. Toronto, ON: Canada.

Gorst, James H. 1973. Letter to Chile Solidarity Committee regarding NDP's position on Chile. October 31. Victoria, BC: Canada.

Inter-Church Committee on Chile. 1975. "Canada–Chile Bulletin." No. 1, May. Toronto, ON: Canada.

Latin American Working Group (LAWG). 1973a. "Canada Aid: Whose Priorities? A Study of the Relationship between Non-governmental Organizations, Business, and the Needs of Latin America." May (reprinted October). Toronto, ON: Canada.

————. 1973b. "Chile 1973: We Lost They Won." July. Toronto, ON: Canada.

————. 1973c. "Chilean History Reveals Background to Coup." In *The Varsity*. September 19. Pages 8–9. Toronto, Canada.

————. 1973d. "News on Chile." Collection of post-coup press releases and pre–coup news clippings. September 14. Toronto, ON: Canada.

———. 1973e. "The Role of the United States in the Overthrow of Allende." September. Toronto, ON: Canada.

———. 1973f. "The Confidential Cables From Ambassador Andrew Ross In Santiago, Chile To External Affairs in Ottawa." November 15. Toronto, ON: Canada.

———. 1974. "LAWG Letter: Special Chile Issue." September, 2(4). Toronto, ON: Canada.

———. 1975a. "LAWG Letter: Women in Chile's Prisons." March–April, 2(6). Toronto, ON: Canada.

———. 1975b. "LAWG Letter: The Land and the People." March, 2(7). Toronto, ON: Canada.

———. 1975c. "LAWG Letter: The Dominican Republic, Ten Years Later." April–May, 2(8). Toronto, ON: Canada.

———. 1975d. "LAWG Letter: Solidarity, Women, Chile, Workers." September–October, 3(1). Toronto, ON: Canada.

———. 1975/1976. "LAWG Letter: 'You Can't Make a Revolution without Them! By Margaret Randall.'" Dec–Jan, 3(2). Toronto, ON: Canada.

———. 1976a. "LAWG Letter: Culture in Latin America." February–March, 3(3). Toronto, ON: Canada.

———. 1976b. "LAWG Letter: The New International Economic Order." June, 3(6). Toronto, ON: Canada.

———. 1977. "LAWG Letter: Cuba – Beyond the Beach." March, 4(3/4). Toronto, ON: Canada.

———. 1980. "LAWG Letter: Peru: Economic Crisis and Daily Bread." May–June, 6(6). Toronto, ON: Canada.

———. n.d. "The 11 Apostles." Document about Eleven "Good Will" Ambassadors Sent out by the Chilean Military Junta. Toronto, ON: Canada.

MAPU (Movimiento de Acción Popular Unitaria). 1974a. "Resistencia: English Version." November, Volume 2.

———. 1974b. "Resistencia: English Version." December, Volume 3.

MAPU Party and Socialist Party (NCR). 1977. "To the Compañeras and Compañeros in Vancouver." Statement on political strategy inside Chile and Vancouver. July.

MIR. n.d. "Revolucionar la Imaginación en la Lucha Contra la Dictadura." Manifesto from artist and cultural workers. Santiago, Chile.

n.a. 1973a. "Chile: No Road to Socialism." In *Latin America*. Vol VII, No. 37. September 14. London, England.

———.1973b. "Chile: Continental Earthquake." In *Latin America*. Vol VII, No. 38. September 21. London, England.

———. 1973c. "Chile: A Corporate State in the Making?" In *Latin America*. September 28. London, England.

———. 1973d. "Solidarity with the People of Chile." Flyer for demonstration, teach–in, and film. November 3. Vancouver, BC: Canada.

———. 1975. "Venceremos." September, 1(4). Vancouver, BC: Canada.

———. 1977a. "Chile Conference: Boycott and Canadian Investments in Chile." Contributors include: Coordinating Committee for Solidarity with Democratic

Chile, Latin American Working Group (LAWG), and Vancouver Chilean Association. September 10.

———. 1977b. "Chile Conference: Political Prisoners and Human Rights in Chile." September 10.

Non-Intervention in Chile (NICH). 1973. "Chile Newsletter." Vol. 1, No. 3, December 31. Berkeley, CA.

Office of Area Relations. 1973. "Trade Topics: Chile," from the Latin America Division. February.

Ortega, Hernan. n.d. "An Open Letter to Vancouver Longshoremen From A Chilean Trade Union Leader." From Hernan Ortega, President of the Industrial Belts of Santiago (workers councils), Co-ordinator [*sic*] of the Chilean Left In Exile.

Paz Paredes, Margarita. "El Crimen Fue En Santiago." Mexico City, Mexico.

Project Chile. n.d. Informational pamphlet (in English). Toronto, ON: Canada.

Proyecto Chile. 1977. Informational pamphlet (in Spanish). April. Toronto, ON: Canada.

Revolutionary Marxist Group (RMG). 1973. "Victory to the Chilean Revolutionary Front." Flyer for "Red Forums." November. Vancouver, BC: Canada.

———. 1974a. "Internal Discussion Bulletin." No. 2. January 14. Toronto, ON: Canada.

———. 1974b. "Internal Discussion Bulletin." No. 4. April 12. Toronto, ON: Canada.

———. 1974c. "Chile Fraction Report." Submitted to a branch conference of the Revolutionary Marxist Group. July 12. Vancouver, BC: Canada.

———. 1974d. Internal report to national branch of the Revolutionary Marxist Group. July 22. Vancouver, BC: Canada.

———. 1974e. "Circular on September Chile Work." Internal document to all branches of the Revolutionary Marxist Group in Canada. July 30. Toronto, ON: Canada.

———. n.d.(a). "Internal Bulletin: Women's Commission Document." Vol. 2, No. 9. Toronto, ON: Canada.

———. n.d.(b). "What's the Use?" Flyer about the continued importance of solidarity work. Vancouver, BC: Canada.

Revolutionary Workers League/Ligue Ouvriere Revolutionanaire (RWL/LOR). n.d. "Solidaridad." Flyer about solidarity work. Vancouver, BC: Canada.

Statistics Canada. 2001. "2001 Census Profile: British Columbia." Census of Population and Housing. Produced by BC STATS. www.bcstats.gov.bc.ca.

Vancouver Chilean Association (VCA). 1978a. "Newsletter: Why Boycott Chile?" May–June, vol. 2. Vancouver, BC: Canada.

———. 1978b. "Canadian Trade with Chile." June, Issue #2. Vancouver, BC: Canada.

World Council of Churches in Geneva. 1973. "Cable From UN Refugee Camps in Santiago." Addressed to: "Parties, political movements, trade unions, committees of wolidarity [*sic*] with Chile, world public opinion." November 26. Circulated by Chile–Canada Solidarity.

Feminist Documents

Aquelarre. n.d. Promotional flyer/subscription form. Vancouver, B.C.

———. n.d. "Marco Ideológico," informational memo about the magazine and organization.

Aquelarre Latin American Women's Cultural Society. 1988a. "Mtgs [*sic*] Chronology – Aquelarre," by Cecilia Tagle. April 13.

———. 1988b. "Revista Reunión 1, Miércoles 13 de Abril de 1988."

———. 1988c. "Revista Reunión 2, Martes 19 de Abril de 1988."

———. 1988d. "Calendario de Trabajo," by Cecilia Tagle. July 4.

———. 1988e. Initial grant application to Exploration Program of The Canada Council. Ottawa, Ontario. September 15.

———. 1989a. *Aquelarre: A Magazine for Latin American Women/Revista de la Mujer Latinoamericana.* Julio Agosto Septiembre/July August September. Issue #1.[2]

———. 1989b. *Aquelarre: A Magazine for Latin American Women/Revista de la Mujer Latinoamericana.* Octubre Noviembre Diciembre/October November December. Issue #2.

———. 1989c. "Historias de Viajes Inesperados/I Wasn't Born Here." Pp. 4–7 in *Aquelarre: A Magazine for Latin American Women/Revista de la Mujer Latinoamericana.* Julio Agosto Septiembre/July August September. Issue #1.

———. 1990a. *Aquelarre: A Magazine for Latin American Women/Revista de la Mujer Latinoamericana.* "Mujeres inmigrantes/Immigrant women."[3] January February March/Enero Febrero Marzo. Issue #3.

———. 1990b. *Aquelarre: A Magazine for Latin American Women/Revista de la Mujer Latinoamericana.* "Women and Art/Mujer Y Arte." Abril Mayo Junio/April May June. Issue #4.

———. 1990c. *Aquelarre: A Magazine for Latin American Women/Revista de la Mujer Latinoamericana.* "Alfabetización/Literacy." Julio Agosto Septiembre/July August September. Issue #5.

———. 1990d. *Aquelarre: A Magazine for Latin American Women/Revista de la Mujer Latinoamericana.* Octubre Noviembre Diciembre/October November December. Issue #6.

———. 1990e. Aquelarre. "Se abre el Aquelarre/getting started." Pg 2 in *Aquelarre: A Magazine for Latin American Women/Revista de la Mujer Latinoamericana.* "Women and Art/Mujer Y Arte." Abril Mayo Junio/April May June. Issue #4.

———. 1991a. *Aquelarre: A Magazine for Latin American Women/Revista de la Mujer Latinoamericana.* "América Latina & el Caribe Feminismo/Latin American & the Caribbean Feminism." Primavera–Verano/Spring–Summer. Issue #7/8.

———. 1991b. *Aquelarre: A Magazine for Latin American Women/Revista de la Mujer Latinoamericana.* "Escritoras Latinoamericanas/Latin American Women Writers." Otoño/Autumn. Issue #9.

———. 1991c. ""Una Semana en la Vida Feminista/A Week in the Life of a Feminist." Pg 2 in *Aquelarre: A Magazine for Latin American Women/Revista de la Mujer Latinoamericana.* "América Latina & el Caribe Feminismo/Latin American & the Caribbean Feminism." Primavera/Verano/Spring/Summer. Issue #7/8.

————.1991/1992. *Aquelarre: A Magazine for Latin American Women/Revista de la Mujer Latinoamericana.* "Mujeres Indígenas de las Américas: 500 Años de Resistencia/First Nations Women of the Americas: 500 Years of Resistance. Invierno/Primavera/Winter/Spring. Issue #10/11.

————. 1992. *Aquelarre: A Magazine for Latin American Women/Revista de la Mujer Latinoamericana.* "La Diferencia Étnica y Cultural/Ethnic and Cultural Diversity." Otoño/Fall. Issue #12/13.

————. 1994a. *Aquelarre: A Magazine for Latin American Women/Revista de la Mujer Latinoamericana.* "¿Globalización de la Economía o del Pobreza?/Globalization of the Economy or of Poverty?" Primavera/Spring. Issue #14.

————. 1994b. *Aquelarre: A Magazine for Latin American Women/Revista de la Mujer Latinoamericana.* "El Trabajo Cultural de las Latinoamericanas en el Canadá/The Cultural Work of Latin American Women in Canada." Otoño/Fall. Issue #15.

————. 1995a. *Aquelarre: A Magazine for Latin American Women/Revista de la Mujer Latinoamericana.* "Violencia Contra La Mujer: ¿Qué Hacer?/Violence Against Women: What Is To Be Done?" Primavera–Verano/Spring–Summer. Issue #16/17.

————. 1995b. *Aquelarre: A Magazine for Latin American Women/Revista de la Mujer Latinoamericana.* "Cuando La Historia Duele/When History Hurts." Otoño/Fall. Issue #18.

————. 1996a. *Aquelarre: A Magazine for Latin American Women/Revista de la Mujer Latinoamericana.* "●Child Labour ●Unpaid Work ●Nafta: two years later/●Explotación Infantil●Trabajo no remunerado●TLC dos años después." Spring/Primavera. Issue #19.

————. 1996b. *Aquelarre: A Magazine for Latin American Women/Revista de la Mujer Latinoamericana.* "Popular Education: from and with women/Educación Popular: desde y con las mujeres." Summer/Fall/Verano/Otoño. Issue #20/21.

Bernabei, Macarena. 1991. "¿Qué es el Feminismo? What is Feminism?" Pp. 14–17 in *Aquelarre: A Magazine for Latin American Women/Revista de la Mujer Latinoamericana.* "América Latina & el Caribe Feminismo/Latin American & the Caribbean Feminism." Primavera–Verano/Spring–Summer. Issue #7/8.

Espinoza, Erika. 1991. "Me Llamo Erika y Soy Lesbiana/My Name is Erika and I am a Lesbian." Pg. 41 in *Aquelarre: A Magazine for Latin American Women/Revista de la Mujer Latinoamericana.* "América Latina & el Caribe Feminismo/Latin American & the Caribbean Feminism." Primavera–Verano/Spring–Summer. Issue #7/8.

Gayle, Noga. 1991. "Desarrollo de un Feminismo Incluyente/Towards the Development of an Inclusive Feminism." Pp. 21–27 in *Aquelarre: A Magazine for Latin American Women/Revista de la Mujer Latinoamericana.* "América Latina & el Caribe Feminismo/Latin American & the Caribbean Feminism." Primavera–Verano/Spring–Summer. Issue #7/8.

n.a. 1987. Flyer/registration form for the "5th Canadian Conference in Solidarity with Women of Latin America." Vancouver, B.C. February 27, 28, and March 1.

Nadir, Nora. 1989. "Crónica De Un Congreso Poco Anunciado ● Chronicle of An Ill–Publicized Conference." Pp. 33–36 in *Aquelarre: A Magazine for Latin American*

Women/Revista de la Mujer Latinoamericana. Julio Agosto Septiembre/July August September. Issue #1.

Rodríguez, Carmen. 1990. "Quinto Encuentro Feminista Latinoamericano y del Caribe: Una Apuesta al Futuro ● Fifth Feminist Conference of Latin America and the Caribbean: A Bet on the Future." Pp. 33–34 in *Aquelarre: A Magazine for Latin American Women/Revista de la Mujer Latinoamericana.* Octubre Noviembre Diciembre/October November December. Issue #6.

Suárez, Estela. 1991. "El Movimiento Feminista en América Latina y el Caribe: Tendencias y Desafíos/The Feminist Movement in Latin America and the Caribbean: Trends and Challenges." Pp. 4–8 in *Aquelarre: A Magazine for Latin American Women/Revista de la Mujer Latinoamericana.* "América Latina & el Caribe Feminismo/Latin American & the Caribbean Feminism." Primavera–Verano/Spring–Summer. Issue #7/8.

PERSONAL INTERVIEWS AND GROUP MEETINGS[4]

Acuña, María Elena. 1999. Member of Bajo Sospecha,[5] interview by author, tape recording, Santiago, Chile.

Aguayo, Carmen Gloria. 1999. Minister for Salvador Allende, interview by author, tape recording, Santiago, Chile.

Aguirre, Alejandra. 2005. Photographer, fitness instructor, mom, interview by author, tape recording, Vancouver, Canada.

Aguirre, Carmen, 2004. Theater artist, interview by author, tape recording, Vancouver, Canada.

Amanda.* 2004. Doctoral student in psychological studies, interview by author, tape recording, Vancouver, Canada.

Andrade, Carmen. 1999. National coordinator of SERNAM's Women Head of Household Program, interview by author, tape recording, Santiago, Chile.

Andrade, Patricia(a). 2004. Former member of the Chilean Socialist Party and member of the Chilean solidarity movement, interview by author, tape recording, Vancouver, Canada.

Andrade, Patricia(b). 2004. Former member of the Chilean Socialist Party, interview by author, tape recording, Vancouver, Canada. (Joint interview with her daughter, Ursula.)

Andrade, Ursula. 2004. Art student, interview by author, tape recording, Vancouver, Canada. (Joint interview with her mother, Patricia.)

Baltra, Mireya. 1999. Minister of Labor under Salvador Allende, interview by author, tape recording, Santiago, Chile.

Basso, Alicia. 1999. Former Communist Party leader, and member of Salvador Allende's presidential advisory group, interview by author, tape recording, Santiago, Chile. (Joint interview with Soledad Parada.)

Boisier, Cecilia. 2004. Visual artist and Educator, interview by author, tape recording, Vancouver, Canada.

Borquez, Graciela. 1999. Co–founder of Mujeres por la Vida; member of the Christian Democrats, interview by author, tape recording, Santiago, Chile.

Cristall, Gary. 2005. Socialist cultural worker and revolutionary socialist activist, interview by author, tape recording, Vancouver, Canada.

Diaz, Andrea.* 2005. Former President Communist Party Youth Sector, interview by author, tape recording, Victoria, Canada.

Díaz Caro, Viviana. 1999. President of Agrupación de Familiares de Detenido y Desaparecido, interview by author, tape recording, Santiago, Chile.

Fuller, Dale. 2005. Former member of the Aquelarre Collective, interview by author, tape recording, Vancouver, Canada.

Gomberoff, Patricia. 2005. Political activist in the Solidarity Movement, interview by author, tape recording, Vancouver, Canada.

González, Ximena. 1999. Journalist in Salvador Allende's communication office, interview by author, tape recording, Santiago, Chile.

de Guevara, Lina. 2004. Founder and artistic director of PUENTE Theater, interview by author, tape recording, Victoria, Canada.

Gutiérrez, Angélica. 2004. Community development worker, public educator, and solidarity, anti-racism, and multiculturalism activist, interview by author, tape recording, Vancouver, Canada.

Gutiérrez, Carla.* 2004. Former member of the Chilean Socialist Party and the Revolutionary Movement of the Left (MIR), interview by author, tape recording, Vancouver, Canada.

Gutiérrez-Diaz, Marilyn. 2004. Survivor of Domestic Violence advocate in Kiwassa Neighbourhood House, interview by author, tape recording, Vancouver, Canada.

———. 2005. Interview by author, tape recording, Vancouver, Canada.

Hola, Eugenia. 1999. Researcher with Centro de Estudios de la Mujer, interview by author, tape recording, Santiago, Chile.

Jara, Lorena. 2004. Solidarity and feminist activist, interview by author, tape recording, Vancouver, Chile.

Jimenez, Rebeca. 2005. Domestic violence counselor, interview by author, tape recording, Vancouver, Canada.

Lazo Carerra, Carmen. 1999. Socialist Party militant, interview by author, tape recording, Santiago, Chile.

López, Isabel. 2004. Former member of the Chilean Socialist Party and cofounder of the Vancouver Chilean Association, interview by author, tape recording, Vancouver, Canada.

Orteaga Araya, Miriam. 1999. Former Member of the Revolutionary Movement of the Left (MIR), coordinator of the Ana Clara Centro de Capacitación para Mujeres, interview by author, tape recording, Santiago, Chile.

Parada, Soleda. 1999. Director of the Ministry of Women under Salvador Allende, interview by author, tape recording, Santiago, Chile. (Joint interview Alicia Basso.)

Policzer, Irene. 2004. Founding member of Aquelarre collective; supporter of the Chilean Solidarity Movement, interview by author, tape recording, Vancouver, Canada.

Pollarolo, Fanny. 1999. Socialist deputy; cofounder of Mujeres por la Vida; psychiatrist, interview by author, tape recording, Santiago, Chile.

Quiroz, Ana María. 2005. International Relations, Ministry of Education in Chile, interview by author, tape recording, Vancouver, Canada.

Rodríguez, Carmen. 2004. Writer and educator, interview by author, tape recording, Vancouver, Canada.

Rodríguez, Carmen, Magaly Varas, Isabel López and Ana María Quiroz. 2005. Focus group discussion with the author, tape recording, Vancouver, Canada.

Rodríguez, Sacha.* 2005. Former member of the Revolutionary Movement of the Left (MIR) in Exile, interview by author, tape recording, Vancouver, Canada.

Tagle, Cecilia. 2004. Former member of the Women's Sector of the Chilean Solidarity Movement and early member of the Chilean Housing Cooperative. Vancouver, Canada.

Tagle, Cecilia, and Irene Policzer. 2005. Focus group discussion with the author, tape recording, Vancouver, Canada.

Vaca, Nina. 2005. Former member of the Revolutionary Movement of the Left (MIR) in Exile, interview by author, tape recording, Vancouver, Canada.

Valdés, Teresa. 1999. Cofounder of Mujeres por la Vida; head of gender studies at FLACSO Chile, interview by author, tape recording, Santiago, Chile.

Valenzuela, María José. 2005. Activist in the Youth Sector of the Solidarity Movement, interview by author, tape recording, Vancouver, Canada.

Varas, Magaly. 2005. Former member of the Aquelarre collective, interview by author, tape recording, Vancouver, Canada.

Weber, Paulina. 1999. Cofounder of MEMCH'83 and co-coordinator of Casa de La Mujer del MEMCH, interview by author, tape recording, Santiago, Chile.

NOTES

1. Nearly all documents referenced here came from Gary Cristall's personal archives. Gary was a member of the Revolutionary Marxist Group and founder of the Chile Solidarity Committee. As a result, I had access to many more documents from those two organizations than Canadians for Democracy in Chile, the other main Canadian solidarity organization. Gary also provided nearly all of the newspaper articles of the period.

2. Some issues have the English first and Spanish second and others vice versa. They are listed in the bibliography as written on the magazine's cover.

3. Some issues had their own title in addition to the date and number.

4. Asterisk implies pseudonym, as per the request of the interviewee.

5. Most titles were chosen by the interviewee.

Index

abortion, 107, 131n9

agency, xviii, xxi, xxvii, xxxiin3, 213

agrarian reform. *See* Popular Unity

AFDD. *See* Association of Relatives of the Detained and Disappeared

Agrupación de Familiares de Detenido y Desaparecido. See Association of Relatives of the Detained and Disappeared

Aguirre, Alejandra, xiii, *36*, 156n7, 223–24

Aguirre, Carmen, xiii–xv, *36*, 84, 151–52, 156n7, 216–17, 218, 219n6, 221–23

Allende, Salvador, xiii, xxxi, 1, 35, 46, 53, 72, 86, 100, 144, 225, 233, 235; downfall of, 11–13; election of, 2–3; suicide of, 13, 29n12, 75. *See also* Popular Unity; Socialist Party in Chile

Allendista Women's Unit, 68, 69

Allesandri, Jorge, 2

Andrade, Patricia, *37*, 53–55, 107, 145–46, 215

Aquelarre, 41, 92, 104, 139, 141, 144, 178–203, 213, 235; audience, 185–89; bilingual, 179, 189; and culture, 180, 181–82, 184, 196–97, 199; feminism issue, 198–201; format, 189–96; funding, 181–82; goals, 180, 201; history of, 176, 177, 179–82; humor in, 191–92, 194–95, 198; inaugural issue, 196–98; and lesbians, 201; organizational efforts, 182–85; topics covered (*see also* feminism issue; inaugural issue), 160, 179, 180, 187, 195–96; witches, xi, 189. *See also* culture; exile feminism

arpilleras/istas, 21, 24, 116, 118, 152–53, 210. *See also* culture

Association of Relatives of the Detained and Disappeared (*Agrupación de Familiares de Detenido y Desaparecido*, AFDD), 18, 20–21, 114. *See also* disappear(ed); Mothers of the Disappeared

Aylwin, Patricio, 25, 122

Bachelet, Michelle, 64, 136

blacklists, 18, 34, 50, 51, 54, 57, 222

Boisier, Cecilia, *36*, 127–28, 221, 225–26

boycotts. *See* solidarity movements

Bussi Soto de Allende, Mercedes Hortensia, 84, 99, 102, 112, 121

275

About the Author

Julie Shayne is a lecturer at the University of Washington, Bothell in the Department of Interdisciplinary Arts and Sciences, and the Center for University Studies and Programs. Her primary research is about revolution, resistance, and feminism in Latin America and the diaspora. Her first book is called *The Revolution Question: Feminisms in El Salvador, Chile, and Cuba* (Rutgers, 2004) and she has been on the family-friendly academic track since 2007.

Breinigsville, PA USA
13 December 2009
229169BV00002B/2/P